C000196854

MotoGP
Source Book

Published in September 2009

A catalogue record for this book is available from the British Library

ISBN 978 1 84425 723 2

Library of Congress catalog card no 2009923212

Haynes Publishing, Sparkford, Yeovil,
Somerset BA22 7JJ, UK
Tel: +44 (0) 1963 442030
Fax: +44 (0) 1963 440001
E-mail: sales@haynes.co.uk
Website: www.haynes.co.uk

Haynes North America, Inc.,
861 Lawrence Drive, Newbury Park,
California 91320, USA

Printed and bound in the UK

MotoGP Source Book

Sixty years of World Championship motorcycle racing
The riders, the races, the records

Julian Ryder & Martin Raines

CONTENTS

BELOW The Moto Guzzis of Fergus Anderson and Enrico Lorenzetti sandwich the NSU of Werner Haas as the leaders of the 1952 250cc GP come off Monza's cobbles and on to the tarmac. (*Elwyn Roberts Collection*)

4
KKE784

INTRODUCTION

Julian Ryder and Martin Raines explain this book's unique approach to recording Grand Prix motorcycle racing's first 60 years

Our objective in writing this book was to chronicle the history of Grand Prix motorcycle racing's first 60 years in a way that would give today's fan an insight into and feeling for the history of the sport. Hopefully, you will be able to recognise and follow trends in machinery development, riders' careers, circuit safety, race organisation and other aspects as well as spotting the major landmarks such as the change from 500cc to MotoGP.

We have also attempted to provide the most accurate record possible of the first 60 years of motorcycle Grand Prix racing within, of course, certain constraints. Chief among them is space. Four pages per year was the only sensible choice in a book of this size, so then we had to decide what to put on those four pages. We decided on two short elements of text, the first of which appears on the opening spread for each year and lists the major players on factory bikes plus any important changes in regulations. The second story, printed on the second spread, explores the most significant event of the year in deeper detail. The remainder of the first spread is taken up with bullet points for each class: incidents that shaped the season, statistics, landmark events in the careers of individual riders or the history of a racing marque. On the second spread you will find a full championship table for the 500cc/MotoGP class plus the top ten in all other solo classes.

In presenting this information, we had to make some decisions on what we could and couldn't do. Here are the ones you need to know about:

GRAND PRIX

A Grand Prix is a race that has been part of the FIM Grand Prix World Championship. We have not included the sidecar class or F750, or any other class whether or not it had World Championship status.

NAMES

We have used the form of address the rider preferred. Hence Les, not Leslie, Graham; Tepi, not Teuvo, Lansivuori; and Max, not Massimiliano, Biaggi.

NATIONALITIES

We have tried to give a rider's nationality rather than the country in which he took out his racing licence. Hence some riders born in Northern Ireland have been listed as British, though they may have been described as Irish by other sources. In cases where a rider was born in one country and brought up in another, such as Gary Hocking or Jim Redman, we have used the nationality the rider officially adopted. Three-letter abbreviations for countries and nationalities follow the ISO's recommendations.

BIKE NAMES

We have endeavoured to give the make of bike used. This is not always a simple matter, especially in the 50/80cc class where many machines were effectively home-made, or in the heyday of 250 and 350 TZ Yamahas where a variety of proprietary frames were used, often with heavily modified engines. The only names we have specifically excluded are those adopted direct from a sponsor.

OPPOSITE On their way to the first ever Grand Prix. Les Graham, the first 500cc World Champion, and his team-mate Bill Doran push the works AJS up the gang plank of the Isle of Man ferry. *(Doran Family Collection)*

LEFT Triple World Champion Werner Haas, Germany's first Champion and the lead rider in NSU's domination of the early 1950s 250 and 125 classes. *(Stuart Dent Archive)*

ABOVE Jarno Saarinen about to start his first race as World Champion – the French 250cc GP of 1973 at Paul Ricard. He won. *(Elwyn Roberts Collection)*

NAMES OF RACES

We have used the title of the Grand Prix, except in the case of the Grand Prix of Nations, as the GP held in Italy was called from 1949 to '90. This was effectively the Italian GP, so we have tagged it as ITA in table headings as there was no other GP held on Italian soil. We are well aware that the British race was until 1976 the Isle of Man TT and the Dutch GP still is, officially, the Dutch TT. However, for simplicity we call them all GPs.

The situation is more complicated where more than one GP was held in one country during one season. Where these were scheduled races, they were usually first given the names of other countries (such as San Marino) then of regions (the Pacific GP for the second race held in Japan) or cities (Catalunya and Valencia for races in Spain). One-off events, usually to replace races cancelled at short notice, usually received odd names like Vitesse du Mans or the FIM GP.

RECORDS

Where we say that a rider was the 'youngest ever' or 'oldest ever' we mean that was the case at the end of the relevant season. For instance, in 1989 when we say Alex Criville was the youngest ever World Champion we mean as of the end of that season. Obviously, as you get towards more recent years that record is more likely to stand, for instance Scott Redding's record as the youngest ever GP winner set at Donington Park in 2008.

POINTS-SCORING SYSTEMS

There have been several systems over the past 60 years, and the one in force for each year is noted on the championship tables.

Where riders finished on equal points, there have been two systems of tiebreaker. Until 1964, when not all results were counted, the system took into account the best discarded result. From 1965 onwards, there has been a different system that compares riders' best scoring results or number of wins, or second places, and so on. This obtained whether a net or gross scoring system was in force; in other words after 1964 discarded results were not used to split riders tied on points.

ACKNOWLEDGEMENTS

Many people have helped in trying to make this book as accurate as possible. In particular, the authors would like to thank the following:

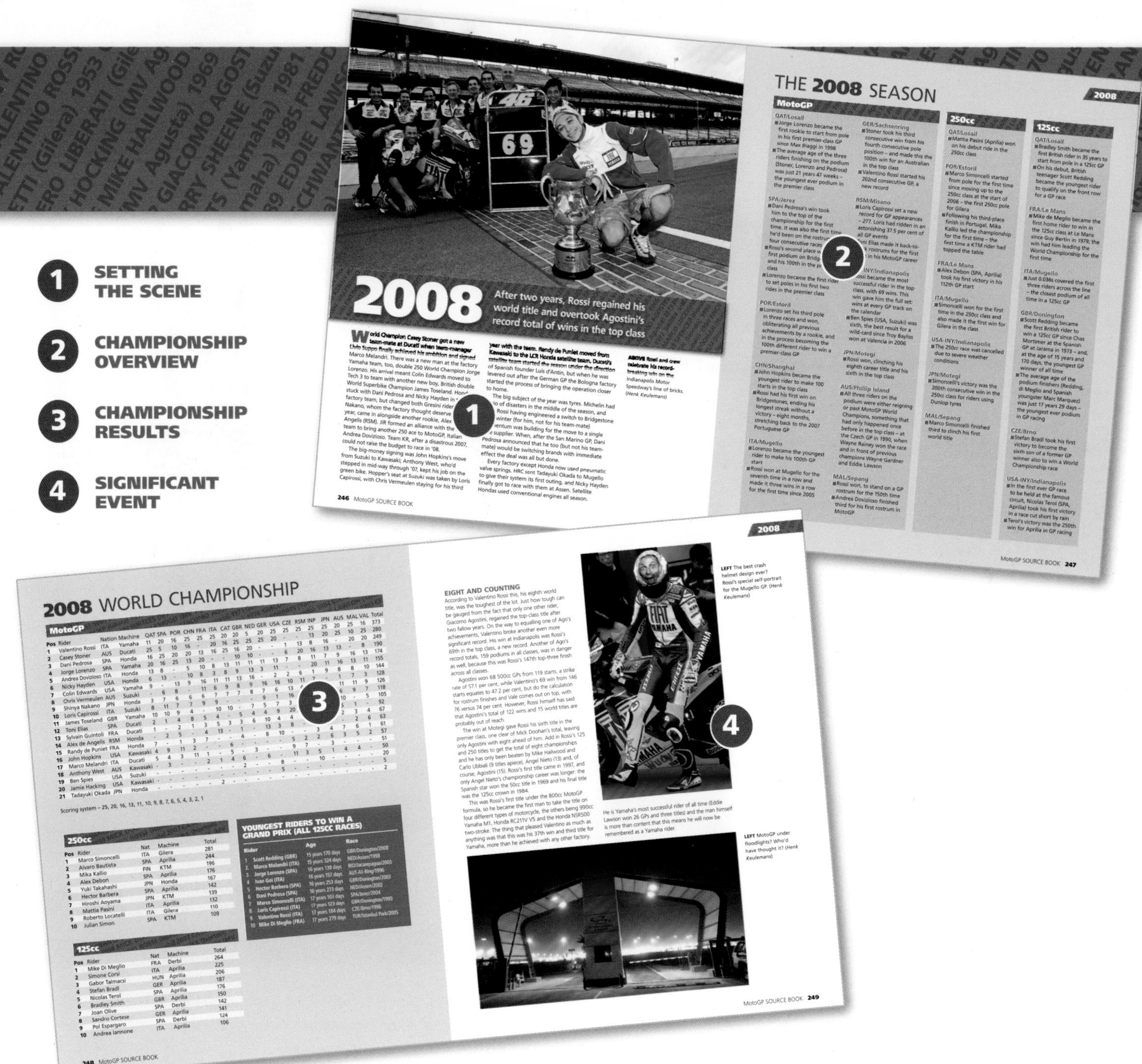

Marc Petrier at the FIM, Ray Battersby, Tommy Robb, Stuart Graham, Jan Leek, Peter Duke, Hans van Loozenoord, Mat Oxley, Dave Ellis and Graham Houlihan for fact-checking and other assistance. Mac Mackay and Yoko Togashi for their help with early Honda history.

PHOTOGRAPHS

The indefatigable Dutch photographer Henk Keulemans was as usual invaluable both in searching his own files as well as advising on the text.

The estimable Welsh collector Elwyn Roberts was as generous as ever with his time and in allowing us access to his comprehensive archive of quality images.

Stuart Dent turned up some remarkable black-and-white pictures from the early 1950s including some truly wonderful portraits – we would have liked to use more of these!

Peggy Doran and family allowed us access to their records of Bill Doran's career and their personal photo albums.

Martin Jordan at JARROTTS.com went to great lengths to help, and unlike the other sources here you can buy his pictures! See him at the big classic shows where you can buy nicely framed big prints – the picture on page 54 would look great on anyone's wall!

Julian Ryder & Martin Raines, August 2009

1949

Les Graham and the AJS *Porcupine* beat Nello Pagani and the Gilera four on countback by the smallest of margins

The most exotic machines on the grid for the first World Championship season were the four-cylinder Gileras of Italians Carlo Bandirola, a stellar but wayward talent with a propensity for crashing, and new boy Arciso Artesiani. Nello Pagani, the most experienced and reliable of the team's riders, was kept on the single-cylinder Saturno until Assen thanks to his prickly relationship with designer Piero Remor.

There was a second Italian 500, Moto Guzzi's 120-degree V-twin but, despite being raced by Enrico Lorenzetti, the factory's longest-serving rider, the bike was outclassed. BMW, who had been very competitive before the Second World War – supercharged Boxer BMWs finished first and second in the 1939 TT – were banned from taking part, along with the other German factories like DKW.

AJS fielded British riders Les Graham, Ted Frend and Jock West, all stars of pre-war racing, alongside Bill Doran who had impressed with second place at the '48 TT on a private Norton. Ireland's Reg Armstrong also rode in the 350s. Norton fielded a variable number of works bikes – seven in Ulster! – but their contracted British riders were Artie Bell and Johnny Lockett in the 500s and Harold Daniell in the 350s. Velocette had DOHC versions of their pre-war singles in both big classes, but only the 350 was competitive.

The 250 class was dominated by Moto Guzzi and their Gamablunghino ('Little Long Legs') flat single. As well as Italian works rider Bruno Ruffo, stars like Irishman Manliff Barrington (a protégé of the great 1930s star Stanley Woods) and the veteran Scottish racer/journalist Fergus Anderson rode Guzzis. Only the Benellis of Italians Dario Ambrosini and Umberto Masetti offered a challenge to their rival marque.

In the 125s three Italian factories – MV Agusta, Mondial and Morini – fought it out. Only Mondial used a four-stroke, a beautiful DOHC single; the other two were two-strokes (yes, an MV stroker) but by the following season both Morini and MV had similar designs on track.

ABOVE Les Graham and the twin-cylinder AJS E90 *Porcupine* on the way to winning the Dutch TT at Assen. (*Author's Collection*)

RIGHT The *Porcupine* poses in the race shop – note traditional makeshift background of oily sheet! The large hole under the nose of the saddle is where the oil tank should be. (*Author's Collection*)

THE **1949** SEASON

500cc

GBR/Isle of Man TT

- Norton factory rider Harold Daniell won the Senior TT – the first ever race counting towards the 500cc World Championship. It was Daniell's one and only GP victory
- Les Graham was leading by two minutes after three hours of racing only to suffer mechanical failure within sight of the flag; he pushed home to finish tenth

BEL/Spa-Francorchamps

- Bill Doran overtook Artesani and Lorenzetti on the last corner of the final lap to record his only 500cc victory. The Gilera rider proceeded to stamp on his goggles in *parc fermé*, while Lorenzetti made do with kicking his Guzzi

ULS/Clady

- Les Graham won the Ulster Grand Prix to become the first 500cc World Champion

350cc

GBR/Isle of Man TT

- Freddie Frith had the honour of winning the first ever race counting towards the World Championship, held on 13 June 1949
- Ben Drinkwater died due to injuries received in a crash on the fourth lap of the race – the first rider to lose his life in a World Championship race

NED/Assen

- Freddie Frith took three wins from three races to clinch the world title

ULS/Clady

- Frith made it a clean sweep of five victories from five races before subsequently retiring from racing

250cc

GBR/Isle of Man TT

- Irish rider Manliff Barrington (Moto Guzzi) won the first 250cc World Championship race

ITA-NAZ/Monza

- Bruno Ruffo finished fourth in the final race of the year to take the first 250cc world title

125cc

SWI/Berne

- Nello Pagani (Mondial) won the first 125cc World Championship race

ITA-NAZ/Monza

- Pagani finished fifth in the final race of the year to clinch the first 125cc world title

OLDEST RIDERS TO WIN THE PREMIER-CLASS TITLE

	Rider	Year	Age
1	Les Graham	1949	37 years 340 days
2	Phil Read	1974	35 years 208 days
3	Mick Doohan	1998	33 years 122 days
4	Giacomo Agostini	1975	33 years 69 days
5	Geoff Duke	1955	32 years 137 days

1949 WORLD CHAMPIONSHIP

500cc

Three best results were counted

Pos	Rider	Nat	Machine	GBR	SWI	NED	BEL	ULS	ITA	Nett	Gross
1	Leslie Graham	GBR	AJS	1	11	8	-	11	-	30	(31)
2	Nello Pagani	ITA	Gilera	-	6	11	5	7	11	29	(40)
3	Arciso Artesiani	ITA	Gilera	-	8	7	9	-	8	25	(32)
4	Bill Doran	GBR	AJS	-	-	-	10	6	7	23	
5	Artie Bell	GBR	Norton	6	-	6	6	8	-	20	(26)
6	Harold Daniell	GBR	Norton	10	7	-	-	-	-	17	
7	Johnny Lockett	GBR	Norton	8	-	5	-	-	-	13	
8	Enrico Lorenzetti	ITA	Moto Guzzi	-	-	-	7	-	-	7	
8	Ernie Lyons	IRL	Velocette	7	-	-	-	-	-	7	
10	Guido Leoni	ITA	Moto Guzzi	-	-	-	-	-	6	6	
11	Bruno Bertacchini	ITA	Moto Guzzi	-	-	-	-	-	5	5	
11	Freddie Frith	GBR	Velocette	-	5	-	-	-	-	5	
11	Sid Jensen	NZE	Triumph	5	-	-	-	-	-	5	
11	Jock West	GBR	AJS	-	-	-	-	5	-	5	

Scoring system – 10, 8, 7, 6, 5, plus 1 point for fastest lap

350cc

Three best results were counted

Pos	Rider	Nat	Machine	Nett	Gross
1	Freddie Frith	GBR	Velocette	33	(54)
2	Reg Armstrong	IRL	AJS	18	
3	Bob Foster	GBR	Velocette	16	
4	Eric McPherson	AUS	AJS	16	
5	Johnny Lockett	GBR	Norton	14	
6	David Whitworth	GBR	Velocette	12	
7	Leslie Graham	GBR	AJS	8	
7	Ernie Lyons	IRL	Velocette	8	
7	Charlie Salt	GBR	Velocette	8	
10	Artie Bell	GBR	Norton	7	
10	Bill Doran	GBR	AJS	7	

250cc

Three best results were counted

Pos	Rider	Nat	Machine	Nett
1	Bruno Ruffo	ITA	Moto Guzzi	24
2	Dario Ambrosini	ITA	Benelli	19
3	Ron Mead	GBR	Norton	13
4	Maurice Cann	GBR	Moto Guzzi	11
5	Claudio Mastellari	ITA	Moto Guzzi	11
6	Manliff Barrington	IRL	Moto Guzzi	10
7	Tommy Wood	GBR	Moto Guzzi	9
8	Fergus Anderson	GBR	Moto Guzzi	8
8	Gianni Leoni	ITA	Moto Guzzi	8
10	Umberto Masetti	ITA	Benelli	7
10	Roland Pike	GBR	Rudge	7

125cc

All races were counted

Pos	Rider	Nat	Machine	Nett
1	Nello Pagani	ITA	Mondial	27
2	Renato Magi	ITA	Morini	14
3	Umberto Masetti	ITA	Morini	13
4	Carlo Ubbiali	ITA	MV Agusta	13
5	Gianni Leoni	ITA	Mondial	11
6	Oscar Clemencigh	ITA	Mondial	8
7	Umberto Braga	ITA	Mondial	7
7	Celeste Cavaciuti	ITA	Mondial	7
9	Franco Bertoni	ITA	MV Agusta	6
10	Giuseppe Matucci	ITA	MV Agusta	5

NEW WORLD ORDER

In truth, the first World Championship did not look too different from pre-war racing, even though 1949 was the first time the sport's governing body had run an official series. All the motorcycles and their riders would have been at home on a pre-1939 grid. In the 1930s, forced induction was the way to go, so AJS's E90 twin and Gilera's four were both designed with supercharging in mind, but that was banned after the war.

A look at the grid shows that telescopic forks and hydraulic rear suspension were far from the norm on a 500, let alone a 125, and that streamlining was a thing of the future. In fact, the British factories were vehemently against any type of fairing on the grounds that fairings had no relevance to road-going motorcycles. Weight was carried far back – 'for traction' – and handlebars were flat; to modern eyes the first World Championship-winning motorcycles look like antiques. But things changed very quickly.

The racetracks, however, did not change. There were only six venues for the first championship, all of them in Europe: the Isle of Man, Berne, Assen, Spa-Francorchamps, Clady and Monza. Only Monza was a purpose-built circuit; closed roads and their attendant dangers would be the norm for two decades and more.

A second factor foreign to the modern spectator was that not every event ran every class, with only the 500s appearing at every round in 1949. The 350 championship consisted of five rounds, the 250 four and the 125 only three events. Championship rounds would multiply, but it would be well into the 1980s before it was normal to see every class at every venue. Indeed, it was common for even factory teams to miss races that were too expensive, or too dangerous, until the demise of the Isle of Man TT as a Grand Prix World Championship round in 1976.

However, the importance of the TT to the whole industry, not just the British factories, cannot be overstated. It was regarded, both before and after the Second World War, as the ultimate test. The Italian GP, or the Gran Premio delle Nazioni, as it was called, ran it a very close second, especially, of course, for the Italian factories.

The third oddity to modern eyes was the fact that racers not only rode in more than one class but also for more than one factory. It was common for riders to have a factory contract for the 500s, say with Gilera, yet ride a Mondial in the 125s. That was exactly what Nello Pagani did for this first season, finishing runner-up in the big class and World Champion in the little one.

OPPOSITE The first 250cc World Champion Bruno Ruffo (ITA) ready for the start of the Italian GP at Monza with his Moto Guzzi single. (*Author's Collection*)

1950

Umberto Masetti wins for Gilera but Norton's new boy Duke is a sensation on the Featherbed Manx

Norton attacked the Italians in the 500 class with a new rider and a new motorcycle. Geoff Duke joined Artie Bell and Johnny Lockett and the old 'garden gate' chassis was replaced by the revolutionary new twin-loop frame dubbed the 'Featherbed' by the veteran Harold Daniell, who retired at the end of the year. The combination was immediately a sensation: TT race and lap records were smashed and Norton monopolised the rostrum in the 500 and 350cc races.

However, Gilera did not send their team to the Isle of Man, well aware of both the difficulty of beating the British racers who'd grown up on the Mountain circuit and the expense of attending the event. They hit back at the second round, Spa, with a relatively unknown new man, Umberto Masetti, replacing Arciso Artesiani. Nello Pagani and Carlo Bandirola were retained with the team under the management of the great polymath Piero Taruffi following Piero Remor's acrimonious departure to MV where Count Domenico Agusta was anxious to enter the 500cc class. Not surprisingly, Remor built him an across-the-frame four not unlike the Gilera. However, the rest of the machine was far from orthodox. The gearbox was aligned down the axis of the bike, the final drive was by shaft and the rear suspension by friction damper. Artesiani was the rider.

AJS lost Bill Doran for the season when he broke his leg in practice for the TT, so Les Graham was backed up by Ted Frend. In the 350cc class, 1949 World Champion Freddie Frith had retired so Bob Foster was joined at Velocette by Reg Armstrong (IRL) and Bill Lomas, with Foster retaining the title for the factory. The other contenders were Norton and AJS, with their 500cc class riders doubling up.

The two smallest classes were almost exclusively Italian affairs. Benelli and Moto Guzzi contested the 250s with DOHC and SOHC singles, respectively. The Benelli was much more sophisticated, the Guzzi had reliability on its side, but the factory withdrew before the end of the year to develop a DOHC four-valve motor. Mondial dominated the 125 class with their DOHC single, Morini providing some opposition with their chain-driven SOHC single.

ABOVE Flat, fast and with an audience well in excess of 100,000; it could only be Assen. (*Keulemans Archive*)

RIGHT Glamour on the grid is nothing new. Belgian privateer Auguste Goffin has some well-dressed help with his Norton. (*Stuart Dent Archive*)

THE 1950 SEASON

500cc

GBR/Isle of Man TT

- Geoff Duke won the Senior TT race for Norton at his very first Grand Prix
- Norton became the first manufacturer to take all three podium places in a 500cc GP, with British riders Geoff Duke, Artie Bell and Johnny Lockett

BEL/Spa-Francorchamps

- Umberto Masetti took his first Grand Prix victory and the honour of being the first rider to win a GP at an average speed of over 100mph/161km/h (his actual average speed was 101.09mph/162.69km/h)
- Artie Bell crashed and suffered injuries that ended his racing career
- Arciso Artesiani finished fifth on the very first Grand Prix outing for the new four-cylinder MV Agusta

NED/Assen

- Umberto Masetti won the Dutch TT to become the first rider to score back-to-back victories in the 500cc class

SWI/Geneva

- After suffering a spill early on, Les Graham won the 500cc race to add to his victory in the earlier 350cc event, thus becoming the first rider to do the 500/350cc double at a Grand Prix

ITA-NAZ/Monza

- In spite of his closest challenger Geoff Duke winning the race, second place was enough for Masetti to clinch the title by a single point

350cc

GBR/Isle of Man TT

- Artie Bell won his one and only Grand Prix, giving Norton their first GP victory in the 350cc class

BEL/Spa-Francorchamps

- Bob Foster (Velocette) took his first Grand Prix victory

ULS/Clady

- Foster won in Ulster to take the 350cc world title

ITA-NAZ/Monza

- Geoff Duke won for the first time in the 350cc class and ended the day with a 350/500cc double victory

250cc

ULS/Clady

- Maurice Cann (GBR, Moto Guzzi) won the race, the only rider to finish in front of Dario Ambrosini (ITA, Benelli) in the four 250cc GP races held during 1950

ITA-NAZ/Monza

- Dario Ambrosini won his home Grand Prix to take the World Championship title

125cc

NED/Assen

- In the opening 125cc race of the year Bruno Ruffo (Mondial) beat his fellow-Italian team-mate Gianni Leoni by just one-tenth of a second after a race lasting 57 minutes

ULS/Clady

- Carlo Ubbiali (ITA, Mondial) took his first Grand Prix victory in a race in which just three riders started and only two finished

ITA-NAZ/Monza

- Ruffo's fourth-place finish was enough to add the 125cc title to the 250cc crown he'd won in 1949, to become the first rider to win world titles in two different classes

1950 WORLD CHAMPIONSHIP

500cc

Four best results were counted

Pos	Rider	Nat	Machine	GBR	BEL	NED	SWI	ULS	ITA	Nett	Gross
1	Umberto Masetti	ITA	Gilera	-	8	8	6	1	6	28	(29)
2	Geoff Duke	GBR	Norton	8	-	-	3	8	8	27	
3	Leslie Graham	GBR	AJS	3	-	-	8	6	-	17	
4	Nello Pagani	ITA	Gilera	-	6	6	-	-	-	12	
5	Carlo Bandirola	ITA	Gilera	-	3	3	4	-	2	12	
6	Johnny Lockett	GBR	Norton	4	-	-	1	4	-	9	
7	Artie Bell	GBR	Norton	6	-	-	-	-	-	6	
8	Arciso Artesiani	ITA	MV Agusta	-	2	-	-	-	4	6	
9	Harry Hinton	AUS	Norton	-	1	4	-	-	-	5	
10	Ted Frend	GBR	AJS	-	4	-	-	-	-	4	
11	Dickie Dale	GBR	Norton	-	-	-	-	3	1	4	
12	Harold Daniell	GBR	Norton	2	-	-	2	-	-	4	
13	Alfredo Milani	ITA	Gilera	-	-	-	-	-	3	3	
14	Eric McPherson	AUS	Norton	-	-	2	-	-	-	2	
14	Jock West	GBR	AJS	-	-	-	-	2	-	2	
16	Reg Armstrong	IRL	AJS	1	-	-	-	-	-	1	
16	Sid Jensen	NZE	Triumph	-	-	1	-	-	-	1	

Scoring system – 8, 6, 4, 3, 2, 1

350cc

Four best results were counted

Pos	Rider	Nat	Machine	Nett	Gross
1	Bob Foster	GBR	Velocette	30	
2	Geoff Duke	GBR	Norton	24	(28)
3	Leslie Graham	GBR	AJS	17	
4	Artie Bell	GBR	Norton	14	
5	Reg Armstrong	IRL	Velocette	11	
6	Harry Hinton	AUS	Norton	9	
7	Bill Lomas	GBR	Velocette	9	
8	Harold Daniell	GBR	Norton	6	
9	Dickie Dale	GBR	Norton/AJS	4	
9	Johnny Lockett	GBR	Norton	4	

250cc

All races were counted

Pos	Rider	Nat	Machine	Nett
1	Dario Ambrosini	ITA	Benelli	30
2	Maurice Cann	GBR	Moto Guzzi	14
3	Fergus Anderson	GBR	Moto Guzzi	6
3	Bruno Ruffo	ITA	Moto Guzzi	6
5	Wilf Billington	GBR	Moto Guzzi	4
5	Dickie Dale	GBR	Benelli	4
5	Bruno Francisci	ITA	Benelli	4
5	Ron Mead	GBR	Velocette	4
9	Arthur Burton	GBR	Excelsior	3
9	Claudio Mastellari	ITA	Moto Guzzi	3
9	Benoit Musy	SWI	Moto Guzzi	3
9	Roland Pike	GBR	Rudge	3

125cc

All races were counted

Pos	Rider	Nat	Machine	Nett
1	Bruno Ruffo	ITA	Mondial	17
2	Gianni Leoni	ITA	Mondial	14
2	Carlo Ubbiali	ITA	Mondial	14
4	Giuseppe Matucci	ITA	Morini	4
4	Luigi Zinzani	ITA	Morini	4
6	Umberto Braga	ITA	Mondial	3
7	Raffaele Alberti	ITA	Mondial	2
7	Felice Benasedo	ITA	MV Agusta	2
9	Gijs Lagerwey	NED	Sparte	1
9	Emilio Soprani	ITA	Morini	1

THE FOURS

There is no doubt that the first recognisably modern multi-cylinder engine was the Gilera four on which Italians Nello Pagani and Arciso Artesiani finished second and third in the first 500cc World Championship, but the origins of the bike go back to the pre-war days of supercharging. In fact, the design can be traced back to two newly graduated engineering students, Carlo Gianni and Piero Remor, who built a number of across-the-frame four motors in the 1920s under the patronage of various noblemen. As far as is known, these were the first across-the-frame fours ever built. According to Raymond Ainscoe's history *Gilera Road Racers* (Osprey, 1987) they were getting the bike to rev to 7000rpm in 1928 but without the reliability to win races despite having the great Piero Taruffi riding. (Taruffi was an engineer, Italian 500cc champion, international tennis player, summer and winter Olympian, Mille Miglia and Targa Floria winner, factory Ferrari and Mercedes driver, and holder of 50 speed records on two, three and four wheels.)

In 1934, with Taruffi now a co-designer as well as team-manager, the bike was reborn under the banner of the CNA aeroplane company as the Rondine ('swallow' in Italian). The 52x58mm water-cooled motor had a semi-automatic gearbox and a Taruffi-designed supercharger, and the cylinders were inclined forward at a very modern-looking 45 degrees. CNA was sold to another plane-maker, Caproni, which quickly sold the racers on to Gilera. Taruffi tested the first Gilera at 137mph/220km/h – unfaired – and reckoned it made 70hp at 8800rpm. This was the bike that Dorino Serafini took to the 1939 European Championship. There was just time for Taruffi to set an absolute speed record of 170.37mph/274.18km/h and a one-hour record of 127 miles/204km before the Italian aerospace industry had things other than racing on its mind.

After the Second World War, Remor redesigned the old motor to take account of the new World Championship regulations: no forced induction was allowed so the engine could be air cooled. However advanced the motor, pre-war orthodoxy on chassis design still ruled. Weight distribution was distinctly rearwards biased, and suspension was by girder forks and friction dampers. There was no doubt that the Italian fours made enormous amounts of power, but not everyone was convinced that multis were the way forward. What was the use of all that power if it couldn't be used? This argument would recur at regular intervals over the next 60 years.

OPPOSITE The first four: the Gilera was the original high-revving, multi-cylinder racer, but check that suspension: girders at the front, friction dampers at the rear. This is Massimo Masserini on the very first post-war design. (*Elwyn Roberts Collection*)

1951

Geoff Duke and the Norton give the archetypal British single-cylinder design its only 500cc world title

Gilera were cottoning on to what made the handling of the Nortons so good. Two of their three riders, Umberto Masetti and Nello Pagani, started the year with their fours equipped with telescopic forks and swinging arms. After the TT, which Gilera again did not attend, Alfredo Milani (who had started the year on a Saturno single) also got a four.

MV Agusta fitted their bikes with modern suspension systems too, but kept the shaft drive, and lured Les Graham to sign for them. The first World Champion was instrumental in taming the four-cylinder MV, which was considered a big, heavy and brutal beast even by the standards of the early 1950s, although his results during the season failed to show it. His Italian team-mates Carlo Bandirola and Arciso Artesiani fared better in the points table.

Norton again fielded Geoff Duke, now recognised as the best rider in the world despite having not yet won a title, and they also signed Dickie Dale. Illness prevented Dale riding so Duke was backed up by fellow-Britons Jack Brett and Johnny Lockett, with Ken Kavanagh (AUS) joining later in the season. Bill Doran, fit again after his 1950 Isle of Man crash, was back for AJS with Irish rider Reg Armstrong as his team-mate.

The contracted 500 riders also rode 350s for their factories, except Graham who was only signed to MV for the 500 class. He rode a Velocette in the 350s.

Moto Guzzi completely dominated the 250cc class after Benelli pulled out following the death of their champion Dario Ambrosini. Guzzi's outdated 500cc V-twin also won in Switzerland, thanks to Fergus Anderson, but he needed the assistance of the weather; Guzzi's second rider, Enrico Lorenzetti, was third. The V-twin would be retired but Guzzi's singles would, like the Manx Norton, be refined year on year by the brilliant engineer and designer Giulio Carcano.

Once again the other Italian factories couldn't compete with Mondial in the 125 class, although the Morini was a considerably improved machine.

ABOVE Duke and the Norton charge past the scoreboard at Assen. (*Keulemans Archive*)

RIGHT AJS factory rider Bill Doran at the bottom of Bray Hill on the Isle of Man – look at that crowd. (*Doran Family Collection*)

THE **1951** SEASON

500cc

SPA/Montjuich

- Umberto Masetti won the 500cc GP on the first visit to Spain for a World Championship event. The average speed for the 34 laps of the 3.7-mile/6.0-km circuit was just 58.3mph/93.9km/h – the slowest ever 500cc Grand Prix race

SWI/Berne

- Aged 42, Fergus Anderson (GBR) won his first Grand Prix and gave the Moto Guzzi factory their first GP success in the 500cc class

FRA/Albi

- Alfredo Milani (ITA, Gilera) took his first GP win on the first visit to France for a GP – the only occasion that a Grand Prix has taken place at the Albi circuit

ULS/Clady

- Geoff Duke won the 500cc race to add to his earlier 350cc success and became the first double World Champion

ITA-NAZ/Monza

- Milani won from team-mates Umberto Masetti and Nello Pagani in what was the first all-Gilera and all-Italian podium

350cc

SWI/Berne

- Les Graham made it ten wins for Velocette riders from the first thirteen GP races in the 350cc class – but Velocette were never again victorious in a GP

ULS/Clady

- Geoff Duke won to take his first world title, which was also the first in the 350cc class for Norton

250cc

SWI/Berne

- 1950 World Champion Dario Ambrosini (Benelli) won the opening 250cc race of the year

FRA/Albi

- Championship leader Dario Ambrosini died from injuries sustained in a crash during practice

ULS/Clady

- Moto Guzzi's Italian team-mates Gianni Leoni and Sante Geminiani were both killed in a collision while testing their machines on the public roads

ITA-NAZ/Monza

- Bruno Ruffo (Moto Guzzi) finished third at his home Grand Prix to regain the 250cc world title he had won in 1949

125cc

SPA/Montjuich

- Guido Leoni (ITA, Mondial) took his first Grand Prix victory. Tragically he died one month later after crashing in an Italian Championship race

GBR/Isle of Man TT

- Ulsterman Cromie McCandless (Mondial) became the first non-Italian rider to win a 125cc GP

ULS/Clady

- The 125cc race at the Ulster GP did not count towards the World Championship classification due to an insufficient number of starters

ITA-NAZ/Monza

- Carlo Ubbiali (Mondial) won the final race of the year to clinch his first world title

1951 WORLD CHAMPIONSHIP

500cc

Five best results were counted

Pos	Rider	Nat	Machine	SPA	SWI	GBR	BEL	NED	FRA	ULS	ITA	Nett	Gross
1	Geoff Duke	GBR	Norton	-	-	8	8	8	2	8	3	35	(37)
2	Alfredo Milani	ITA	Gilera	-	-	-	6	6	8	3	8	31	
3	Umberto Masetti	ITA	Gilera	8	-	-	-	-	3	4	6	21	
4	Bill Doran	GBR	AJS	-	-	6	-	-	6	1	1	14	
5	Nello Pagani	ITA	Gilera	-	-	-	2	-	4	-	4	10	
6	Reg Armstrong	IRL	AJS	-	6	-	3	-	-	-	-	9	
7	Fergus Anderson	GBR	Moto Guzzi	-	8	-	-	-	-	-	-	8	
8	Enrico Lorenzetti	ITA	Moto Guzzi	-	4	-	-	4	-	-	-	8	
9	Ken Kavanagh	AUS	Norton	-	-	-	-	-	-	6	-	6	
9	Tommy Wood	GBR	Norton	6	-	-	-	-	-	-	-	6	
11	Johnny Lockett	GBR	Norton	-	-	-	1	3	-	2	-	6	
12	Carlo Bandirola	ITA	MV Agusta	2	3	-	-	-	-	-	-	5	
13	Arciso Artesiani	ITA	MV Agusta	4	-	-	-	-	-	-	-	4	
13	Sante Geminiani	ITA	Moto Guzzi	-	-	-	4	-	-	-	-	4	
13	Cromie McCandless	GBR	Norton	-	-	4	-	-	-	-	-	4	
16	Tommy McEwan	GBR	Norton	-	-	3	-	-	-	-	-	3	
16	Roger Montane	SPA	Norton	3	-	-	-	-	-	-	-	3	
18	Jack Brett	GBR	Norton	-	-	-	-	2	1	-	-	3	
19	Manliff Barrington	IRL	Norton	-	-	2	-	-	-	-	-	2	
19	Benoit Musy	SWI	Moto Guzzi	-	2	-	-	-	-	-	-	2	
19	Bruno Ruffo	ITA	Moto Guzzi	-	-	-	-	-	-	-	2	2	
22	Willy Lips	SWI	Norton	-	1	-	-	-	-	-	-	1	
22	Len Parry	GBR	Norton	-	-	1	-	-	-	-	-	1	
22	Len Perry	NZE	Norton	-	-	-	-	1	-	-	-	1	
22	Ernesto Vidal	SPA	Norton	1	-	-	-	-	-	-	-	1	

Scoring system – 8, 6, 4, 3, 2, 1

350cc

Five best results were counted

Pos	Rider	Nat	Machine	Nett
1	Geoff Duke	GBR	Norton	40
2	Bill Doran	GBR	AJS	19
3	Johnny Lockett	GBR	Norton	19
4	Ken Kavanagh	AUS	Norton	16
5	Jack Brett	GBR	Norton	15
6	Leslie Graham	GBR	Velocette	14
7	Reg Armstrong	IRL	AJS	11
8	Bill Petch	GBR	AJS	10
9	Cecil Sandford	GBR	Velocette	9
10	Tommy Wood	GBR	Velocette	8

250cc

Four best results were counted

Pos	Rider	Nat	Machine	Nett
1	Bruno Ruffo	ITA	Moto Guzzi	26
2	Tommy Wood	GBR	Moto Guzzi	21
3	Dario Ambrosini	ITA	Benelli	14
4	Enrico Lorenzetti	ITA	Moto Guzzi	12
5	Gianni Leoni	ITA	Moto Guzzi	10
6	Maurice Cann	GBR	Moto Guzzi	6
7	Arthur Wheeler	GBR	Velocette	6
8	Fergus Anderson	GBR	Moto Guzzi	3
8	Wilf Hutt	GBR	Moto Guzzi	3
8	Alano Montanari	ITA	Moto Guzzi	3
8	Benoit Musy	SWI	Moto Guzzi	3

125cc

All races were counted

Pos	Rider	Nat	Machine	Nett
1	Carlo Ubbiali	ITA	Mondial	20
2	Gianni Leoni	ITA	Mondial	12
3	Cromie McCandless	GBR	Mondial	11
4	Luigi Zinzani	ITA	Morini	10
5	Guido Leoni	ITA	Mondial	8
6	Vincenzo Zanzi	ITA	Morini	7
7	Romolo Ferri	ITA	Mondial	6
8	Leslie Graham	GBR	MV Agusta	4
9	Juan-Soler Bulto	SPA	Montesa	4
10	Raffaele Alberti	ITA	Mondial	3
10	Nello Pagani	ITA	Mondial	3

YEAR OF THE MANX

How did a single-cylinder Norton, making perhaps 40hp, outpace a field full of four-cylinder Gileras and MVs with around 55hp at their disposal? The answer is two Northern Irishmen and a Pole. The first Ulsterman was ex-racer turned tuner and race team boss, the acerbic Joe Craig. He refined the essentially pre-war single to a peak of usability and reliability. The second was Rex McCandless who, with brother Cromie and Artie Bell, designed the modern racing cycle. This is no exaggeration for, until 1950, the prevailing wisdom was that weight distribution had to be biased towards the rear for good traction – and many riders, including Les Graham, were suspicious of telescopic forks. Rear suspension could be anything from rigid to sliding pillar to dry friction dampers. McCandless went against all this, going so far as to produce his own hydraulic rear suspension units based on Citroën parts and realising very early on that telescopic forks were the way to go. The real breakthrough, however, was the twin-loop frame with substantial bracing around the steering head and swinging arm pivot; crucially he also moved the weight of both engine and rider forward. Compare the look of a Manx Norton to a contemporary Italian four, especially the distance between front wheel and engine. The single looks like a modern motorcycle, while the multi looks like a museum piece. The Italian factories would spend the next year or two working this out for themselves.

The Pole was Leo Kuzmicki, who was sweeping the floor at the Norton factory when someone discovered that before he fled from the Nazi advance to join the Free Polish Airforce in the UK he had been a senior academic in the mechanical engineering department at Warsaw University, specialising in internal combustion. His squish piston increased the 350 Manx's power output by over 25 per cent almost overnight before doing much the same for the 500. Geoff Duke, in particular, has always had a high regard for Kuzmicki, who designed the Vanwall F1 engine before moving to the Rootes group where he designed the Hillman Imp's alloy engine.

The combined efforts of these disparate characters refined the single-cylinder Norton racer to such a pitch that the same basic design that won the world title in 1951 was still able to win a GP in 1969.

OPPOSITE LEFT Les Graham on the 500 MV Agusta which his work made competitive. (*Elwyn Roberts Collection*)

OPPOSITE RIGHT Legendary Norton tuner Joe Craig on the grid with Ray Amm, who would go on to carry the single-cylinder banner when Duke left. (*Stuart Dent Archive*)

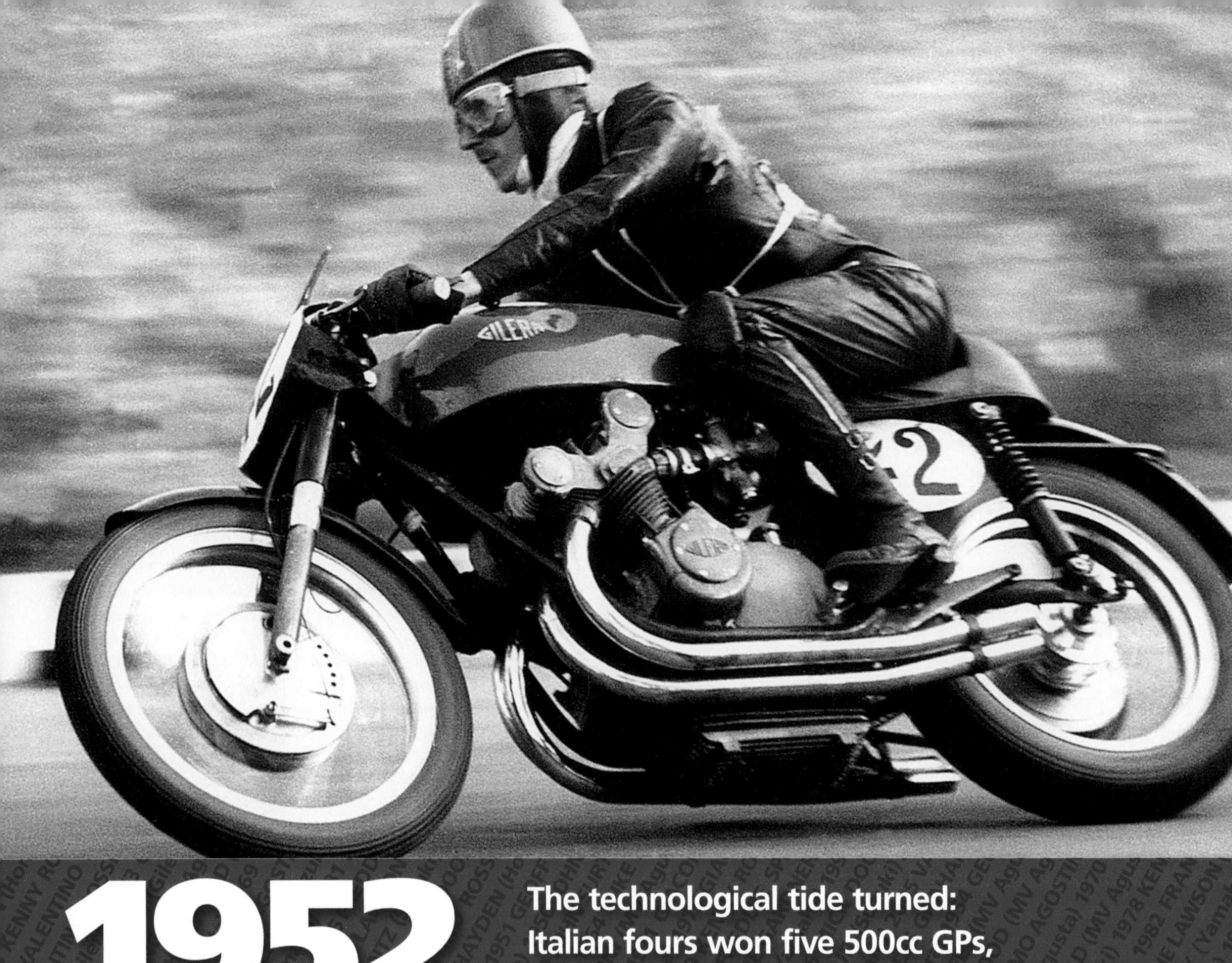

1952

The technological tide turned: Italian fours won five 500cc GPs, British singles two

Geoff Duke stayed at Norton but dabbled in sports car racing as well; Aussie Ken Kavanagh was retained, with Reg Armstrong recruited from AJS. Young Dave Bennett was added to the team as an investment for the future. Jack Brett went from Norton to AJS to join Bill Doran and New Zealander Rod Coleman. Injury and worse, however, would seriously affect the Norton team. Bennett was killed at the first race of the year, his bikes later being given to Ray Amm, the Rhodesian who had impressed on a private Norton in the first race of the year. Duke crashed in a non-championship race, broke an ankle and missed the second half of the season, while Amm was hurt in practice for the German GP and replaced for two races by Briton Syd Lawton.

Gilera retained Umberto Masetti, Nello Pagani and Alfredo Milani and brought in their own young Italian hopeful, Giuseppe Colnago. Over at MV, their 500 now had the benefit of Les Graham's input. Gone was the in-line gearbox, parallelogram swinging arm and shaft drive to be replaced by conventional chain-drive transmission. Rear suspension was conventional twin shock, but Graham preferred leading-link Earles forks to telescopics. After a season of niggling problems with the bike, which also had a new engine, Graham won the last two races of the year convincingly on the Monza and Montjuich tracks, two very different challenges. A second MV with Carlo Bandirola aboard only appeared in six of the eight 500cc races.

The status quo was maintained in the 350 and 250 classes, which were ruled by Norton and Moto Guzzi, respectively. However, Mondial's domination of the 125 class came to an end at the hands of MV Agusta's DOHC single and their British rider Cecil Sandford. It was another case of modernity winning. This was the machine that gave MV Agusta their first Grand Prix win and their first World Championship.

Italian domination of the smaller classes, however, was about to be challenged and destroyed by another resurgent nation's industry.

ABOVE Umberto Masetti (Gilera) just beat Les Graham (MV) to the 500 title. (*Maurice Bula*)

RIGHT The design of the racing bike was still not set in stone: MV Agusta continued to favour this Earles fork. (*Stuart Dent Archive*)

THE **1952** SEASON

500cc

SWI/Berne

- Jack Brett took the win from team-mate Bill Doran – his only Grand Prix victory – on his debut on the factory AJS machine. This was the last 500cc GP victory by AJS
- New recruit to the Norton factory squad, Dave Bennett, died after crashing on the penultimate lap while battling for the lead with fellow-Britons Brett and Doran

GBR/Isle of Man TT

- Reg Armstrong's (Norton) chain snapped as he crossed the line to win the race

GER/Solitude

- At the first Grand Prix to be held in Germany, Irishman Reg Armstrong (Norton) won the 500cc race to add to his earlier 350cc success in front of a reported 400,000 spectators

ULS/Clady

- Riding a factory Gilera as a substitute for the injured Alfredo Milani, Cromie McCandless won his home Grand Prix

ITA-NAZ/Monza

- Les Graham gave MV Agusta their first Grand Prix victory in the 500cc class

SPA/Montjuich

- Despite winning the final race of the year, Graham missed out on the world title by just three points to second man home in Spain, Umberto Masetti (Gilera)

350cc

BEL/Spa-Francorchamps

- Geoff Duke made it four wins from the first four races of the year to retain the 350cc world title – the last ever world title to be won by the rider of a British-made motorcycle
- One week late Duke crashed in a non-championship race at the Schotten circuit in Germany and suffered injuries which kept him out of the rest of the season's GP events

ULS/Clady

- Ken Kavanagh (Norton) became the first Australian rider to win a GP

ITA-NAZ/Monza

- Norton's Ray Amm became the first rider from Rhodesia to take a GP victory

250cc

SWI/Berne

- Fergus Anderson (Moto Guzzi) won the opening race of the year to become the first rider to win in both the 500cc and 250cc classes

GER/Solitude

- Rudi Felgenheier (GER) scored his only GP win to give the DKW factory their first World Championship success
- This was the first Grand Prix to be won by a two-stroke machine

ITA-NAZ/Monza

- Enrico Lorenzetti won the season's final 250cc GP from Werner Hass (NSU) and took the world title. The two riders were so close across the line they could not be separated by the timekeepers

125cc

GBR/Isle of Man TT

- Cecil Sandford gave MV Agusta their first ever Grand Prix victory

GER/Solitude

- Werner Haas scored his first GP victory and the first for the NSU factory

ULS/Clady

- Cecil Sandford won the race, to become the first non-Italian rider to take the 125cc world title

ITA-NAZ/Monza

- Emilio Mendogni won to give Morini their first GP victory

1952 WORLD CHAMPIONSHIP

500cc

Five best results were counted

Pos	Rider	Nat	Machine	SWI	GBR	NED	BEL	GER	ULS	ITA	SPA	Nett	Gross
1	Umberto Masetti	ITA	Gilera	-	-	8	8	-	-	6	6	28	
2	Leslie Graham	GBR	MV Agusta	-	6	-	-	3	-	8	8	25	
3	Reg Armstrong	IRL	Norton	-	8	3	-	8	-	1	2	22	
4	Rod Coleman	NZE	AJS	2	3	2	2	-	6	-	-	15	
5	Jack Brett	GBR	AJS	8	-	-	3	-	3	-	-	14	
6	Ken Kavanagh	AUS	Norton	-	-	4	-	6	-	-	4	14	
7	Geoff Duke	GBR	Norton	-	-	6	6	-	-	-	-	12	
8	Nello Pagani	ITA	Gilera	3	-	1	1	-	-	4	3	12	
9	Cromie McCandless	GBR	Gilera/Norton	-	1	-	-	-	8	-	-	9	
10	Ray Amm	RHO	Norton	1	4	-	4	-	-	-	-	9	
11	Carlo Bandirola	ITA	MV Agusta	4	-	-	-	-	-	3	-	7	
12	Bill Doran	GBR	AJS	6	-	-	-	-	-	-	-	6	
13	Bill Lomas	GBR	MV Agusta/AJS	-	2	-	-	-	4	-	-	6	
14	Syd Lawton	GBR	Norton	-	-	-	-	4	-	-	1	5	
15	Phil Carter	GBR	Norton	-	-	-	-	-	2	-	-	2	
15	Giuseppe Colnago	ITA	Gilera	-	-	-	-	-	-	2	-	2	
15	Auguste Goffin	BEL	Norton	-	-	-	-	2	-	-	-	2	
18	Hans Baltisberger	GER	BMW	-	-	-	-	1	-	-	-	1	
18	John Surtees	GBR	Norton	-	-	-	-	-	1	-	-	1	

Scoring system – 8, 6, 4, 3, 2, 1

350cc

Four best results were counted

Pos	Rider	Nat	Machine	Nett	Gross
1	Geoff Duke	GBR	Norton	32	
2	Reg Armstrong	IRL	Norton	24	(31)
3	Ray Amm	RHO	Norton	21	
4	Rod Coleman	NZE	AJS	20	(24)
5	Ken Kavanagh	AUS	Norton	16	
6	Jack Brett	GBR	AJS	12	(13)
7	Bill Lomas	GBR	AJS	9	
8	Syd Lawton	GBR	AJS/Norton	7	
9	Robin Sherry	GBR	AJS	4	
10	Ernie Ring	AUS	AJS	3	

250cc

Four best results were counted

Pos	Rider	Nat	Machine	Nett	Gross
1	Enrico Lorenzetti	ITA	Moto Guzzi	28	(34)
2	Fergus Anderson	GBR	Moto Guzzi	24	
3	Leslie Graham	GBR	Velocette/Benelli	11	
4	Maurice Cann	GBR	Moto Guzzi	10	
5	Rudi Felgenheier	GER	DKW	8	
6	Bruno Ruffo	ITA	Moto Guzzi	7	
7	Werner Haas	GER	NSU	6	
7	Heinrich Thorn-Prikker	GER	Moto Guzzi	6	
9	Alano Montanari	ITA	Moto Guzzi	6	
10	Herman Gablenz	GER	Horex	4	
10	Syd Lawton	GBR	Moto Guzzi	4	

125cc

Four best results were counted

Pos	Rider	Nat	Machine	Nett	Gross
1	Cecil Sandford	GBR	MV Agusta	28	(32)
2	Carlo Ubbiali	ITA	Mondial	24	
3	Emilio Mendogni	ITA	Morini	16	
4	Leslie Graham	GBR	MV Agusta	10	
5	Luigi Zinzani	ITA	Morini	9	
6	Werner Haas	GER	NSU	8	
7	Angelo Copeta	ITA	MV Agusta	7	
8	Bill Lomas	GBR	MV Agusta	6	
9	Guido Sala	ITA	MV Agusta	5	
10	Len Parry	GBR	Mondial	4	
10	Charlie Salt	GBR	MV Agusta	4	

THE GERMANS ARE COMING

Germany was readmitted to the FIM (or FICM as it then was) in 1951, enabling her racers to compete on the international stage again in the following year. BMW, who had been pre-war winners with their supercharged flat twin, did not re-enter the fray immediately, but DKW and NSU took part. Like the rest, these factories had been working on forced induction when hostilities commenced so had had to come up with brand-new designs to suit GPs where supercharging was specifically banned.

In the 1930s DKW had raced a strange two-stroke twin with an extra smaller cylinder acting as a pump to pressurise the intake side, and they now kept their faith with the two-stroke, fielding a 250 twin and then a 350 triple. They maintained the tradition of the pre-war bike by producing machines that were incredibly loud, very thirsty, wayward both in corners and on straights, and extremely fast.

NSU used their 1939 supercharged DOHC twin as the starting point for a generation of racers, producing a new motor with unit gearbox, wet-sump lubrication and giant camboxes. It looked, and was, the most modern and efficient engine in the world and for years was the only naturally aspirated motor with a specific power output of over 125hp per litre. The 125cc Rennfox single and Rennmax twin both had pressed steel forks, and spine frames like the company's SOHC road bikes that they were designed to promote, to which end the company ran the largest racing department in the world.

The NSU factory's efforts were enhanced by the discovery of a very talented young racer called Werner Haas. He won first time out on the Rennfox with a team-mate fifth, and at Monza chased new 250cc World Champion Enrico Lorenzetti (Moto Guzzi) home on the Rennmax. There were other German makers who looked as if they could be competitive, notably Horex and Adler, but NSU's attack on GP racing was a thoroughly modern, high-technology effort by a large company intent on promoting its products. NSU's bikes and methods of working were much admired by one Soichiro Honda when he saw the factory team in operation on his first visit to Europe.

OPPOSITE Fergus Anderson (Moto Guzzi) and Werner Haas (NSU) check out each other's bikes before the 250cc GP at Monza. (*Stuart Dent Archive*)

1953

Geoff Duke left Norton to join Gilera and won his second title, but MV Agusta's progress was halted by Les Graham's death

The tide turned finally and decisively against the British single-cylinder 500. Geoff Duke joined the Gilera team and accelerated the process of 'Nortonising' the four to the formula so brilliantly deduced by Rex McCandless. The Gilera was lower, with shorter, stronger forks and rear suspension units, and clip-ons replaced the old handlebars. Reg Armstrong and Dickie Dale also joined the Italian squad, while reigning champion Umberto Masetti (who walked out after Assen) and fellow-Italians Alfredo Milani and Giuseppe Colnago were retained.

MV Agusta, and indeed the whole paddock, were badly shaken by the death of their lead rider Les Graham at the TT. The 1949 World Champion had developed the MV to the point where it could beat the Gileras, but in the aftermath of Graham's death Carlo Bandirola could not continue the progress.

Norton only won at the TT and in Ulster, with Rhodesia's Ray Amm as their lead rider backed up by Briton Jack Brett and Ken Kavanagh.

Another Italian factory also upped their game. Moto Guzzi moved away from their traditional power base in the 250 class, with Fergus Anderson and Enrico Lorenzetti now also riding in the 350cc class with what was essentially a bored and stroked version of their 250. (MV were also experimenting with a 350, a sleeved version of the 500.) The new Guzzi proceeded to blow the British singles, which had dominated the 350cc class, out of the water. And Moto Guzzi didn't stop there. They entered the 500cc class with an entirely new design, an in-line four with shaft drive and mechanical fuel injection.

BMW had more sophisticated fuel injection on their new DOHC boxer twin raced by Walter Zeller. The BMW factory also led the way in aerodynamics, fielding a fully enclosed bike at Monza. NSU, well on their way to becoming for a short but glorious period the biggest motorcycle manufacturer in the world, arrived in the 125 and 250 classes in full force. The 125 revved to at least 1000rpm more than the MVs, the 250 twin to over 2000rpm more than the Guzzi singles which were its main rivals.

ABOVE The Gilera team riders – Duke, Colnago, Milani and Masetti – with their mechanics and, between Duke and Colnago, team manager Piero Taruffi. (*Keulemans Archive*)

RIGHT, ABOVE Fergus Anderson – the oldest racer to win a 500cc or MotoGP race. (*Stuart Dent Archive*)

RIGHT Frantic action at the start of the 250cc Monza race. (*Stuart Dent Archive*)

THE **1953** SEASON

500cc

GBR/Isle of Man TT

- Ray Amm won the Senior TT for Norton to make it a double success after winning the 350cc race earlier in the week
- Les Graham lost his life after crashing his MV Agusta on the second lap

NED/Assen

- Geoff Duke won for the first time since joining the Gilera factory team

GER/Schotten

- Both the 500 and 350cc GP races scheduled to take place were downgraded to international events (not counting towards the World Championship) after the major factory riders objected to the dangerous nature of the circuit. Ironically, winners Walter Zellen and Carlo Bandirola never got to win a GP that counted for the World Championship

ULS/Dundrod

- The Dundrod circuit hosted the Ulster GP for the first time, with Ken Kavanagh becoming the first Australian rider to win a 500cc Grand Prix

SPA/Montjuich

- Aged 44, Fergus Anderson (Moto Guzzi) became the oldest ever rider to win a premier-class Grand Prix

350cc

NED/Assen

- Enrico Lorenzetti (Moto Guzzi) became the first Italian rider to win a 350cc GP
- This was also the first 350cc GP not to be won by a British-manufactured motorcycle

ULS/Dundrod

- Ken Mudford (Norton) took his only Grand Prix win to become the first rider from New Zealand to win a GP

SWI/Berne

- Fergus Anderson (Moto Guzzi) took victory to become World Champion for the first time and the first rider to win the 350cc title on an Italian machine

250cc

GBR/Isle of Man TT

- Former World Champion Bruno Ruffo (Moto Guzzi) suffered serious injuries which ended his career following a crash during practice

NED/Assen

- Werner Haas gave the NSU factory their first GP victory in the 250cc class

SPA/Montjuich

- Although he did not compete here, Werner Haas took the 250cc title as closest challenger Reg Armstrong did not enter the race either
- With this title success Haas became the first rider to win both 125 and 250cc titles in the same season

125cc

GBR/Isle of Man TT

- Les Graham took his only 125cc GP win just days before his tragic accident in the 500cc race

NED/Assen

- Werner Haas (NSU) won the 125cc race to add to his earlier 250cc success

ITA-NAZ/Monza

- Hass's win in Italy made him the first German rider to take a world title

OLDEST RIDERS TO WIN A PREMIER-CLASS RACE

	Rider	Age at last victory	Race
1	**Fergus Anderson**	44 years 237 days	SPA/Montjuich/1953
2	**Jack Findlay**	42 years 85 days	AUT/Salzburgring/1977
3	**Les Graham**	41 years 21 days	SPA/Montjuich/1952
4	**Jack Ahearn**	39 years 327 days	FIN/Imatra/1964
5	**Harold Daniell**	39 years 240 days	GBR/Isle of Man TT/1949
6	**Frantisek Stastny**	38 years 247 days	DDR/Sachsenring/1966
7	**Nello Pagani**	37 years 328 days	ITA-NAZ/Monza/1949
8	**Troy Bayliss**	37 years 213 days	VAL/Ricardo Tormo/2006
9	**Phil Read**	36 years 235 days	CZE/Brno/1975
10	**Geoff Duke**	35 years 120 days	SWE/Hedemora/1958

1953 WORLD CHAMPIONSHIP

500cc

Five best results were counted

Pos	Rider	Nat	Machine	GBR	NED	BEL	FRA	ULS	SWI	ITA	SPA	Nett	Gross
1	Geoff Duke	GBR	Gilera	-	8	-	8	6	8	8	-	38	
2	Reg Armstrong	IRL	Gilera	4	6	4	6	3	4	3	-	24	(30)
3	Alfredo Milani	ITA	Gilera	-	-	8	4	-	6	-	-	18	
4	Ken Kavanagh	AUS	Norton	-	4	3	3	8	-	-	-	18	
5	Ray Amm	RHO	Norton	8	-	6	-	-	-	-	-	14	
6	Jack Brett	GBR	Norton	6	2	-	1	4	-	-	-	13	
7	Dickie Dale	GBR	Gilera	-	-	1	-	-	-	6	4	11	
8	Giuseppe Colnago	ITA	Gilera	-	3	-	2	-	3	-	3	11	
9	Fergus Anderson	GBR	Moto Guzzi	-	-	-	-	-	-	-	8	8	
10	Rod Coleman	NZE	AJS	3	-	2	-	-	2	-	-	7	
11	Carlo Bandirola	ITA	MV Agusta	-	-	-	-	-	-	-	6	6	
12	Libero Liberati	ITA	Gilera	-	-	-	-	-	-	4	-	4	
13	Bill Doran	GBR	AJS	2	1	-	-	-	-	-	-	3	
13	Derek Farrant	GBR	AJS	-	-	-	-	2	1	-	-	3	
15	Nello Pagani	ITA	Gilera	-	-	-	-	-	-	-	2	2	
15	Cecil Sandford	GBR	MV Agusta	-	-	-	-	-	-	2	-	2	
17	Peter Davey	GBR	Norton	1	-	-	-	-	-	-	-	1	
17	Ken Mudford	NZE	Norton	-	-	-	-	1	-	-	-	1	
17	Hermann-Paul Muller	GER	MV Agusta	-	-	-	-	-	-	1	-	1	
17	Tommy Wood	GBR	Norton	-	-	-	-	-	-	-	1	1	

Scoring system – 8, 6, 4, 3, 2, 1

350cc

Four best results were counted

Pos	Rider	Nat	Machine	Nett	Gross
1	Fergus Anderson	GBR	Moto Guzzi	30	(34)
2	Enrico Lorenzetti	ITA	Moto Guzzi	26	
3	Ray Amm	RHO	Norton	18	
4	Ken Kavanagh	AUS	Norton	18	
5	Jack Brett	GBR	Norton	12	
6	Rod Coleman	NZE	AJS	9	
7	Ken Mudford	NZE	Norton	8	
8	Bob McIntyre	GBR	AJS	6	
8	Pierre Monneret	FRA	AJS	6	
10	Duilio Agostini	ITA	Moto Guzzi	4	

250cc

Four best results were counted

Pos	Rider	Nat	Machine	Nett	Gross
1	Werner Haas	GER	NSU	28	(35)
2	Reg Armstrong	IRL	NSU	23	
3	Fergus Anderson	GBR	Moto Guzzi	22	(26)
4	Enrico Lorenzetti	ITA	Moto Guzzi	22	(25)
5	Alano Montanari	ITA	Moto Guzzi	19	
6	Ken Kavanagh	AUS	Moto Guzzi	6	
7	Siegfried Wunsche	GER	DKW	6	
8	August Hobl	GER	DKW	6	
9	Otto Daiker	GER	NSU	6	
10	Arthur Wheeler	GBR	Moto Guzzi	4	

125cc

Four best results were counted

Pos	Rider	Nat	Machine	Nett	Gross
1	Werner Haas	GER	NSU	30	(36)
2	Cecil Sandford	GBR	MV Agusta	20	
3	Carlo Ubbiali	ITA	MV Agusta	18	
4	Angelo Copeta	ITA	MV Agusta	17	
5	Leslie Graham	GBR	MV Agusta	8	
6	Otto Daiker	GER	NSU	7	
7	Emilio Mendogni	ITA	Morini	6	
8	Wolfgang Brandt	GER	NSU	5	
9	Reg Armstrong	IRL	NSU	4	
9	Rupert Hollaus	AUT	NSU	4	

DUKE DEFECTS

Geoff Duke knew the day of the single was over, but Norton kept him hanging on with promises of a new, water-cooled four-cylinder motor. When it was finally admitted there was no possibility of the rumours becoming hardware, Duke decided to concentrate on his burgeoning car racing career with Aston Martin. That didn't go quite to plan either, so he accepted an offer from Gilera. This was a brave decision by both parties. The British press regarded the move as something akin to treason, while the Italian media wasn't keen on the idea of importing foreign riders. How brave, then, was Piero Taruffi to employ three of them in 1953? He was rewarded with a clean sweep of the top-three places in the championship, with Duke and Armstrong finishing first and second ahead of Italian Alfredo Milani.

Duke was widely regarded as the best rider in the world, and not just in the UK. Not only was he a superb racer, he was also technically very astute, and became the first example of a new breed, a rider on whom a factory could focus their efforts to improve their machine. Duke did for Gilera what Les Graham had been in the process of doing with the four-cylinder MV. John Surtees would eventually do the same job, just as Giacomo Agostini would with the MV Agusta triple and men like Wayne Rainey and Mick Doohan would do for Yamaha and Honda respectively. Geoff's attention to detail was legendary, and not merely on the bike. In 1950 he realised the baggy riding kit of the time was aerodynamically inefficient and asked his tailor to make him a one-piece suit.

Geoff Duke was also the first nationally famous motorcycle racer in the UK. He was awarded an OBE in 1953, and won one of the first 'Sportsman of the Year' polls. Duke was, in short, the first modern motorcycle racer.

OPPOSITE BMW came to GPs a year after NSU and DKW, but, like the other German factories, they brought some advanced thinking. This streamliner, ridden by Walter Zeller, appeared at the final GP of the year at Monza and led to the universal adoption of 'dustbin' fairings on faster circuits. Note the absence of carburettors as BMW used fuel injection; the company had also used telescopic forks on their pre-war racers. The German motorcycle industry was booming and, for a few short but spectacular years, would be the biggest and most innovative in the world. (*Stuart Dent Archive*)

1954

Duke wins his third title, Guzzi dominate the 350 class, NSU win all the races they enter in the 250 and 125s

Gilera significantly upgraded their engine for the men who had finished first, second and third in the previous year's championship – Geoff Duke, Reg Armstrong and Alfredo Milani – plus Umberto Masetti and Frenchman Pierre Monneret. Nello Pagani and Dickie Dale had been poached by MV Agusta, who retained the ever-combative Carlo Bandirola.

Moto Guzzi gave Ken Kavanagh a full-time contract after his try-out at the end of 1953, and he and Fergus Anderson rode the 500-four for just a couple of races; after that the single, much preferred by all the riders, was brought back out. The 350cc version of Guzzi's single was ridden by the two 500 pilots plus veteran Enrico Lorenzetti, with fellow-Italian Duilio Agostini as reserve.

Norton also had a new works Manx for Ray Amm and Jack Brett in both 500 and 350 classes. AJS again fielded Rod Coleman with new team-mate Bob McIntyre (GBR). They persevered for one last year with the *Porcupine* in the 500s but had a much happier time in the 350s.

Once again, NSU dominated the smaller classes. Werner Haas and Rupert Hollaus (AUT) became 250 and 125cc champions, respectively – and up until Monza, the penultimate event of the season, not only did they win every race, but every 250cc rostrum position bar one was also filled by an NSU rider. It is difficult to think of any manufacturer dominating not one but two classes so comprehensively.

This was the year that Mr Soichiro Honda visited Europe for the first time, and was so impressed by the NSU teams. Unhappily, their run was bought to an end by the death of Hollaus in practice for Monza, after which the team withdrew from the championship. Only the great Carlo Ubbiali (MV Agusta) could give the NSUs a race in the 125cc class, although he and Mondial's Tarquinio Provini were only winners once NSU had gone home.

At the end of the season both NSU and Norton would withdraw their works teams from GPs, but they did continue to sell customer bikes.

ABOVE Geoff Duke prepares to start the Isle of Man TT. He finished second after the race was red-flagged early: Duke had stopped for fuel, but Ray Amm (Norton) hadn't and won by a minute. (*Stuart Dent Archive*)

RIGHT Rupert Hollaus, motorcycle racing's only posthumous world champion, on the fully faired 250 NSU. (*Stuart Dent Archive*)

THE **1954** SEASON

500cc

FRA/Reims
- The French GP was held at Reims for the first time and Pierre Monneret won his home 500cc race on a Gilera, to add to his 350 victory earlier in the day on an AJS – the first GP victories by a French rider

GBR/Isle of Man TT
- Ray Amm repeated his victory of the previous year

ULS/Dundrod
- Won by Ray Amm, this victory did not count towards the World Championship classification because, due to adverse weather conditions, the race distance was reduced to 112 miles/179km, which was below the minimum length of 125 miles/200km for a 500cc GP event at that time

BEL/Spa-Francorchamps
- Geoff Duke took his first Grand Prix victory of the year in defence of his world title

SWI/Berne
- Duke became the first rider to win the 500cc World Championship three times with victory at the Swiss Grand Prix

SPA/Montjuich
- Britain's Dickie Dale gave MV Agusta their only victory of the year in the 500cc class

350cc

GBR/Isle of Man TT
- AJS team-mates Rod Coleman and Derek Farrant finished first and second – the last Grand Prix victory by AJS

NED/Assen
- Reigning World Champion Fergus Anderson took his first victory of the year

ITA-NAZ/Monza
- Fergus Anderson's victory at Monza was enough to retain the 350cc world title

250cc

FRA/Reims
- Reigning champion Werner Haas led home an all-NSU top four at an average speed of 101.03mph/162.59km/h – the first 250cc GP to average over 100mph/161km/h

NED/Assen
- Haas made it four straight wins from the first four races of the year to become the first rider to retain the 250cc world title

GER/Solitude
- At his home race Haas became the first rider to win five successive races in the 250cc class, in front of a crowd estimated to be half a million strong

SWI/Berne
- Werner Haas's winning streak came to an end with a crash on the first lap, allowing team-mate Rupert Hollaus to take his only 250cc GP victory

ITA-NAZ/Monza
- At the age of 38, Arthur Wheeler (Moto Guzzi) took his first Grand Prix victory

125cc

GBR/Isle of Man TT
- Austrian Rupert Hollaus took his first GP victory for NSU at the opening race of the year for the 125cc class

GER/Solitude
- Hollaus made it four wins from four races to clinch the 125cc world title

ITA-NAZ/Monza
- Rupert Hollaus lost his life after crashing and sustaining fatal injuries during the last practice period. As a mark of respect the NSU factory team withdrew from the event
- In the absence of the NSU factory machines, Guido Sala (ITA) took his only GP win to give MV their sole 125cc victory of the year

SPA/Montjuich
- Italian Tarquinio Provini (Mondial) took his first Grand Prix victory

1954 WORLD CHAMPIONSHIP

500cc

Five best results were counted

Pos	Rider	Nat	Machine	FRA	GBR	BEL	NED	GER	SWI	ITA	SPA	Nett	Gross
1	Geoff Duke	GBR	Gilera	-	6	8	8	8	8	8	-	40	(46)
2	Ray Amm	RHO	Norton	-	8	-	-	6	6	-	-	20	
3	Ken Kavanagh	AUS	Moto Guzzi	-	-	6	-	3	-	1	6	16	
4	Dickie Dale	GBR	MV Agusta	-	-	-	2	-	-	3	8	13	
5	Reg Armstrong	IRL	Gilera	-	3	-	-	4	4	2	-	13	
6	Pierre Monneret	FRA	Gilera	8	-	-	-	-	-	-	-	8	
7	Fergus Anderson	GBR	Moto Guzzi	-	-	-	6	2	-	-	-	8	
8	Carlo Bandirola	ITA	MV Agusta	-	-	-	4	-	-	4	-	8	
9	Jack Brett	GBR	Norton	-	4	-	-	1	3	-	-	8	
10	Umberto Masetti	ITA	Gilera	-	-	-	-	-	-	6	-	6	
10	Alfredo Milani	ITA	Gilera	6	-	-	-	-	-	-	-	6	
12	Rod Coleman	NZE	AJS	-	-	-	3	-	2	-	-	5	
13	Jacques Collot	FRA	Norton	4	-	-	-	-	-	-	-	4	
13	Leon Martin	BEL	Gilera	-	-	4	-	-	-	-	-	4	
13	Nello Pagani	ITA	MV Agusta	-	-	-	-	-	-	-	4	4	
16	Bob McIntyre	GBR	AJS	-	-	3	1	-	-	-	-	4	
17	Luigi Taveri	SWI	Norton	3	-	-	-	-	-	-	-	3	
17	Tommy Wood	GBR	Norton	-	-	-	-	-	-	-	3	3	
19	Rudy Allison	RSA	Norton	-	2	-	-	-	-	-	-	2	
19	Keith Campbell	AUS	Norton	-	-	2	-	-	-	-	-	2	
19	Auguste Goffin	BEL	Norton	-	-	-	-	-	-	-	2	2	
19	Bob Matthews	GBR	Norton	2	-	-	-	-	-	-	-	2	
23	Harold Clark	GBR	Norton	-	-	-	-	-	-	-	1	1	
23	Derek Farrant	GBR	AJS	-	-	-	-	-	1	-	-	1	
23	Cyril Julian	GBR	Norton	1	-	-	-	-	-	-	-	1	
23	Gordon Laing	AUS	Norton	-	1	-	-	-	-	-	-	1	
23	Peter Murphy	NZE	Matchless	-	-	1	-	-	-	-	-	1	

Scoring system – 8, 6, 4, 3, 2, 1

LEFT Fergus Anderson and the innovative but unloved Moto Guzzi straight four; it was fuel-injected and the petrol held in pannier tanks in the flanks of the dustbin fairing. (*Stuart Dent Archive*)

RIGHT A 125 NSU flat out at Dundrod. The teams' mechanics decided the nose of the fairing looked like the beak of a dolphin – and the term 'dolphin fairing' was born. (*Stuart Dent Archive*)

350cc

Five best results were counted

Pos	Rider	Nat	Machine	Nett
1	Fergus Anderson	GBR	Moto Guzzi	38
2	Ray Amm	RHO	Norton	22
3	Rod Coleman	NZE	AJS	20
4	Ken Kavanagh	AUS	Moto Guzzi	18
5	Enrico Lorenzetti	ITA	Moto Guzzi	15
6	Jack Brett	GBR	Norton	14
7	Duilio Agostini	ITA	Moto Guzzi	9
8	Bob McIntyre	GBR	AJS	9
9	Leo Simpson	NZE	AJS	9
10	Pierre Monneret	FRA	AJS	8

250cc

Four best results were counted

Pos	Rider	Nat	Machine	Nett	Gross
1	Werner Haas	GER	NSU	32	(40)
2	Rupert Hollaus	AUT	NSU	26	(30)
3	Hermann-Paul Muller	GER	NSU	17	(19)
4	Arthur Wheeler	GBR	Moto Guzzi	15	
5	Hans Baltisberger	GER	NSU	14	
6	Georg Braun	GER	NSU	6	
6	Romolo Ferri	ITA	Moto Guzzi	6	
8	Roberto Colombo	ITA	Moto Guzzi	5	
9	Reg Armstrong	IRL	NSU	4	
9	Helmut Hallmeier	GER	Adler	4	
9	Kurt Knopf	GER	NSU	4	

125cc

Four best results were counted

Pos	Rider	Nat	Machine	Nett
1	Rupert Hollaus	AUT	NSU	32
2	Carlo Ubbiali	ITA	MV Agusta	18
3	Hermann-Paul Muller	GER	NSU	15
4	Tarquinio Provini	ITA	Mondial	14
5	Werner Haas	GER	NSU	11
6	Hans Baltisberger	GER	NSU	10
7	Guido Sala	ITA	MV Agusta	8
8	Cecil Sandford	GBR	MV Agusta	8
9	Roberto Colombo	ITA	MV Agusta	6
10	Jose-Antonio Elizalde	SPA	Montesa	4

ENTER THE DUSTBIN

This was the year aerodynamics were taken seriously, with Moto Guzzi – who had a wind tunnel at their factory – leading the way. They'd pioneered small nose-cone fairings, often integrated with the long, thin tanks of the day, and then in 1952 they extended the bodywork down around the engine to produce a look not unlike today's 'dolphin' fairing. Guzzi, though, had a beak-like front mudguard projecting from under the front number plate as opposed to attached to the front forks.

NSU followed a similar path, using the wind tunnel at Stuttgart Technical Institute, only their fairing for the 1954 125 bike covered the handlebars and the whole engine. The 250 sported a giant, flat-sided wedge. It was the NSU team who first used the term 'dolphin' after someone decided the Rennfox fairing's beak resembled the nose of the marine mammal.

Moto Guzzi, aware that their highly evolved single-cylinder designs needed all the help they could get against the multis, pioneered full streamlining: the so-called 'dustbin' fairing that fully enclosed the front wheel. It was tried on the straight-four machine at the end of 1953; not everyone was convinced it was a good idea.

MV Agusta, conscious that their 500 still had a reputation as a difficult-to-handle brute, tried a variety of designs. There was a strange fairing that looked like a dustbin with the bit covering the front wheel taken off, something else that looked very like a dolphin design, and they also raced with no fairing at all. However, like every other manufacturer, MV had no hesitation in adopting full streamlining for the smaller capacity classes. Norton had the strange 'proboscis' fairing with an elongated nose; only AJS, who had never used any streamlining, did not experiment.

Gilera also tried a dolphin design that was really their integrated nose-cone/tank design with panels added to cover either side of the engine, but at Monza they had a full dustbin and Geoff Duke promptly set new race record and lap speeds with it. From the following season onwards full streamlining was used by nearly every factory on most courses, and especially at the fast tracks like Monza and Assen.

1955

Gilera and Duke win again, Guzzi continue to dominate the 350s, but a customer bike wins the 250 title

This was meant to be the year that Geoff Duke had a real challenger. When Norton announced they would not be contesting the GPs, Ray Amm, who had been Norton's lead rider since Duke left, signed for MV Agusta, only to be killed in his first race, an international at Imola. Thus the old Gilera team of Nello Pagani, Umberto Masetti and Carlo Bandirola found themselves reunited at MV. They were up against what was now the established Gilera line-up of Duke and Reg Armstrong backed up by Pierre Monneret, Libero Liberati and Giuseppe Colnago. Gilera won every race they contested, except the one that mattered most – Monza.

Moto Guzzi were still there, with Fergus Anderson now team-manager. Ken Kavanagh was joined by Dickie Dale, Diulio Agostini and, after the TT, Briton Bill Lomas. The 500 was not competitive, although Lomas did win on it in Ulster, but the 350 was literally unbeatable – it won every GP.

The Norton factory, unhappy with the trend towards streamlining and away from pure road circuits, only entered the TT with a factory team: Jack Brett backed up by two British youngsters, John Surtees and John Hartle. The bikes were no longer full works prototypes but development versions of customer machines. BMW looked like they might fill the gap. They entered Walter Zeller (GER) and John Surtees at the Nürburgring but dithered about making the commitment to field a factory team.

NSU may also have withdrawn their works machines but they sold a tuned version of their 250cc single-cylinder road bike, called the Sportmax. It was good enough to win the championship and be competitive for several years to come. NSU's competition in the 250 class came from the previous year's factory Guzzi, in the hands of Cecil Sandford, and from MV with a bored-out version of their DOHC 125cc single. At the class minimum of 203cc it was nevertheless fast enough for Bill Lomas to win the TT. It would also give the other Italian factories, Mondial and Morini, a clue as to how they too could be competitive in the 250 class.

ABOVE You could buy an NSU Sportmax over the counter, Hermann-Paul Muller did and won the 250cc World Championship. (*Stuart Dent Archive*)

TOP RIGHT The appearance of a woman in GPs, sidecar passenger Ingeborg Stoll, was viewed as scandalous in some quarters. (*Stuart Dent Archive*)

BOTTOM RIGHT Luigi Taveri was a winner on MV before becoming one of Honda's pioneers. (*Stuart Dent Archive*)

THE **1955** SEASON

500cc

SPA/Montjuich
- Reg Armstrong took his first victory since joining the Gilera factory squad

GER/Nürburgring
- Walter Zeller finished second in his home race to give BMW their first podium result in Grand Prix racing

BEL/Spa-Francorchamps
- Following the retirement of team-mate Geoff Duke when in a clear lead, Giuseppe Colnago took his only GP victory

ULS/Dundrod
- Bill Lomas took his only GP victory in the 500cc class and the last ever 500cc GP win for Moto Guzzi
- Neither Geoff Duke nor closest championship challenger Reg Armstrong appeared, because the Gilera team were unable to reach a financial agreement with the organisers. This resulted in Duke taking the world title for the fourth and final time

350cc

GBR/Isle of Man TT
- After his first GP victory in the 250cc race earlier in the week, Bill Lomas (Moto Guzzi) doubled up by winning the 350cc race

NED/Assen
- More than a dozen riders pulled into the pits after completing one lap, in protest at the inadequate start money provided by the organisers. Following this strike 13 riders were suspended from racing for six months
- Bill Lomas finished second to clinch his first World Championship title

250cc

GER/Nürburgring
- At the age of 45, Hermann-Paul Muller (NSU) took his first GP victory on the first visit to the Nürburgring circuit for the German Grand Prix

NED/Assen
- Bill Lomas (MV Agusta) crossed the line in first place but was demoted to second behind Taveri by the International Jury after a protest was upheld claiming he had refuelled without stopping his engine

ULS/Dundrod
- At only his sixth GP, John Surtees (NSU) took his first Grand Prix victory

ITA-NAZ/Monza
- Bill Lomas cruised home to take fifth place and the 250cc title from Hermann-Paul Muller. However, at the FIM congress in October it was decided to eliminate Lomas completely from the Dutch TT results and Muller thus became World Champion at the age of 45 – the oldest rider to win a world title

125cc

SPA/Montjuich
- Luigi Taveri (MV Agusta) became the first Swiss rider to win a Grand Prix

NED/Assen
- Carlo Ubbiali (MV Agusta) took victory at the Dutch TT to regain the world title he had previously won four years earlier

1955 WORLD CHAMPIONSHIP

500cc

Five best results were counted

Pos	Rider	Nat	Machine	SPA	FRA	GBR	GER	BEL	NED	ULS	ITA	Nett	Gross
1	Geoff Duke	GBR	Gilera	-	8	8	8	-	8	-	4	36	
2	Reg Armstrong	IRL	Gilera	8	4	6	-	-	6	-	6	30	
3	Umberto Masetti	ITA	MV Agusta	4	-	-	3	-	4	-	8	19	
4	Giuseppe Colnago	ITA	Gilera	-	-	-	2	8	-	-	3	13	
5	Carlo Bandirola	ITA	MV Agusta	6	-	-	4	-	-	-	-	10	
6	Bill Lomas	GBR	Moto Guzzi	-	-	-	-	-	-	8	-	8	
7	John Hartle	GBR	Norton	-	-	-	-	-	-	6	-	6	
7	Libero Liberati	ITA	Gilera	-	6	-	-	-	-	-	-	6	
7	Pierre Monneret	FRA	Gilera	-	-	-	-	6	-	-	-	6	
7	Walter Zeller	GER	BMW	-	-	-	6	-	-	-	-	6	
11	Bob McIntyre	GBR	Norton	-	-	2	-	-	-	3	-	5	
12	Dickie Dale	GBR	Moto Guzzi	-	-	-	-	-	-	4	-	4	
12	Ken Kavanagh	AUS	Moto Guzzi	-	-	4	-	-	-	-	-	4	
12	Leon Martin	BEL	Gilera	-	-	-	-	4	-	-	-	4	
15	Tito Forconi	ITA	MV Agusta	1	3	-	-	-	-	-	-	4	
16	Duilio Agostini	ITA	Moto Guzzi	-	-	-	-	3	-	-	-	3	
16	Jack Brett	GBR	Norton	-	-	3	-	-	-	-	-	3	
16	Orlando Valdinoci	ITA	Gilera	3	-	-	-	-	-	-	-	3	
16	Drikus Veer	NED	Gilera	-	-	-	-	-	3	-	-	3	
20	Bob Brown	AUS	Matchless	-	-	-	-	-	2	-	-	2	
20	Jacques Collot	FRA	Norton	-	2	-	-	-	-	-	-	2	
20	Auguste Goffin	BEL	Norton	-	-	-	-	2	-	-	-	2	
20	Alfredo Milani	ITA	Gilera	-	-	-	-	-	-	-	2	2	
20	Peter Murphy	NZE	Matchless	-	-	-	-	-	-	2	-	2	
20	Nello Pagani	ITA	MV Agusta	2	-	-	-	-	-	-	-	2	
26	Jack Ahearn	AUS	Norton	-	-	-	1	-	-	-	-	1	
26	John Clark	GBR	Matchless	-	-	-	-	-	-	1	-	1	
26	Firmin Dauwe	BEL	Norton	-	1	-	-	-	-	-	-	1	
26	Derek Ennett	GBR	Matchless	-	-	1	-	-	-	-	-	1	
26	Eddie Grant	RSA	Norton	-	-	-	-	-	1	-	-	1	
26	Ernst Riedelbauch	GER	BMW	-	-	-	-	-	-	-	1	1	
26	John Storr	GBR	Norton	-	-	-	-	1	-	-	-	1	

Scoring system – 8, 6, 4, 3, 2, 1

350cc

Four best results were counted

Pos	Rider	Nat	Machine	Nett	Gross
1	Bill Lomas	GBR	Moto Guzzi	32	(44)
2	Dickie Dale	GBR	Moto Guzzi	18	
3	August Hobl	GER	DKW	17	
4	Ken Kavanagh	AUS	Moto Guzzi	14	
5	Cecil Sandford	GBR	Moto Guzzi	13	
6	John Surtees	GBR	Norton	11	
7	Duilio Agostini	ITA	Moto Guzzi	8	
8	Bob McIntyre	GBR	Norton	8	
9	John Hartle	GBR	Norton	7	
10	Roberto Colombo	ITA	Moto Guzzi	7	

250cc

Four best results were counted

Pos	Rider	Nat	Machine	Nett	Gross
1	Hermann-Paul Muller	GER	NSU	19	(20)
2	Cecil Sandford	GBR	Moto Guzzi	14	
3	Bill Lomas	GBR	MV Agusta	13	
4	Luigi Taveri	SWI	MV Agusta	11	
5	Umberto Masetti	ITA	MV Agusta	11	
6	Sammy Miller	IRL	NSU	10	
7	John Surtees	GBR	NSU	8	
7	Carlo Ubbiali	ITA	MV Agusta	8	
9	Hans Baltisberger	GER	NSU	6	
9	Wolfgang Brandt	GER	NSU	6	

125cc

Four best results were counted

Pos	Rider	Nat	Machine	Nett	Gross
1	Carlo Ubbiali	ITA	MV Agusta	32	(44)
2	Luigi Taveri	SWI	MV Agusta	26	
3	Remo Venturi	ITA	MV Agusta	16	
4	Guiseppe Lattanzi	ITA	Mondial	11	
5	Angelo Copeta	ITA	MV Agusta	8	
6	Romolo Ferri	ITA	Mondial	7	
7	Bill Webster	GBR	MV Agusta	5	
8	Rudolf Grimas	AUT	Mondial	4	
9	August Hobl	GER	DKW	3	
9	Bill Lomas	GBR	MV Agusta	3	
9	Karl Lottes	GER	MV Agusta	3	
9	Tarquinio Provini	ITA	Mondial	3	

STRIKE

The events of the 1955 350cc race at the Dutch TT would have far-reaching consequences. Race organisers habitually exploited riders, paying derisory start and prize money. As the Dutch TT, then as now, attracted enormous crowds the privateers decided this was the time for action. After the demands of the riders were rejected they told the organisers they would pull out of the 350 race. Sure enough, a dozen riders pulled in after doing one lap at a processional pace.

Further panicky negotiations now took place, with Geoff Duke and the rest of the Gilera team threatening to back up the privateers, thus putting the 500cc race in jeopardy. That extracted some cash from the notoriously tight-fisted promoters and the 500 event went ahead.

Sportsmen do not usually make good trades unionists, but Duke and Reg Armstrong acted in solidarity because of events which had taken place at the Italian GP two years earlier, when the promoters had arbitrarily decided not to pay start money to British riders racing for Italian teams. On that occasion Fergus Anderson, a Scot riding for Moto Guzzi, delivered a letter of protest signed by every competitor and the organisers relented. For Duke and Armstrong, supporting the privateers' aims at Assen was repaying that debt, although they did not approve the threat of strike action.

There was, of course, retribution. In November the FIM's sporting committee suspended Duke, Armstrong and twelve others from all competition for six months, and three Italian riders for four months. No doubt the severer punishment for Duke and Armstrong was *pour encourager les autres.*

The FIM eventually relented after Duke made a public apology – much against his better judgement – but only allowed him to race in domestic competition. The Grand Prix ban stood and would ensure that he and the rest of the factory Gilera team missed the first two races of the 1956 season, the Isle of Man TT and Assen.

LEFT Geoff Duke's actions at Assen would have severe repercussions for his 1956 season. Here he stands on the German GP rostrum of 1954 with Assen co-conspirator and fellow Gilera man Reg Armstrong (right) and Norton's Ray Amm. (*Stuart Dent Archive*)

1956

John Surtees gave MV their first 500cc title as the Italian factory won three championships; only Moto Guzzi held out in the 350s

With Geoff Duke and the rest of the Gilera team suspended for six months in the aftermath of the previous season's Assen strike, MV Agusta's John Surtees was able to rack up victories at the Isle of Man TT and the Dutch TT. Umberto Masetti was the other MV rider.

BMW finally decided to contest a whole season with Walter Zeller on the fuel-injected short-stroke Rennsport flat-twin. The combination didn't win a race but Zeller did get on the rostrum – and not just when the Gilera team was absent. Moto Guzzi contested all classes except the 125 with Aussie Ken Kavanagh, Brits Bill Lomas and Dickie Dale, and Italy's Duilio Agostini. However, the 500cc single was now uncompetitive and the factory raced the still quite astounding water-cooled V8. The Guzzi 350 was still good enough to see off the new four-cylinder designs from MV and Gilera comfortably, although the screaming three-cylinder two-stroke DKWs of August Hobl (GER) and Cecil Sandford were more of a problem.

MV's new 250 – a full 249cc as opposed to the old enlarged 125, which would only stretch to 220cc – was too good for even Enrico Lorenzetti and the Moto Guzzi. Carlo Ubbiali dominated both the 250 and 125 championships, winning 10 of the 12 races. Add in the very competitive and important Italian Championship and he won 18 races out of 20 in the season! The 250 GP that Ubbiali missed out on was won by Luigi Taveri on another MV, but the 125 race they failed to win was a victory for the fast but fragile newcomer, Gilera's twin, the Gilerino. The rider was Romolo Ferri (ITA), poached from Mondial, whose effort was again fronted by the indefatigable Tarquinio Provini.

This was the year that MV Agusta finally achieved their first 500cc title, plus three constructors' titles to go with their three riders' championships. The highlight was their clean sweep of all four races at the Belgian GP at Spa-Francorchamps, the 500 and 350cc wins being taken by Surtees, the two smaller classes by Ubbiali.

ABOVE The 125s blast off at Monza. Nearest the camera is Provini on Mondial number 21, and number 4 is an MV Agusta (the rider may be Roberto Colombo). Provini set the fastest lap but was beaten by Ubbiali by 0.4sec. *(Stuart Dent Archive)*

RIGHT, ABOVE John Surtees and the 500cc MV Agusta, with his father, Jack, issuing last-minute instructions. *(Stuart Dent Archive)*

RIGHT Tarquinio Provini: there may have been tougher racers, but no-one is quite sure who they might be. *(Stuart Dent Archive)*

THE 1956 SEASON

500cc

GBR/Isle of Man TT
- John Surtees won the Senior TT on his World Championship debut on the MV Agusta factory bike

BEL/Spa-Francorchamps
- Surtees took his third successive win after Geoff Duke, making his return to racing after his six-month ban, retired with mechanical failure when holding a one-minute lead

ULS/Dundrod
- John Hartle (GBR) won his first GP and gave Norton their first 500cc GP victory for more than two years
- In spite of missing the event, John Surtees won his first world title after his closest challenger Walter Zeller (BMW) retired from the race with mechanical problems

ITA-NAZ/Monza
- Defending champion Geoff Duke took his only points of the year with a victory at Monza

250cc

GER/Solitude
- Carlo Ubbiali won the first four races of the year to clinch the 250cc world title for the first time

ULS/Dundrod
- Luigi Taveri took the second of his two career victories in the 250 class, the only rider other than Ubbiali to win a 250cc race in 1956

350cc

BEL/Spa-Francorchamps
- John Surtees gave MV Agusta their first victory in the 350cc class
- This was also the first 350cc win by a four-cylinder machine

GER/Solitude
- Surtees crashed on lap eight and suffered injuries that caused him to miss the remainder of the season

ULS/Dundrod
- Bill Lomas took his third victory of the year to retain the 350cc world title, as closest challenger August Hobl (DKW) finished seventh and failed to score any points

ITA-NAZ/Monza
- Libero Liberati gave Gilera their first 350cc GP victory

125cc

GER/Solitude
- Romolo Ferri gave Gilera their first GP win in the 125cc class; it took another 45 years before Gilera achieved their second 125cc victory, with Manuel Poggiali (RSM) at the French GP of 2001
- Carlo Ubbiali's record run of eight successive victories came to an end when he finished second to Romolo Ferri, but he did retain the 125cc world title

ULS/Dundrod
- Luigi Taveri took the second of his two career victories in the 250 class, the only rider other than Ubbiali to win a 250cc race in 1956
- Frank Cope (MV) finishes fifth at the age of 60, the oldest points scorer in GPs

1956 WORLD CHAMPIONSHIP

500cc

Four best results were counted

Pos	Rider	Nat	Machine	GBR	NED	BEL	GER	ULS	ITA	Nett	Gross
1	John Surtees	GBR	MV Agusta	8	8	8	-	-	-	24	
2	Walter Zeller	GER	BMW	3	6	6	-	-	1	16	
3	John Hartle	GBR	Norton	6	-	-	-	8	-	14	
4	Pierre Monneret	FRA	Gilera	-	-	4	4	-	4	12	
5	Reg Armstrong	IRL	Gilera	-	-	-	8	-	3	11	
6	Umberto Masetti	ITA	MV Agusta	-	-	3	6	-	-	9	
7	Geoff Duke	GBR	Gilera	-	-	-	-	-	8	8	
8	Bob Brown	AUS	Matchless	-	-	-	-	6	-	6	
8	Libero Liberati	ITA	Gilera	-	-	-	-	-	6	6	
10	Eddie Grant	RSA	Norton	-	4	-	2	-	-	6	
11	Jack Brett	GBR	Norton	4	-	-	-	1	-	5	
12	Peter Murphy	NZE	Matchless	-	-	-	-	4	-	4	
13	Keith Bryen	AUS	Norton	-	3	-	1	-	-	4	
14	Gerold Klinger	AUT	BMW	-	-	-	3	-	-	3	
14	Geoff Tanner	GBR	Norton	-	-	-	-	3	-	3	
16	Carlo Bandirola	ITA	MV Agusta	-	-	-	-	-	2	2	
16	Paul Fahey	NZE	Matchless	-	2	-	-	-	-	2	
16	Wilf Herron	GBR	Norton	-	-	-	-	2	-	2	
16	Bill Lomas	GBR	Moto Guzzi	2	-	-	-	-	-	2	
16	Alfredo Milani	ITA	Gilera	-	-	2	-	-	-	2	
21	Derek Ennett	GBR	Matchless	1	-	-	-	-	-	1	
21	Auguste Goffin	BEL	Norton	-	-	1	-	-	-	1	
21	Ernst Hiller	GER	BMW	-	1	-	-	-	-	1	

Scoring system – 8, 6, 4, 3, 2, 1

LEFT The final version of the astounding 500cc Moto Guzzi V8. (*Ian Falloon*)

OPPOSITE Moto Guzzi's genius engineer Giulio Carcano with assistants Enrico Cantoni and Umberto Todero. (*Ian Falloon*)

350cc

Four best results were counted

Pos	Rider	Nat	Machine	Nett	Gross
1	Bill Lomas	GBR	Moto Guzzi	24	
2	Dickie Dale	GBR	Moto Guzzi	17	
2	August Hobl	GER	DKW	17	
4	John Surtees	GBR	MV Agusta	14	
5	Cecil Sandford	GBR	DKW	13	(15)
6	Ken Kavanagh	AUS	Moto Guzzi	10	
7	Libero Liberati	ITA	Gilera	8	
8	John Hartle	GBR	Norton	8	
9	Derek Ennett	GBR	AJS	6	
10	Karl Hofmann	GER	DKW	6	

250cc

Four best results were counted

Pos	Rider	Nat	Machine	Nett	Gross
1	Carlo Ubbiali	ITA	MV Agusta	32	(40)
2	Luigi Taveri	SWI	MV Agusta	26	(29)
3	Enrico Lorenzetti	ITA	Moto Guzzi	10	
4	Roberto Colombo	ITA	MV Agusta	9	
5	Horst Kassner	GER	NSU	9	
6	Remo Venturi	ITA	MV Agusta	8	
7	Sammy Miller	IRL	NSU	7	
8	Hans Baltisberger	GER	NSU	7	
9	Arthur Wheeler	GBR	Moto Guzzi	5	
10	Bob Coleman	NZE	NSU	3	
10	Kees Koster	NED	NSU	3	

125cc

Four best results were counted

Pos	Rider	Nat	Machine	Nett	Gross
1	Carlo Ubbiali	ITA	MV Agusta	32	(46)
2	Romolo Ferri	ITA	Gilera	14	
3	Luigi Taveri	SWI	MV Agusta	12	
4	Tarquinio Provini	ITA	Mondial	10	
5	Fortunato Libanori	ITA	MV Agusta	9	
6	Marcelo Cama	SPA	Montesa	6	
7	August Hobl	GER	DKW	6	
8	Karl Hofmann	GER	DKW	5	
9	Francisco Gonzales	SPA	Montesa	4	
9	Pierre Monneret	FRA	Gilera	4	
9	Renato Sartori	ITA	Mondial	4	
9	Bill Webster	GBR	MV Agusta	4	

GUZZI, CARCANO AND THE V8

Moto Guzzi's designer, Giulio Carcano, was responsible for the astonishing single-cylinder racers that won the 350cc world title between 1953 and 1957, as well as for the most ambitious racer of any era, the Guzzi V8. He understood that the only way for the single to compete with multi-cylinder designs was with low weight, efficient aerodynamics and increased revs. Over the years, the horizontal single was painstakingly refined with both SOHC and DOHC heads. The final 350 of 1957 weighed just 215lb/98kg thanks to much use of aluminium and magnesium; it revved to 8400rpm and made 38hp.

Although Carcano had faith in the single-cylinder layout as the way forward in the 350 class, he was well aware the 500 couldn't compete with the Gileras and MVs. The in-line four of 1953 that was disliked by everyone who rode it was not a Carcano design, and the team quickly reverted to the lightweight single. Carcano was finally allowed to pursue his vision, and the result was the V8. The 90-degree across-the-frame motor had a one-piece magnesium crankcase, over-square bore and stroke, very narrow (5mm) valve stems, and it made 68hp at 12,000rpm. The motor weighed just 123lb/56kg, with all-up weight 331lb/150kg.

The original design was first raced in 1955 but suffered from serious handling problems in fast corners, and a lack of reliability: it always broke down, usually while in the lead, and didn't finish a race until a new crankshaft design was used for the '57 season, by which time it was making 73hp. Reliability was much improved and Dickie Dale scored fourths on it in the first two GPs of 1957. Spa was the nearest the V8 came to winning a GP. Australia's Keith Campbell was leading by a distance, had smashed the lap record and been timed at 178mph/286km/h when a battery lead came off. Giuseppe Colnago did, however, win an Italian Championship race on it. It is tempting to speculate on what could have been achieved had the Italian factories not withdrawn from Grand Prix racing at the end of 1957. Nevertheless, the V8 Moto Guzzi remains one of the great racing designs of any era and a lasting reminder of Giulio Carcano's genius.

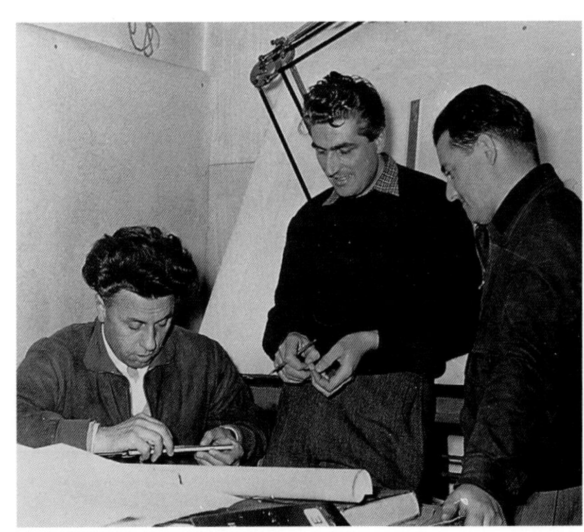

1957

Gilera took the 500 title back from MV and finally broke the 100mph barrier on the Isle of Man

This was Gilera's year. Libero Liberati won the 500cc title, with team-mate Bob McIntyre runner-up. Geoff Duke's season was ruined by shoulder injury sustained in a pre-season race at Imola, and Aussie Bob Brown replaced him at the TT.

MV Agusta's hopes were carried alone by reigning champion John Surtees, but he only managed one race win. MV unveiled a six-cylinder 500 in practice for the Monza GP but did not race it. Moto Guzzi's V8 added reliability to its undoubted speed, although its high-speed handling led to more than one rider refusing to race it. Bill Lomas, Dickie Dale and Keith Campbell started the season for Guzzi, with another Australian, Keith Bryen, joining them at Spa. Giuseppe Colnago was reserve, racing primarily in the Italian Championship.

The 350cc Guzzi single was still able to dominate Gilera's smaller four and the Norton Manx, while in the 250 and 125 classes Mondial swept the board with riders Cecil Sandford, Tarquinio Provini and Ireland's Sammy Miller. A new single replaced the twin in the 250 class and comprehensively outperformed the MV to finish first, second and third. Things were closer in the 125 class, but the uprated, seven-speed Mondial was good enough for Provini to see off the MV armada led by Luigi Taveri and Carlo Ubbiali.

At the end of the year the Italian factories announced their withdrawal from the sport, although MV, who had originally planned to go along with the pull-out, later thought better of it. Gilera's decision was affected by the death of Ferruccio Gilera, son of the company owner and a driving force behind the team. Their bikes would be back on track with Scuderia Duke in 1963.

Moto Guzzi, with its three top riders badly injured and its aerodynamic advantage about to be negated by the banning of full streamlining, cited the downturn in street-bike sales, as did the comparatively small Mondial concern. Single-cylinder Guzzis were still raced, notably by British veteran Arthur Wheeler.

ABOVE Libero Liberati on the fully-faired factory 500 Gilera. (Elwyn Roberts Collection)

RIGHT John Hartle impressed enough for John Surtees to recommend him to MV Agusta. John won on a 250 MV in Belgium that year, his only win in the class. He won three in 500s. (*Stuart Dent Archive*)

THE 1957 SEASON

500cc

GER/Hockenheim

- Libero Liberati (Gilera) took his first 500cc GP win and made it a double, having taken 350cc victory earlier in the day
- This was the first time that an average speed of 124mph/200km/h had been achieved in a Grand Prix race

GBR/Isle of Man TT

- To celebrate the 50th anniversary of the first Isle of Man TT, the race was increased to eight laps, a distance of 302 miles/486km – the longest Grand Prix ever
- On his way to winning the Senior TT, Bob McIntyre (Gilera) became the first rider to lap the TT course at more than 100mph/161km/h; his race time was 3h 2m 57s

NED/Assen

- Bill Lomas, riding the Moto Guzzi V8, crashed in practice, his injuries eliminating him from the season's remaining races and leading to his subsequent retirement when Guzzi pulled out of GP racing at the end of the year
- John Surtees (MV Agusta) took his only GP victory of the year in defence of his World Championship title
- Championship leader Bob McIntyre crashed and suffered injuries that prevented him racing at the next GP in Belgium

BEL/Spa-Francorchamps

- Libero Liberati won the race, only to be disqualified for changing his machine without notifying the officials. (He'd used team-mate Bob Brown's machine for the race)
- This handed victory to Jack Brett (GBR, Norton), but Liberati was later reinstated as winner on appeal after the racing season was over

ITA-NAZ/Monza

- Liberati won the final race of the year to confirm his world title irrespective of the result of the disputed Belgian race

350cc

ULS/Dundrod

- Keith Campbell took his third successive victory to become the first Australian World Champion
- This was the fifth successive year that a Moto Guzzi rider was 350cc champion – but this was also the last championship win by a Guzzi rider

ITA-NAZ/Monza

- Bob McIntyre gave Gilera their last 350cc GP win

250cc

GER/Hockenheim

- Carlo Ubbiali won the opening race of the year in defence of his world title, but it was his only points-scoring ride of the year in the class

GBR/Isle of Man TT

- Cecil Sandford (Mondial) won his first 250cc GP after a race-long battle with team-mate Sammy Miller, who crashed with less than a mile to go to the chequered flag

ULS/Dundrod

- Cecil Sandford won to become the first British rider to take the 250cc world title

125cc

GBR/Isle of Man TT

- Carlo Ubbiali's second-place finish was the last in a record sequence of 14 successive podium finishes in the 125cc class

NED/Assen

- Ubbiali crashed during practice and suffered injuries that eliminated him from the Belgian and Ulster events

BEL/Spa-Francorchamps

- Roberto Colombo (MV) died after crashing in practice

ULS/Dundrod

- A second-place finish for Tarquinio Provini was enough to give him his first World Championship title

1957 WORLD CHAMPIONSHIP

500cc

Four best results were counted

Pos	Rider	Nat	Machine	GER	GBR	NED	BEL	ULS	ITA	Nett	Gross
1	Libero Liberati	ITA	Gilera	8	-	6	8	8	8	32	(38)
2	Bob McIntyre	GBR	Gilera	6	8	-	-	6	-	20	
3	John Surtees	GBR	MV Agusta	-	6	8	-	-	3	17	
4	Geoff Duke	GBR	Gilera	-	-	-	-	4	6	10	
5	Jack Brett	GBR	Norton	-	-	3	6	-	-	9	
6	Walter Zeller	GER	BMW	4	-	4	-	-	-	8	
7	Keith Bryen	AUS	Norton/Moto Guzzi	-	-	1	4	2	-	7	
8	Dickie Dale	GBR	Moto Guzzi	3	3	-	-	-	-	6	
9	Bob Brown	AUS	Gilera	-	4	-	-	-	-	4	
9	Alfredo Milani	ITA	Gilera	-	-	-	-	-	4	4	
11	Terry Shepherd	GBR	MV Agusta	2	-	-	-	1	1	4	
12	Derek Minter	GBR	Norton	-	-	-	3	-	-	3	
12	Geoff Tanner	GBR	Norton	-	-	-	-	3	-	3	
14	Ernst Hiller	GER	BMW	1	-	2	-	-	-	3	
15	Keith Campbell	AUS	Moto Guzzi	-	2	-	-	-	-	2	
15	Umberto Masetti	ITA	MV Agusta	-	-	-	-	-	2	2	
15	Mike O'Rourke	GBR	Norton	-	-	-	2	-	-	2	
18	Hans Gunter Jager	GER	BMW	-	-	-	1	-	-	1	
18	Alan Trow	GBR	Norton	-	1	-	-	-	-	1	

Scoring system – 8, 6, 4, 3, 2, 1

350cc

Four best results were counted

Pos	Rider	Nat	Machine	Nett	Gross
1	Keith Campbell	AUS	Moto Guzzi	30	
2	Libero Liberati	ITA	Gilera	22	(26)
3	Bob McIntyre	GBR	Gilera	22	
4	Keith Bryen	AUS	Moto Guzzi/Norton	12	
5	John Hartle	GBR	Norton	11	
6	Giuseppe Colnago	ITA	Moto Guzzi	7	
7	Bob Brown	AUS	Gilera	6	
8	Helmut Hallmeier	GER	NSU	4	
9	Adelmo Mandolini	ITA	Moto Guzzi	4	
10	Alano Montanari	ITA	Moto Guzzi	3	
10	Jack Brett	GBR	Norton	3	
10	Umberto Masetti	ITA	MV Agusta	3	
10	Alfredo Milani	ITA	Gilera	3	
10	John Surtees	GBR	MV Agusta	3	

250cc

Four best results were counted

Pos	Rider	Nat	Machine	Nett	Gross
1	Cecil Sandford	GBR	Mondial	26	(33)
2	Tarquinio Provini	ITA	Mondial	16	
3	Sammy Miller	IRL	Mondial	14	
4	Roberto Colombo	ITA	MV Agusta	10	
5	John Hartle	GBR	MV Agusta	8	
5	Carlo Ubbiali	ITA	MV Agusta	8	
7	Luigi Taveri	SWI	MV Agusta	8	
8	Dave Chadwick	GBR	MV Agusta	7	
9	Enrico Lorenzetti	ITA	Moto Guzzi	7	
10	Remo Venturi	ITA	MV Agusta	6	

125cc

Four best results were counted

Pos	Rider	Nat	Machine	Nett	Gross
1	Tarquinio Provini	ITA	Mondial	30	(36)
2	Luigi Taveri	SWI	MV Agusta	22	(28)
3	Carlo Ubbiali	ITA	MV Agusta	22	
4	Sammy Miller	IRL	Mondial	12	
5	Roberto Colombo	ITA	MV Agusta	11	
6	Cecil Sandford	GBR	Mondial	9	
7	Remo Venturi	ITA	MV Agusta	6	
8	Fortunato Libanori	ITA	MV Agusta	5	
9	Frantisek Bartos	CZE	CZ	3	
9	Dave Chadwick	GBR	MV Agusta	3	
9	Horst Fugner	GER	MZ	3	

THE MAGIC TON

The Isle of Man Mountain circuit's 100mph/161km/h barrier was finally breached by Bob McIntyre (Gilera) in the TT's golden jubilee year. Geoff Duke had come so near to the magic ton two years previously, in 1955, only to have what was announced as a lap at exactly 100mph rounded down to 99.97mph. (The Gilera team was then suspended for the first two GPs of 1956.) In 1957 McIntyre started the longest ever GP, the Senior TT – eight laps of the Island instead of the usual seven, in honour of the jubilee – with a lap of 99.99mph from a standing start. That was a new lap record; then came a lap of 101.03mph and three more at three-figure speeds: 100.54, 101.12 and 100.35mph. His race average was 98.99mph. No other rider, in a field that included John Surtees on the MV, Bob Brown on the other Gilera and the Guzzis of Dickie Dale and Keith Campbell, could manage even one lap at over a hundred. Surtees, though, would do the ton the following year and take the lap record in '59.

When Gilera pulled out of racing the factory embarked on a spree of record breaking using both the 350 and 500-fours at Monza in November. Alfredo Milani set a new one-hour record of 134.4 miles/216.3km on the 500 before flying to compete in a winter series in Argentina. McIntyre then used the 350 to do 141.37 miles/227.5km. That record wasn't beaten until 1964, and it took the combination of Mike Hailwood, MV Agusta and the Daytona banking to do it.

Bob McIntyre died after a wet-weather crash at Oulton Park in 1962. At a tribute meeting later that same year Geoff Duke rode one of the Gileras and formed the idea of running his own team, Scuderia Duke. Thus the Gilera four, one of the seminal racing motorcycle designs of all time, returned to the track for a final outing.

OPPOSITE Bob McIntyre on the Gilera four during the record-breaking Senior TT. (*JARROTTS.com*)

ABOVE Bob McIntyre, the very epitome of the gritty Scot. The '57 TT was his only GP win. (*Elwyn Roberts Collection*)

1958

In the absence of the other Italian factories, MV Agusta won every class and Surtees was all but unbeatable

The look of racing changed over winter as the FIM banned full-enclosure streamlining: both wheels and (most of) the rider's arms and legs now had to be visible from the side. The shape of sporting motorcycles as we now know them was fixed.

The withdrawal of Gilera, Moto Guzzi and Mondial left MV alone in the bigger classes, but they still had stiff Italian competition in the smaller ones in the shape of Ducati in the 125s, plus Morini, making a comeback to GPs, in the 250s. There was also a new challenge emerging from a most unexpected quarter: the East German MZ factory and their Walter Kaaden-designed two-strokes.

John Surtees dominated both the 500 and 350 classes with support from new team-mate and fellow-Brit John Hartle. Geoff Duke started the year on a BMW but soon reverted to Norton, as did most of the ex-employees of the Italian factories. MV had both Carlo Ubbiali and Tarquinio Provini in the smaller classes, not an easy pair to manage, but the factory decided Provini should be the lead man for the 250s and Ubbiali for the 125s. This arrangement kept these two very different but equally strong characters happy, at least for a while.

Ducati had first raced, and won, with their 125 Desmo in 1956 but this was the first year they contested the full World Championship. The team was led by Luigi Taveri with support from fellow-Italians Alberto Gandossi, Romolo Ferri, Bruno Spaggiari and Francesco Villa, plus Britain's Dave Chadwick. Morini's new 250 only appeared for the final race of the year, Monza, but Italians Emilio Mendogni and Gianpiero Zubani finished first and second there. The other challenge to MV in the quarter-litre class was from MZ's Horst Fügner, with Ernst Degner (both DDR) backing him up in the 125s.

A good rider could still get on the rostrum with an NSU Sportmax, however, as a British youngster called Mike Hailwood demonstrated.

ABOVE John Surtees on the 500cc four-cylinder MV Agusta. (*JARROTTS.com*)

RIGHT Bob Brown and Mike Hailwood on NSU Sportmaxes during the Lightweight (250cc) TT. This was Hailwood's first GP meeting – he finished third in the 250s and got to the flag in all four classes. (*JARROTTS.com*)

THE **1958** SEASON

500cc

GBR/Isle of Man TT

- John Surtees opened the year with a 500/350cc double victory

BEL/Spa-Francorchamps

- Reigning 350cc champion Keith Campbell (Norton) took his best ever result in the 500cc class, finishing second behind John Surtees
- Sadly, just one week later, Campbell was to lose his life on the first lap of a non-championship 500cc race at the Cadours circuit in France, having already won the 350cc race at the same event

GER/Nürburgring

- John Surtees made it four wins from the first four races to regain the world title
- Riding at only his third Grand Prix event, 20-year-old Rhodesian Gary Hocking (Norton) finished third behind the four-cylinder factory MVs of Surtees and Hartle

SWE/Hedemora

- At the first Swedish Grand Prix counting towards the World Championship, Geoff Duke (Norton) became the only rider other than John Surtees to win in the 500cc class during 1958, having won the 350cc race earlier in the day
- This win was the last of Duke's 33 Grand Prix victories

ITA-NAZ/Monza

- John Surtees won at the final race of the year to make it 12 wins from 12 starts in 1958's two biggest classes
- John Hartle gave the new six-cylinder MV Agusta its debut and, after being last away, moved up to fourth before retiring on lap 19

350cc

GER/Nürburgring

- John Surtees repeated his success in the 500cc class by winning the opening four races of the year to take his first 350cc world title and the first for a multi-cylinder machine

SWE/Hedemora

- Geoff Duke took the last of his 11 wins in the 350cc class and the first for Norton in four years

250cc

GBR/Isle of Man TT

- Aged 18, Mike Hailwood (NSU), competing in his first Grand Prix, finished third

SWE/Hedemora

- Horst Fügner became the first rider to take a Grand Prix victory on an MZ motorcycle

ULS/Dundrod

- Tarquinio Provini (MV Agusta) made this his fourth win of the year to take the 250cc world title

ITA-NAZ/Monza

- Morini debuted their new 250cc machine and took first and second places with Emilio Mendogni and Gianpiero Zubani

125cc

GBR/Isle of Man TT

- Carlo Ubbiali (MV) won from Romolo Ferri and Dave Chadwick, the first riders on Ducati machinery to finish on the podium

BEL/Spa-Francorchamps

- Alberto Gandossi gave Ducati their first Grand Prix victory

ULS/Dundrod

- Ubbiali won at the Ulster GP to take the 125cc title for the fourth time

1958 WORLD CHAMPIONSHIP

500cc

Four best results were counted

Pos	Rider	Nat	Machine	GBR	NED	BEL	GER	SWE	ULS	ITA	Nett	Gross
1	John Surtees	GBR	MV Agusta	8	8	8	8	-	8	8	32	(48)
2	John Hartle	GBR	MV Agusta	-	6	4	6	-	4	-	20	
3	Geoff Duke	GBR	BMW/Norton	-	-	3	-	8	2	-	13	
4	Dickie Dale	GBR	BMW	-	2	2	2	6	1	3	13	(16)
5	Derek Minter	GBR	Norton	3	4	-	-	-	3	-	10	
6	Gary Hocking	RHO	Norton	-	1	-	4	3	-	-	8	
7	Ernst Hiller	GER	BMW	-	3	-	3	2	-	-	8	
8	Bob Anderson	GBR	Norton	6	-	1	-	-	-	-	7	
9	Keith Campbell	AUS	Norton	-	-	6	-	-	-	-	6	
9	Bob McIntyre	GBR	Norton	-	-	-	-	-	6	-	6	
9	Remo Venturi	ITA	MV Agusta	-	-	-	-	-	-	6	6	
12	Bob Brown	AUS	Norton	4	-	-	1	1	-	-	6	
13	Umberto Masetti	ITA	MV Agusta	-	-	-	-	-	-	4	4	
13	Terry Shepherd	GBR	Norton	-	-	-	-	4	-	-	4	
15	Dave Chadwick	GBR	Norton	2	-	-	-	-	-	1	3	
16	Carlo Bandirola	ITA	MV Agusta	-	-	-	-	-	-	2	2	
17	John Anderson	NZE	Norton	1	-	-	-	-	-	-	1	

Scoring system – 8, 6, 4, 3, 2, 1

350cc

Four best results were counted

Pos	Rider	Nat	Machine	Nett	Gross
1	John Surtees	GBR	MV Agusta	32	(48)
2	John Hartle	GBR	MV Agusta	24	(30)
3	Geoff Duke	GBR	Norton	17	
4	Dave Chadwick	GBR	Norton	13	
5	Bob Anderson	GBR	Norton	11	
6	Mike Hailwood	GBR	Norton	9	
7	Keith Campbell	AUS	Norton	8	
8	Terry Shepherd	GBR	Norton	7	
9	Derek Minter	GBR	Norton	7	
10	Geoff Tanner	GBR	Norton	4	

250cc

Four best results were counted

Pos	Rider	Nat	Machine	Nett
1	Tarquinio Provini	ITA	MV Agusta	32
2	Horst Fügner	DDR	MZ	16
3	Carlo Ubbiali	ITA	MV Agusta	16
4	Mike Hailwood	GBR	NSU	13
5	Dieter Falk	GER	Adler	11
6	Emilio Mendogni	ITA	Morini	8
7	Tommy Robb	GBR	NSU	6
7	Giampiero Zubani	ITA	Morini	6
9	Gunter Beer	GER	Adler	6
10	Dave Chadwick	GBR	MV Agusta	4
10	Geoff Monty	GBR	NSU	4

125cc

Four best results were counted

Pos	Rider	Nat	Machine	Nett	Gross
1	Carlo Ubbiali	ITA	MV Agusta	32	(38)
2	Alberto Gandossi	ITA	Ducati	25	(28)
3	Luigi Taveri	SWI	Ducati	20	(21)
4	Tarquinio Provini	ITA	MV Agusta	17	
5	Dave Chadwick	GBR	Ducati	14	(16)
6	Romolo Ferri	ITA	Ducati	12	
7	Ernst Degner	DDR	MZ	9	
8	Bruno Spaggiari	ITA	Ducati	8	
9	Horst Fügner	DDR	MZ	7	
10	Francesco Villa	ITA	Ducati	4	

THE BIRTH OF THE MODERN TWO-STROKE

When DKW stopped racing after winning just one GP, prevailing wisdom had it that the two-stroke really couldn't challenge the four-stroke in any class of racing. At the tiny East German MZ firm, though, engineer Walter Kaaden had come to a deeper understanding than anyone else of how the two-stroke worked. He knew that efficiency came from harnessing the pressure waves that reflect and resonate in the exhaust. This gave rise to the expansion chamber. He understood the need for asymmetric port timing, hence disc-valve induction. Finally, he rediscovered an old Zundapp concept, the third transfer – or boost – port.

Unfortunately, in post-war Communist East Germany it was difficult to get hold of modern metals, let alone state-of-the art ignitions or carburettors. Nevertheless, the small team first scored points under the IFA name in 1955, unnoticed by everyone except British journalist Vic Willoughby, who did more than anyone to throw light on the genius of Kaaden, a man who was liked as well as respected by all who worked with or rode for him.

By 1958 the bikes, now called MZs, were very fast but fussy and fragile. The standard technique for a rider on another make of bike was to try and slipstream the MZs while keeping a sharp eye on the two-stroke's exhaust. As soon as the first tell-tale signs of blue smoke appeared it was necessary to dive to one side to avoid the rapidly slowing MZ.

However, a rider with mechanical sympathy and an acute enough ear to juggle with an air-lever control (a bit like a choke) while racing these machines could make them last. Horst Fügner was good enough to do all that. He finished the season second, splitting the factory MVs and taking the MZ's first GP victory. The following season, foreign riders started taking an interest in riding MZs. The factory went on to win 13 GPs, the last in 1971, but never won the world title that Walter Kaaden's work deserved (see the chapter on 1961 for the reasons why). However, that should not obscure the fact that one man, working behind the Iron Curtain without access to modern techniques or materials, deduced the principles of the modern two-stroke racer.

OPPOSITE An original MZ factory publicity postcard showing their first GP winner Horst Fügner. Note the antiquated Earles forks. *(Elwyn Roberts Collection)*

ABOVE Ernst Degner, MZ's lead rider who would play such a part in the momentous events of 1961. *(Stuart Dent Archive)*

1959

John Surtees won every race as MV Agusta dominated the big classes, Gary Hocking emerged as a future champion

Once again MV won everything, with John Surtees victorious in every 350 and 500cc race, a unique achievement. His back-up in the big class was Remo Venturi (ITA) and, in the 350s, John Hartle. In both classes the opposition again came from privately entered and tuned Nortons, with young Rhodesian Gary Hocking on the Dearden Manx being particularly impressive. BMW tried for a final season, this time with Dickie Dale on board.

Hocking was one of the riders who had shrewdly assessed the potential of MZ's two-strokes and, when Horst Fügner suffered career-ending injuries at Spa, Gary rode the 250 MZ and won first time out. He won next time out, too – and MV immediately signed him up for 1960. MZ's Walter Kaaden later told the Swedish journalist Jan Leek how Hocking never blew up one of his ultra-sensitive engines, despite being so blazingly fast. By comparison Luigi Taveri, the first non-East German rider to sign for MZ, started 16 races for them but only finished five, although as Kaaden said in the same interview, it was the Swiss rider who'd first showed that his bikes could win. The MZ team's 125 riders, Ernst Degner and Britain's Derek Minter, couldn't get near the MVs, apart from a brilliant Degner victory at Monza.

MV's Carlo Ubbiali and Tarquinio Provini were by now as intent on stabbing each other in the back as they were on retaining their titles. Ubbiali ended up winning both 125 and 250 championships, with Provini departing for Moto Morini at the end of the year. In the 250 class Morini-mounted Emilio Mendogni and Minter, plus Mike Hailwood on an ex-works Mondial, were MV's other opposition. Hailwood again featured in the 125s, this time on a Ducati Desmo single, with Bruno Spaggiari and Walter Villa receiving similar machinery. Luigi Taveri started the year on a Ducati twin before switching to MZ, while Ken Kavanagh bought a DOHC single and received some additional factory support.

ABOVE John Surtees blasts through Parliament Square on the 350cc MV Agusta during the Junior TT. (*JARROTTS.com*)

RIGHT MV Agusta's other double champion, Carlo Ubbiali. (*JARROTTS.com*)

THE **1959** SEASON

500cc

FRA/Clermont-Ferrand
- At the first Grand Prix event to be held at the newly constructed Clermont-Ferrand circuit, John Surtees opened the season with another 500/350cc double victory

NED/Assen
- For the second successive year Surtees won the championship with four wins from the first four races

ITA-NAZ/Monza
- John Surtees made it seven wins from seven races to become the first rider to have a perfect winning season in the 500cc class
- Geoff Duke (Norton) finished third on his last Grand Prix appearance before retiring from motorcycle racing

350cc

SWE/Kristianstad
- John Surtees won the opening four races of the year to retain the 350cc world title

ITA-NAZ/Monza
- Surtees made it six wins from six races to become the first rider since Freddie Frith in 1949 to have a perfect winning season in the 350cc class

250cc

GBR/Isle of Man TT
- Tarquinio Provini won the opening races of the season for both 125 and 250cc classes

GER/Hockenheim
- Carlo Ubbiali won after a race-long battle with Emilio Mendogni and Horst Fügner
- Third-placed Fügner finished just 0.8s behind Ubbiali – the first time in the 250cc class that the three podium finishers were covered by less than a second

NED/Assen
- Derek Minter finished third on his debut for the Morini factory team

SWE/Kristianstad
- Gary Hocking scored his first Grand Prix victory on his debut riding for the factory MZ team

ULS/Dundrod
- In spite of not attending the Ulster GP, Ubbiali regained the 250cc world title as his closest challenger and team-mate, Provini, was also absent from the event

125cc

GBR/Isle of Man TT
- Honda made their World Championship debut, winning the team prize with a best result of sixth for Naomi Taniguchi

BEL/Spa-Francorchamps
- MZ factory rider Horst Fügner crashed in practice and suffered career-ending injuries

ULS/Dundrod
- At 19, Mike Hailwood (Ducati) became the youngest rider to win a Grand Prix

ITA-NAZ/Monza
- Ernst Degner (MZ) took his first GP victory, but the Italian authorities banned the playing of the East German national anthem and the raising of its flag
- Carlo Ubbiali finished second at the final race of the year to retain his world title

1959 WORLD CHAMPIONSHIP

500cc

Four best results were counted

Pos	Rider	Nat	Machine	FRA	GBR	GER	NED	BEL	ULS	ITA	Nett	Gross
1	John Surtees	GBR	MV Agusta	8	8	8	8	8	8	8	32	(56)
2	Remo Venturi	ITA	MV Agusta	6	-	6	4	2	-	6	22	(24)
3	Bob Brown	AUS	Norton	-	4	4	6	3	2	3	17	(22)
4	Geoff Duke	GBR	Norton	-	-	-	-	4	4	4	12	
5	Gary Hocking	RHO	Norton	4	-	-	-	6	-	-	10	
6	Bob McIntyre	GBR	Norton	-	2	-	-	-	6	-	8	
7	Alastair King	GBR	Norton	-	6	-	-	-	1	-	7	
8	Dickie Dale	GBR	BMW	3	-	-	3	-	-	-	6	
9	Terry Shepherd	GBR	Norton	2	-	-	-	-	3	-	5	
10	John Hempleman	NZE	Norton	-	-	2	-	-	-	2	4	
11	Ken Kavanagh	AUS	Norton	-	-	3	-	-	-	-	3	
11	Derek Powell	GBR	Matchless	-	3	-	-	-	-	-	3	
13	Paddy Driver	RSA	Norton	1	1	-	-	-	-	1	3	
14	Jim Redman	RHO	Norton	-	-	-	2	-	-	-	2	
15	Bob Anderson	GBR	Norton	-	-	-	-	1	-	-	1	
15	Alois Huber	GER	BMW	-	-	1	-	-	-	-	1	
15	Ron Miles	AUS	Norton	-	-	-	1	-	-	-	1	

Scoring system – 8, 6, 4, 3, 2, 1

350cc

Four best results were counted

Pos	Rider	Nat	Machine	Nett	Gross
1	John Surtees	GBR	MV Agusta	32	(48)
2	John Hartle	GBR	MV Agusta	16	
3	Bob Brown	AUS	Norton	14	
4	Gary Hocking	RHO	Norton	12	
5	Geoff Duke	GBR	Norton	10	
6	Remo Venturi	ITA	MV Agusta	6	
7	Dickie Dale	GBR	AJS	6	
8	John Hempleman	NZE	Norton	6	
9	Bob Anderson	GBR	Norton	5	
10	Alastair King	GBR	Norton	4	
10	Ernesto Brambilla	ITA	MV Agusta	4	

250cc

Four best results were counted

Pos	Rider	Nat	Machine	Nett	Gross
1	Carlo Ubbiali	ITA	MV Agusta	28	(34)
2	Gary Hocking	RHO	MZ	16	
2	Tarquinio Provini	ITA	MV Agusta	16	
4	Ernst Degner	DDR	MZ	14	
5	Mike Hailwood	GBR	Mondial	13	
6	Emilio Mendogni	ITA	Morini	10	
7	Derek Minter	GBR	Morini	7	
8	Tommy Robb	GBR	GMS/MZ	7	
9	Horst Fügner	DDR	MZ	6	
10	Geoff Duke	GBR	Benelli	5	

125cc

Four best results were counted

Pos	Rider	Nat	Machine	Nett	Gross
1	Carlo Ubbiali	ITA	MV Agusta	30	(38)
2	Tarquinio Provini	ITA	MV Agusta	28	(30)
3	Mike Hailwood	GBR	Ducati	20	(23)
4	Luigi Taveri	SWI	Ducati/MZ	14	
5	Ernst Degner	DDR	MZ	13	
6	Bruno Spaggiari	ITA	Ducati	8	
7	Derek Minter	GBR	MZ	8	
8	Ken Kavanagh	AUS	Ducati	8	
9	Gary Hocking	RHO	MZ/MV Agusta	7	
10	Horst Fügner	DDR	MZ	6	

ENTER HONDA

Early in 1954 Soichiro Honda had announced that his company would race at the Isle of Man TT. What he saw when he visited the Island later that year shocked him. The gulf between the bikes competing there, especially the NSU team, and what Japanese industry could produce was enormous. The TT was at its height, the most important race in the world, and any success there translated directly into sales.

The first team from a Japanese factory to race in Europe consisted of four Japanese riders recruited from the company's Speed Club, Giichi Suzuki, Junzo Suzuki, Naomi Taniguchi and Teisuke Tanaka, plus American Bill Hunt (an employee of the nascent American Honda) who acted as liaison man as well as riding. The Japanese riders had never ridden on full tarmac because their experience was on dirt roads in events like the Asama Plains race and the Mount Fuji Hillclimb. They were managed by Kiyoshi Kawashima, who managed the Honda team and went on to become the second President of the Honda Motor Company.

The Japanese raced in just one class, the 125, in 1959 on the short Clypse course. Their bike was the RC142, a bevel-drive DOHC twin with four-valve heads, and it was a neat and efficient motor reckoned to make 18hp, about 10 per cent less than the Ducatis and MVs. But Honda knew next to nothing about racing on road circuits and the chassis with its leading-link forks was totally outclassed by the Italian and East German opposition. Nevertheless, they achieved their objective of winning the team prize, with Taniguchi finishing sixth and scoring Honda's first World Championship point. Some Europeans still sniggered at the funny little motorcycles, but astute privateers like Tom Phillis (AUS) had taken note of the team's efficiency and started making discreet enquiries about Honda's intentions for the 1960 season.

While Honda made satisfied noises about their Island debut they knew they were a long way behind the opposition. Over winter, Kawashima signed Phillis and prepared to return, not just for the TT but for the whole European season. Honda arrived with a completely redesigned 125 and a new 250. Those sniggering Europeans were now astonished by the company's pace of development – and that was a feeling that wouldn't go away.

OPPOSITE Honda's first team photographed behind the grandstand at the Isle of Man TT. Left to right: riders Teisuke Tanaka and Giichi Suzuki, team manager Kiyoshi Kawashima, riders Naomi Taniguchi and Junzo Suzuki, American rider and co-ordinator Bill Hunt, and chief mechanic Hisakazu Sekiguchi. (*Honda*)

1960

MV Agusta and John Surtees dominate again, but there are signs of what's to come as Honda score their first points

This was truly MV Agusta's *annus mirabilis*. For the third year running they won every championship, and this time they won every race but two. Britain's John Hartle, riding a Norton, won the 500cc race in Ulster, but only after John Surtees had stopped to replace a broken gear pedal. Perhaps, therefore, the victory of Ernst Degner on an MZ in the 125cc Belgian GP should be counted as the only time MV were beaten all year. The two-strokes really were getting rather fast, Degner's race average for eight laps of the old Spa circuit hitting over 100mph/161km/h.

At MV, Surtees again had Remo Venturi as team-mate along with the experienced Emilio Mendogni, who retired at the end of the season. John Hartle rode MVs in the 350 and 500 TTs but thereafter reverted to his Nortons. There was an interesting newcomer in the 350 class, a bevel-drive DOHC twin from Jawa, ridden with panache by Frantisek Stastny (CZE).

In the 250 and 125 classes the MVs of Ubbiali and Hocking carried all before them. Tarquinio Provini had left MV on far from amicable terms and now rode for Morini. He concentrated on the Italian Championship for them while developing their bike into the most effective 250 single, with which he would put the fear of God into the 250 field for the next four years.

Degner led the MZ team and rode in both the 125 and 250 classes. Fellow-East German Werner Musiol rode a 250, and various non-DDR riders like John Hempleman, Dickie Dale, Bob Anderson and Italian Alberto Gandossi backed him up in both classes. Another team with foreign riders was Honda, who signed Aussie Tom Phillis to ride alongside their Japanese teamsters. This was a vital cultural exchange, allowing the factory to receive critical input from an experienced racer, not automatic deference to superiors. However, it was a Japanese rider, Teisuke Tanaka, who scored Honda's first Grand Prix podium in the 250cc race in Germany.

In many ways, Phillis's most significant act of the year was to break his collarbone at Assen, because he recommended that his ride be taken by Rhodesian racer Jim Redman.

ABOVE John Hartle (MV Agusta) and Bob McIntyre (AJS) hurtle past the coach parties at Ginger Hall during the Junior (350cc) Isle of Man TT. (*JARROTTS.com*)

RIGHT The 19-year-old Mike Hailwood (Norton), 1960 was the first season he scored points in the 500s. (*Elwyn Roberts Collection*)

THE 1960 SEASON

500cc

FRA/Clermont-Ferrand
- John Surtees won the opening race of the year in defence of his world title
- Fumio Ito (BMW) finished sixth to become the first Japanese rider to score 500cc championship points

GBR/Isle of Man TT
- Surtees won the Senior TT for the third successive year and in doing so became the first rider to average over 100mph/161km/h for a full TT race

NED/Assen
- Remo Venturi took his only GP victory to end a sequence of 11 successive victories for Surtees, who crashed out of the race

GER/Solitude
- John Surtees won four of the first five races of the year to take his fourth and last 500cc world title

ULS/Dundrod
- John Hartle (Norton) took victory and ended a sequence of 14 successive 500cc victories by MV Agusta

ITA-NAZ/Monza
- John Surtees won the final race of the year before retiring from Grand Prix racing – the only time that a rider has retired as 500cc World Champion

350cc

FRA/Clermont-Ferrand
- Gary Hocking, having his first outing on the 350cc MV Agusta, won the opening race of the year despite taking a tumble on the second lap
- For the first time since 1957 John Surtees failed to win a GP in which he started – he finished third after pulling into the pits to rectify a misfiring engine
- Frantisek Stastny finished second to give the Czech Jawa factory their first Grand Prix podium

ULS/Dundrod
- John Surtees clinched the 350cc title with a win to become double World Champion for the third year in succession

250cc

GER/Solitude
- Kenjiro Tanaka finished third to give Honda their first ever podium finish in Grand Prix racing

ITA-NAZ/Monza
- Carlo Ubbiali won the final race of the year to clinch his ninth and final world title

125cc

BEL/Spa-Francorchamps
- Ernst Degner became the only non-MV Agusta rider to win in 1960 in the smaller classes

ULS/Dundrod
- Victory in the Ulster GP gave Carlo Ubbiali the 125cc world title for the sixth and last time

1960 WORLD CHAMPIONSHIP

500cc

Four best results were counted

Pos	Rider	Nat	Machine	FRA	GBR	NED	BEL	GER	ULS	ITA	Nett	Gross
1	John Surtees	GBR	MV Agusta	8	8	-	8	8	6	8	32	(46)
2	Remo Venturi	ITA	MV Agusta	6	-	8	6	6	-	-	26	
3	John Hartle	GBR	Norton/MV Augusta	-	6	-	-	-	8	2	16	
4	Bob Brown	AUS	Norton	4	1	6	4	-	-	-	15	
4	Emilio Mendogni	ITA	MV Agusta	-	-	4	1	4	-	6	15	
6	Mike Hailwood	GBR	Norton	-	4	2	3	-	-	4	13	
7	Paddy Driver	RSA	Norton	3	-	3	-	-	-	3	9	
8	Dickie Dale	GBR	Norton	-	2	1	-	3	-	-	6	
9	Jim Redman	RHO	Norton	-	-	-	2	-	2	1	5	
10	Alan Shepherd	GBR	Matchless	-	-	-	-	-	4	-	4	
11	Tom Phillis	AUS	Norton	-	3	-	-	-	1	-	4	
12	Ralph Rensen	GBR	Norton	-	-	-	-	-	3	-	3	
13	John Hempleman	NZE	Norton	-	-	-	-	2	-	-	2	
13	Ladislaus Richter	AUT	Norton	2	-	-	-	-	-	-	2	
15	Rudolf Glaser	GER	Norton	-	-	-	-	1	-	-	1	
15	Fumio Ito	JPN	BMW	1	-	-	-	-	-	-	1	

Scoring system – 8, 6, 4, 3, 2, 1

350cc

Three best results were counted

Pos	Rider	Nat	Machine	Nett	Gross
1	John Surtees	GBR	MV Agusta	22	(26)
2	Gary Hocking	RHO	MV Agusta	22	
3	John Hartle	GBR	MV Agusta/Norton	18	
4	Frantisek Stastny	CZE	Jawa	12	
5	Bob Anderson	GBR	Norton	9	(10)
6	Bob Brown	AUS	Norton	6	
7	Hugh Anderson	NZE	AJS	5	
8	Dickie Dale	GBR	Norton	5	
9	Paddy Driver	RSA	Norton	5	
10	Bob McIntyre	GBR	AJS	4	

125cc

Three best results were counted

Pos	Rider	Nat	Machine	Nett	Gross
1	Carlo Ubbiali	ITA	MV Agusta	24	(36)
2	Gary Hocking	RHO	MV Agusta	18	(22)
3	Ernst Degner	DDR	MZ	16	(18)
4	Bruno Spaggiari	ITA	MV Agusta	12	
5	John Hempleman	NZE	MZ	10	
6	Luigi Taveri	SWI	MV Agusta	6	
7	Jim Redman	RHO	Honda	6	
8	Alberto Gandossi	ITA	MZ	4	
9	Bob Anderson	GBR	MZ	2	
10	Mike Hailwood	GBR	Ducati	1	
10	Giichi Suzuki	JPN	Honda	1	
10	Kunimitsu Takahashi	JPN	Honda	1	
10	Naomi Taniguchi	JPN	Honda	1	

250cc

Four best results were counted

Pos	Rider	Nat	Machine	Nett	Gross
1	Carlo Ubbiali	ITA	MV Agusta	32	(44)
2	Gary Hocking	RHO	MV Agusta	28	
3	Luigi Taveri	SWI	MV Agusta	11	
4	Jim Redman	RHO	Honda	10	
5	Mike Hailwood	GBR	Ducati/Mondial	8	
6	Tom Phillis	AUS	Honda	6	
7	Kunimitsu Takahashi	JPN	Honda	6	
8	Ernst Degner	DDR	MZ	5	
9	Tarquinio Provini	ITA	Morini	4	
9	Kenjiro Tanaka	JPN	Honda	4	

OPPOSITE Two of MV's great champions with 16 world titles between them both retired at the end of the 1960 season. Carlo Ubbiali, seen here with Nello Pagani – another MV great who went on to be team manager – and, on the far right, John Surtees. (*Stuart Dent Archive*)

MV AND THEIR CHAMPIONS RETIRE

At the end of the season, Count Agusta decided to withdraw his machines from racing. The expanding number of Grands Prix, including a planned trip to Argentina in 1961, meant the expense of running four-strokes was prohibitive. Also, both John Surtees and Carlo Ubbiali, with seven and nine world titles, respectively, to their names, decided to retire from motorcycle competition. (The 500 MVs did, however, appear at most GPs in '61. They were lent to Gary Hocking and sported a 'Privat' logo on their tanks.)

John Surtees, of course, went on to achieve the unique distinction of becoming World Champion on both two and four wheels. It is increasingly unlikely that that feat will ever be equalled. His departure may have been slightly acrimonious, John feeling that as he wasn't allowed to race MVs in non-championship events, he wasn't getting enough racing. However, as he pointed out in his autobiography, he was the only MV rider to have been given one of his bikes so they must have forgiven him for leaving. It is often said that Surtees had little competition in his championship years, and that may be true, but it was his skill which developed the four from an unruly monster into something close to four-stroke perfection.

Carlo Ubbiali retired because he was now aged 30 and had business interests to look after. Like Surtees, he was a perfectionist about set-up and a calculating racer who remained a little aloof from the competition. Tarquinio Provini, for years his main opponent, was Ubbiali's polar opposite and their clashes on and off the track were the stuff of legend. By any measure, Ubbiali was among the all-time greats of motorcycle racing, and he was certainly Italy's greatest before Giacomo Agostini and Valentino Rossi came along.

JOHN SURTEES'S GRAND PRIX STATISTICS

	Starts	Wins	Podium finishes
500cc	34	22	24
350cc	32	15	20
250cc	3	1	1
Total	69	38	45

CARLO UBBIALI'S GRAND PRIX STATISTICS

	Starts	Wins	Podium finishes
250cc	27	13	21
125cc	60	26	47
Total	87	39	68

1961

Gary Hocking took over where Surtees had left off at MV Agusta, Honda won their first world title in the 125cc class

Count Domenico Agusta decided in January that the increased number of GPs and the expense involved meant he had to stop racing. The retirements of two MV greats, Carlo Ubbiali and John Surtees, doubtless had their effect as well. Thankfully this draconian decision was diluted by April and 1960-spec MVs were supplied to several racers, notably Gary Hocking, who promptly cleaned up in the 500 and 350 classes. The word 'Privat' appeared prominently next to the MV badge to show these weren't works bikes.

Hocking had also started the season competing in the 250 class, and won the first race, but the strength of six Hondas, three factory and three leased, proved overwhelming – one of them claimed Honda's first world title, thanks to Mike Hailwood. Two other Brits, John Hartle and Bob McIntyre, also got bikes through the UK importer. The factory squad comprised another Rhodesian rider, Jim Redman, along with Aussie Tom Phillis and Japanese Kunimitsu Takahashi. In the 125 class Phillis and Redman rode alongside Swiss veteran Luigi Taveri.

Yamaha ventured into Europe for the first time with all-Japanese entries in the 125 and 250cc classes. They didn't do a full season but raced at the TT, Assen and Spa-Francorchamps early in the year before reappearing at the last round in Argentina.

Mike Hailwood won the Isle of Man TT on a private 500cc Norton tuned by Bill Lacey, and followed Hocking home in the next four races. Count Agusta knew talent when he saw it and provided an MV for Hailwood for the Italian GP, which Mike won when Hocking fell chasing him. The Rhodesian got his revenge next time out. The final race of the year took place in Argentina, the first time Grand Prix motorcycle racing had ventured outside Europe. However, not many of the top runners, especially in the 500cc class, went to the time, trouble and expense of attending. This is why many of the 'one hit wonders' of Grand Prix history appear in the record books with their names attached to early South American races.

ABOVE Welsh-born but brought up in Rhodesia, Gary Hocking was a natural talent who could surely have won more than two championships. (*JARROTTS.com*)

RIGHT The Nortons of John Hartle and Mike Hailwood lead the field at the start of the Ulster GP. (*JARROTTS.com*)

THE 1961 SEASON

500cc

GER/Hockenheim

- Gary Hocking opened the year with a first Grand Prix victory in the 500cc class

GBR/Isle of Man TT

- Mike Hailwood took his first 500cc GP victory to become the youngest rider to win in the top class at that time
- Hailwood's victory in the 500cc class on a private Norton followed wins on Hondas in the 125 and 250cc classes, making him the first rider to win three Grand Prix classes at one event

ULS/Dundrod

- Gary Hocking took his sixth win in the first seven races to clinch the 500cc world title

ITA-NAZ/Monza

- Mike Hailwood won first time out riding the MV Agusta after Hocking crashed while battling for the victory

ARG/Buenos Aires

- Jorge Kissling (Matchless) became the first Argentine rider to win a Grand Prix on the first occasion a World Championship event was staged outside Europe

350cc

GER/Hockenheim

- Frantisek Stastny became the first Czech rider to win a Grand Prix, and also the first to win riding a Jawa

GBR/Isle of Man TT

- Britain's Phil Read (Norton) scored his first GP win on his debut in Grand Prix racing

ITA-NAZ/Monza

- Gary Hocking took victory, to add the 350cc title to the 500cc championship he'd already won

250cc

SPA/Montjuich

- Gary Hocking gave MV Agusta their 26th and last GP victory in the 250cc class

GER/Hockenheim

- Kunimitsu Takahashi (Honda) became the first Japanese rider to win a Grand Prix. This was also Honda's first 250cc win

FRA/Clermont-Ferrand

- Tom Phillis won the 250cc race, having already taken victory in the 125cc class – the first Honda rider to win two classes on the same day
- Phillis won from Mike Hailwood and Kunimitsu Takahashi – the first all-Honda podium in Grand Prix racing

BEL/Spa-Francorchamps

- Jim Redman took his first Grand Prix victory for Honda

SWE/Kristianstad

- Mike Hailwood won the race, to become the youngest ever World Champion and the first to win a championship on Japanese machinery

125cc

SPA/Montjuich

- Tom Phillis gave Honda their first GP victory after Mike Hailwood (EMC), leading by half a minute with seven laps to go, was slowed by a split exhaust

GER/Hockenheim

- Ernst Degner (DDR) won the race from Alan Shepherd (GBR) and Walter Brehme (DDR) – the only GP race at which MZ riders took all three podium places

FRA/Clermont-Ferrand

- Yamaha entered Grand Prix racing for the first time with Japanese factory rider Fumio Ito

DDR/Sachsenring

- Ernst Degner, riding an MZ built in East Germany, won the first ever GP race to be held in that country

ARG/Buenos Aires

- In the absence of Degner, Tom Phillis took the required GP victory to give him and Honda the 125cc world title

1961 WORLD CHAMPIONSHIP

500cc

Six best results were counted

Pos	Rider	Nat	Machine	GER	FRA	GBR	NED	BEL	DDR	ULS	ITA	SWE	ARG	Nett	Gross
1	Gary Hocking	RHO	MV Agusta	8	8	-	8	8	8	8	-	8	-	48	(56)
2	Mike Hailwood	GBR	Norton/MV Agusta	3	6	8	6	6	6	6	8	6	-	40	(55)
3	Frank Perris	GBR	Norton	6	-	-	2	-	-	-	-	4	4	16	
4	Bob McIntyre	GBR	Norton	-	-	6	4	4	-	-	-	-	-	14	
5	Alastair King	GBR	Norton	-	-	3	-	-	-	4	6	-	-	13	
6	Bert Schneider	AUT	Norton	-	-	-	-	-	4	-	2	3	-	9	
7	Jorge Kissling	ARG	Matchless	-	-	-	-	-	-	-	-	-	8	8	
8	Ron Langston	GBR	Matchless	-	-	2	-	2	-	3	-	-	-	7	
9	Juan Carlos Salatino	ARG	Norton	-	-	-	-	-	-	-	-	-	6	6	
10	Paddy Driver	RSA	Norton	-	-	-	-	1	-	-	4	-	-	5	
11	Mike Duff	CAN	Matchless	-	-	-	-	3	-	-	-	2	-	5	
12	Hans Gunter Jager	GER	BMW	4	-	-	-	-	-	-	-	-	-	4	
12	Antoine Paba	FRA	Norton	-	4	-	-	-	-	-	-	-	-	4	
12	Tom Phillis	AUS	Norton	-	-	4	-	-	-	-	-	-	-	4	
15	John Farnsworth	NZE	Norton	-	-	-	-	-	3	-	-	-	-	3	
15	Gyula Marsovszky	SWI	Norton	-	3	-	-	-	-	-	-	-	-	3	
15	Alberto Pagani	ITA	Norton	-	-	-	-	-	-	-	3	-	-	3	
15	Juan Carlos Perkins	ARG	Norton	-	-	-	-	-	-	-	-	-	3	3	
15	Phil Read	GBR	Norton	-	-	-	3	-	-	-	-	-	-	3	
20	Jack Findlay	AUS	Norton	-	-	-	-	-	2	-	1	-	-	3	
21	Peter Chatterton	GBR	Norton	-	-	-	-	-	-	2	-	-	-	2	
21	Ernst Hiller	GER	BMW	2	-	-	-	-	-	-	-	-	-	2	
21	Fritz Messerli	SWI	Matchless	-	2	-	-	-	-	-	-	-	-	2	
21	Eduardo Salatino	ARG	Norton	-	-	-	-	-	-	-	-	-	2	2	
25	Horacio Costa	URU	Norton	-	-	-	-	-	-	-	-	-	1	1	
25	Roland Foll	GER	Matchless	-	1	-	-	-	-	-	-	-	-	1	
25	Tony Godfrey	GBR	Norton	-	-	1	-	-	-	-	-	-	-	1	
25	Lothar John	GER	BMW	1	-	-	-	-	-	-	-	-	-	1	
25	Ron Miles	AUS	Norton	-	-	-	1	-	-	-	-	-	-	1	
25	Peter Pawson	NZE	Norton	-	-	-	-	-	-	-	-	1	-	1	
25	Anssi Resko	FIN	Norton	-	-	-	-	-	1	-	-	-	-	1	
25	Tom Thorp	GBR	Norton	-	-	-	-	-	-	1	-	-	-	1	

Scoring system – 8, 6, 4, 3, 2, 1

350cc

Four best results were counted

Pos	Rider	Nat	Machine	Nett	Gross
1	Gary Hocking	RHO	MV Agusta	32	(38)
2	Frantisek Stastny	CZE	Jawa	26	(32)
3	Gustav Havel	CZE	Jawa	19	
4	Phil Read	GBR	Norton	13	
5	Bob McIntyre	GBR	Bianchi	10	
6	Ralph Rensen	GBR	Norton	7	
6	Rudi Thalhammer	AUT	Norton	7	
8	Mike Hailwood	GBR	MV Agusta	6	
8	Alastair King	GBR	Bianchi	6	
10	Ernesto Brambilla	ITA	Bianchi	5	
10	Alan Shepherd	GBR	Bianchi/AJS	5	

250cc

Six best results were counted

Pos	Rider	Nat	Machine	Nett	Gross
1	Mike Hailwood	GBR	Honda	44	(54)
2	Tom Phillis	AUS	Honda	38	(45)
3	Jim Redman	RHO	Honda	36	(51)
4	Kunimitsu Takahashi	JPN	Honda	29	(30)
5	Bob McIntyre	GBR	Honda	14	
6	Tarquinio Provini	ITA	Morini	10	
7	Silvio Grassetti	ITA	Benelli	10	
8	Gary Hocking	RHO	MV Agusta	8	
9	Fumio Ito	JPN	Yamaha	7	
10	Luigi Taveri	SWI	Honda	6	

125cc

Six best results were counted

Pos	Rider	Nat	Machine	Nett	Gross
1	Tom Phillis	AUS	Honda	44	(56)
2	Ernst Degner	DDR	MZ	42	(45)
3	Luigi Taveri	SWI	Honda	30	(31)
4	Jim Redman	RHO	Honda	28	(37)
5	Kunimitsu Takahashi	JPN	Honda	24	
6	Mike Hailwood	GBR	EMC/Honda	16	
7	Alan Shepherd	GBR	MZ	12	
8	Walter Brehme	DDR	MZ	7	
9	Teisuke Tanaka	JPN	Honda	6	
10	Werner Musiol	DDR	MZ	5	
10	Sadao Shimazaki	JPN	Honda	5	

LEFT Tom Phillis takes the flag at Montjuich to mark up Honda's first GP win. (*Honda*)

FAR LEFT The Honda team that monopolised the 125cc rostrum at the TT: Phillis (3rd), Taveri (2nd) and Hailwood (1st). (*Honda*)

DEGNER DEFECTS

Honda and MZ were locked in a battle for the 125cc title as the season came to an end. Sweden was due to be the penultimate round, with Argentina completing the season, but there were doubts over the South American race. The East German factory's 125 had just become the first motor in history to generate a specific power output of over 200hp/litre, and lead rider Ernst Degner was heading the championship and favourite for the title.

How had a tiny company locked away in East Germany with no means of buying top riders, modern alloys or state-of-the-art parts like carbs and ignitions been able to do this? The answer was the genius of one man, Walter Kaaden. Single-handedly he had deduced the modern two-stroke from first principles by treating it as a resonating device not as a pump – like a four-stroke machine – no matter that he had to use old saw blades to fabricate disc valves. And all this took place with MZ pitted against Honda's highly paid works stars and the Italian armada.

Not long before the Swedish GP, in September 1961, the situation of the East German team was made even more precarious because their government built the Berlin Wall, plunging the Cold War well and truly into the deep freeze. Some people think that Degner's plans were already well advanced before the Wall went up, and on the way to Kristianstad he learnt that his family had been successfully smuggled to the West, drugged in the boot of a car.

Instead of running a conservative race and taking the title, Degner shot into the lead but the engine only lasted two laps. Most histories state that Degener deliberately over-revved his bike, but why would a man as self-centred as Degner pass up the chance of calling himself a World Champion? Especially as his status as an international sportsman enabled him to travel freely and he could have escaped relatively easily once he knew his family was safe?

With the help of Suzuki, he immediately defected and joined his family. Suzuki weren't helping for humanitarian reasons, though: their two-strokes were cringingly slow next to both Honda's four-strokes and the MZs, and they wanted Kaaden's secrets. Degner provided a quick route.

In 1962 Ernst Degner became the first rider to win a World Championship on a two-stroke – a 50cc Suzuki – and the following year Hugh Anderson won both the 125 and 50cc titles for Suzuki.

What did Degner take with him? He always maintained he just took what was in his head. Walter Kaaden thought otherwise, feeling sure Degner took a good deal of hardware too. Most of all, he resented the selling of years of his team's work, and when Suzuki painted their bikes blue and silver, the same as MZ, Kaaden had his machines painted green and silver.

There are also fanciful stories about Degner's death, some claiming that he was murdered by the East German secret service, the Stasi. The truth is more prosaic. He died young of a heart attack, as did his father and grandfather.

1962

World 500 Champion Gary Hocking retired after the first race, leaving Mike Hailwood to carry the MV Agusta banner

Mike Hailwood joined Gary Hocking on 500 'Privat' MVs and the pair won every race they attended. The only works bikes on the grid were the Jawa twin of Frantisek Stastny and Phil Read's single-cylinder Manx Norton. The story was very different in the smaller classes. Honda fielded Jim Redman, Tom Phillis, Luigi Taveri, Kunimitsu Takahashi, Bob McIntyre and new recruit, Ulsterman Tommy Robb, as factory riders. McIntyre was supposed to win the 350s, Redman the 250s and Takahashi the 125s. Britain's Derek Minter did his best to upset the applecart by unknowingly beating the factory bikes at the 250cc Isle of Man TT on a Honda supplied by the British importer. He never rode a Honda again.

It was a grisly year. Phillis died in the 350cc TT, McIntyre after crashing at a British national meeting. Gary Hocking, appalled by the death of his great friend Phillis, quit motorcycle racing and went back to South Africa and a career on four wheels. Before the end of the year he too was dead. Like Jarno Saarinen in the 1970s, Hocking was an astonishing talent cut down in his prime. He won 19 GPs, two on MZs, the rest on MVs. He won the first time he sat on a two-stroke, at Sweden's Kristianstad circuit in 1959, and he was good enough to race Hailwood at lap-record pace on equal machinery around the Isle of Man. No-one who saw him or raced against him doubts he could have added to his two world titles.

Jim Redman persevered grimly and won both the 250 and 350 championships. This was the first year Honda raced in the 350 class, using their 250-four bored out to 285cc. They finished first and second, Tommy Robb taking victory in the last race of the season, in Finland, to claim the runner-up spot. In the 250s it was another one–two, this time with McIntyre taking second place – and only three of the championship top ten weren't on a Honda. In the 125cc class Taveri won, with the other three Honda riders second, third and fourth.

However, they didn't have it their own way in the new 50cc class. Taveri and Robb were faced with a new phenomenon: two-strokes that were both fast and reliable, with Ernst Degner taking the title on a Suzuki.

ABOVE Mike Hailwood on the 500c MV Agusta. (*JARROTTS.com*)

THE **1962** SEASON

500cc

GBR/Isle of Man TT

- Gary Hocking (MV Agusta) won the opening race of the year and then retired from racing

ITA-NAZ/Monza

- Mike Hailwood (MV Agusta) won for the fifth successive race to become the youngest ever 500cc World Champion – a record he held until Freddie Spencer won the title in 1983

FIN/Tampere

- In the absence of the MV Team, Alan Shepherd (Matchless) won the 500cc race at the first ever Grand Prix event to be held in Finland

ARG/Buenos Aires

- Argentina's Benedicto Caldarella (Matchless) took his only GP victory in a poorly supported race in which the fourth rider home was lapped five times

125cc

GBR/Isle of Man TT

- Winner of the opening two races of the year, Kunimitsu Takahashi crashed on the opening lap and suffered injuries that kept him out of racing for the remainder of the season

ULS/Dundrod

- In the absence of Takahashi, Luigi Taveri's victory at the Ulster GP gave him his first world title

ARG/Buenos Aires

- Hugh Anderson (NZE) gave Suzuki their first Grand Prix victory in the 125cc class

350cc

GBR/Isle of Man TT

- Mike Hailwood won the race after a tremendous battle with MV team-mate Gary Hocking, less than six seconds covering the pair after more than two hours of racing
- Reigning 125cc World Champion Tom Phillis (Honda) lost his life after crashing on the second lap while lying in third place

NED/Assen

- Jim Redman gave Honda their first Grand Prix victory in the 350cc class

ITA-NAZ/Monza

- Redman's fourth victory of the year added the 350cc World Championship to the 250cc title he'd already won

250cc

SPA/Montjuich

- Jim Redman won the opening 250cc race of the year after Silvio Grassetti (ITA), giving the new Benelli four-cylinder machine its first GP outing, suffered mechanical failure while battling for the lead

FRA/Clermont-Ferrand

- Just half a second covered the three podium finishers, Honda riders Redman, Bob McIntyre and Tom Phillis, with all three riders lapping every other rider in the race at least once

GER/Solitude

- Bob McIntyre finished second in his last GP before tragically losing his life due to injuries suffered in a non-championship race at Oulton Park in England

ULS/Dundrod

- Tommy Robb (Honda) took his first Grand Prix victory at his home event

DDR/Sachsenring

- Nikolai Sevostyanov finished fifth to back up his sixth in the earlier 350cc race – the first Russian rider to score World Championship points

ARG/Buenos Aires:

- Arthur Wheeler (Moto Guzzi), who made his GP debut at the first championship race in 1949, took victory at the age of 46 – the oldest rider to win a Grand Prix.
- This was also the last of 45 GP victories for Moto Guzzi

50cc

SPA/Montjuich

- Hans-Georg Anscheidt (Kreidler) won the first Grand Prix for 50cc machines from home rider José Busquets, riding a Derbi – the first GP points for the Spanish manufacturer

GBR/Isle of Man TT

- Ernst Degner (GER) gave Suzuki their first win in Grand Prix racing
- Beryl Swain (GBR, Itom) became the first female rider to compete in a TT race and finished in 22nd position

ARG/Buenos Aires

- In the final race of the year, Degner finished second in front of his closest championship challenger, fellow-German Anscheidt, to clinch the world title – the first ever by a Suzuki rider

OLDEST RIDERS TO WIN ACROSS ALL SOLO GP CLASSES

	Rider	Age	Race
1	Arthur Wheeler	46 years 70 days	ARG/Buenos Aires/1962/250cc
2	Fergus Anderson	45 years 236 days	SPA/Montjuich/1954/350cc
3	Hermann-Paul Muller	45 years 217 days	GER/Nürburgring/1955/250cc
4	Enrico Lorenzetti	42 years 273 days	SPA/Montjuich/1953/250cc
5	Jack Findlay	42 years 85 days	AUT/Salzburgring/1977/500cc
6	Les Graham	41 years 270 days	GBR/Isle of Man TT/1953/125cc
7	Maurice Cann	41 years 144 days	ULS/Clady/1952/250cc
8	Marcellino Lucchi	41 years 65 days	ITA/Mugello/1998/250cc
9	Freddie Frith	40 years 82 days	ULS/Clady/1949/350cc
10	Jack Ahearn	39 years 327 days	FIN/Imatra/1964/500cc

1962 WORLD CHAMPIONSHIP

500cc

Five best results were counted

Pos	Rider	Nat	Machine	GBR	NED	BEL	ULS	DDR	ITA	FIN	ARG	Nett	Gross
1	Mike Hailwood	GBR	MV Agusta	-	8	8	8	8	8	-	-	40	
2	Alan Shepherd	GBR	Matchless	-	3	6	6	6	-	8	-	29	
3	Phil Read	GBR	Norton	-	4	-	4	-	3	-	-	11	
4	Bert Schneider	AUT	Norton	3	2	-	-	4	1	-	-	10	
5	Benedicto Caldarella	ARG	Matchless	-	-	-	-	-	-	-	8	8	
5	Gary Hocking	RHO	MV Agusta	8	-	-	-	-	-	-	-	8	
7	Frantisek Stastny	CZE	Jawa	-	-	-	-	3	-	4	-	7	
8	Tony Godfrey	GBR	Norton	-	1	4	2	-	-	-	-	7	
9	Paddy Driver	RSA	Norton	-	-	3	-	2	2	-	-	7	
10	Ellis Boyce	GBR	Norton	6	-	-	-	-	-	-	-	6	
10	Esso Gunnarsson	SWE	Norton	-	-	-	-	-	-	6	-	6	
10	Derek Minter	GBR	Norton	-	6	-	-	-	-	-	-	6	
10	Juan Carlos Salatino	ARG	Norton	-	-	-	-	-	-	-	6	6	
10	Remo Venturi	ITA	MV Agusta	-	-	-	-	-	6	-	-	6	
15	Fred Stevens	GBR	Norton	4	-	1	-	-	-	-	-	5	
16	Silvio Grassetti	ITA	Bianchi	-	-	-	-	-	4	-	-	4	
16	Eduardo Salatino	ARG	Norton	-	-	-	-	-	-	-	4	4	
18	Pablo Gamberini	CHL	Matchless	-	-	-	-	-	-	-	3	3	
18	Ron Langston	GBR	Norton	-	-	-	3	-	-	-	-	3	
18	Anssi Resko	FIN	Matchless	-	-	-	-	-	-	3	-	3	
21	Jack Findlay	AUS	Norton	-	-	2	-	-	-	-	-	2	
21	Roy Ingram	GBR	Norton	2	-	-	-	-	-	-	-	2	
21	Harald Karlsson	FIN	Norton	-	-	-	-	-	-	2	-	2	
21	Amleta Pomesano	ARG	Norton	-	-	-	-	-	-	-	2	2	
25	Roland Foll	GER	Matchless	-	-	-	-	1	-	1	-	2	
26	Brian Setchell	GBR	Norton	1	-	-	-	-	-	-	-	1	
26	Manuel Soler	URG	Norton	-	-	-	-	-	-	-	1	1	
26	Ray Spence	GBR	Norton	-	-	-	1	-	-	-	-	1	

Scoring system – 8, 6, 4, 3, 2, 1

350cc

Four best results were counted

Pos	Rider	Nat	Machine	Nett	Gross
1	Jim Redman	RHO	Honda	32	(38)
2	Tommy Robb	GBR	Honda	22	
3	Mike Hailwood	GBR	MV Agusta	20	
4	Frantisek Stastny	CZE	Jawa	16	
5	Silvio Grassetti	ITA	Bianchi	8	
6	Alan Shepherd	GBR	MZ/AJS	7	
7	Gustav Havel	CZE	Jawa	7	
8	Gary Hocking	RHO	MV Agusta	6	
9	Mike Duff	CAN	AJS	5	
10	Esso Gunnarsson	SWE	Norton	3	
10	Roy Ingram	GBR	Norton	3	

250cc

Six best results were counted

Pos	Rider	Nat	Machine	Nett	Gross
1	Jim Redman	RHO	Honda	48	(66)
2	Bob McIntyre	GBR	Honda	32	
3	Arthur Wheeler	GBR	Moto Guzzi	19	
4	Tom Phillis	AUS	Honda	12	
5	Tarquinio Provini	ITA	Morini	10	
6	Derek Minter	GBR	Honda	8	
6	Tommy Robb	GBR	Honda	8	
8	Luigi Taveri	SWI	Honda	8	
9	Alberto Pagani	ITA	Honda/Aermacchi	8	
10	Dan Shorey	GBR	Bultaco	8	

125cc

Six best results were counted

Pos	Rider	Nat	Machine	Nett	Gross
1	Luigi Taveri	SWI	Honda	48	(67)
2	Jim Redman	RHO	Honda	38	(47)
3	Tommy Robb	GBR	Honda	30	(33)
4	Kunimitsu Takahashi	JPN	Honda	16	
5	Mike Hailwood	GBR	EMC	12	
6	Teisuke Tanaka	JPN	Honda	11	
7	Hugh Anderson	NZE	Suzuki	11	
8	Hans Fischer	DDR	MZ	7	
9	Raoul Kissling	ARG	DKW	6	
10	Paddy Driver	RSA	EMC	6	

50cc

Six best results were counted

Pos	Rider	Nat	Machine	Nett	Gross
1	Ernst Degner	GER	Suzuki	41	
2	Hans-Georg Anscheidt	GER	Kreidler	36	(43)
3	Luigi Taveri	SWI	Honda	29	(33)
4	Jan Huberts	NED	Kreidler	29	
5	Mitsuo Itoh	JPN	Suzuki	23	(24)
6	Tommy Robb	GBR	Honda	17	
7	Hugh Anderson	NZE	Suzuki	16	
8	Seiichi Suzuki	JPN	Suzuki	10	
9	Kunimitsu Takahashi	JPN	Honda	7	
10	José Busquets	SPA	Derbi	6	

SUZUKI JOIN THE PARTY

The effect of the East German star Ernst Degner's defection to the West soon became apparent. He had secretly done a deal with Suzuki and, over winter, their bikes went from wheezing also-rans to state-of-the-art racers. Degner always maintained he only took the information that was in his head, but in his seminal book *Team Suzuki* Ray Battersby quotes Suzuki team-managers and mechanics affirming that he brought plenty of hardware as well.

The MZ factory, affected not just by the loss of their star rider but also by even severer restrictions on their already strictly controlled movements, simply didn't figure. From now on East German riders hardly ever appeared away from their home race or the Czechoslovakian GP. MZ's presiding genius Walter Kaaden ran the racing effort by remote control, with Britain's Alan Shepherd as his main 350cc rider and guest appearances by a variety of others, the most memorable of which was Mike Hailwood's ride at the 250cc East German GP at the Sachsenring just a few kilometres from the MZ factory. In front of over a quarter of a million spectators Hailwood duelled for the whole race with Jim Redman on the factory Honda, over a minute and a half ahead of the rest of the field, only losing out on the win by a fifth of a second.

In the 50cc class, the new Suzuki and another German two-stroke, the Kreidler, fought it out with the four-stroke Hondas. Kreidler was a West German moped factory and their race team, including rider Hans-Georg Anscheidt, were all factory employees. However, the bike was ultra-modern with disc-valve induction and the first use of silicate coatings on cylinder bore. In the 125 class the Hondas were unbeatable, but in the 50s the new generation of two-strokes was making itself felt. Honda had to start multiplying the ratios in the gearbox to get competitive. The Honda ended the season with a nine-speed gearbox but didn't win a race until the penultimate round of the year. This was the start of Honda's attempts to keep competitive with the disc-valve inlet, expansion-chamber exhaust two-stroke giving their four-strokes more and more cylinders and gear ratios that would give rise to the six-cylinder 250 and five-cylinder 21,500rpm 125 of 1966.

BELOW Suzuki's 50cc armada at Spa: Isao Morishita, Hugh Anderson, Michio Icino and Ernst Degner. (*Elwyn Roberts Collection*)

1963

MV and Mike Hailwood retained the 500 title easily but for the second year running couldn't beat Jim Redman and Honda in the 350s

By far the most interesting World Championship class in 1963 was the 250. Honda development was stalled and the team understaffed, Yamaha burst on to the scene with a two-stroke twin and Italian double World Champion Tarquinio Provini had a new iteration of the Morini single which he rode as if his life depended on it. It was one of those time windows when a lighter, less powerful bike was able to compete with the more powerful but clumsier machines, and Provini pushed Honda's team leader Jim Redman all the way. The other Honda 250 riders were Tommy Robb and Luigi Taveri. Benelli had a new four-stroke four for Silvio Grassetti, while MZ's two-stroke twin in the hands of Britain's Alan Shepherd was still on the pace.

The real surprise was how competitive the Yamaha RD56 was. Unfortunately the team only had finances for three races: the Isle of Man TT, Assen and Spa. Fumio Ito finished second to Redman in the first two races, then won the third with his team-mates getting two fourths and a second. Phil Read got to ride the Yamaha at the last race of the season and immediately signed up for '64. Suzuki debuted a square-four machine at the same race.

Honda's trio had similar problems in the 125 class. Their twin was outclassed by the Suzuki disc-valve two-strokes of Hugh Anderson, Ernst Degner, Frank Perris (GBR) and Bert Schneider (AUT). Honda didn't contest the 50cc class, so Suzuki's only opposition came from Kreidler, at least until Honda raced a new twin at Suzuka and Taveri won on it.

The 350 class was a straight fight between Redman and Mike Hailwood on the MV Agusta, which the Honda man won. Mike the Bike cakewalked the 500s on the MV with the dogged and versatile Alan Shepherd second on a Matchless single. The Gilera fours were taken out of mothballs for one last season and run by Geoff Duke under the banner of Scuderia Duke: British riders John Hartle and Derek Minter were contracted, with Phil Read taking over when Minter was injured.

ABOVE Double World Champion for the second year running – Jim Redman on the 125 Honda at the French GP. (*Honda*)

TOP RIGHT Luigi Taveri (Honda) prepares for the start of the 125cc Ulster GP. (*Elwyn Roberts Collection*)

BOTTOM RIGHT The 50s head for the first corner at Assen led by Hugh Anderson. (Suzuki) (*Keulemans Archive*)

THE **1963** SEASON

500cc

GBR/Isle of Man TT
- Mike Hailwood (MV Agusta) took the opening race of the year from Scuderia Duke team-mates John Hartle and Phil Read, their Gileras appearing for the first time since 1957

NED/Assen
- John Hartle won from Phil Read – the first GP win for Gilera since 1957 and their last ever victory in the 500cc class

FIN/Tampere
- Mike Hailwood lapped every other rider at least once in taking the win to retain the world title

350cc

ULS/Dundrod
- Jim Redman made it four wins from four races in the 350cc class to retain his 350cc world title

DDR/Sachsenring
- Mike Hailwood (MV Agusta) became the first rider to defeat Jim Redman in the 350cc class in the 1963 season

250cc

SPA/Montjuich
- At the opening race of the year Tarquinio Provini gave the single-cylinder Morini its first victory for five years

FRA/Clermont-Ferrand
- The 250cc race was first delayed and then cancelled due to torrential rain, with the riders already formed up on the grid

GBR/Isle of Man TT
- In the absence of Provini, who had won the opening two races, Jim Redman gave Honda their first 250cc victory of the year
- Fumio Ito finished second, the Japanese rider giving Yamaha their first podium finish in any class of GP racing

BEL/Spa-Francorchamps
- Fumio Ito gave Yamaha their first Grand Prix victory

DDR/Sachsenring
- Mike Hailwood won the 250cc race on the locally built MZ, having already won the 350cc (held the previous day) and 500cc races on his factory MV Agustas

ITA-NAZ/Monza
- Giacomo makes his GP debut on a Morini. He led the race before mechanical failure put him out

ARG/Buenos Aires
- Tarquinio Provini won the penultimate race of the year to go level on points with Jim Redman
- This was the last GP win for Morini and the last win in the 250cc class for a four-stroke single-cylinder machine

JPN/Suzuka
- Jim Redman won the final race of the year, on the GPs' first visit to Japan, to retain his 250cc world title

125cc

GBR/Isle of Man TT
- Hugh Anderson, on a Suzuki, became the first rider to win an Isle of Man 125cc TT on a two-stroke machine

NED/Assen
- After winning both the 250 and 350cc races Jim Redman crashed while battling for a top-six finish, breaking his collarbone and missing the next GP in Belgium

DDR/Sachsenring
- Hugh Anderson took victory to become the first rider to win the 125cc world title on a Suzuki, and the first on a two-stroke

JPN/Suzuka
- Ernst Degner crashes and suffers serious burns on the corner now called Degner

50cc

GER/Hockenheim
- Hugh Anderson won the race and was joined on the podium by team-mates Isao Morishita (JPN) and Ernst Degner – the first all-Suzuki podium in Grand Prix racing

GBR/Isle of Man TT
- Mitsuo Itoh (Suzuki) became the first Japanese rider to win a race over the Isle of Man TT course

JPN/Suzuka
- After championship leader Hans-Georg Anscheidt (Kreidler) suffered machine failure, Hugh Anderson finished second to add the 50cc world title to the 125cc crown he'd already won

1963 WORLD CHAMPIONSHIP

500cc

Five best results were counted

Pos	Rider	Nat	Machine	GBR	NED	BEL	ULS	DDR	FIN	ITA	ARG	Nett	Gross
1	Mike Hailwood	GBR	MV Agusta	8	-	8	8	8	8	8	8	40	(56)
2	Alan Shepherd	GBR	Matchless	-	4	4	3	4	6	-	-	21	
3	John Hartle	GBR	Gilera	6	8	-	6	-	-	-	-	20	
4	Phil Read	GBR	Gilera	4	6	6	-	-	-	-	-	16	
5	Fred Stevens	GBR	Norton	1	2	3	-	-	3	4	-	13	
6	Mike Duff	CAN	Matchless	3	-	-	1	3	4	-	-	11	
7	Derek Minter	GBR	Gilera	-	-	-	4	6	-	-	-	10	
8	Jack Findlay	AUS	Matchless	-	-	-	-	2	-	6	-	8	
9	Jorge Kissling	ARG	Norton	-	-	-	-	-	-	-	6	6	
10	Jack Ahearn	AUS	Norton	-	3	2	-	-	-	-	-	5	
11	Benedicto Caldarella	ARG	Matchless	-	-	-	-	-	-	-	4	4	
12	Victorio Minguzzi	ARG	Matchless	-	-	-	-	-	-	-	3	3	
12	Bill Smith	GBR	Norton	-	-	-	-	-	-	3	-	3	
14	Ralph Bryans	GBR	Norton	-	-	-	2	-	-	-	-	2	
14	Joe Dunphy	GBR	Norton	2	-	-	-	-	-	-	-	2	
14	Sid Mizen	GBR	Matchless	-	-	-	-	-	2	-	-	2	
14	Ladislaus Richter	AUT	Norton	-	-	-	-	-	-	2	-	2	
14	Raul Villaveiran	URU	Norton	-	-	-	-	-	-	-	2	2	
19	Jose Acosta	URU	Norton	-	-	-	-	-	-	-	1	1	
19	Vernon Cottle	GBR	Norton	-	-	-	-	1	-	-	-	1	
19	Esso Gunnarsson	SWE	Norton	-	1	-	-	-	-	-	-	1	
19	Vasco Loro	ITA	Norton	-	-	-	-	-	-	1	-	1	
19	Gyula Marsovzsky	SWI	Matchless	-	-	1	-	-	-	-	-	1	
19	Nikolai Sevostyanov	RUS	CKB	-	-	-	-	-	1	-	-	1	

Scoring system – 8, 6, 4, 3, 2, 1

350cc

Four best results were counted

Pos	Rider	Nat	Machine	Nett	Gross
1	Jim Redman	RHO	Honda	32	(50)
2	Mike Hailwood	GBR	MV Agusta	28	
3	Luigi Taveri	SWI	Honda	16	
4	Frantisek Stastny	CZE	Jawa	7	
5	Gustav Havel	CZE	Jawa	7	
6	John Hartle	GBR	Gilera	6	
6	Alan Shepherd	GBR	MZ	6	
6	Remo Venturi	ITA	Bianchi	6	
9	Mike Duff	CAN	AJS	5	
9	Nikolai Sevostyanov	RUS	CKB	5	

250cc

Six best results were counted

Pos	Rider	Nat	Machine	Nett	Gross
1	Jim Redman	RHO	Honda	44	(58)
2	Tarquinio Provini	ITA	Morini	42	(49)
3	Fumio Ito	JPN	Yamaha	26	
4	Tommy Robb	GBR	Honda	20	(21)
5	Luigi Taveri	SWI	Honda	13	
6	Alan Shepherd	GBR	MZ	11	
7	Yoshikaza Sunako	JPN	Yamaha	9	
8	Mike Hailwood	GBR	MZ	8	
9	Kunimitsu Takahashi	JPN	Honda	7	
10	Umberto Masetti	ITA	Morini	4	
10	Phil Read	GBR	Yamaha	4	
10	Bill Smith	GBR	Honda	4	

125cc

Seven best results were counted

Pos	Rider	Nat	Machine	Nett	Gross
1	Hugh Anderson	NZE	Suzuki	54	(62)
2	Luigi Taveri	SWI	Honda	38	(47)
3	Jim Redman	RHO	Honda	35	
4	Frank Perris	GBR	Suzuki	24	
5	Bert Schneider	AUT	Suzuki	23	
6	Ernst Degner	GER	Suzuki	17	
7	Kunimitsu Takahashi	JPN	Honda	14	
8	Alan Shepherd	GBR	MZ	11	
9	Tommy Robb	GBR	Honda	11	
10	Laslo Szabo	HUN	MZ	7	

50cc

Five best results were counted

Pos	Rider	Nat	Machine	Nett	Gross
1	Hugh Anderson	NZE	Suzuki	34	(47)
2	Hans-Georg Anscheidt	GER	Kreidler	32	(36)
3	Ernst Degner	GER	Suzuki	30	
4	Isao Morishita	JPN	Suzuki	23	(26)
5	Mitsuo Itoh	JPN	Suzuki	20	(21)
6	Michio Ichino	JPN	Suzuki	14	
7	Alberto Pagani	ITA	Kreidler	9	
8	Luigi Taveri	SWI	Honda	8	
9	José Busquets	SPA	Derbi	7	
10	Shunkichi Masuda	JPN	Suzuki	4	

GILERA'S FINAL FLING

Gilera's four-cylinder 350s and 500s had been hidden away since the end of 1957, but Geoff Duke persuaded the factory to let him enter them for the 1963 season. It was a measure of how little the 500 class had progressed in the intervening five years that the bigger bikes were competitive, whereas it was quickly obvious that the 350 was significantly inferior not just to the Honda and the MV but to Jawa as well. It was quickly parked.

Hailwood's MV was generally superior and only when it hit mechanical problems at Assen did Scuderia Duke achieve a win, courtesy of John Hartle. This was not a proper works effort, though, because the only factory contribution was a couple of mechanics. Promised sponsorship never materialised (some things never change) so Duke's riders were allowed to ride other bikes at events not on the team's schedule. Derek Minter, the Scuderia's lead rider, was hurt at Brands Hatch and missed the first three GPs; Phil Read took over. The bikes looked different, with dolphin fairings, but were essentially the '57 machines. Only at the Italian GP did Minter receive an updated motor. However, the effort was not only short of factory support and finance but also riven by personality clashes. It was the last time Gilera contested the GPs with a team.

The last burst of Gilera glory came via Benedicto Caldarella, winner of his home 500cc GP in Argentina in 1962. He had an ex-Scuderia Duke bike for end-of-season internationals in South America and was quick enough to be allowed to keep it for '64. At the opening GP of the year at Daytona he gave Mike Hailwood a serious race before the bike broke, proving that the win at his sparsely attended home race did mean something. However, Caldarella had the same problems as Scuderia Duke, and his only scoring ride in 1964 was a close second place behind Hailwood at Monza. Both Derek Minter and Remo Venturi (ITA) tried to race Gileras again in '67, but to no avail. The racing career of the bike that pioneered the ubiquitous double-overhead-camshaft across-the-frame four-cylinder layout was over.

LEFT Derek Minter on the Scuderia Duke Gilera. (*JARROTTS.com*)

1964

Two-strokes broke through to win the 250 championship for the first time, as Hailwood and Redman added to their titles

Honda went on the attack in the war against the invading two-strokes with their 50cc twin and 125cc four. Luigi Taveri duly won the 125 title with Jim Redman, now effectively Honda's team-manager as well as lead rider, second. Suzuki, despite the absence of Degner for most of the season, retained the 50cc title with Hugh Anderson, although he was run close by Honda's new recruit Ralph Bryans (GBR).

With Gilera deciding not to repeat the experiment of Scuderia Duke, the 500cc class provided an easy victory for Mike Hailwood and the MV Agusta. It was a similar story in the 350s, only this time it was Redman and Honda who had an even more dominant season, winning all eight races.

Interest again centred on the 250 class, both in terms of technical development and rider talent. Honda fielded Redman and Taveri, while Tarquinio Provini moved from Morini to Benelli and won one GP. Morini stayed at home to compete in the Italian Championship with a promising young rider called Giacomo Agostini who caught all eyes when Morini raced their home GP at Monza. The combination of Alan Shepherd and MZ was still good enough to win a race, and Suzuki joined in with their fast but fragile square-four machine – known to its riders as Whispering Death. With factory man Fumio Ito injured, Yamaha started with Phil Read on his own, only bringing in a second rider, Mike Duff (CAN) when it became apparent that the title was a possibility. A 125cc version of the Yamaha twin appeared at Assen but was quickly shelved to avoid deflecting effort from the fight for the 250 crown.

Despite early-season flourishes from Benelli and MZ, the 250cc World Championship was an epic confrontation between Read and Redman. Honda's response to the challenge was to give Redman a six-cylinder 250, the RC165, but even that wasn't enough to stave off the inevitable advance of the two-stroke.

ABOVE Mike Hailwood (Honda) shadows Benedicto Caldarella (Gilera) during the US GP. (*Elwyn Roberts Collection*)

RIGHT Ralph Bryans (Honda) leads Ernst Degner (Suzuki) over Ballaugh Bridge during the 50cc Isle of Man TT. (*Honda*)

THE **1964** SEASON

500cc

USA/Daytona

- At the first Grand Prix to be held in the USA, Mike Hailwood won the 500cc event after being challenged mid-race by Argentine Benedicto Caldarella riding a Gilera

GER/Solitude

- Mike Hailwood took maximum points from the first five races of the year to take the world title for the third successive year

ULS/Dundrod

- In the absence of Hailwood, Phil Read (Norton) scored his first 500cc Grand Prix victory

FIN/Imatra

- Australian privateer Jack Ahearn (Norton) took his one and only GP victory more than ten years after making his Grand Prix debut

ITA-NAZ/Monza

- Caldarella finished second, Gilera's last 500cc podium

350cc

DDR/Sachsenring

- This was the first appearance of the four-cylinder Russian-built Vostok machines, which suffered mechanical problems in the race after qualifying second and third fastest

ULS/Dundrod

- Jim Redman made it a clean sweep of the first five races of the year to retain the 350cc World Championship

JPN/Suzuka

- Redman completed a perfect season of eight wins from eight races

250cc

USA/Daytona

- Alan Shepherd took the race win followed by two riders with claims to be the first Americans to finish on the podium in GPs. Ron Grant (Parilla) was second, racing with an American licence and living in the USA, but originally from London, while third-place finisher was Bo Gehring (Bultaco) from Washington DC

SPA/Montjuich

- Tarquinio Provini gave the new four-cylinder Benelli its first World Championship victory

FRA/Clermont-Ferrand

- Yamaha-mounted Phil Read won his first 250cc Grand Prix

BEL/Spa-Francorchamps

- Mike Duff (Yamaha) took his first GP victory, the only Canadian ever to win a World Championship race

GER/Solitude

- Giacomo Agostini made his Grand Prix debut, riding for Morini

DDR/Sachsenring

- Having already won the 500cc race, Mike Hailwood crashed out of the 250s while leading and suffered injuries that kept him out of the next race in Ulster

ITA-NAZ/Monza

- Despite Honda providing Jim Redman with a new six-cylinder machine, Phil Read won the race to clinch his first world title
- This was the first world title for Yamaha and the first by a two-stroke machine in the 250cc class

125cc

USA/Daytona

- Hugh Anderson (Suzuki) made a strong start to the defence of his world titles by winning the 125cc race to add to his success in the 50cc event earlier in the day

NED/Assen

- Jim Redman took the win after earlier victories in the 250 and 350cc races, to become the first rider to win three Grand Prix races in a single day
- Phil Read finished second on the debut outing for the new 125cc twin-cylinder Yamaha – the first podium for Yamaha in the 125cc class

FIN/Imatra

- Luigi Taveri (Honda) won the race to regain the world title he had previously won in 1962

50cc

SPA/Montjuich

- Angel Nieto (SPA, Derbi) finished fifth on his Grand Prix debut

NED/Assen

- Britain's Ralph Bryans won his first GP and gave Honda their first victory of the year in the 50cc class

FIN/Imatra

- Hugh Anderson (Suzuki) retained the 50cc world title with a win in the final race of the year after closest challenger Ralph Bryans suffered ignition failure while leading

1964 WORLD CHAMPIONSHIP

500cc

Five best results were counted

Pos	Rider	Nat	Machine	USA	GBR	NED	BEL	GER	DDR	ULS	FIN	ITA	Nett	Gross
1	Mike Hailwood	GBR	MV Agusta	8	8	8	8	8	8	-	-	8	40	(56)
2	Jack Ahearn	AUS	Norton	-	-	3	3	6	1	4	8	4	25	(29)
3	Phil Read	GBR	Matchless/Norton	6	-	1	6	4	-	8	-	-	25	
4	Mike Duff	CAN	Matchless	3	-	-	-	-	6	-	6	3	18	
5	Paddy Driver	RSA	Matchless	2	-	4	4	-	4	-	2	-	16	
6	Fred Stevens	GBR	Matchless	-	4	2	-	1	-	1	-	-	8	
7	Gyula Marsovszky	SWI	Matchless	-	-	-	-	3	-	-	4	-	7	
8	Benedicto Caldarella	ARG	Gilera	-	-	-	-	-	-	-	-	6	6	
8	Dick Creith	GBR	Norton	-	-	-	-	-	-	6	-	-	6	
8	Derek Minter	GBR	Norton	-	6	-	-	-	-	-	-	-	6	
8	Remo Venturi	ITA	Bianchi	-	-	6	-	-	-	-	-	-	6	
12	Nikolai Sevostyanov	RUS	CKB	-	-	-	-	-	3	-	3	-	6	
13	Derek Woodman	GBR	Matchless	-	3	-	1	-	2	-	-	-	6	
14	John Hartle	GBR	Norton	4	-	-	-	-	-	-	-	-	4	
15	Jack Findlay	AUS	Matchless	-	-	-	2	-	-	-	-	2	4	
16	Robin Fitton	GBR	Norton	-	-	-	-	-	-	3	-	-	3	
17	Chris Conn	GBR	Norton	-	-	-	-	-	-	2	-	-	2	
17	Griff Jenkins	GBR	Norton	-	2	-	-	-	-	-	-	-	2	
17	Morrie Low	NZE	Norton	-	-	-	-	2	-	-	-	-	2	
20	Billy McCosh	GBR	Matchless	-	1	-	-	-	-	-	-	-	1	
20	Buddy Parriott	USA	Norton	1	-	-	-	-	-	-	-	-	1	
20	Walter Scheimann	GER	Norton	-	-	-	-	-	-	-	-	1	1	
20	Lewis Young	GBR	Matchless	-	-	-	-	-	-	-	1	-	1	

Scoring system – 8, 6, 4, 3, 2, 1

350cc

Five best results were counted

Pos	Rider	Nat	Machine	Nett	Gross
1	Jim Redman	RHO	Honda	40	(64)
2	Bruce Beale	RHO	Honda	24	
3	Mike Duff	CAN	AJS	20	(24)
4	Mike Hailwood	GBR	MV Agusta/MZ	12	
5	Gustav Havel	CZE	Jawa	10	
6	Phil Read	GBR	AJS	6	
7	Paddy Driver	RSA	AJS	5	
8	Isamu Kasuya	JPN	Honda	4	
8	Endel Kiisa	RUS	CKB	4	
8	Stanislav Malina	CZE	CZ	4	
8	Remo Venturi	ITA	Bianchi	4	

250cc

Six best results were counted

Pos	Rider	Nat	Machine	Nett	Gross
1	Phil Read	GBR	Yamaha	46	(50)
2	Jim Redman	RHO	Honda	42	(58)
3	Alan Shepherd	GBR	MZ	23	
4	Mike Duff	CAN	Yamaha	20	
5	Tarquinio Provini	ITA	Benelli	15	
6	Luigi Taveri	SWI	Honda	11	
7	Isamu Kasuya	JPN	Honda	10	
8	Bruce Beale	RHO	Honda	9	
9	Tommy Robb	GBR	Yamaha	7	
10	Ron Grant	USA	Parilla	6	

125cc

Six best results were counted

Pos	Rider	Nat	Machine	Nett	Gross
1	Luigi Taveri	SWI	Honda	46	(64)
2	Jim Redman	RHO	Honda	36	(37)
3	Hugh Anderson	NZE	Suzuki	34	
4	Bert Schneider	AUT	Suzuki	22	(24)
5	Ralph Bryans	GBR	Honda	21	
6	Ernst Degner	GER	Suzuki	12	
7	Frank Perris	GBR	Suzuki	10	
8	Mitsuo Itoh	JPN	Suzuki	6	
8	Phil Read	GBR	Yamaha	6	
10	Walter Scheimann	GER	Honda	6	

50cc

Five best results were counted

Pos	Rider	Nat	Machine	Nett	Gross
1	Hugh Anderson	NZE	Suzuki	38	(42)
2	Ralph Bryans	GBR	Honda	30	
3	Hans-Georg Anscheidt	GER	Kreidler	29	(38)
4	Isao Morishita	JPN	Suzuki	25	(32)
5	Mitsuo Itoh	JPN	Suzuki	19	(21)
6	Jean-Pierre Beltoise	FRA	Kreidler	6	
7	Luigi Taveri	SWI	Kreidler	5	
8	José Busquets	SPA	Derbi	3	
9	Rudi Kunz	GER	Kreidler	3	
10	Peter Eser	GER	Honda	2	
10	Angel Nieto	SPA	Derbi	2	
10	Cees van Dongen	NED	Kreidler	2	

YAMAHA'S FIRST

Yamaha had been the pre-eminent Japanese racing marque right up until the point that Soichiro Honda sent his team to the 1959 Isle of Man TT. Suddenly, success in domestic competition wasn't enough and Yamaha too had to venture overseas. They had first appeared at a Grand Prix in 1961 with air-cooled disc-valve two-stroke racers, a single-cylinder 125, the RA41, and a 250 twin, the RD48, for the French, British, Dutch and Belgian races. The bigger bike was good enough to score points at all but the first race. Yamaha only raced once outside Japan in 1962, and that was in a non-championship event, but the factory was busy applying the lessons they had learnt. The result was the RD56. The motor was little changed, but the chassis now looked modern: duplex cradle frame, Girling rear shocks, forks with internal springs and a flat-sided tank. With Fumio Ito leading the team, Yamaha made a massive impression when they raced at the Isle of Man TT, Assen and Spa in 1963.

Still short of budget, the Yamaha factory didn't want to do a full season in '64 but Phil Read talked them into it. He started the 250cc GP season on the RD56 he had ridden at Suzuka at the end of the previous season, and received the revised model in time for the Isle of Man TT, the fourth round of the year. It incorporated more modern porting to give it an estimated 50bhp, but it looked even fresher thanks to that iconic red and white colour scheme that would feature on all Yamaha racers up to and including the YZR500.

The Honda, by contrast, was considerably more powerful but also a lot heavier. The Achilles heel of all the two-strokes was still reliability, but the points-scoring system meant that in the 250cc class riders counted their six best results from eleven races, so the failures that Read did experience were not as damaging as they would be nowadays. Read thus became Yamaha's first World Champion, but it is easy to overlook the contribution of Fumio Ito. The Japanese rode at Catalina in the USA in 1958, the factory's first venture outside Japan; he was the team's lead rider when they came to GPs and he scored their first victory, although his first GP point actually came when he was riding a 500cc BMW in 1960. Ito also recorded a pop single and was arrested for possession of a firearm! He moved to the USA in 1967 and was variously employed as a taxi driver in Los Angeles, in the tourist business in Hawaii and was rumoured to have been running a Japanese restaurant in Florida when he died in 1990.

BELOW Phil Read on the 250cc twin-cylinder Yamaha RD56. (*Keulemans Archive*)

1965

Mike Hailwood got a fast new team-mate at MV Agusta: Giacomo Agostini

Yamaha's RD56 air-cooled twin dominated the 250cc class in 1965, with Phil Read and Mike Duff finishing first and second; even Jim Redman and the Honda six couldn't worry them. However, Yamaha didn't rest on their laurels and came out with their own monster in the 125 class. First a water-cooled version of the 125cc twin appeared at the TT and Assen, winning both races before being shipped home. Then, 12 months after Honda had unveiled their 250-six at Monza, Yamaha took the sheets off their V4, effectively two contra-rotating RA97 125cc engines mounted in a 70-degree Vee. It turned out to be neither as effective nor as pretty as the RA65.

Suzuki's team of Hugh Anderson, Frank Perris and Ernst Degner were joined full time by Yoshimi Katayama who had scored a rostrum finish on the 125 at Suzuka the previous year. The square-four 250 continued to be problematic and didn't appear again after Spa, despite Perris having got it on the rostrum at the TT – the RZ's second and final top-three finish. However, Suzuki got their revenge in the 125 class as they added water-cooling to their twin and so outpaced the Honda fours of Luigi Taveri and Ralph Bryans that the four-strokes were withdrawn after Assen.

Honda showed their intention by unveiling their five-cylinder 125 at the final race of the year at Suzuka, where it set the fastest lap, and some satisfaction was obtained when Bryans won the 50cc title on the 20,000rpm nine-speed RC115 twin. At that Japanese GP the 250 race took place last, as was then usual. Having won the 350 race for MV, Mike Hailwood hopped on a six-cylinder Honda and won the 250 race by a minute and a half.

Honda left Jim Redman on his own not just in the 250 class, but in the 350s as well, where he came under serious pressure from MV Agusta's new recruit, Giacomo Agostini. MV were still using their old two-valves-per-cylinder four in the 500cc class – and it was good enough for Mike Hailwood and his new team-mate to finish first and second in the championship – but in the 350s they now had a lightweight four-valve triple.

ABOVE MV Agusta team-mates at Assen: Giacomo Agostini leads Mike Hailwood. (*Keulemans Archive*)

RIGHT Frank Perris on the new, water-cooled, 125cc Suzuki RK66. (*JARROTTS.com*)

THE **1965** SEASON

500cc

USA/Daytona
- Mike Hailwood won the opening race of the year at Daytona for the second successive year
- Buddy Parriott (Norton) finished second to become the first American rider to stand on the podium in the 500cc class

GER/Nürburgring
- Giacomo Agostini finished second on his debut in the 500cc class

GBR/Isle of Man TT
- Hailwood won the Senior TT for the third successive year after crashing in a rain-lashed race and remounting

DDR/Sachsenring
- Mike Hailwood made it a clean sweep of six wins in six races to become the first rider to win four successive 500cc world titles

ULS/Dundrod
- In the absence of the MVs, local Ulster rider Dick Creith (Norton) won from South African Paddy Driver (Matchless) and Chris Conn (GBR, Norton)
- This was the last time the top three were all on single-cylinder bikes, and also the last time that all podium finishers were riding British-made machinery

FIN/Imatra
- Having won the 350cc race earlier in the day, Giacomo Agostini took the first of his 68 victories in the 500cc class

350cc

GER/Nürburgring
- Giacomo Agostini won first time out on the new three-cylinder MV Agusta
- Reigning champion Jim Redman crashed while battling with Agostini and his injuries kept him out of both the 250cc race and the next GP in Spain

ULS/Dundrod
- Redman crashed on the last lap while holding a massive lead; his injuries kept him out of the 250cc race

JPN/Suzuka
- Mike Hailwood won on his very last GP ride for MV Agusta
- Jim Redman finished second to clinch his fourth successive 350cc world title

125cc

GBR/Isle of Man TT
- Phil Read gave the new water-cooled twin-cylinder Yamaha a win on its debut
- This was the first of 47 GP wins for Yamaha in the 125cc class

NED/Assen
- Canadian Mike Duff made it two wins from two races for the new 125cc Yamaha, after which its only appearance was at the final GP of the year in Japan

ULS/Dundrod
- Ernst Degner's victory was the last of his 15 GP wins

ITA-NAZ/Monza
- Hugh Anderson won from team-mate Frank Perris to regain the 125cc world title he had won previously in 1963

JPN/Suzuka
- Honda debuted their new five-cylinder machine in the hands of Luigi Taveri. It led the race until two-thirds' distance before suffering an oil leak, Taveri dropping back to finish second behind Anderson's Suzuki

250cc

FRA/Rouen
- At the only GP ever to be held at the Rouen circuit, Phil Read made it four wins from four races after Jim Redman suffered mechanical failure mid-race while leading by 13 seconds

GBR/Isle of Man TT
- Phil Read became the first rider to lap the TT course at an average speed of more than 100mph/161km/h on a 250cc machine before breaking down on the second lap

CZE/Brno
- At the first GP visit to Brno the 250cc race provided the best entertainment for over 300,000 spectators, with Yamaha team-mates Read and Mike Duff finishing ahead of Honda factory rider Redman

ULS/Dundrod
- In Redman's absence, Phil Read took his seventh 250cc win of the year to retain the world title

ITA-NAZ/Monza
- Read finished down in seventh place after suffering mechanical problems on the debut of the new four-cylinder Yamaha in a race won by Provini (Benelli)

JPN/Suzuka
- Having won the earlier 350cc race on an MV Agusta, Mike Hailwood won the 250cc race riding a 'private' Honda

50cc

JPN/Suzuka
- Ralph Bryans finished second to team-mate Luigi Taveri to give Honda their one and only 50cc world title – the only four-stroke machine ever to win the 50cc title

1965 WORLD CHAMPIONSHIP

500cc

Six best results were counted

Pos	Rider	Nat	Machine	USA	GER	GBR	NED	BEL	DDR	CZE	ULS	FIN	ITA	Nett	Gross
1	Mike Hailwood	GBR	MV Agusta	8	8	8	8	8	8	8	-	-	8	48	(64)
2	Giacomo Agostini	ITA	MV Agusta	-	6	-	6	6	6	6	-	8	6	38	(44)
3	Paddy Driver	RSA	Matchless	-	-	-	4	3	4	3	6	6	-	26	
4	Fred Stevens	GBR	Matchless	-	-	-	-	2	2	2	2	4	3	15	
5	Jack Ahearn	AUS	Norton	-	-	-	2	-	3	4	-	-	-	9	
6	Dick Creith	GBR	Norton	-	-	-	-	-	-	-	8	-	-	8	
7	Jack Findlay	AUS	Matchless	-	3	-	-	-	-	-	3	2	-	8	
8	Joe Dunphy	GBR	Norton	-	-	6	-	-	-	-	-	-	-	6	
8	Buddy Parriott	USA	Norton	6	-	-	-	-	-	-	-	-	-	6	
10	Frantisek Stastny	CZE	Jawa	-	-	-	-	-	-	1	-	-	4	5	
11	Roger Beaumont	CAN	Norton	4	-	-	-	-	-	-	-	-	-	4	
11	Chris Conn	GBR	Norton	-	-	-	-	-	-	-	4	-	-	4	
11	Mike Duff	CAN	Matchless	-	-	4	-	-	-	-	-	-	-	4	
11	Derek Minter	GBR	Norton	-	-	-	-	4	-	-	-	-	-	4	
11	Walter Scheimann	GER	Norton	-	4	-	-	-	-	-	-	-	-	4	
16	Ian Burne	RSA	Norton	-	-	3	-	-	1	-	-	-	-	4	
17	John Cooper	GBR	Norton	-	-	-	3	-	-	-	-	-	-	3	
17	Ken King	CAN	Norton	3	-	-	-	-	-	-	-	-	-	3	
17	Jouko Ryhanen	FIN	Matchless	-	-	-	-	-	-	-	-	3	-	3	
20	Selwyn Griffiths	GBR	Matchless	-	-	2	-	-	-	-	-	-	-	2	
20	Ed Labelle	USA	Norton	2	-	-	-	-	-	-	-	-	-	2	
20	Eduard Lenz	AUT	Norton	-	2	-	-	-	-	-	-	-	-	2	
20	Giuseppe Mandolini	ITA	Moto Guzzi	-	-	-	-	-	-	-	-	-	2	2	
20	Gyula Marsovszky	SWI	Matchless	-	-	-	-	1	-	-	-	-	1	2	
25	Robin Fitton	GBR	Norton	-	-	-	-	-	-	-	1	-	-	1	
25	Dave Lloyd	CAN	Norton	1	-	-	-	-	-	-	-	-	-	1	
25	Billy McCosh	GBR	Matchless	-	-	1	-	-	-	-	-	-	-	1	
25	Billie Nelson	GBR	Norton	-	1	-	-	-	-	-	-	-	-	1	
25	Dan Shorey	GBR	Norton	-	-	-	1	-	-	-	-	-	-	1	
25	Lewis Young	GBR	Matchless	-	-	-	-	-	-	-	-	1	-	1	

Scoring system – 8, 6, 4, 3, 2, 1

350cc

Five best results were counted

Pos	Rider	Nat	Machine	Nett	Gross
1	Jim Redman	RHO	Honda	38	
2	Giacomo Agostini	ITA	MV Agusta	32	(34)
3	Mike Hailwood	GBR	MV Agusta	20	
4	Bruce Beale	RHO	Honda	15	
5	Frantisek Stastny	CZE	Jawa	14	
6	Derek Woodman	GBR	MZ	14	
7	Gustav Havel	CZE	Jawa	12	
8	Renzo Pasolini	ITA	Aermacchi	9	
9	Silvio Grassetti	ITA	Bianchi	6	
9	Phil Read	GBR	Yamaha	6	

250cc

Seven best results were counted

Pos	Rider	Nat	Machine	Nett	Gross
1	Phil Read	GBR	Yamaha	56	(68)
2	Mike Duff	CAN	Yamaha	42	(50)
3	Jim Redman	RHO	Honda	34	
4	Heinz Rosner	DDR	MZ	18	
5	Derek Woodman	GBR	MZ	15	
6	Bruce Beale	RHO	Honda	14	
7	Tarquinio Provini	ITA	Benelli	11	
8	Ramon Torras	SPA	Bultaco	10	
9	Frank Perris	GBR	Suzuki	9	
10	Mike Hailwood	GBR	Honda	8	

125cc

Seven best results were counted

Pos	Rider	Nat	Machine	Nett	Gross
1	Hugh Anderson	NZE	Suzuki	56	(62)
2	Frank Perris	GBR	Suzuki	44	(48)
3	Derek Woodman	GBR	MZ	28	(30)
4	Ernst Degner	GER	Suzuki	23	
5	Luigi Taveri	SWI	Honda	14	
6	Mike Duff	CAN	Yamaha	12	
7	Klaus Enderlein	DDR	MZ	11	
8	Ralph Bryans	GBR	Honda	11	
9	Joachim Leitert	DDR	MZ	10	
10	Phil Read	GBR	Yamaha	8	

50cc

Five best results were counted

Pos	Rider	Nat	Machine	Nett	Gross
1	Ralph Bryans	GBR	Honda	36	(38)
2	Luigi Taveri	SWI	Honda	32	(39)
3	Hugh Anderson	NZE	Suzuki	32	(37)
4	Ernst Degner	GER	Suzuki	26	
5	Mitsuo Itoh	JPN	Suzuki	16	
6	Michio Ichino	JPN	Suzuki	6	
7	Hans-Georg Anscheidt	GER	Kreidler	6	
8	José Busquets	SPA	Derbi	4	
9	Jacques Roca	FRA	Derbi	4	
10	Harou Koshino	JPN	Suzuki	3	
10	Charlie Mates	GBR	Honda	3	

AGO ARRIVES

It is impossible to overestimate Giacomo Agostini's impact on motorcycle racing. Count Agusta had been waiting for an Italian rider capable of winning on his machines, so when Ago appeared the triple was created specifically for him. It was built to the Count's specific orders to be smaller and lighter than the old bike, and was based on the 250 twin that had last raced in 1961. The machine first surfaced in 350cc form in domestic competition, notably without the 'Privat' logo on the tank, and won its first Grand Prix at the Nürburgring in Germany in 1965. Mike Hailwood rode the old four.

Why did MV test their new concept in the 350 class? There was no real challenge to their domination of the 500s with what was, essentially, a 15-year-old design, but in the 350s Honda had won the last three titles with Jim Redman. Count Agusta wanted to fight back. The new MV was so fast that Redman crashed chasing it in Germany, but the champ then hit back with a run of four straight wins. Neither Redman nor Ago scored in Ulster, then Ago won two in a row, so the fight went all the way down to the last round in Japan. Agostini maintains to this day that he would have been champion if his ignition hadn't malfunctioned, but that failure allowed Redman to cruise to second place behind Hailwood's MV, and the Rhodesian rider retained the title for the fourth year in succession.

The advent of the MV triple was just the first of a series of seismic shifts in the power balance of motorcycle racing. The '65 350 crown was to be Redman's last world title; the man who did more than any other to put Honda on the racing map would soon have to hand over to Hailwood for the company's assault on the 500cc class. The combination of Giacomo Agostini and the MV triple, however, would bestride the next seven years of Grand Prix racing in the two biggest capacity classes, first in epic confrontations with Mike Hailwood and the Honda six, and then fighting a heroic rearguard action against the advance of the two-strokes.

ABOVE Giacomo Agostini – devastatingly fast, impeccably organised, and handsome with it. (*JARROTTS.com*)

1966

Mike Hailwood moved to Honda and with their new 500 took the fight to Agostini and MV Agusta

Honda attacked on all fronts as they entered the 500 class for the first time. Jim Redman and Mike Hailwood rode the RC181, like the other Hondas an air-cooled DOHC but, perhaps surprisingly, with only four cylinders. Hailwood and Redman also rode six-cylinder Hondas in the 250 and 350 classes while Luigi Taveri and Ralph Bryans contested the 50 and 125cc classes. When Jim Redman was injured at the Belgian GP, Stuart Graham (GBR) was employed to back up Hailwood.

The opposition to Honda's onslaught came, as was now the pattern, from MV Agusta in the two biggest classes, from Yamaha in the 125 and 250s, and from Suzuki in the 50s. The Italian factory concentrated all its efforts behind Giacomo Agostini and brought out a 420cc version of their triple to counter the threat of the new 500cc Honda. Yamaha persisted with their unwieldy V4 in the 250 class but countered Honda's five-cylinder 125 with their own water-cooled V4 late in the season. The (in)famous team of Phil Read and Bill Ivy (GBR) rode both classes, Little Bill getting the job after he replaced the injured Mike Duff at the last race of '65.

Suzuki kept Frank Perris, Yoshimi Katayama and Hugh Anderson on their 125s and the latter two were joined by Hans-Georg Anscheidt on the 50s. The German was recruited after his previous employers, Kreidler, quit GPs. Suzuki had a new water-cooled twin, the RK66, on which Anscheidt would prove almost unbeatable over the next three years. However, he needed a Honda boycott of the last race of the year, as usual the Japanese GP, to win his first title. Ostensibly, Honda refused to race at the Fisco Circuit (also known as Fuji) because of safety concerns. The alternative theory was that the company was irked at the event being moved from Suzuka, Honda's own circuit.

Honda may not have won the 500 or 50cc Riders' Championships but they did something just as remarkable. They won the Constructors' Championship in all five solo classes in what was arguably the season which saw the technology of racing advance further than in any other year.

ABOVE Mike Hailwood on the bike with which he is identified more than any other – the six-cylinder, 18,000rpm, 250cc Honda RC166. (*JARROTTS.com*)

RIGHT Derek Woodman kept the MZ flying. (*JARROTTS.com*)

THE 1966 SEASON

500cc

GER/Hockenheim
- Jim Redman gave the new four-cylinder Honda the perfect debut with a victory in the opening race of the year, 26 seconds ahead of closest challenger Giacomo Agostini on the MV Agusta
- There was confusion at the end of the race when the leaders were shown the chequered flag one lap early and the final results were taken at the end of 19 laps instead of the planned 20

NED/Assen
- After Mike Hailwood crashed while leading on his debut on the 500cc Honda, Redman made it two wins from two starts
- Agostini came home a close second, debuting the new three-cylinder MV Agusta

BEL/Spa-Francorchamps
- Agostini took his first victory of the year after Jim Redman crashed and Mike Hailwood retired with gearbox trouble
- Redman suffered a bad wrist injury after crashing and retired from Grand Prix racing at the end of the season

DDR/Sachsenring
- After Hailwood retired and Agostini crashed when leading by more than a lap, Frantisek Stastny gave Jawa their only win in the 500cc class – and also the only victory in the premier class by a Czech rider

CZE/Brno
- Having won the 250 and 350cc races earlier in the day, Mike Hailwood won the 500cc race and joined Jim Redman as the only riders to have taken three GP victories in a single day. This was also Hailwood's first 500cc victory on a Honda

GBR/Isle of Man TT
- Mike Hailwood gave Honda their first Senior TT victory and put himself just two points behind championship leader Giacomo Agostini going into the final race of the year

ITA-NAZ/Monza
- Hailwood broke down and Giacomo Agostini won the race to clinch his first world title

350cc

DDR/Sachsenring
- After taking three wins from the first three races of the year, Mike Hailwood suffered mechanical failure while leading, leaving Giacomo Agostini on his MV Agusta to take his first 350cc win of the year

ULS/Dundrod
- Hailwood took his sixth win from the first seven races of the year to win the 350cc world title for the first time

JPN/Fisco
- Read takes Yamaha's first 350cc victory

250cc

SPA/Montjuich
- Mike Hailwood opened his season as a Honda factory rider with a victory at the first race of the year

CZE/Brno
- Hailwood won the first seven races of the year to regain the 250cc world title he had previously won in 1961

ULS/Dundrod
- Ginger Molloy (NZE) scored his only Grand Prix victory and gave Bultaco their sole win in the 250cc class

125cc

SPA/Montjuich
- Bill Ivy (Yamaha) took his first GP victory in the opening event of the year

ITA-NAZ/Monza
- Luigi Taveri (Honda) won at Monza to clinch the last of his three world titles in the 125cc class

50cc

GBR/Isle of Man TT
- Ralph Bryans gave Honda their last 50cc GP victory – and also the last 50cc GP won by a four-stroke

ITA-NAZ/Monza
- Hans-Georg Anscheidt (Suzuki) won his second race of the year, taking him to third place in the championship table with one race to go, just a single point behind Honda team-mates and joint championship leaders Taveri and Bryans

JPN/Fisco
- Anscheidt won the 50cc world title with a second-place finish; the event was not attended by the Honda factory team in protest at the event being held at the Fisco circuit

1966 WORLD CHAMPIONSHIP

500cc

Five best results were counted

Pos	Rider	Nat	Machine	GER	NED	BEL	DDR	CZE	FIN	ULS	GBR	ITA	Nett	Gross
1	Giacomo Agostini	ITA	MV Agusta	6	6	8	-	6	8	6	6	8	36	(54)
2	Mike Hailwood	GBR	Honda	-	-	-	-	8	6	8	8	-	30	
3	Jack Findlay	AUS	Matchless	-	1	-	6	3	4	3	-	4	20	(21)
4	Frantisek Stastny	CZE	Jawa	-	4	-	8	-	-	4	1	-	17	
5	Jim Redman	RHO	Honda	8	8	-	-	-	-	-	-	-	16	
6	Jack Ahearn	AUS	Norton	-	-	4	4	2	3	-	-	-	13	
6	Gyula Marsovszky	SWI	Matchless	4	-	3	2	4	-	-	-	-	13	
8	Stuart Graham	GBR	Matchless	3	2	6	-	-	-	-	-	-	11	
9	Peter Williams	GBR	Matchless/AJS	-	-	-	-	-	-	1	-	6	7	
10	Chris Conn	GBR	Norton	-	-	-	-	-	-	2	4	-	6	
11	Ron Chandler	GBR	Matchless	-	-	1	3	-	-	-	2	-	6	
12	John Blanchard	GBR	Matchless	-	-	-	-	-	-	-	3	-	3	
12	John Cooper	GBR	Norton	-	3	-	-	-	-	-	-	-	3	
12	Fred Stevens	GBR	Paton	-	-	-	-	-	-	-	-	3	3	
15	Lewis Young	GBR	Matchless	2	-	-	-	-	1	-	-	-	3	
16	John Mawby	GBR	Norton	-	-	2	-	-	-	-	-	-	2	
16	Walter Scheimann	GER	Norton	-	-	-	-	-	-	-	-	2	2	
16	Malcolm Stanton	AUS	Norton	-	-	-	-	-	2	-	-	-	2	
19	Eduard Lenz	AUT	Matchless	1	-	-	-	-	-	-	-	1	2	
20	John Dodds	AUS	Norton	-	-	-	1	-	-	-	-	-	1	
20	Eric Hinton	AUS	Norton	-	-	-	-	1	-	-	-	-	1	

Scoring system – 8, 6, 4, 3, 2, 1

350cc

Six best results were counted

Pos	Rider	Nat	Machine	Nett	Gross
1	Mike Hailwood	GBR	Honda	48	
2	Giacomo Agostini	ITA	MV Agusta	42	(48)
3	Renzo Pasolini	ITA	Aermacchi	17	
4	Frantisek Stastny	CZE	Jawa	13	
5	Gustav Havel	CZE	Jawa	12	
6	Alberto Pagani	ITA	Aermacchi	11	
7	Heinz Rosner	DDR	MZ	10	
8	Phil Read	GBR	Yamaha	8	
9	Jack Ahearn	AUS	Norton	8	
10	Bruce Beale	RHO	Honda	7	

250cc

Seven best results were counted

Pos	Rider	Nat	Machine	Nett	Gross
1	Mike Hailwood	GBR	Honda	56	(80)
2	Phil Read	GBR	Yamaha	34	
3	Jim Redman	RHO	Honda	20	
4	Derek Woodman	GBR	MZ	18	
5	Stuart Graham	GBR	Honda	15	
6	Heinz Rosner	DDR	MZ	15	
7	Jack Findlay	AUS	Bultaco	14	
8	Frantisek Stastny	CZE	Jawa	11	
9	Mike Duff	CAN	Yamaha	9	
10	Hiroshi Hasegawa	JPN	Yamaha	8	
10	Ginger Molloy	NZE	Bultaco	8	

125cc

Six best results were counted

Pos	Rider	Nat	Machine	Nett	Gross
1	Luigi Taveri	SWI	Honda	46	(58)
2	Bill Ivy	GBR	Yamaha	40	(44)
3	Ralph Bryans	GBR	Honda	32	(33)
4	Phil Read	GBR	Yamaha	29	(37)
5	Hugh Anderson	NZE	Suzuki	15	
6	Yoshimi Katayama	JPN	Suzuki	14	
7	Frank Perris	GBR	Suzuki	10	
8	Akiyasu Motohashi	JPN	Yamaha	5	
9	Mitsuo Itoh	JPN	Suzuki	4	
10	Mike Duff	CAN	Yamaha	4	

50cc

Four best results were counted

Pos	Rider	Nat	Machine	Nett	Gross
1	Hans-Georg Anscheidt	GER	Suzuki	28	(31)
2	Luigi Taveri	SWI	Honda	26	(29)
3	Ralph Bryans	GBR	Honda	26	(30)
4	Hugh Anderson	NZE	Suzuki	16	(22)
5	Yoshimi Katayama	JPN	Suzuki	10	
6	Mitsuo Itoh	JPN	Suzuki	3	
6	Ernst Degner	GER	Suzuki	3	
8	Barry Smith	AUS	Derbi	3	
9	Tommy Robb	GBR	Bridgestone	2	
9	Angel Nieto	SPA	Derbi	2	
9	Oswald Dittrich	GER	Kreidler	2	
9	Brian Gleed	GBR	Honda	2	

HONDA AND REDMAN

No other rider, not even Mike Hailwood, was as important to Honda in their early years as Jim Redman. He first rode for Honda in 1960 when he replaced his injured friend, Aussie Tom Phillis, joining the factory full time the following year. He went on to win six titles, including two 250/350 doubles, in four years. In 1964 he won the 125, 250 and 350cc races at the Dutch TT on the same day, a feat equalled only by Hailwood. He also acted as Honda's team captain, advising the factory on rider recruitment, and he had enough power to decide that the team should boycott the US GP in 1964 and '65. Jim enjoyed the confidence and respect of Mr Honda himself and the second President of the Honda Motor Company, Mr Kawashima. Company legend has it that when the bikes started becoming competitive and there was a queue of better known riders asking to ride them, Mr Kawashima said: 'Jim-san and Tom-san rode them when they were slow, they will ride them now they are fast.' That loyalty worked both ways. No-one ever heard Redman say anything bad about his bikes, no matter how wayward their handling. Even though he was never a fan of the TT, Jim won the same two races three years running on the Island, a fact of which he remains extremely proud.

No-one has won more world titles on a Honda, and 1966 was supposed to be the year when Redman added the 500c crown to his two 250 and four 350 championships. Hailwood was originally supposed to concentrate on the 250 and 350 classes. Jim won the first two rounds, then crashed at Spa, badly breaking his wrist. He tried to come back four races later but he had not fully recovered. He retired at the end of the season, as he'd always planned, without completing the year and without a 500cc title to his name.

English by birth, Redman emigrated to Rhodesia to avoid his young twin brother and sister being taken into care when he was called up for National Service. Not surprisingly, he turned out to be a difficult man to beat.

He wasn't just tough on the track, Redman was one of the first riders to challenge the exploitation of riders by organisers. Unlike many of his contemporaries, Jim Redman is still with us and can be seen giving the Honda museum's treasures a run at tracks around the world.

BELOW Jim Redman, Honda's most successful rider. *(Elwyn Roberts Collection)*

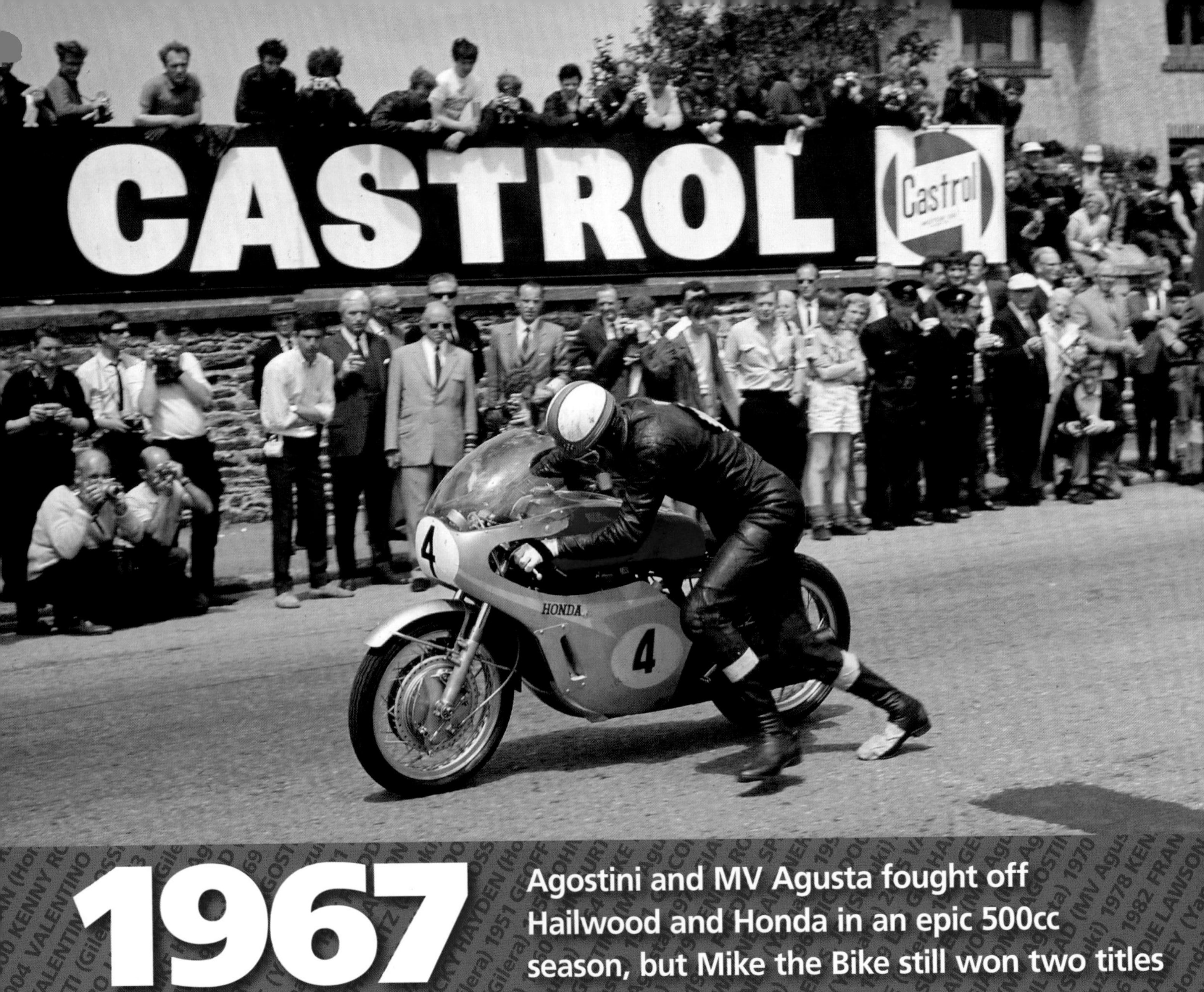

1967

Agostini and MV Agusta fought off Hailwood and Honda in an epic 500cc season, but Mike the Bike still won two titles

For once the 250s were eclipsed by the 500s and 350s. This was the year of the epic duel between Giacomo Agostini on the three-cylinder MV Agusta and Mike Hailwood on the much-improved but still wayward-handling Honda four. Their confrontation at the Isle of Man saw Hailwood set a lap record that would stand for nine years and, by common consent, the 1967 Senior TT was the greatest race ever on the Mountain circuit. The Honda RC181 500 wasn't good enough for Hailwood to get on terms with Ago, but the six-cylinder 350, the RC174, which was actually a 250 over-bored to 297cc, was perfection. Mike won every GP he rode it in.

The resources taken up by Honda's attack on Formula 1 – or it may have been the inexorable march of the two-strokes – led to a reduction in the factory's effort on two wheels. Mike Hailwood contested the three big classes – 250, 350, 500cc – with Ralph Bryans supporting him in the two smaller classes; Mike was on his own in the 500s. Honda did not contest the 50 and 125cc championships.

Gauge the status of the 250s by the fact that every GP promoter ran the class – 13 rounds – whereas 10 ran the 500s and just 8 the 350s. Yamaha again had the pairing of Phil Read and Bill Ivy on V4s in both the 125 and 250cc classes. Nothing could touch their 125, and although Hailwood won more 250 races than Read, only seven races were counted for the scoring system, which put the pair level on points. Hailwood won on countback. Suzuki were as dominant in the 50cc class as the Yamahas were in the 125s. Hans-Georg Anscheidt just rode the 50 (and won the title again), Stuart Graham and Yoshimi Katayama doubled up with the 125 as well, and Graham got to ride the new V4 125cc Suzuki at the Japanese GP.

As usual, the end-of-season Japanese Grand Prix was awash with rumours of exotic new machinery for the following year – a 50cc Suzuki triple, a six-cylinder Honda 500, even a V8 250. None of it was to happen.

ABOVE Hailwood pushes off on the 500 Honda at the start of the greatest-ever TT: he set a lap record that would stand for nine years. (*JARROTTS.com*)

RIGHT Hans-Georg Anscheidt (GER) retained the 50cc title for Suzuki. (*JARROTTS.com*)

THE **1967** SEASON

500cc

GER/Hockenheim

- Giacomo Agostini won the opening race of the year in defence of his world title after Mike Hailwood's Honda suffered crankshaft failure

GBR/Isle of Man TT

- Hailwood won the 500cc TT race to add to his victories in the 250 and 350cc classes, repeating his 1961 feat of three World Championship TT victories in the same week

NED/Assen

- For the second successive GP Mike Hailwood took wins in the 250, 350 and 500cc classes. On this occasion all three races were on the same day, covering a total of 273 miles over more than three hours of racing

ITA-NAZ/Monza

- Agostini won his home GP, with Hailwood trailing home in second place after his machine stuck in top gear while he was leading the race comfortably with just three laps to go
- Agostini now needed to score just a single point at the final race in Canada to be sure of retaining his world title

CAN/Mosport

- Mike Hailwood won his last GP on a Honda on the only occasion a Grand Prix event has been held in Canada; Agostini finished second to retain the title

350cc

GER/Hockenheim

- Mike Hailwood opened the defence of his 350cc title with a win on the new six-cylinder Honda, and with a margin of almost a minute over Giacomo Agostini (MV Agusta)

CZE/Brno

- Mike Hailwood made it five wins from five races to retain the 350cc world title

ULS/Dundrod

- In Hailwood's absence, Agostini took his first 350cc victory of the year after a battle with Ralph Bryans, the Briton riding the six-cylinder Honda in the 350cc class for the first time

JPN/Suzuka

- Mike Hailwood took the last of his 76 Grand Prix victories

250cc

SPA/Montjuich

- Phil Read opened the year with a win after Mike Hailwood suffered a puncture while leading by 35 seconds

GER/Hockenheim

- World Champion Hailwood retired for the second successive race, allowing team-mate Ralph Bryans to take his first 250cc GP victory

FRA/Clermont-Ferrand

- Having won the earlier 125cc race, Bill Ivy (Yamaha) scored his first double with victory in the 250cc race in front of team-mate Phil Read and the Honda of Hailwood

CAN/Mosport

- Mike Hailwood's win made him level on points with Phil Read with one race left

JPN/Fisco

- Both title challengers, Hailwood and Read, failed to finish the race resulting in the title going to Mike with five wins during the year to Phil's four

125cc

SPA/Montjuich

- Bill Ivy gave the new four-cylinder Yamaha its first Grand Prix victory

GER/Hockenheim

- Factory Suzuki rider Yoshimi Katayama won his only 125cc GP after both Yamaha riders were taken out in a single incident when lapping a backmarker who fell

FRA/Clermont-Ferrand

- Dave Simmonds (GBR) finished fifth to give Kawasaki their first points-scoring finish in GP racing

FIN/Imatra

- Simmonds finished third, scoring Kawasaki's first podium in Grand Prix racing

ITA-NAZ/Monza

- Bill Ivy clinched the world title with victory in Italy, having stopped mid-race with overheating problems when in a huge lead, restarted in second place and then won by 0.2s on the sprint to the line

50cc

GBR/Isle of Man TT

- Stuart Graham (Suzuki), whose father Les was the first 500cc World Champion, became the first son of a Grand Prix winner also to win a GP

NED/Assen

- Angel Nieto (Derbi) finished on a GP podium for the first time, taking second place behind Suzuki factory rider Yoshimi Katayama

BEL/Spa-Francorchamps

- Hans-Georg Anscheidt retained the 50cc world title with a win for Suzuki

1967 WORLD CHAMPIONSHIP

500cc

Six best results were counted

Pos	Rider	Nat	Machine	GER	GBR	NED	BEL	DDR	CZE	FIN	ULS	ITA	CAN	Nett	Gross
1	Giacomo Agostini	ITA	MV Agusta	8	-	6	8	8	6	8	-	8	6	46	(58)
2	Mike Hailwood	GBR	Honda	-	8	8	6	-	8	-	8	6	8	46	(52)
3	John Hartle	GBR	Matchless	-	1	-	-	6	2	6	6	1	-	22	
4	Peter Williams	GBR	Matchless	6	6	4	-	-	-	-	-	-	-	16	
5	Jack Findlay	AUS	Matchless	4	-	-	3	4	-	-	4	-	-	15	
6	Fred Stevens	GBR	Paton	-	2	-	4	-	-	2	-	3	-	11	
7	John Cooper	GBR	Norton	-	3	-	-	-	4	-	1	-	-	8	
8	Gyula Marsovszky	SWI	Matchless	-	-	2	2	-	3	-	-	-	-	7	
9	Billie Nelson	GBR	Norton	2	-	-	-	-	-	4	-	-	-	6	
9	Steve Spencer	GBR	Norton	-	4	-	-	-	-	-	2	-	-	6	
11	Angelo Bergamonti	ITA	Paton	-	-	-	-	-	-	-	-	4		4	
11	Mike Duff	CAN	Matchless	-	-	-	-	-	-	-	-	-	4	4	
13	John Dodds	AUS	Norton	-	-	-	-	3	1	-	-	-	-	4	
13	Dan Shorey	GBR	Norton	-	-	3	-	1	-	-	-	-	-	4	
15	John Blanchard	GBR	Seeley	-	-	-	-	-	-	-	3	-	-	3	
15	Robin Fitton	GBR	Norton	3	-	-	-	-	-	-	-	-	-	3	
15	Bo Granath	SWE	Matchless	-	-	-	-	-	-	3	-	-	-	3	
15	Ivor Lloyd	GBR	Matchless	-	-	-	-	-	-	-	-	-	3	3	
19	Andreas Georgeades	CAN	Velocette	-	-	-	-	-	-	-	-	-	2	2	
19	Rod Gould	GBR	Norton	-	-	-	-	2	-	-	-	-	-	2	
19	Giuseppe Mandolini	ITA	Moto Guzzi	-	-	-	-	-	-	-	-	2	-	2	
22	Chris Conn	GBR	Norton	-	-	1	-	-	-	-	-	-	-	1	
22	Maurice Hawthorne	GBR	Norton	-	-	-	-	-	-	1	-	-	-	1	
22	Griff Jenkins	GBR	Norton	1	-	-	-	-	-	-	-	-	-	1	
22	Derek Minter	GBR	Norton	-	-	-	1	-	-	-	-	-	-	1	
22	George Rockett	USA	Norton	-	-	-	-	-	-	-	-	-	1	1	

Scoring system – 8, 6, 4, 3, 2, 1

350cc

Five best results were counted

Pos	Rider	Nat	Machine	Nett	Gross
1	Mike Hailwood	GBR	Honda	40	(48)
2	Giacomo Agostini	ITA	MV Agusta	32	
3	Ralph Bryans	GBR	Honda	20	
4	Heinz Rosner	GER	MZ	18	
5	Derek Woodman	GBR	MZ	14	
6	Alberto Pagani	ITA	Aermacchi	11	
7	Kel Carruthers	AUS	Aermacchi	9	
8	Renzo Pasolini	ITA	Benelli	8	
9	Silvio Grassetti	ITA	Benelli	6	
10	Shigeyoshi Mimuro	JPN	Yamaha	4	

250cc

Seven best results were counted

Pos	Rider	Nat	Machine	Nett	Gross
1	Mike Hailwood	GBR	Honda	50	(54)
2	Phil Read	GBR	Yamaha	50	(56)
3	Bill Ivy	GBR	Yamaha	46	(51)
4	Ralph Bryans	GBR	Honda	40	(58)
5	Derek Woodman	GBR	MZ	18	
6	Heinz Rosner	GER	MZ	13	
7	Ginger Molloy	NZE	Bultaco	9	
8	Gyula Marsovszky	SWI	Bultaco	8	
9	Akiyasu Motohashi	JPN	Yamaha	6	
10	Tommy Robb	GBR	Bultaco	5	
10	Dave Simmonds	GBR	Kawasaki	5	

125cc

Seven best results were counted

Pos	Rider	Nat	Machine	Nett	Gross
1	Bill Ivy	GBR	Yamaha	56	(76)
2	Phil Read	GBR	Yamaha	40	
3	Stuart Graham	GBR	Suzuki	38	(44)
4	Yoshimi Katayama	JPN	Suzuki	19	
5	Laszlo Szabo	HUN	MZ	13	
6	Hans-Georg Anscheidt	GER	Suzuki	12	
7	Dave Simmonds	GBR	Kawasaki	9	
8	Kel Carruthers	AUS	Honda	7	
9	Tim Coopey	CAN	Yamaha	6	
10	Thomas Heuschkel	GER	MZ	5	
10	Walter Scheimann	GER	Honda	5	

50cc

Four best results were counted

Pos	Rider	Nat	Machine	Nett	Gross
1	Hans-Georg Anscheidt	GER	Suzuki	30	(42)
2	Yoshimi Katayama	JPN	Suzuki	28	
3	Stuart Graham	GBR	Suzuki	22	
4	Angel Nieto	SPA	Derbi	12	
5	Barry Smith	AUS	Derbi	12	
6	Mitsuo Itoh	JPN	Suzuki	8	
7	Rolf Schmalzle	GER	Kreidler	6	
8	José Busquets	SPA	Derbi	4	
8	Benjamin Grau	SPA	Derbi	4	
8	Hiroyuki Kawasaki	JPN	Suzuki	4	
8	Tommy Robb	GBR	Suzuki	4	

MIKE THE BIKE

Mike Hailwood is regarded by many if not all authorities on racing as the greatest, most versatile rider who ever lived. The 1967 season shows why this view still prevails. Mike carried the Honda banner alone in the 500 class, pushing Ago all the way, and he retained his 250 and 350 titles. Twice he won three races at one event, at the TT and at Assen, with the Dutch hat-trick coming all on one day. No wonder even the supremely laid-back Hailwood thought the year was a bit too much like hard work. In earlier seasons he'd ridden MVs of all sizes and also raced NSU, Norton, Ducati, Mondial, AJS, production BSA and Triumph twins, EMC and MZ bikes, and won on all of them.

This was Mike's last season in GP racing on two wheels. Honda pulled out over the winter but gave him a large salary, a 350-six and a 500-four to keep racing in international meetings in 1968. Honda did not want to lose the link with Mike the Bike. The next three seasons were quiet on the bike front, although Hailwood did lead the Daytona 200 on a BSA triple. Then, in 1972, Mike went car racing, winning the European F2 Championship and moving to F1 with John Surtees. He retired from racing in 1975.

His comeback started in 1977 with a one-off fun race at the Castrol Six Hour in Australia, where he rode a 750 Ducati. The following year was the stuff of legend. Mike went back to the TT on an F1 Ducati and, eleven years after he'd last raced there, he won the race and set a new lap record. And it is often forgotten that he went back the following year and won again, this time the Senior TT on a 500cc two-stroke Suzuki, once more setting a new record lap.

Mike Hailwood died along with his daughter Michelle in a road traffic accident in March 1981.

	Starts	Wins	Podiums
500cc	66	37	48
350cc	46	16	26
250cc	56	21	32
125cc	28	2	6
Total	196	76	112

LEFT Racing in three classes in '67 was too much even for Mike Hailwood. (*Keulemans Archive*)

MIKE HAILWOOD STATISTICS

- At the 1959 Ulster GP, riding a Ducati, Mike Hailwood became the first teenage rider to win a Grand Prix
- At the Isle of Man TT in 1961 he became the youngest rider to win a 250cc race – a record that stood until Alan Carter won the French GP in 1983
- In 1961 Hailwood won the 250cc World Championship to become the youngest rider to win a world title in any class
- At the Isle of Man TT in 1961 he became the youngest rider to win a 500cc race – a record he held until Randy Mamola won in Belgium in 1980
- In 1962 Mike became the youngest ever rider to win the 500cc world title. Since then only two riders have won the premier-class title at a younger age – Freddie Spencer and Casey Stoner
- Mike Hailwood was the first rider to win the 500cc title in four successive years
- He won three races at the same GP event on five occasions; twice these three races were on the same day
- Hailwood was one of only four riders to have won GP races in the 125cc, 250cc, 350cc and 500cc classes
- He was a Grand Prix winner on the following different machines: 125cc Ducati, 125cc Honda, 250cc Honda, 250cc MZ, 350cc MV Agusta, 350cc Honda, 500cc Norton, 500cc MV Agusta and 500cc Honda

1968

With Honda gone Giacomo Agostini cruised to two more titles, attention focused on the civil war at Yamaha

The Honda Motor Company announced in February that it was withdrawing from motorcycle GPs. Suzuki followed suit shortly afterwards, but agreed to supply Stuart Graham with a 125 twin for non-GP events. Hans-Georg Anscheidt did a similar deal with Suzuki but he was given a 50cc bike as well, which he was allowed to race in the World Championship – and that turned out to be a good decision, because the German rider made it a hat-trick of titles and then retired from racing.

Neither Suzuki nor any other manufacturer could have lived with Yamaha in the intensely competitive 250 class, now most definitely the race with the most interest. The V4 Yamahas of Ivy and Read were the most advanced motorcycles in the paddock and they dominated both the 125 and 250 classes, winning every race bar one. A third Yamaha finished fourth in the 250 class, ridden by Rod Gould (GBR). This was an over-the-counter racer, a TD1C – Yamaha had actually been producing them since 1962 – but it was the first time one was sent to the GPs. Gould housed the motor in a Bultaco chassis. A factory MZ prevented a Yamaha one–two–three in the 250s.

The Spanish industry was now taking a serious interest in the smaller classes. Ginger Molloy (NZE) and Salvador Canellas (SPA) put Bultacos on the rostrum in the 125 class, while Barry Smith (AUS) and Angel Nieto did the same for Derbi in the 50s. There was also a win for the Dutch Jamathi bike in the 50s.

In the bigger classes Giacomo Agostini embarked on a run of sustained domination by winning every race on the 350 and 500cc calendar. In the 350s he was pursued by a new Italian hero, the bespectacled Renzo Pasolini on a four-cylinder Benelli, who would take the fight to Ago both in the Italian Championship and in GPs. In the big class, a herd of antiquated British singles had their own race, minutes adrift of the MV four. That at least let the epitome of the privateer, Aussie Jack Findlay, focus of the cult 1972 film *Continental Circus* which documented the precarious lives of the privateer racers to a prog rock soundtrack by Gong, achieve his career-best championship position with second place.

ABOVE Bill Ivy leads Phil Read in the 250cc Dutch TT; Ivy won by a tenth of a second with Pasolini's Benelli one and three quarter minutes behind in third. (*Keulemans Archive*)

RIGHT Ivy on the four-cylinder Yamaha, the first 125 to lap the Isle of Man at over 100mph. (*JARROTTS.com*)

THE **1968** SEASON

500cc

GER/Nürburgring

- Giacomo Agostini opened the defence of his title with a comfortable win – he had already lapped all the other riders when the race was stopped prematurely because a fire started accidentally by spectators spread onto the track

GBR/Isle of Man TT

- Agostini became the first Italian rider to win the Senior TT

DDR/Sachsenring

- Agostini made it six wins from six races to clinch his third 500cc world title

ITA-NAZ/Monza

- Giacomo Agostini won the final race of the year to make a clean sweep of ten wins from ten races, one of only two occasions in the 500cc class where a rider has had a perfect season – the other being John Surtees's seven wins from seven starts in 1959
- Mike Hailwood made a one-off appearance on the new four-cylinder factory Benelli but crashed in the wet conditions on lap three when challenging Agostini for the lead. Hailwood had been due to race an MV Agusta – and practised on it – but withdrew when told he would be required to finish second to Agostini
- Agostini was followed across the line by four other Italian riders (Renzo Pasolini, Angelo Bergamonti, Alberto Pagani and Silvano Bertarelli), the only occasion on which Italian riders took the top five places in a premier-class GP

350cc

CZE/Brno

- Giacomo Agostini made it five wins from five starts to clinch the 350cc world title for the first time and to become the first Italian rider to do the 350/500cc double

ITA-NAZ/Monza

- Agostini took seven wins from seven races to equal the 1959 feat of John Surtees in winning all 350cc and 500cc races in a single season

250cc

CZE/Brno

- After winning the 125cc race and securing the world title, Phil Read went against team orders to win the 250cc event from team-mate Bill Ivy

ULS/Dundrod

- Bill Ivy won the race to maintain his lead in the 250cc title race

ITA-NAZ/Monza

- With cancellation of the scheduled final race of the year in Japan, it was winner take all for the two factory Yamaha riders
- Phil Read won from Bill Ivy, putting both riders equal on points, and the title was decided by combined times in races both had completed, handing the title to Read

125cc

SPA/Montjuich

- After the retirement of both Yamaha factory riders, Salvador Canellas gave the Spanish Bultaco factory their first victory in the 125cc class

GBR/Isle of Man TT

- Bill Ivy became the first rider to lap the TT course at over 100mph/161km/h on a 125cc machine, then slowed on the final lap to allow Phil Read to win the race

CZE/Brno

- Phil Read won the race to clinch the world title

50cc

GBR/Isle of Man TT

- Les Griffiths (GBR, Honda) finished third at the age of 54, the oldest ever GP podium finisher

NED/Assen

- Dutch rider Paul Lodewijkx gave the Dutch-built Jamathi its first GP victory at their home race at Assen

BEL/Spa-Francorchamps

- Hans-Georg Anscheidt took his third win of the year to take the world title for Suzuki for the third successive year, the last time the 50cc title was won by a Japanese manufacturer

1968 WORLD CHAMPIONSHIP

500cc

Six best results were counted

Pos	Rider	Nat	Machine	GER	SPA	GBR	NED	BEL	DDR	CZE	FIN	ULS	ITA	Nett	Gross
1	Giacomo Agostini	ITA	MV Agusta	8	8	8	8	8	8	8	8	8	8	48	(80)
2	Jack Findlay	AUS	Matchless	-	6	-	6	6	4	6	6	2	-	34	(36)
3	Gyula Marsovszky	SWI	Matchless	3	2	-	-	-	-	4	1	-	-	10	
4	Robin Fitton	GBR	Norton	-	-	-	-	3	-	-	-	6	-	9	
4	Alberto Pagani	ITA	Linto	-	-	-	-	-	6	-	-	-	3	9	
6	Peter Williams	GBR	Matchless	4	-	-	3	-	-	2	-	-	-	9	
7	Derek Woodman	GBR	Seeley	-	-	-	-	4	-	-	4	-	-	8	
8	John Cooper	GBR	Seeley	-	-	-	4	1	3	-	-	-	-	8	
9	Dan Shorey	GBR	Norton	6	-	-	-	-	-	1	-	-	-	7	
10	Angelo Bergamonti	ITA	Paton	-	3	-	-	-	-	-	-	-	4	7	
11	Kel Carruthers	AUS	Norton	-	-	1	2	2	-	-	-	1	1	7	
12	Brian Ball	GBR	Seeley	-	-	6	-	-	-	-	-	-	-	6	
12	Renzo Pasolini	ITA	Benelli	-	-	-	-	-	-	-	-	-	6	6	
14	John Dodds	AUS	Norton	-	4	-	-	-	-	-	2	-	-	6	
15	Billie Nelson	GBR	Paton	-	-	-	-	-	2	3	-	-	-	5	
16	John Hartle	GBR	Metisse	-	-	-	-	-	-	-	-	4	-	4	
16	Barry Randle	GBR	Norton	-	-	4	-	-	-	-	-	-	-	4	
18	Nikolai Sevostyanov	RUS	Vostok	-	-	-	-	-	-	-	3	-	-	3	
18	Bill Smith	GBR	Matchless	-	-	3	-	-	-	-	-	-	-	3	
18	Percy Tait	GBR	Triumph	-	-	-	-	-	-	-	-	3	-	3	
21	Silvano Bertarelli	ITA	Paton	-	-	-	-	-	-	-	-	-	2	2	
21	Bernie Lund	GBR	Matchless	-	-	2	-	-	-	-	-	-	-	2	
21	Bohumil Stasa	CZE	CZ	2	-	-	-	-	-	-	-	-	-	2	
24	Rex Butcher	GBR	Norton	-	1	-	-	-	-	-	-	-	-	1	
24	Ron Chandler	GBR	Seeley	-	-	-	1	-	-	-	-	-	-	1	
24	Rod Gould	GBR	Norton	1	-	-	-	-	-	-	-	-	-	1	
24	Godfrey Nash	GBR	Norton	-	-	-	-	-	1	-	-	-	-	1	

Scoring system – 8, 6, 4, 3, 2, 1

350cc

Four best results were counted

Pos	Rider	Nat	Machine	Nett	Gross
1	Giacomo Agostini	ITA	MV Agusta	32	(56)
2	Renzo Pasolini	ITA	Benelli	18	
3	Kel Carruthers	AUS	Aermacchi	17	
4	Heinz Rosner	DDR	MZ	12	
5	Ginger Molloy	NZE	Bultaco	12	
6	Derek Woodman	GBR	Aermacchi	9	
7	Frantisek Stastny	CZE	Jawa	8	
8	Bohumil Stasa	CZE	CZ	7	
9	Silvio Grassetti	ITA	Benelli	4	
9	Gilberto Milani	ITA	Aermacchi	4	
9	Bill Smith	GBR	Honda	4	
9	Brian Steenson	GBR	Aermacchi	4	

250cc

Six best results were counted

Pos	Rider	Nat	Machine	Nett	Gross
1	Phil Read	GBR	Yamaha	46	(52)
2	Bill Ivy	GBR	Yamaha	46	(52)
3	Heinz Rosner	DDR	MZ	32	(39)
4	Rod Gould	GBR	Yamaha	21	(25)
5	Ginger Molloy	NZE	Bultaco	19	
6	Renzo Pasolini	ITA	Benelli	10	
7	Santiago Herrero	SPA	Ossa	8	
8	Kent Andersson	SWE	Yamaha	6	
9	Laszlo Szabo	HUN	MZ	5	
9	Malcolm Uphill	GBR	Suzuki	5	

125cc

Five best results were counted

Pos	Rider	Nat	Machine	Nett	Gross
1	Phil Read	GBR	Yamaha	40	(60)
2	Bill Ivy	GBR	Yamaha	34	
3	Ginger Molloy	NZE	Bultaco	15	
4	Heinz Rosner	DDR	MZ	12	
5	Salvador Canellas	SPA	Bultaco	11	
6	Laszlo Szabo	HUN	MZ	11	
7	Dieter Braun	GER	MZ	11	
8	Hans-Georg Anscheidt	GER	Suzuki	10	
9	Gunter Bartusch	DDR	MZ	8	
10	Kel Carruthers	AUS	Honda	6	

50cc

Three best results were counted

Pos	Rider	Nat	Machine	Nett	Gross
1	Hans-Georg Anscheidt	GER	Suzuki	24	(30)
2	Paul Lodewijkx	NED	Jamathi	17	
3	Barry Smith	AUS	Derbi	15	
4	Angel Nieto	SPA	Derbi	10	
5	Rudi Kunz	GER	Kreidler	6	
5	Chris Walpole	GBR	Honda	6	
6	Rolf Schmalzle	GER	Kreidler	6	
7	Les Griffiths	GBR	Honda	4	
7	Aalt Toersen	NED	Kreidler	4	
9	Jan de Vries	NED	Kreidler	3	
8	Ludwig Fassbender	GER	Kreidler	3	
9	Dave Lock	GBR	Honda	3	

IVY AND READ

It was usual practice in this era for factory teams to decide which of their riders they wanted to win a particular championship – hardly surprising since it was normal for riders to compete in at least two and often three classes at each GP. Yamaha were so far ahead of the competition in '68 that they could effectively decide who should be the 125 and 250 World Champions. Their decision was that Bill Ivy should win the 250s and Phil Read the 125s.

Ivy, very much an innocent abroad compared to the calculating Read, duly rode shotgun for his team-mate until the 125 championship was decided. At the Czech GP, however, Read announced that he was riding to win the 250cc class as well. This was more than simple double-dealing. Read had his reasons, prime among them a desire to get Yamaha to commit to the '69 season, or at least to tell him whether they would be racing or not because it was strongly rumoured that they would be pulling out at the end of the year. When he received no such assurance Read made his announcement. There is also no doubt that Phil felt that it was he who had done the hard work developing the original 250, he who had won the first titles for Yamaha, and that he should be allowed to race for another one. The 250 class, don't forget, was the one that mattered most. According to his friend and biographer Alan Peck, Bill Ivy saw the world in a much simpler light. He simply couldn't imagine reneging on a deal.

It came down to the last race of the year, at Monza, where Read won the race and the title. Both riders were prepared to protest against the other – and Ivy did so on, it must be said, trivial grounds which deflected some of the criticism from Read. Peck's book, *No Time to Lose*, records that Ivy became much more difficult to deal with after this episode and that he really wanted to quit bike racing. He dabbled in cars, where his talent was as obvious as it was on two wheels. Ivy announced his retirement from bike racing but would, tragically, be tempted back. Phil Read had been right about Yamaha, though: they pulled their works team out of GPs at the end of the season.

LEFT Yamaha team-mates Read and Ivy, not seeing eye-to-eye as usual. (*Elwyn Roberts Collection*)

1969

Japan Inc abandoned GPs so Agostini and MV Agusta were left to steamroller what opposition was left

The exotic multi-cylinder Japanese machines disappeared from the grids before the new legislation outlawing them came into force, leaving a strange-looking assortment of machinery battling for honours. In the 350 and 500 classes Agostini and MV Agusta again won every race they contested. In the 500s the Linto, basically two Aermacchi 250cc cylinders on a common crankcase, was now reliable enough to put the Hungarian-born Swiss Gyula Markovszky regularly on the rostrum, and he took second place in the championship. The completely home-made Paton, brainchild of ex-Mondial engineer Giuseppe Patoni, was almost as successful for Billie Nelson (GBR), but this was a one-off motorcycle; it was possible to buy a Linto. Ago's hegemony of the 350s was threatened by Bill Ivy and the powerful but fickle V4 Jawa two-stroke, but that threat was snuffed out when Little Bill died at the Sachsenring.

In the smaller classes, the titles were really open to anyone who could put together a good season. That turned out to be Kel Carruthers (AUS) in the 250 class: the Benelli factory continued to race their four for one last season and were rewarded with the last quarter-litre title to be won by a four-stroke. The two-stroke banner was now carried by the production parallel-twin air-cooled Yamahas rather than the water-cooled V4s. Rod Gould got some Yamaha factory parts at Daytona, Kent Andersson (SWE) took a little longer but still won races, but Spanish ace Santiago Herrero and the monocoque-framed single-cylinder Ossa were the surprise contenders. They won three races and led the 250 class until the final race.

In the 125s, Britain's Dave Simmonds nursed a fragile three-year-old Kawasaki to eight wins and the title in front of similarly aged Suzukis. MZ came up with a new tandem-twin design that proved fast but fragile; they also changed too many things on their 250 twin. The 50cc championship was even closer than the 250. Angel Nieto and Aussie Barry Smith on Derbis battled with a horde of Kreidlers and the Dutch Jamathis, with Nieto eventually winning the first of his 13 titles.

ABOVE The grid for the 350 race at the Sachsenring, with a wreath where Bill Ivy should be. Agostini looks like he'd rather be somewhere – anywhere – else. (*Roland Priess Collection*)

OPPOSITE Dave Simmonds on a Kawasaki took the 125 title – the only title won by a Japanese marque in '69. (*Elwyn Roberts Collection*)

THE 1969 SEASON

500cc

BEL/Spa-Francorchamps
- Giacomo Agostini (MV Agusta) won the race, lapping the entire field with the exception of Percy Tait (GBR) who gave Triumph their one and only GP podium finish

DDR/Sachsenring
- Agostini made it a perfect seven wins from seven races to take the 500cc title for the fourth successive year

ITA-NAZ/Imola
- In the absence of Agostini, Alberto Pagani (Linto) took victory to become the first son of a former 500cc Grand Prix winner also to win a 500cc GP

YUG/Opatija
- Godfrey Nash (GBR) took his one and only GP victory, the last ever GP win for Norton and the last by a single-cylinder machine in the 500cc class

350cc

SPA/Jarama
- Bill Ivy made his debut on the four-cylinder Jawa but retired with mechanical problems when catching the leaders after making a bad start

NED/Assen
- Ivy took second place at Assen after leading eventual victor Giacomo Agostini until the Jawa started to misfire
- Agostini broke the lap record in chasing Ivy and the final race time was six seconds faster than the same-length 500cc race

DDR/Sachsenring
- Billy Ivy lost his life after crashing during practice for the East German Grand Prix

CZE/Brno
- Giacomo Agostini clinched his second 350cc title with a victory at Brno

ITA-NAZ/Imola
- After winning the 250cc race, Phil Read did the double with a win in the 350cc event
- This was the first GP win in the 350cc class by a privateer Yamaha twin-cylinder machine

250cc

SPA/Jarama
- At the championship's first visit to the circuit, Santiago Herrero became the first Spanish rider to win a 250cc GP
- This was the first win for the Ossa single-cylinder two-stroke machine

GER/Hockenheim
- Kent Andersson (Yamaha) became the first Swedish rider to win a Grand Prix
- This was the first win for Yamaha's range of twin-cylinder racers manufactured for general sale

GBR/Isle of Man TT
- On his very first race on the four-cylinder factory Benelli, Kel Carruthers took his maiden Grand Prix victory

NED/Assen
- Italy's Renzo Pasolini took his first GP victory in front of Benelli team-mate Carruthers

YUG/Opatija
- Arriving at the season's final event the three top riders, Herrero, Carruthers and Andersson, were separated by just two points, with the Australian winning the race to become the last rider to win the 250cc world title on a four-stroke machine

125cc

GER/Hockenheim
- Dave Simmonds took his first GP victory, and the first Grand Prix win for Kawasaki

FRA/Le Mans
- Jean Aureal (Yamaha) became the first French rider to win a 125cc Grand Prix

DDR/Sachsenring
- With victory in East Germany, Dave Simmonds became the first rider to win a World Championship title riding Kawasaki machinery
- Simmonds was the last British rider to become 125cc World Champion

50cc

DDR/Sachsenring
- Angel Nieto, riding the factory Derbi, scored his first Grand Prix victory

YUG/Opatija
- Finishing second at the final race of the year was enough to give Spain's Nieto his first world title by a single point from Dutch rider Aalt Toersen (Kreidler)

1969 WORLD CHAMPIONSHIP

500cc

Seven best results were counted

Pos	Rider	Nat	Machine	SPA	GER	FRA	GBR	NED	BEL	DDR	CZE	FIN	ULS	ITA	YUG	Nett	Gross
1	Giacomo Agostini	ITA	MV Agusta	15	15	15	15	15	15	15	15	15	15	-	-	105	(150)
2	Gyula Marsovszky	SWI	Linto	8	5	5	-	5	8	-	12	-	-	4	-	47	
3	Godfrey Nash	GBR	Norton	6	2	6	-	4	-	-	2	10	-	-	15	45	
4	Billie Nelson	GBR	Paton	-	-	12	-	2	-	12	4	12	-	-	-	42	
5	Alan Barnett	GBR	Metisse	-	-	-	12	10	10	-	-	-	-	-	-	32	
6	Steve Ellis	GBR	Linto	-	-	3	-	-	-	10	-	3	-	-	10	26	
7	Ron Chandler	GBR	Seeley	-	1	-	5	3	6	-	-	-	5	5	-	25	
8	Gilberto Milani	ITA	Aermacchi	-	4	-	-	8	-	-	-	-	-	12	-	24	
9	Robin Fitton	GBR	Norton	-	6	-	-	-	5	-	-	-	8	-	-	19	
10	Brian Steenson	GBR	Seeley	-	-	-	-	-	-	-	-	-	12	6	-	18	
11	John Dodds	AUS	Linto	-	8	-	-	-	-	-	-	-	-	10	-	18	
12	Terry Dennehy	AUS	Honda	-	-	-	-	-	-	6	-	4	-	8	-	18	
13	Jack Findlay	AUS	Linto/Aermacchi	-	10	-	-	6	-	-	-	-	-	-	-	16	
14	Alberto Pagani	ITA	Linto	-	-	-	-	-	-	-	-	-	-	15	-	15	
15	Lewis Young	GBR	Matchless	-	-	-	-	-	-	-	-	6	-	-	8	14	
16	Karl Auer	AUT	Matchless	-	-	10	-	1	2	-	-	-	-	-	-	13	
17	Pentti Lehtela	FIN	Matchless	-	-	-	-	-	-	3	-	5	-	-	5	13	
18	Angelo Bergamonti	ITA	Paton	12	-	-	-	-	-	-	-	-	-	-	-	12	
18	Karl Hoppe	GER	Metisse	-	12	-	-	-	-	-	-	-	-	-	-	12	
18	Percy Tait	GBR	Triumph	-	-	-	-	-	12	-	-	-	-	-	-	12	
18	Franco Trabalzini	ITA	Norton	-	-	-	-	-	-	-	-	-	-	-	12	12	
18	Peter Williams	GBR	Matchless	-	-	-	-	12	-	-	-	-	-	-	-	12	
23	Bohumil Stasa	CZE	CZ	-	-	-	-	-	-	-	10	-	2	-	-	12	
24	Tom Dickie	GBR	Seeley	-	-	-	10	-	1	-	-	-	-	-	-	11	
25	Dan Shorey	GBR	Matchless	-	-	2	-	-	3	-	6	-	-	-	-	11	
26	Ginger Molloy	NZE	Bultaco	10	-	-	-	-	-	-	-	-	-	-	-	10	
26	Malcolm Uphill	GBR	Norton	-	-	-	-	-	-	-	-	-	10	-	-	10	
28	Theo Louwes	NED	Norton	-	-	8	-	-	-	-	-	-	-	2	-	10	
29	John Findlay	GBR	Norton	-	-	-	6	-	-	-	-	-	4	-	-	10	
30	Walter Scheimann	GER	Norton	-	-	1	-	-	4	-	5	-	-	-	-	10	
31	Werner Bergold	AUT	Matchless	-	-	-	-	-	-	8	1	-	-	-	-	9	
31	Hannu Kuparinen	FIN	Matchless	-	-	-	-	-	-	-	-	8	-	1	-	9	
33	Silvano Bertarelli	ITA	Paton	-	-	-	-	-	-	-	8	-	-	-	-	8	
33	Derek Woodman	GBR	Seeley	-	-	-	8	-	-	-	-	-	-	-	-	8	
35	Andre-Luc Appietto	FRA	Paton	-	-	4	-	-	-	-	3	-	-	-	-	7	
36	Barry Scully	GBR	Norton	-	-	-	-	-	-	-	-	-	6	-	-	6	
36	Keith Turner	NZE	Linto	-	-	-	-	-	-	-	-	-	-	-	6	6	
38	Gunther Fischer	GER	Matchless	5	-	-	-	-	-	-	-	-	-	-	-	5	
38	Phil O'Brien	AUS	Matchless	-	-	-	-	-	-	5	-	-	-	-	-	5	
40	Maurice Hawthorne	GBR	Matchless	-	-	-	-	-	-	4	-	-	-	-	1	5	
41	Gilbert Argo	SWI	Matchless	4	-	-	-	-	-	-	-	-	-	-	-	4	
41	Paul Eickelberg	GER	Norton	-	-	-	-	-	-	-	-	-	-	-	4	4	
41	Steve Jolly	GBR	Seeley	-	-	-	4	-	-	-	-	-	-	-	-	4	
44	Paolo Campanelli	ITA	Seeley	-	-	-	-	-	-	-	-	-	-	3	-	3	
44	Kel Carruthers	AUS	Aermacchi	-	3	-	-	-	-	-	-	-	-	-	-	3	
44	Selwyn Griffiths	GBR	Matchless	-	-	-	3	-	-	-	-	-	-	-	-	3	
44	Emanuele Maugliani	ITA	Norton	-	-	-	-	-	-	-	-	-	-	-	3	3	
44	John Williams	GBR	Metisse	-	-	-	-	-	-	-	-	-	3	-	-	3	
49	Peter Darvill	GBR	Norton	-	-	-	2	-	-	-	-	-	-	-	-	2	
49	Ross Hannan	AUS	Norton	-	-	-	-	-	-	-	-	-	-	-	2	2	
49	Osmo Hansen	FIN	Matchless	-	-	-	-	-	-	-	-	2	-	-	-	2	
49	Jack Lindh	SWE	Seeley	-	-	-	-	-	-	2	-	-	-	-	-	2	
53	Endel Kiisa	RUS	Vostok	-	-	-	-	-	-	1	-	-	-	-	-	1	

53	Alan Lawton	GBR	Norton	-	-	-	-	-	-	-	-	-	1	-	-	1
53	Steve Spencer	GBR	Metisse	-	-	-	1	-	-	-	-	-	-	-	-	1
53	Wolfgang Stropek	AUT	MV Agusta	-	-	-	-	-	-	-	-	1	-	-	-	1

Scoring system – 15, 12, 10, 8, 6, 5, 4, 3, 2, 1

350cc

Six best results were counted

Pos	Rider	Nat	Machine	Nett	Gross
1	Giacomo Agostini	ITA	MV Agusta	90	(120)
2	Silvio Grassetti	ITA	Yamaha/Jawa	47	
3	Guiseppe Vicenzi	ITA	Yamaha	45	
4	Heinz Rosner	DDR	MZ	38	
5	Rod Gould	GBR	Yamaha	36	
6	Jack Findlay	AUS	Yamaha/Aermacchi	34	
7	Kel Carruthers	AUS	Aermacchi	29	
8	Bohumil Stasa	CZE	CZ	27	
9	Frantisek Stastny	CZE	Jawa	26	
10	Bill Ivy	GBR	Jawa	24	

250cc

Seven best results were counted

Pos	Rider	Nat	Machine	Nett	Gross
1	Kel Carruthers	AUS	Benelli	89	(103)
2	Kent Andersson	SWE	Yamaha	84	(108)
3	Santiago Herrero	SPA	Ossa	83	(88)
4	Renzo Pasolini	ITA	Benelli	45	
5	Borje Jansson	SWE	Kawasaki/Yamaha	45	
6	Rod Gould	GBR	Yamaha	44	
7	Heinz Rosner	DDR	MZ	28	
8	Frank Perris	GBR	Suzuki	25	
9	Lothar John	GER	Suzuki/Yamaha	21	
10	Dieter Braun	GER	MZ	20	

125cc

Six best results were counted

Pos	Rider	Nat	Machine	Nett	Gross
1	Dave Simmonds	GBR	Kawasaki	90	(144)
2	Dieter Braun	GER	Suzuki	59	
3	Cees van Dongen	NED	Suzuki	51	
4	Kent Andersson	SWE	Maico	36	
5	Heinz Kriwanek	AUT	Rotax	33	
6	Ginger Molloy	NZE	Bultaco	29	
7	Ryszard Mankiewicz	POL	MZ	27	
8	Laszlo Szabo	HUN	MZ	26	
9	Friedhelm Kohlar	DDR	MZ	24	
10	Kel Carruthers	AUS	Aermacchi	20	

50cc

Six best results were counted

Pos	Rider	Nat	Machine	Nett	Gross
1	Angel Nieto	SPA	Derbi	76	
2	Aalt Toersen	NED	Kreidler	75	(93)
3	Barry Smith	AUS	Derbi	69	(73)
4	Jan de Vries	NED	Kreidler	64	(73)
5	Paul Lodewijkx	NED	Jamathi	63	
6	Gilberto Parlotti	ITA	Tomos	31	
7	Santiago Herrero	SPA	Derbi	28	
8	Rudi Kunz	GER	Kreidler	26	
9	Ludwig Fassbender	GER	Kreidler	25	
10	Martin Mijwaart	NED	Jamathi	18	

BILL IVY AND THE JAWA

According to his friend and biographer Alan Peck, Bill Ivy didn't really want to race bikes again after the feud with Phil Read in 1968. However, he had tried car racing and was good at it – more than good, in fact, as Jackie Stewart, Graham Hill and others noted. Typically, Ivy wanted to go straight into Formula 2 and needed to finance his new career. The Czech Jawa factory had a radical 350cc V4 two-stroke bike designed by Zdenek Tichy, no doubt after careful observation of MZ and Yamaha's progress. The two underdogs liked each other.

The Jawa was undoubtedly fast and powerful but it was underdeveloped, like all the other machines that emerged from behind the Iron Curtain. The factory's lack of access to modern ignition, suspension and carburettors was also a major handicap. Nevertheless, Ivy gave Ago a serious scare at Hockenheim, then twice overtook him at Assen before the machine faltered. At the next event, the East German GP, the Jawa seized in practice and Ivy sustained fatal injuries. It was thought he might have been adjusting his helmet when the incident happened so did not have time to grab the clutch lever.

There is little doubt that Ivy would have been successful at car racing. His few competitive events saw him racing with big names like Stewart, Hill, Jean-Pierre Beltoise and Jochen Rindt – he was a natural on four wheels, just as he was on two. Bill was the first man to lap the Isle of Man at over 100mph/161km/h on a 125 and his 1968 250cc lap record of 105.5mph/169.8km/h stood until 1979.

The V4 continued to race but never again showed the form it had in Bill Ivy's hands, and those of veteran factory rider Frantisek Stastny who had won four GPs for Jawa, three in the 350 class and one in the 500s, earlier in his long career. Versatile Italian Silvio Grassetti did win the final race of '69 on it, in Yugoslavia, but the MV team did not enter that event.

1970

There was still no-one to compete with Agostini in the 500 and 350cc classes, but Yamaha's 250cc TD2 showed how Japan was going to change everything

There was still no coherent challenge to Giacomo Agostini and the MV Agusta in the 500cc class in 1970. Nevertheless, Count Agusta saw fit to field a second bike for Angelo Bergamonti from Monza onwards. There wasn't enough time for the Italian to secure second in the championship, but when Ago did not attend the final race of the year, at Montjuich, 'Berga' won both 350 and 500 races in record time and with two new lap records to his name. Ago himself won every race he contested, in both classes. It is worth noting, however, that despite the lack of serious opposition the MV was continually refined – perfected might be a better adjective – and race and lap records were often broken. Giacomo Agostini never did complacency, as anyone who worked with or for him will readily testify.

Kawasaki sold a run of 40 H1R racers based on their three-cylinder road-bike engine. Experienced privateer Ginger Molloy traded in his Bultaco for one and made it on to the rostrum four times. This was in no small part due to the Kiwi rider's abilities as a tuner and mechanic, talents a privateer needed if he were to make a living, and he duly finished second in the 500cc championship table.

In the 350 class Ago had to cope with real pressure from Benelli riders Kel Carruthers and Renzo Pasolini, and also Rod Gould on a Yamaha. Gould and Kent Andersson were officially employed by Yamaha (unlike the previous season, when there was no 'works' team). In what was now a familiar pattern, they rode development bikes that would form the basis of the B-model TR2 and TD2 that would be sold for the '71 season. The TD2 instantly turned the 250 class into a Yamaha benefit. Only the mercurial Spaniard Santiago Herrero and the remarkable Ossa single looked like stemming the tide, but a crash at the Isle of Man TT, probably on melting tar, ended his life.

In the 125s the big German Dieter Braun and an aging Suzuki somehow saw off Nieto and the Derbi, but the Spaniard made no mistake in the 50s, retaining his title, again with Aalt Toersen in second, although the Dutchman had abandoned Kreidler in favour of Jamathi.

ABOVE ABOVE Angel Nieto, the greatest ever 50/125cc racer, retained his 50cc title with the factory Derbi. (*Elwyn Roberts Collection*)

RIGHT Kawasaki's production-based H1R was the privateer's preferred mount. This is Christian Ravel (FRA) on his way to third place at Spa. (*Elwyn Roberts Collection*)

THE **1970** SEASON

500cc

FRA/Le Mans
- Ginger Molloy finished second – the first ever 500cc GP podium for Kawasaki

BEL/Spa-Francorchamps
- With a victory in Belgium, Giacomo Agostini became the first rider to win the 500cc world title for five years in succession

SPA/Montjuich
- MV Agusta's new signing Angelo Bergamonti won the final race of the year in the absence of team-mate Agostini

350cc

CZE/Brno
- Giacomo Agostini won at Brno to become double World Champion for the third year in succession

SPA/Montjuich
- Angelo Bergamonti repeated his win in the earlier 500cc race to complete a double victory – his only Grand Prix wins

250cc

GER/Nürburgring
- Reigning champion Kel Carruthers, having swapped to Yamaha, opened the defence of his world title with a victory

FRA/Le Mans
- Rod Gould (Yamaha) scored his first Grand Prix victory

YUG/Opatija
- Santiago Herrero won on the Ossa to take the lead in the World Championship, the last GP victory by a single-cylinder machine in the 250cc class

GBR/Isle of Man TT
- Santiago Herrero lost his life after crashing on the last lap

NED/Assen
- Finland's Jarno Saarinen (Yamaha) finished on the podium for the first time in only his fifth Grand Prix

ITA-NAZ/Monza
- Rod Gould clinched the 250cc world title with a victory after a race-long battle with Carruthers and Phil Read, less than a second covering the three riders at the chequered flag

125cc

GER/Nürburgring
- John Dodds (AUS) scored his first GP victory and also became the first rider to win a Grand Prix riding an Aermacchi

NED/Assen
- Dieter Braun (Suzuki) won his fourth successive race to take a commanding lead in the World Championship standings

BEL/Spa-Francorchamps
- Angel Nieto (Derbi) won for the first time in the 125cc class

CZE/Brno
- Gilberto Parlotti (ITA) scored his first Grand Prix victory, the first GP victory for Morbidelli

FIN/Imatra
- Although he failed to score in Finland, Dieter Braun became the 125cc World Champion

SPA/Montjuich
- After leading the race for five laps, Barry Sheene (GBR), making his GP debut riding an ex-Stuart Graham factory Suzuki, finished second to Spanish favourite Angel Nieto

50cc

ITA-NAZ/Monza
- In spite of failing to finish the race, Angel Nieto retained the 50cc world title

1970 WORLD CHAMPIONSHIP

500cc

Seven best results were counted

Pos	Rider	Nat	Machine	GER	FRA	YUG	GBR	NED	BEL	DDR	FIN	ULS	ITA	SPA	Nett	Gross
1	Giacomo Agostini	ITA	MV Agusta	15	15	15	15	15	15	15	15	15	15	-	90	(150)
2	Ginger Molloy	NZE	Kawasaki/Bultaco	6	12	4	-	8	-	-	12	12	5	12	62	(71)
3	Angelo Bergamonti	ITA	Aermacchi/MV Agusta	-	8	12	-	12	-	-	-	-	12	15	59	
4	Tommy Robb	GBR	Seeley	10	-	-	-	1	10	1	6	-	-	8	36	
5	Alberto Pagani	ITA	Linto	-	10	-	-	10	-	-	10	-	-	-	30	
6	Alan Barnett	GBR	Seeley	12	4	-	-	-	-	8	-	-	-	-	24	
7	Christian Ravel	FRA	Kawasaki	-	3	-	-	-	12	6	-	-	-	3	24	
8	Jack Findlay	AUS	Seeley	-	-	8	8	-	-	-	-	8	-	-	24	
9	Martti Pesonen	FIN	Yamaha	4	-	6	-	-	3	-	3	4	-	4	24	
10	Peter Williams	GBR	Matchless	-	-	-	12	4	-	-	-	6	-	-	22	
11	Roberto Gallina	ITA	Paton	-	-	10	-	-	-	-	-	-	4	6	20	
12	Martin Carney	GBR	Kawasaki	-	-	-	-	-	-	10	-	5	-	5	20	
13	Gyula Marsovszky	SWI	Linto/Kawasaki	-	5	3	-	2	-	-	-	-	8	-	18	
14	Eric Offenstadt	FRA	Kawasaki	-	2	-	-	-	-	4	8	-	-	-	14	
15	John Dodds	AUS	Linto	-	-	-	-	-	-	12	-	-	-	-	12	
16	Silvano Bertarelli	ITA	Kawasaki	-	-	-	-	-	-	-	-	-	10	-	10	
16	Giuseppe Mandolini	ITA	Moto Guzzi	-	-	-	-	-	-	-	-	-	-	10	10	
16	Bill Smith	GBR	Kawasaki	-	-	-	10	-	-	-	-	-	-	-	10	
16	Percy Tait	GBR	Seeley	-	-	-	-	-	-	-	-	10	-	-	10	
20	Dave Simmonds	GBR	Kawasaki	-	-	5	-	-	-	3	-	-	-	2	10	
21	Karl Auer	AUT	Matchless	-	-	-	-	-	8	-	-	-	-	-	8	
21	Karl Hoppe	GER	Munch URS	8	-	-	-	-	-	-	-	-	-	-	8	
23	John Williams	GBR	Matchless	-	-	-	6	-	-	-	-	2	-	-	8	
23	Giampiero Zubani	ITA	Kawasaki	-	-	2	-	-	-	-	-	-	6	-	8	
25	Godfrey Nash	GBR	Norton	-	-	-	-	-	-	2	5	-	-	-	7	
25	Billie Nelson	GBR	Paton	2	-	-	-	-	-	5	-	-	-	-	7	
27	Ernst Hiller	GER	Kawasaki	3	-	-	-	-	4	-	-	-	-	-	7	
28	Paul Smart	GBR	Seeley	-	-	-	-	6	-	-	-	-	-	-	6	
28	Brian Steenson	GBR	Seeley	-	6	-	-	-	-	-	-	-	-	-	6	
28	Lewis Young	GBR	Honda	-	-	-	-	-	6	-	-	-	-	-	6	
31	Terry Dennehy	AUS	Honda	1	-	-	-	-	5	-	-	-	-	-	6	
32	Rob Bron	NED	Suzuki	-	-	-	-	5	-	-	-	-	-	-	5	
32	Tony Jefferies	GBR	Matchless	-	-	-	5	-	-	-	-	-	-	-	5	
32	Walter Rungg	SWI	Aermacchi	5	-	-	-	-	-	-	-	-	-	-	5	
35	Steve Ellis	GBR	Linto/Matchless	-	-	-	-	-	1	-	4	-	-	-	5	
36	Ron Chandler	GBR	Seeley	-	-	-	-	3	2	-	-	-	-	-	5	
37	Selwyn Griffiths	GBR	Matchless	-	-	-	4	-	-	-	-	-	-	-	4	
38	Brian Adams	GBR	Norton	-	-	-	3	-	-	-	-	-	-	-	3	
38	Gerry Mateer	GBR	Norton	-	-	-	-	-	-	-	-	3	-	-	3	
38	Gianni Perrone	ITA	Kawasaki	-	-	-	-	-	-	-	-	-	3	-	3	
41	Hans Butenuth	GER	BMW	-	-	-	-	-	-	-	2	-	-	-	2	
41	Paolo Campanelli	ITA	Kawasaki	-	-	-	-	-	-	-	-	-	2	-	2	
41	Vincent Duckett	GBR	Seeley	-	-	-	2	-	-	-	-	-	-	-	2	
44	Jean Campiche	SWI	Honda	-	-	1	-	-	-	-	1	-	-	-	2	
45	Andre-Luc Appietto	FRA	Paton	-	1	-	-	-	-	-	-	-	-	-	1	
45	Charlie Dobson	GBR	Seeley	-	-	-	-	-	-	-	-	1	-	-	1	
45	Gordon Keith	RHO	Velocette	-	-	-	-	-	-	-	-	-	-	1	1	
45	Vasco Loro	ITA	Kawasaki	-	-	-	-	-	-	-	-	-	1	-	1	
45	Steve Spencer	GBR	Norton	-	-	-	1	-	-	-	-	-	-	-	1	

Scoring system – 15, 12, 10, 8, 6, 5, 4, 3, 2, 1

350cc

Six best results were counted

Pos	Rider	Nat	Machine	Nett	Gross
1	Giacomo Agostini	ITA	MV Agusta	90	(135)
2	Kel Carruthers	AUS	Yamaha/Benelli	58	
3	Renzo Pasolini	ITA	Benelli	46	
4	Kent Andersson	SWE	Yamaha	44	
5	Martti Pesonen	FIN	Yamaha	38	
6	Rod Gould	GBR	Yamaha	28	
7	Angelo Bergamonti	ITA	MV Agusta	27	
8	Gunter Bartusch	DDR	MZ	20	
9	Alan Barnett	GBR	Aermacchi	20	
10	Tommy Robb	GBR	Yamaha	18	

250cc

Seven best results were counted

Pos	Rider	Nat	Machine	Nett	Gross
1	Rod Gould	GBR	Yamaha	102	(124)
2	Kel Carruthers	AUS	Yamaha	84	
3	Kent Andersson	SWE	Yamaha	67	
4	Jarno Saarinen	FIN	Yamaha	57	
5	Borje Jansson	SWE	Yamaha	34	
6	Chas Mortimer	GBR	Yamaha/Villa	30	
7	Gyula Marsovszky	SWI	Yamaha	28	
8	Santiago Herrero	SPA	Ossa	27	
9	Bo Granath	SWE	Yamaha	25	
10	Silvio Grassetti	ITA	Yamaha/MZ	24	

125cc

Six best results were counted

Pos	Rider	Nat	Machine	Nett	Gross
1	Dieter Braun	GER	Suzuki	84	(92)
2	Angel Nieto	SPA	Derbi	72	
3	Borje Jansson	SWE	Maico	62	(73)
4	Dave Simmonds	GBR	Kawasaki	57	
5	Laszlo Szabo	HUN	MZ	34	
6	Toni Gruber	GER	Maico	33	
7	Aalt Toersen	NED	Suzuki	31	
8	John Dodds	AUS	Aermacchi	24	
9	Gunter Bartusch	DDR	MZ	22	
10	Heinz Kriwanek	AUT	Rotax	21	

50cc

Six best results were counted

Pos	Rider	Nat	Machine	Nett	Gross
1	Angel Nieto	SPA	Derbi	87	(105)
2	Aalt Toersen	NED	Jamathi	75	(84)
3	Rudi Kunz	GER	Kreidler	66	(88)
4	Salvador Canellas	SPA	Derbi	63	(74)
5	Jan de Vries	NED	Kreidler	60	(66)
6	Jos Schurgers	NED	Kreidler	41	
7	Martin Mijwaart	NED	Jamathi	40	(45)
8	Ludwig Fassbender	GER	Kreidler	17	
9	Gilberto Parlotti	ITA	Tomos	15	
10	Harald Bartol	AUT	Kreidler	11	

ALL CHANGE

The FIM decided that, as from the start of the 1970 season, the technical regulations should undergo a major change. All machines were to be limited to six-speed gearboxes and the number of cylinders allowed in each class would be one for the 50s, two for the 125s and 250s, and four for the 350s and 500s.

This would outlaw, at a stroke, such exotica as the five-cylinder 125cc Honda and the V4 125 and 250 Yamahas that were proving too expensive even for the giant Japanese corporations to develop. It would also allow the rise of machines of all capacities based on production bikes, just as NSU had done with the Sportmax in the mid-1950s. Chief among these were the Yamaha TD2 and TR2 250 and the 350cc air-cooled twins that could trace their ancestry directly to the YR2 roadster. These bikes would lead directly to the water-cooled TZs, and in both guises these Yamahas would be the mainstay of privateer racers for two decades. In the right hands, and with the right treatment, they were capable of winning not just GPs but world titles. Sweden's Kent Andersson had won on the TD2 at Hockenheim in 1969 at an average speed of 100mph/161km/h, a major milestone in Yamaha's racing history. It won again in Finland and Andersson finished the year as runner-up in the 250cc World Championship. The Kawasaki on which Ginger Molloy finished as runner-up in the 500s in 1970 was also street-bike derived.

A look at the smaller classes shows a wave of new machines from smaller European manufacturers like Maico, Bultaco, Tomos and Ossa, who put tuned versions of their road or motocross two-stroke singles into road racers. The Dutch Jamathi which won the 50cc Assen GP in 1968 and was a thorn in the side of Derbi and Kreidler was different again. This was a home-built machine, the brainchild of two engineers, Jan Thiel and Martin Mijwaart. The 50cc (later 80cc) class would continue to provide a home for this sort of enterprise, but the Jamathi is one of a very small number of such 'home-made' bikes to have won a GP.

1971

MV and Agostini still ruled the big classes unchallenged, but Yamaha's two-stroke twins now dominated the 250s and were threatening the established order in the 350s

There were some signs that the established order was about to change. Giacomo Agostini and the MV still ruled the 500cc class, but the old three-cylinder design was at the end of its life and a four was debuted at Monza by Alberto Pagani (son of Nello). Ago rode triples in the 350 and 500 classes and both had breakdowns – a totally unprecedented occurrence. Pagani was drafted into the MV team after Angelo Bergamonti was killed in an Italian Championship race. Agostini won the first eight races of the season on the bounce, and out of the remaining three rounds only raced at Monza. That let in Jack Findlay (Suzuki) and Dave Simmonds (Kawasaki) to take the first two-stroke wins in the 500cc class. MV's honour was almost salvaged by Pagani's win at Monza.

Findlay rode a TR500 supplied by the Italian importer, while Rob Bron (NED) and Keith Turner (NZE) got semi-works Suzukis through similar arrangements. Simmonds took over Ginger Molloy's Kawasaki H1R but housed it in a frame built by Reynolds' legend of the welding torch, Ken Sprayson.

Agostini's majestic progress to another 350 title was interrupted only by mechanical failures, although there was a warning of what was to come. Jarno Saarinen received 250 and 350 Yamahas through the Finnish importer and won races on both. He also set a new lap record at his home 250cc race. It is worth remembering, though, that despite being second in the 350 race, Jarno was almost lapped by Ago! Apart from the MV, the 250 and 350 classes were now totally dominated by Yamahas, although MZ's Silvio Grassetti managed two wins in the 250 class and Peter Williams (GBR) won a wet 350cc Ulster race.

Another youngster burst on the scene in the 125 class. Barry Sheene and his father Frank had bought a four-year-old ex-works Suzuki off Stuart Graham, and Barry promptly scored more points on it than Angel Nieto on the factory Derbi, although the Spaniard won the title because only a rider's six best results were counted. Sheene also had a win on a 50cc Kreidler as he supported champion Jan de Vries (NED) against Nieto and Derbi in the smallest class.

ABOVE The 125s skirt the barrier at the Salzburgring: Braun (GER, Suzuki) leads Parlotti (ITA, Morbidelli), Nieto (SPA, Derbi) and Sheene (GBR, Suzuki). (*Elwyn Roberts Collection*)

RIGHT Giacomo Agostini gets some air over Ago's Leap on his way to winning the Senior TT. (*Elwyn Roberts Collection*)

THE **1971** SEASON

500cc

AUT/Salzburgring

- Giacomo Agostini scored a 500/350cc double victory in the first ever Austrian Grand Prix counting towards the World Championship classification

DDR/Sachsenring

- Agostini made it six wins from the first six 500cc GPs of the year to clinch his sixth successive premier-class title

ULS/Dundrod

- Jack Findlay (Suzuki) became the first rider to win a 500cc Grand Prix race on a two-stroke machine

SPA/Jarama

- Dave Simmonds gave Kawasaki their first victory in the GP 500cc class

350cc

CZE/Brno

- Jarno Saarinen (Yamaha) scored his first Grand Prix win – the first ever GP victory by a Finnish rider

FIN/Imatra

- Giacomo Agostini took his sixth 350cc victory of the year to become the most successful rider of all time, with ten World Championship titles

ULS/Dundrod

- Peter Williams gave MZ their one and only victory in the 350cc class, and also their final GP win

250cc

BEL/Spa-Francorchamps

- Silvio Grassetti gave MZ the last of their seven victories in the 250cc class

DDR/Sachsenring

- West German rider Dieter Braun won for the first time in the 250cc class to cause great celebration among the 250,000 German fans, mainly from the eastern section of the country

CZE/Brno

- Janos Drapal (Yamaha) became the first Hungarian rider to win a Grand Prix race
- Championship leader Phil Read crashed during practice and suffered a broken shoulder, causing him to miss the race and the following GP in Sweden

ULS/Dundrod

- Local rider Ray McCullough won the 250cc race on the last occasion the Ulster GP counted towards the World Championship

ITA-NAZ/Monza

- Aged 35, Swiss rider Gyula Marsovszky took the only win of his GP career more than ten years after making his debut
- Fourth-place finisher Rod Gould was just 0.41s behind the winner – the first time that the top four in a GP race were covered by less than half a second

SPA/Jarama

- Five riders went to the final race of the year with a chance of taking the title – Phil Read, Rod Gould, Jarno Saarinen, John Dodds and Dieter Braun, but second place was enough to give Read his fourth 250cc world title

125cc

GER/Hockenheim

- Dave Simmonds scored the last of Kawasaki's ten victories in the 125cc class, all of them with Simmonds as rider

BEL/Spa-Francorchamps

- Twenty-year-old Barry Sheene (Suzuki) took his first GP victory at only his sixth GP event to become the youngest GP winner since Mike Hailwood in 1959

SPA/Jarama

- Angel Nieto won his home GP to take the 125cc title for the first time, with Barry Sheene second in the table

50cc

CZE/Brno

- Barry Sheene (Kreidler) won first time out in the 50cc class
- With his later victories in the 500cc class Sheene was the only rider to win GPs in both the 50cc and 500cc classes

SPA/Jarama

- With Angel Nieto crashing on the first lap, Jan de Vries took his first title, the first ever World Championship for a Dutch rider and also the first for Kreidler

1971 WORLD CHAMPIONSHIP

500cc

Seven best results were counted

Pos	Rider	Nat	Machine	AUT	GER	GBR	NED	BEL	DDR	SWE	FIN	ULS	ITA	SPA	Nett	Gross
1	Giacomo Agostini	ITA	MV Agusta	15	15	15	15	15	15	15	15	-	-	-	90	(120)
2	Keith Turner	NZE	Suzuki	12	-	4	8	-	12	12	8	-	5	6	58	(67)
3	Rob Bron	NED	Suzuki	-	12	-	12	8	3	-	10	12	-	-	57	
4	Dave Simmonds	GBR	Kawasaki	-	-	-	10	-	-	5	12	-	10	15	52	
5	Jack Findlay	AUS	Suzuki	8	-	-	-	10	-	1	6	15	6	5	50	(51)
6	Eric Offenstadt	FRA	Kawasaki	10	-	-	-	12	-	-	-	-	-	10	32	
7	Tommy Robb	GBR	Seeley	-	5	-	4	-	-	10	2	10	-	-	31	
8	Alberto Pagani	ITA	MV Agusta/Linto	4	6	-	-	-	-	-	4	-	15	-	29	
9	Kaarlo Koivuniemi	FIN	Seeley	-	-	-	-	-	6	6	-	-	-	12	24	
10	Ron Chandler	GBR	Kawasaki	-	10	-	-	6	-	-	-	3	-	-	19	
11	Frank Perris	GBR	Suzuki	-	-	10	-	4	-	-	-	-	-	-	14	
12	Lothar John	GER	Yamaha	6	-	-	-	-	-	-	3	-	4	-	13	
13	Peter Williams	GBR	Matchless	-	-	12	-	-	-	-	-	-	-	-	12	
13	Giampiero Zubani	ITA	Kawasaki	-	-	-	-	-	-	-	-	-	12	-	12	
15	Bo Granath	SWE	Husqvarna	-	-	-	3	-	-	3	-	5	1	-	12	
16	Billie Nelson	GBR	Paton	5	-	-	5	1	-	-	-	-	-	-	11	
17	Ernst Hiller	GER	Kawasaki	-	-	-	-	-	10	-	-	-	-	-	10	
18	Hansrudolf Brungger	SWI	Bultaco	-	-	-	-	-	8	-	-	-	-	-	8	
18	Benjamin Grau	SPA	Bultaco	-	-	-	-	-	-	-	-	-	-	8	8	
18	Selwyn Griffiths	GBR	Matchless	-	-	8	-	-	-	-	-	-	-	-	8	
18	Maurice Hawthorne	GBR	Kawasaki	-	8	-	-	-	-	-	-	-	-	-	8	
18	Ulf Nilsson	SWE	Seeley	-	-	-	-	-	-	8	-	-	-	-	8	
18	Phil Read	GBR	Ducati	-	-	-	-	-	-	-	-	-	8	-	8	
18	Percy Tait	GBR	Seeley	-	-	-	-	-	-	-	-	8	-	-	8	
25	Kurt Ivan Carlsson	SWE	Yamaha	-	-	-	-	5	-	-	-	-	-	2	7	
26	Jim Curry	GBR	Seeley	-	-	-	6	-	-	-	-	-	-	-	6	
26	Gerry Mateer	GBR	Norton	-	-	-	-	-	-	-	-	6	-	-	6	
26	Gordon Pantall	GBR	Kawasaki	-	-	6	-	-	-	-	-	-	-	-	6	
29	Karl Auer	AUT	Matchless	-	-	-	-	-	5	-	-	-	-	-	5	
29	Matti Salonen	FIN	Yamaha	-	-	-	-	-	-	-	5	-	-	-	5	
29	Roger Sutcliffe	GBR	Matchless	-	-	5	-	-	-	-	-	-	-	-	5	
32	Hans Butenuth	GER	BMW	-	4	1	-	-	-	-	-	-	-	-	5	
33	Piet van der Wal	NED	Kawasaki	-	-	-	-	2	-	-	-	-	3	-	5	
34	Jean Campiche	SWI	Honda	-	-	-	-	-	4	-	-	-	-	-	4	
34	Wilf Herron	GBR	Seeley	-	-	-	-	-	-	-	-	4	-	-	4	
34	Peter Jones	AUS	Suzuki	-	-	-	-	-	-	-	-	-	-	4	4	
34	Morgan Radberg	SWE	Monark	-	-	-	-	-	-	4	-	-	-	-	4	
38	Willi Bertsch	GER	BMW	-	3	-	-	-	-	-	-	-	-	-	3	
38	Juan Bordons	SPA	Bultaco	-	-	-	-	-	-	-	-	-	-	3	3	
38	Jerry Lancaster	GBR	Yamaha	-	-	-	-	3	-	-	-	-	-	-	3	
38	Charlie Sanby	GBR	Seeley	-	-	3	-	-	-	-	-	-	-	-	3	
42	Paul Eickelberg	GER	Yamaha	-	-	-	2	-	-	-	1	-	-	-	3	
43	Johnny Bengtson	SWE	Kawasaki	-	-	-	-	-	-	2	-	-	-	-	2	
43	Tom Dickie	GBR	Matchless	-	-	2	-	-	-	-	-	-	-	-	2	
43	Horst Dzierzawa	GER	Yamaha	-	2	-	-	-	-	-	-	-	-	-	2	
43	Pentti Lehtela	FIN	Yamaha	-	-	-	-	-	2	-	-	-	-	-	2	
43	Giordano Mongardi	ITA	Ducati	-	-	-	-	-	-	-	-	-	2	-	2	
43	Dudley Robinson	GBR	Yamaha	-	-	-	-	-	-	-	-	2	-	-	2	
49	John Dodds	AUS	Konig	-	1	-	-	-	-	-	-	-	-	-	1	
49	Emanuele Maugliani	ITA	Seeley	-	-	-	-	-	-	-	-	-	-	1	1	
49	Rob Noorlander	NED	Norton	-	-	-	1	-	-	-	-	-	-	-	1	
49	Stan Woods	GBR	Norton	-	-	-	-	-	-	-	-	1	-	-	1	

Scoring system – 15, 12, 10, 8, 6, 5, 4, 3, 2, 1

350cc

Six best results were counted

Pos	Rider	Nat	Machine	Nett	Gross
1	Giacomo Agostini	ITA	MV Agusta	90	
2	Jarno Saarinen	FIN	Yamaha	63	
3	Kurt Ivan Carlsson	SWE	Yamaha	39	
4	Theo Bult	NED	Yamaha	36	
5	Paul Smart	GBR	Yamaha	34	
6	Werner Pfirter	SWI	Yamaha	33	
7	Bo Granath	SWE	Yamaha/Ducati	30	
8	Laszlo Szabo	HUN	Yamaha	29	
9	Tony Jefferies	GBR	Yamaha	25	
10	Tepi Lansivuori	FIN	Yamaha	25	

250cc

Seven best results were counted

Pos	Rider	Nat	Machine	Nett	Gross
1	Phil Read	GBR	Yamaha	73	
2	Rod Gould	GBR	Yamaha	68	
3	Jarno Saarinen	FIN	Yamaha	64	(67)
4	John Dodds	AUS	Yamaha	59	
5	Dieter Braun	GER	Yamaha	58	
6	Gyula Marsovszky	SWI	Yamaha	57	(65)
7	Silvio Grassetti	ITA	MZ	43	
8	Chas Mortimer	GBR	Yamaha	42	
9	Janos Drapal	HUN	Yamaha	26	
10	Theo Bult	NED	Yamaha	22	

125cc

Six best results were counted

Pos	Rider	Nat	Machine	Nett	Gross
1	Angel Nieto	SPA	Derbi	87	
2	Barry Sheene	GBR	Suzuki	79	(109)
3	Borje Jansson	SWE	Maico	64	
4	Dieter Braun	GER	Maico/Suzuki	54	
5	Chas Mortimer	GBR	Yamaha/Maico	48	(52)
6	Dave Simmonds	GBR	Kawasaki	48	
7	Gert Bender	GER	Maico	41	
8	Gilberto Parlotti	ITA	Morbidelli	39	
9	Kent Andersson	SWE	Yamaha	30	
10	Jurgen Lenk	DDR	MZ	27	

50cc

Five best results were counted

Pos	Rider	Nat	Machine	Nett	Gross
1	Jan de Vries	NED	Kreidler	75	(97)
2	Angel Nieto	SPA	Derbi	69	(89)
3	Jos Schurgers	NED	Kreidler	42	
4	Herman Meijers	NED	Jamathi	41	(45)
5	Rudi Kunz	GER	Kreidler	36	
6	Aalt Toersen	NED	Jamathi	24	
7	Barry Sheene	GBR	Kreidler	23	
8	Gilberto Parlotti	ITA	Derbi	22	
9	Frederico van Dehoeven	NED	Derbi	22	
10	Jan Bruins	NED	Kreidler	19	

TWO-STROKE POWER BALANCE

The TD and TR Yamahas were now freely available to privateers, and importers also acted as channels for semi-works machines. Rod Gould rode the factory's development bike, which formed the basis for the 1972 TD3 and TR3 models. After the 1968 bust-up with Bill Ivy and the factory over team orders Phil Read was never going to be one of the favoured few, so he bought his own Yamahas. With the remarkable German engineer and sidecar champion Helmut Fath tuning the engines, aided by Ferry Brouwer (later to become the European distributor for Arai helmets), and a lightweight Reynolds frame, Read was able to win the title for the first time since '68, defeating the factory men in the process. Phil's bikes also featured electronic ignition, which would quickly become a standard modification, and a six-speed Quaife gearbox, dry clutch and disc brakes. Most of these modifications anticipated the '72 customer bikes' features, but Read's 250cc World Championship in 1971 was a true privateer victory, albeit a well-financed one.

TD, TR and later TZ Yamahas were mass-produced racers, a completely new phenomenon. They provided the basis for any good rider to prepare a machine capable of winning a Grand Prix. On the other side of the paddock, the company that led the two-stroke-revolution, MZ, won their last GP. The East German authorities were more interested in motocross and enduro, disciplines in which they could win not just the occasional race but world titles. Events after the East German 250cc GP probably also contributed. The race was won by West German rider Dieter Braun, which entailed the playing of the German anthem 'Deutschland über alles'. The massive crowd, hundreds of thousands of them, was going wild. In his biography Giacomo Agostini says hundreds of police emerged from under the grandstand and lined up facing the crowd with sub-machine guns. Silence fell. The East German GP only ran for one more year.

None of which should detract from the memory of the genius of Walter Kaaden, a man respected and admired by every rider, German or foreigner, who rode for MZ.

1972

Yamaha's two-stroke twins now invaded the 500 class as well as dominating 350 and 250 GPs

Giacomo Agostini and MV Agusta yet again dominated the 500 class, although there was considerable pressure on them in the 350s. Ago and team-mate Alberto Pagani won all the 500 GPs they contested (Pagani won in Yugoslavia when Ago stopped). They didn't bother going to the last round of the year in Spain and Chas Mortimer (GBR) won on an over-bored 350 Yamaha. TZs wouldn't be available until the following year but plenty of water-cooled pre-production models got to GPs in the hands of factory-supported riders. Mortimer even tested his before the start of the season; his bike was assembled at Yamaha's Dutch HQ by Ferry Brouwer.

The Yamaha that really gave Ago trouble was the 350 of Jarno Saarinen. MV had seen the trouble coming and developed a new four-cylinder 350, which they ran alongside the old triple through the '72 season. MV's 500-four didn't appear until the following year. Phil Read was recruited by MV but only rode in the 350 class. Yamaha supported four other riders through various importers, as well as Saarinen and Mortimer, but the 250 class was a fight between Saarinen and Italian Renzo Pasolini on the new two-stroke Aermacchi. The 125 class was won by Angel Nieto (Derbi) from the factory Yamahas of Mortimer and Kent Andersson (SWE), who was given free rein to develop the bike over the next couple of years. The story of the class might have been very different but for the death of Gilberto Parlotti on the Isle of Man.

The real drama came in the 50s, where Nieto and his great rival Jan de Vries finished equal on points and couldn't be split on countback. The rules stated that the title be decided on the aggregate time of the races in which they both finished, so Nieto won the title by 21.32 seconds. The Derbi factory then quit racing, only returning in 1984 when they had another Spanish hero as their rider, Jorge 'Aspar' Martinez.

ABOVE Jarno Saarinen won his only world title on the Finnish importer's Yamaha 250. *(Elwyn Roberts Collection)*

RIGHT Who would have thought these two Champions ever met? Geoff Duke greets Jarno Saarinen at a British international meeting. *(Elwyn Roberts Collection)*

THE 1972 SEASON

500cc

GER/Nürburgring
- Giacomo Agostini won the opening race of the season for a record sixth successive year
- Kim Newcombe's third-place finish was the first GP podium for both the Kiwi rider and the Konig

ITA-NAZ/Imola
- Bruno Spaggiari (ITA) finished third to give Ducati their only GP podium in the 500cc class

GBR/Isle of Man TT
- Agostini took the last victory for MV Agusta over the Isle of Man TT course

YUG/Opatija
- Italian Alberto Pagani won his second race on MV Agusta machinery when team-mate Agostini suffered head-gasket failure on lap 15 while in a commanding lead

BEL/Spa-Francorchamps
- Giacomo Agostini took his seventh successive 500cc title with seven wins from the first eight races of the year

DDR/Sachsenring
- Agostini won the 500cc race – the last Grand Prix to be held on the East German road circuit

FIN/Imatra
- Agostini won his 11th race of the year, setting a new record for most 500cc GP wins in a single season. (This record stood until Mick Doohan won 12 in 1997)

SPA/Montjuich
- Chas Mortimer became the first rider to win on a Yamaha in the 500cc class. This was the last occasion on which a 500cc GP was held at the circuit

350cc

GER/Nürburgring
- Jarno Saarinen won the opening race of the year and became the first person to get the better of Agostini in a head-to-head battle since Mike Hailwood in 1967

FRA/Clermont-Ferrand
- Saarinen repeated his victory of the week before and was followed home by fellow Finn Tepi Lansivuori and Renzo Pasolini on the new Aermacchi
- Agostini finished in fourth – the first time he'd failed to make the podium since 1967

AUT/Salzburgring
- Giacomo Agostini gave the new four-cylinder MV its first Grand Prix victory

ITA-NAZ/Imola
- Phil Read had his first Grand Prix ride for MV Agusta

YUG/Opatija
- Janos Drapal becomes the first Hungarian to win a 350cc GP race

DDR/Sachsenring
- Read won for the first time on an MV Agusta

FIN/Imatra
- Agostini took his fifth successive 350cc world title with a victory in front of his closest title challenger, Jarno Saarinen

250cc

GER/Nürburgring
- Hideo Kanaya (JPN, Yamaha) took his only GP victory in the 250cc class

FRA/Clermont-Ferrand
- After missing the first race of the year, Phil Read won first time out in defence of his world title

AUT/Salzburgring
- Sweden's Borje Jansson gave the Derbi factory their only GP victory in the 250cc class

ITA-NAZ/Imola
- Renzo Pasolini took the Aermacchi factory to their first GP victory in the 250cc class, despite crashing while leading and remounting in third place

BEL/Spa-Francorchamps
- Jarno Saarinen took his first 250cc victory of the year

CZE/Brno
- Saarinen won the 250cc race, having already taken victory in the earlier 350cc event – the first time he made it two GP wins on the same day

FIN/Imatra
- Saarinen's fourth 250cc victory of the year clinched the world title

125cc

GBR/Isle of Man TT
- World Championship leader Gilberto Parlotti lost his life after crashing on lap two while leading the race

DDR/Sachsenring
- Borje Jansson gave Maico their first Grand Prix victory

SPA/Montjuich
- Angel Nieto retained the 125cc world title for Derbi with a third-place finish at home in Spain

23 OCTOBER
- British racer Dave Simmonds, 125cc World Champion in 1969, was killed in a gas explosion in the paddock while competing in a non-championship race at the Rungis circuit on the outskirts of Paris

50cc

SPA/Montjuich
- Angel Nieto's victory in the final race of the year was enough to give him the world title from Jan de Vries (Kreidler) – the two were equal on points and separated only by accumulated time in the races they both finished

1972 WORLD CHAMPIONSHIP

500cc

Seven best results were counted

Pos	Rider	Nat	Machine	GER	FRA	AUT	ITA	GBR	YUG	NED	BEL	DDR	CZE	SWE	FIN	SPA	Nett	Gross
1	Giacomo Agostini	ITA	MV Agusta	15	15	15	15	15	-	15	15	15	15	15	15	-	105	(165)
2	Alberto Pagani	ITA	MV Agusta	12	-	-	12	12	15	12	12	-	-	-	12	-	87	
3	Bruno Kneubuhler	SWI	Yamaha	-	8	3	6	-	-	10	-	8	10	4	-	8	54	(57)
4	Rod Gould	GBR	Yamaha	-	-	-	-	-	-	-	10	12	8	12	10	-	52	
5	Bo Granath	SWE	Husqvarna	5	5	10	-	-	6	-	6	5	4	10	-	-	47	(51)
6	Chas Mortimer	GBR	Yamaha	-	-	-	-	-	12	6	-	6	-	3	-	15	42	
7	Dave Simmonds	GBR	Kawasaki	8	-	-	-	-	-	8	-	-	-	8	6	12	42	
8	Jack Findlay	AUS	Jada	4	-	-	-	-	-	5	-	-	12	-	-	10	31	
9	Billie Nelson	GBR	Yamaha/Paton/Honda	3	4	-	-	-	-	2	3	-	6	2	8	5	31	(33)
10	Kim Newcombe	NZE	Konig	10	1	-	-	-	-	-	-	10	-	6	-	-	27	
11	Guido Mandracci	ITA	Suzuki	-	3	12	-	-	8	1	-	-	-	-	-	-	24	
12	Christian Bourgeois	FRA	Yamaha	-	12	6	-	-	-	-	2	-	-	-	-	-	20	
13	Rob Bron	NED	Suzuki	-	10	8	-	-	-	-	-	-	-	-	-	-	18	
14	Esso Gunnarsson	SWE	Kawasaki	-	-	-	-	-	-	-	-	-	5	5	-	6	16	
15	Jerry Lancaster	GBR	Suzuki/Yamaha	-	-	-	-	-	2	4	4	-	-	-	4	-	14	
16	Paul Eickelberg	GER	Konig	-	-	-	-	-	10	3	-	-	-	-	-	-	13	
17	Mick Grant	GBR	Kawasaki	-	-	-	-	10	-	-	-	-	-	-	-	-	10	
17	Bruno Spaggiari	ITA	Ducati	-	-	-	10	-	-	-	-	-	-	-	-	-	10	
19	Giampiero Zubani	ITA	Kawasaki	-	-	5	-	-	4	-	-	-	-	-	-	-	9	
20	Sergio Baroncini	ITA	Ducati	-	-	2	4	-	3	-	-	-	-	-	-	-	9	
21	Lothar John	GER	Yamaha/Suzuki	1	-	-	3	-	-	-	1	-	3	-	1	-	9	
22	Kevin Cowley	GBR	Seeley	-	-	-	-	8	-	-	-	-	-	-	-	-	8	
22	Hideo Kanaya	JPN	Yamaha	-	-	-	-	-	-	-	8	-	-	-	-	-	8	
22	Paul Smart	GBR	Ducati	-	-	-	8	-	-	-	-	-	-	-	-	-	8	
25	Piet van der Wal	NED	Kawasaki/Suzuki	-	-	-	-	-	-	-	-	3	-	-	-	4	7	
26	Derek Chatterton	GBR	Yamaha	-	-	-	-	6	-	-	-	-	-	-	-	-	6	
26	Ernst Hiller	GER	Konig	6	-	-	-	-	-	-	-	-	-	-	-	-	6	
26	Andre Pogolotti	FRA	Suzuki	-	6	-	-	-	-	-	-	-	-	-	-	-	6	
29	Charlie Dobson	GBR	Kawasaki	-	-	-	-	-	5	-	-	-	-	-	-	-	5	
29	Klaus Huber	GER	Kawasaki	-	-	-	5	-	-	-	-	-	-	-	-	-	5	
29	Pentti Korhonen	FIN	Yamaha	-	-	-	-	-	-	-	-	-	-	-	5	-	5	
29	Eric Offenstadt	FRA	Kawasaki	-	-	-	-	-	-	-	5	-	-	-	-	-	5	
29	Charlie Williams	GBR	Yamaha	-	-	-	-	5	-	-	-	-	-	-	-	-	5	
34	Kurt Ivan Carlsson	SWE	Yamaha	-	2	-	-	-	-	-	-	-	1	-	-	2	5	
35	Silvano Bertarelli	ITA	Kawasaki	-	-	4	-	-	-	-	-	-	-	-	-	-	4	
35	Selwyn Griffiths	GBR	Matchless	-	-	-	-	4	-	-	-	-	-	-	-	-	4	
35	Alois Maxwald	AUT	Rotax	-	-	-	-	-	-	-	-	4	-	-	-	-	4	
38	Clive Brown	GBR	Suzuki	-	-	-	-	3	-	-	-	-	-	-	-	-	3	
38	Paul Cott	GBR	Seeley	-	-	-	-	3	-	-	-	-	-	-	-	-	3	
38	Derek Lee	GBR	Suzuki	-	-	-	-	-	-	-	-	-	-	-	3	-	3	
38	Getulio Marcaccini	ITA	Aermacchi	-	-	-	-	-	-	-	-	-	-	-	-	3	3	
42	Carlo Marelli	ITA	Paton/Kawasaki	-	-	1	2	-	-	-	-	-	-	-	-	-	3	
43	Ken Araoka	JPN	Kawasaki	2	-	-	-	-	-	-	-	-	-	-	-	-	2	
43	Johnny Bengtson	SWE	Husqvarna	-	-	-	-	-	-	-	-	-	-	-	2	-	2	
43	Arpad Juhos	HUN	Metisse	-	-	-	-	-	-	-	-	2	-	-	-	-	2	
43	Seppo Kangasniemi	FIN	Yamaha	-	-	-	-	-	-	-	-	-	2	-	-	-	2	
47	Roberto Gallina	ITA	Paton	-	-	-	-	-	1	-	-	-	-	-	-	-	1	
47	Maurice Hawthorne	GBR	Kawasaki	-	-	-	-	-	-	-	-	-	-	-	-	1	1	
47	Ulf Nilsson	SWE	Suzuki	-	-	-	-	-	-	-	-	-	-	1	-	-	1	
47	Josef Ozelt	AUT	Matchless	-	-	-	-	-	-	-	-	1	-	-	-	-	1	
47	Charlie Sanby	GBR	Suzuki	-	-	-	-	1	-	-	-	-	-	-	-	-	1	

Scoring system – 15, 12, 10, 8, 6, 5, 4, 3, 2, 1

350cc

Seven best results were counted

Pos	Rider	Nat	Machine	Nett	Gross
1	Giacomo Agostini	ITA	MV Agusta	102	(110)
2	Jarno Saarinen	FIN	Yamaha	89	(97)
3	Renzo Pasolini	ITA	Aermacchi	78	(102)
4	Dieter Braun	GER	Yamaha	54	
5	Phil Read	GBR	MV Agusta	51	
6	Bruno Kneubuhler	SWI	Yamaha	45	(47)
7	Tepi Lansivuori	FIN	Yamaha	42	
8	Janos Drapal	HUN	Yamaha	41	
9	Hideo Kanaya	JPN	Yamaha	41	
10	Jack Findlay	AUS	Yamaha	17	

250cc

Seven best results were counted

Pos	Rider	Nat	Machine	Nett	Gross
1	Jarno Saarinen	FIN	Yamaha	94	(122)
2	Renzo Pasolini	ITA	Aermacchi	93	(103)
3	Rod Gould	GBR	Yamaha	88	(101)
4	Phil Read	GBR	Yamaha	58	
5	Tepi Lansivuori	FIN	Yamaha	46	(54)
6	John Dodds	AUS	Yamaha	42	
7	Kent Andersson	SWE	Yamaha	39	
8	Borje Jansson	SWE	Yamaha/Derbi/Maico	36	
9	Silvio Grassetti	ITA	MZ	30	
10	Werner Pfirter	SWI	Yamaha	28	

125cc

Seven best results were counted

Pos	Rider	Nat	Machine	Nett	Gross
1	Angel Nieto	SPA	Derbi	97	
2	Kent Andersson	SWE	Yamaha	87	(103)
3	Chas Mortimer	GBR	Yamaha	87	(121)
4	Borje Jansson	SWE	Maico	78	(100)
5	Gilberto Parlotti	ITA	Morbidelli	52	
6	Dave Simmonds	GBR	Kawasaki	44	
7	Harald Bartol	AUT	Suzuki	37	
8	Dieter Braun	GER	Maico	25	
9	Jos Schurgers	NED	Bridgestone	23	
10	Bernd Kohler	DDR	MZ	23	

50cc

Five best results were counted

Pos	Rider	Nat	Machine	Nett	Gross
1	Angel Nieto	SPA	Derbi	69	(81)
2	Jan de Vries	NED	Kreidler	69	(81)
3	Theo Timmer	NED	Jamathi	50	
4	Jan Bruins	NED	Kreidler	39	
5	Otello Buscherini	ITA	Malanca	32	
6	Hans Hummel	AUT	Kreidler	26	
7	Harald Bartol	AUT	Kreidler	26	
8	Jan Huberts	NED	Kreidler	25	
9	Rudi Kunz	GER	Kreidler	17	
10	Benjamin Grau	SPA	Derbi	12	

DEATH AND THE ISLAND

Italian racer Gilberto Parlotti had won the opening two rounds of the 125cc championship while his great rival Angel Nieto failed to score. The Spaniard came back with wins in Austria and Italy, but Parlotti was on the rostrum both times. This was shaping up to be a tight championship; but the next round was at the Isle of Man TT.

In the wake of the death of Santiago Herrero, riding an Ossa on the Mountain circuit two years earlier, the Spanish Federation had banned its riders from competing in the TT and saw no reason to alter their ruling. Parlotti felt this was a way of taking an advantage and entered against the advice of the Morbidelli factory, seeking guidance from his good friend, Giacomo Agostini. Ago even took him for a lap in his car the night before the race. The weather was filthy and Parlotti crashed at the Veranda, a succession of high-speed lefts high on Snaefell, while leading on the second lap. There was, of course, no run-off. Ago was preparing for the Senior TT (the 500 race) when news of the fatal accident came through. He raced, and won, that afternoon but had already decided not to return to the TT.

Barry Sheene had made his feelings known in 1971, the only year he raced on the Island, and now Agostini was backed up by Count Agusta, Phil Read, Rod Gould and most of the top GP men – although Read was tempted back for the TT F1 series that was initially created as a one-race World Championship in 1978 and then extended to – mainly – roads circuits. (Technical regulations were not unlike those for the new MotoGP2 class.) F1 survived for a couple of years after the advent of the World Superbike Championship in 1988.

The Isle of Man TT continued as the UK's Grand Prix until 1976, but the factories never went back. Many of the one-hit wonders in the record books won their sole GP on the Isle of Man circuit against less than stellar opposition, although that is not a charge that can only be levelled at the TT: there was still no compulsion to compete in every round of the World Championship, so end-of-season races at tracks like Imatra and Montjuich were often undersubscribed.

1973

Yamaha entered the 500 class with a four and the class was relevant again, at least until the events at Monza

ABOVE Phil Read, MV's last 500cc champion. (*JARROTTS.com*)

RIGHT It looked agricultural but it was effective. Kim Newcmbe's Konig. (*Elwyn Roberts Collection*)

Phil Read won the first of his two 500cc titles on an MV – despite the fact that he was team-mate to the great Agostini. The British rider was never a man to take too much notice of team orders, so it is safe to assume that MV, having had a look at him on their 350 the previous season, put him on the 500 to keep their multiple World Champion honest, just as they'd done when employing Angelo Bergamonti two years earlier. However, for the first time since 1965, Giacomo Agostini did not become 500cc World Champion. He failed to finish the first four races of the year, won three of the final six, but Read took four victories to become the oldest rider to win the 500cc world title since Les Graham in 1949.

All of these MV victories might have been irrelevant but for the events of 20 May at Monza and the accident that killed Jarno Saarinen and Renzo Pasolini. The Finn had been 250cc World Champion in 1972, and was now racing in 500s too, on the new four-cylinder across-the-frame Yamaha. He won the first two races on it, and was leading the third, at Hockenheim, when his chain broke. Then came Monza.

The next two rounds were the Isle of Man TT and the Yugoslavian GP at the equally fearsome Opatija circuit, neither contested by the factory teams, so it wasn't until Assen that the championship really got going again after a three-race hiatus. Ago was stronger on the run-in, but Read was able to protect his lead. The biggest surprise of the season was the race win in Yugoslavia, and second place in the championship, for New Zealander Kim Newcombe on the Konig, a bike he'd help develop while working as an engineer for the eponymous West German outboard motor company, using one of their flat-four two-strokes mated to Manx Norton transmission parts.

Newcombe died at a non-championship race at Silverstone, and racing lost a man who could have taken the two-stroke challenge to MV. In 2006 a film entitled *Love, Speed & Loss* was released. Narrated by Kim's widow, Jeneen. It is worth seeing not just for the insight it gives into racing 35 years ago but as a record of a remarkable privateer achievement.

THE 1973 SEASON

500cc

FRA/Paul Ricard
- Circuit used for the first time
- The new 500cc four-cylinder two-stroke Yamaha made its debut in the hands of Hideo Kanaya and Jarno Saarinen, with the Japanese qualifying in pole position
- Jarno Saarinen won on his debut in 500cc GPs, the first Finnish rider to claim victory in the class and the first 500cc race win by a four-cylinder two-stroke machine

ITA-NAZ/Monza
- The 500cc race was cancelled following the fatal crash in the 250cc race, after which the Yamaha factory withdrew their team for the remainder of the season

GBR/Isle of Man TT
- Jack Findlay (AUS, Suzuki) became the first rider to win the Senior TT riding a two-stroke machine, and the first to win a 500cc World Championship race using Michelin tyres

YUG/Opatija
- After appearing for the first practice session MV factory riders Agostini and Read withdrew from the Yugoslavian GP due to safety issues
- Kim Newcombe's maiden win in Yugoslavia was the only Grand Prix victory for Konig

SWE/Anderstorp
- Phil Read (MV Agusta) wins the race and takes his first world title in the 500cc class

350cc

FIN/Imatra
- Giacomo Agostini won the last ever 350cc title for MV Agusta and the last for a four-stroke machine
- Agostini's closest challenger was Jarno Saarinen's close friend and fellow-countryman, Tepi Lansivuori. The Finn scored more points overall than Agostini but was relegated to second place in the championship as only a rider's best six results counted

SPA/Jarama
- Adu Celso-Santos became the first Brazilian rider to win a Grand Prix

50cc

SPA/Jarama
- Dutch rider Jan de Vries (Kreidler) took the world title by winning five of the class's seven races

250cc

GER/Hockenheim
- Defending champion Saarinen won the opening three races of the year; on each occasion his Yamaha team-mate Hideo Kanaya finished second

ITA-NAZ/Monza
- Jarno Saarinen and Renzo Pasolini (Harley Davidson) both died following an accident on the first lap of the race in which 15 riders fell at Curva Grande

FIN/Imatra
- Following the accident at Monza, West German rider Dieter Braun won four of the remaining eight races to take the world title, with Tepi Lansivuori again finishing second, as he had in the 350 class

125cc

YUG/Opatija
- Kent Andersson of Sweden, riding a Yamaha, won five of the opening six races of the year

NED/Assen
- Andersson crashed and suffered a broken foot which resulted in him not competing in the next two races, but he had enough of a margin to retain his championship-winning lead

BEL/Spa-Francorchamps
- Jos Schurgers (NED) took his sole Grand Prix victory riding a Bridgestone, the only GP win for this machine

SPA/Jarama
- Chas Mortimer (Yamaha) won the final race of the year – the last British winner in the 125cc class for 35 years – to take second place in the championship

1973 WORLD CHAMPIONSHIP

500cc

Six best results were counted

Pos	Rider	Nat	Machine	FRA	AUT	GER	GBR	YUG	NED	BEL	CZE	SWE	FIN	SPA	Nett	Gross
1	Phil Read	GBR	MV Agusta	12	-	15	-		15	12	12	15	12	15	84	(108)
2	Kim Newcombe	NZE	Konig	6	10	-	-	15	12	8	-	10	8	-	63	(69)
3	Giacomo Agostini	ITA	MV Agusta	-	-	-	-	-	-	15	15	12	15	-	57	
4	Werner Giger	SWI	Yamaha	-	5	12	-	6	5	-	-	6	4	10	44	(48)
5	Jack Findlay	AUS	Suzuki	1	-	-	15	-	6	10	6	-	-	-	38	
6	Bruno Kneubuhler	SWI	Yamaha	-	2	-	-	-	-	-	10	-	10	12	34	
7	Jarno Saarinen	FIN	Yamaha	15	15	-	-	-	-	-	-	-	-	-	30	
8	Hideo Kanaya	JAP	Yamaha	10	12	-	-	-	-	-	-	-	-	-	22	
9	Alex George	GBR	Yamaha	-	-	2	8	5	-	-	-	-	-	4	19	
10	Billie Nelson	GBR	Yamaha	2	3	6	-	-	3	1	-	4	1	-	19	(20)
11	Christian Bourgeois	FRA	Yamaha	-	-	-	-	-	10	-	-	5	2	-	17	
12	Eric Offenstadt	FRA	Kawasaki	4	-	-	-	-	2	-	8	-	3	-	17	
13	Reinhard Hiller	GER	Konig	-	-	5	-	-	-	4	-	-	5	-	14	
14	Guido Mandracci	ITA	Suzuki	5	8	-	-	-	-	-	-	-	-	-	13	
15	Steve Ellis	GBR	Yamaha	-	-	-	-	12	-	-	-	-	-	-	12	
15	Peter Williams	GBR	Matchless	-	-	-	12	-	-	-	-	-	-	-	12	
17	Bo Granath	SWE	Husqvarna	-	4	-	-	-	-	-	3	-	-	5	12	
18	Paul Eickelberg	GER	Konig	-	-	-	-	-	-	5	-	-	6	-	11	
19	Gianfranco Bonera	ITA	Harley Davidson	-	-	-	-	10	-	-	-	-	-	-	10	
19	Ernst Hiller	GER	Konig	-	-	10	-	-	-	-	-	-	-	-	10	
19	Charlie Sanby	GBR	Suzuki	-	-	-	10	-	-	-	-	-	-	-	10	
22	Seppo Kangasniemi	FIN	Yamaha	-	-	-	-	8	-	-	-	2	-	-	10	
23	Borge Nielsen	DEN	Yamaha	-	-	-	-	-	-	-	-	8	-	1	9	
23	Georg Pohlmann	GER	Yamaha	-	-	8	-	-	1	-	-	-	-	-	9	
25	Wil Hartog	NED	Yamaha	-	-	-	-	-	8	-	-	-	-	-	8	
25	Christian Leon	FRA	Kawasaki	8	-	-	-	-	-	-	-	-	-	-	8	
25	Chas Mortimer	GBR	Yamaha	-	-	-	-	-	-	-	-	-	-	8	8	
28	Marcel Ankone	NED	Yamaha	-	-	-	-	-	-	2	-	-	-	6	8	
29	Roberto Gallina	ITA	Paton	-	6	-	-	-	-	-	-	-	-	-	6	
29	Roger Nichols	GBR	Suzuki	-	-	-	6	-	-	-	-	-	-	-	6	
29	Michel Rougerie	FRA	Harley Davidson	-	-	-	-	-	-	6	-	-	-	-	6	
32	Dave Hughes	GBR	Matchless	-	-	-	5	-	-	-	-	-	-	-	5	
32	Bohumil Stasa	CZE	Yamaha	-	-	-	-	-	-	-	5	-	-	-	5	
34	Derek Chatterton	GBR	Yamaha	-	-	-	-	-	4	-	-	-	-	-	4	
34	Mario Lega	ITA	Yamaha	-	-	-	-	-	-	-	4	-	-	-	4	
34	Gyula Marsovszky	SWI	Yamaha	-	-	-	-	4	-	-	-	-	-	-	4	
34	Dudley Robinson	GBR	Suzuki	-	-	-	4	-	-	-	-	-	-	-	4	
34	Peter Stocksiefen	GER	Suzuki	-	-	4	-	-	-	-	-	-	-	-	4	
39	Esso Gunnarson	SWE	Kawasaki	-	-	1	-	-	-	-		3	-	-	4	
39	Piet van der Wal	NED	Yamaha	-	-	-	-	-	-	3	1	-	-	-	4	
41	Jean-Francois Balde	FRA	Kawasaki	3	-	-	-	-	-	-	-	-	-	-	3	
41	Kurt Ivan Carlsson	SWE	HM	-	-	-	-	-	-	-	-	-	-	3	3	
41	Udo Kochanski	GER	Konig	-	-	3	-	-	-	-	-	-	-	-	3	
41	Derek Lee	GBR	Suzuki	-	-	-	-	3	-	-	-	-	-	-	3	
41	John Taylor	GBR	Suzuki	-	-	-	3	-	-	-	-	-	-	-	3	
46	Jean-Paul Boinet	FRA	Kawasaki	-	-	-	-	-	-	-	-	-	-	2	2	
46	Selwyn Griffiths	GBR	Matchless	-	-	-	2	-	-	-	-	-	-	-	2	
46	Ted Janssen	GER	Konig	-	-	-	-	2	-	-	-	-	-	-	2	
46	Lothar John	GER	Suzuki	-	-	-	-	-	-	-	2	-	-	-	2	
50	Graham Bailey	GBR	Kawasaki	-	-	-	1	-	-	-	-	-	-	-	1	
50	Bo Brolin	SWE	Suzuki	-	-	-	-	-	-	-	-	1	-	-	1	
50	Alois Maxwald	AUT	Rotax	-	1	-	-	-	-	-	-	-	-	-	1	
50	Jerome van Haeltert	BEL	Suzuki	-	-	-	-	1	-	-	-	-	-	-	1	

Scoring system – 15, 12, 10, 8, 6, 5, 4, 3, 2, 1

350cc

Six best results were counted

Pos	Rider	Nat	Machine	Nett	Gross
1	Giacomo Agostini	ITA	MV Agusta	84	
2	Tepi Lansivuori	FIN	Yamaha	77	(87)
3	Phil Read	GBR	MV Agusta	56	
4	John Dodds	AUS	Yamaha	49	
5	Billie Nelson	GBR	Yamaha	38	
6	Kent Andersson	SWE	Yamaha	38	
7	Adu Celso-Santos	BRA	Yamaha	33	
8	Dieter Braun	GER	Yamaha	33	
9	Janos Drapal	HUN	Yamaha	30	
10	Pentti Korhonen	FIN	Yamaha	25	

250cc

Six best results were counted

Pos	Rider	Nat	Machine	Nett	Gross
1	Dieter Braun	GER	Yamaha	80	
2	Tepi Lansivuori	FIN	Yamaha	64	
3	John Dodds	AUS	Yamaha	58	(62)
4	Jarno Saarinen	FIN	Yamaha	45	
5	Michel Rougerie	FRA	Harley Davidson	45	
6	Chas Mortimer	GBR	Yamaha	40	(41)
7	Hideo Kanaya	JPN	Yamaha	36	
8	Roberto Gallina	ITA	Yamaha	32	
9	Bruno Kneubuhler	SWI	Yamaha/Harley Davidson	28	
10	Silvio Grassetti	ITA	MZ/Yamaha	21	

125cc

Seven best results were counted

Pos	Rider	Nat	Machine	Nett	Gross
1	Kent Andersson	SWE	Yamaha	99	
2	Chas Mortimer	GBR	Yamaha	75	
3	Jos Schurgers	NED	Bridgestone	70	(72)
4	Borje Jansson	SWE	Maico	64	
5	Eugenio Lazzarini	ITA	Piovaticci/Maico	59	(62)
6	Otello Buscherini	ITA	Malanca	51	
7	Angel Nieto	SPA	Morbidelli	46	
8	Rolf Minhoff	GER	Maico	42	
9	Matti Salonen	FIN	Yamaha	32	
10	Pentti Salonen	FIN	Yamaha	28	

50cc

Four best results were counted

Pos	Rider	Nat	Machine	Nett	Gross
1	Jan de Vries	NED	Kreidler	60	(75)
2	Bruno Kneubuhler	SWI	Kreidler	51	(63)
3	Theo Timmer	NED	Jamathi	47	(61)
4	Gerhard Thurow	GER	Kreidler	36	(42)
5	Henk van Kessel	NED	Kreidler	27	
6	Herbert Rittberger	GER	Kreidler	22	(27)
7	Ulrich Graf	SWI	Kreidler	21	
8	Jan Huberts	NED	Kreidler	21	(29)
9	Rudi Kunz	GER	Kreidler	14	
10	Wolfgang Gedlich	GER	Kreidler	13	

A YEAR OF TRAGEDY

The facts are brutal enough – a 15-bike pile-up at Curva Grande on the first lap of the 250cc GP delle Nazione at Monza resulted in the deaths of Jarno Saarinen and Renzo Pasolini. What caused it? Was it Walter Villa's Benelli leaking oil during the closing laps of the 350 race, as the Italian toured round to try and pick up a point? Australian John Dodds thought so and tried to tell the organisers. He was threatened with expulsion from the race and the police were called to eject him from Race Control. The French journalist Christian Lacombe suffered similar treatment when he tried to get marshals to show an oil flag.

Pasolini arrived at the corner first and fell. His bike then bounced back off the Armco that closely bordered the track, right into Saarinen's path. Both men died on the spot. The German journalist Volker Rauch collected statements from Hideo Kanaya, Dieter Braun, Borje Jansson, Kent Andersson and others who all stated categorically that there was oil on the track.

The Italian inquiry decided that the accident was caused by Pasolini's bike seizing. This was widely regarded as a whitewash until photos of Paso's engine internals emerged in 1993 showing that the right piston was indeed seized. One fact is incontrovertible: the proximity of the crash barriers was a major factor. At the next race at Monza, an Italian junior meeting, Dr Costa Snr was refused permission to station an ambulance at Curva Grande. Three riders died in another mass pile-up and it took 20 minutes for an ambulance to reach the scene.

JARNO SAARINEN

Finnish ice-racing champion in 1965 before entering the GP arena

- First Finnish rider to win a Grand Prix
- Only Finnish rider to have won a world title
- Won on his debut in the 500cc class at the French GP in 1973

WORLD CHAMPIONSHIP CLASSIFICATIONS

1970: 250cc – 4th
1971: 250cc – 3rd, 350cc – 2nd
1972: 250cc – 1st, 350cc – 2nd

RENZO PASOLINI

- Six wins, all in 250cc class:
- 1969 (Benelli): NED/Assen; DDR/Sachsenring; CZE/Brno
- 1972 (Harley Davidson): ITA-NAZ/Imola; YUG/Opatija; SPA/Montjuich.

1974

Phil Read retained the 500 title, the last won by a four-stroke, while Ago took some revenge by winning the 350 – on a two-stroke

MV Agusta again swept the board, but this time without Giacomo Agostini. Because he both disliked Phil Read intensely and realised the power of the approaching two-stroke tsunami, Ago decamped to Yamaha and promptly won both the Daytona and Imola 200-milers. Neither was a Grand Prix race, but at that time they carried enormous prestige and earned him massive kudos with the factory. However, a crash in Sweden due to water leaking from Barry Sheene's Suzuki effectively torpedoed the Italian's chances of the 500 title, although Ago still believes that but for this crash and his ensuing broken shoulder he would have won the 500 championship in his first season on a two-stroke. (He didn't have to wait too long: the following year saw him claim victory.) Compensation in 1974 came in the form of the 350 title, Yamaha's first in the class, on the magnesium-engined TZ ridden by Tepi Lansivuori the previous year. The Finn stayed on as Ago's team-mate in both the 350 and 500 classes. Read did race the 350 MV in the first few GPs but suffered mechanical problems and it was parked for the rest of the year.

Yamaha did not defend the 250 title with a factory effort and their customer racers were beaten by Walter Villa on the factory Harley Davidson. Phil Read became MV's lead rider and marched to the 500 title with the help of Gianfranco Bonera (ITA) and the four-cylinder MV.

The most significant event of the year was the appearance of a brand-new 500cc Suzuki in the hands of Barry Sheene and Australian Jack Findlay. The RG500 was a square-four disc-valve two-stroke in which the DNA of Walter Kaaden's work at MZ could clearly be detected. The bike was fast but fragile; nevertheless, Sheene put it on the rostrum first time out.

Perhaps there was another candidate for event of the year: in the 250 class at Assen a young American Yamaha rider called Kenny Roberts made his Grand Prix debut. He set pole position and fastest lap before finishing third behind Villa and Bruno Kneubuhler (SWI, Yamaha).

ABOVE Jack Findlay (AUS) on the Suzuki RG500 at the French GP, the first race outing for the new water-cooled square-four 500 two-stroke. *(Elwyn Roberts Collection)*

RIGHT Factory Yamaha mechanics working in the open in the Assen paddock, the days of air-conditioned garages were still well in the future (*Henk Keulemans*)

THE 1974 SEASON

500cc

FRA/Clermont-Ferrand
- Barry Sheene finished on the podium for the first time in the 500cc class, taking second place in the debut outing of the new square-four RG500 Suzuki

GER/Nürburgring
- All the top riders boycotted the race, citing insufficient safety measures, in particular lack of protection for the metal barriers lining the circuit

AUT/Salzburgring
- Giacomo Agostini scored his first 500/350cc double race win on Yamaha machinery

ITA-NAZ/Imola
- Gianfranco Bonera (ITA, MV) took his only victory in the 500cc class and a 12-point lead in the championship standings

GBR/Isle of Man TT
- Phil Carpenter (GBR, Yamaha) won the Senior TT race in dreadful conditions, his one and only points-scoring ride in the 500cc class

NED/Assen
- Giacomo Agostini followed up his win in the 350cc race with victory in the 500cc event. This was the last of the 36 occasions when he won two GP races on the same day

BEL/Spa-Francorchamps
- Phil Read regained the lead in the championship with a stunning display, winning the race by 72 seconds from Agostini

SWE/Anderstorp
- Agostini's championship challenge ended after he crashed out of the race trying to avoid Barry Sheene, who had fallen when his Suzuki locked up
- Tepi Lansivuori took his only victory in the 500cc class

FIN/Imatra
- Phil Read won the race, retaining his world title with one race to spare. This was the last 500cc world title won by a four-stroke machine

CZE/Brno
- Read won from team-mate Gianfranco Bonera – the final one–two for MV Agusta

350cc

FRA/Clermont-Ferrand
- Giacomo Agostini won his first race on the 350cc Yamaha after pole-man Phil Read (MV Agusta) retired with mechanical problems

YUG/Opatija
- Agostini scored a start-to-finish victory to become the first rider to take the 350cc title riding a two-stroke machine

SPA/Montjuich
- Victor Palomo (Yamaha) became the only Spanish rider to win a 350cc Grand Prix

250cc

ITA-NAZ/Imola
- Walter Villa took his first GP victory and in the process scored a first GP win for the Harley Davidson factory

NED/Assen
- Kenny Roberts, making his GP debut, qualified his Yamaha on pole before finishing third

BEL/Spa-Francorchamps
- Just one week after making his GP debut at the Dutch TT, Takazumi Katayama (JPN, Yamaha) qualified on pole and finished third

SWE/Anderstorp
- Katayama scored his first victory at only his third Grand Prix

CZE/Brno
- Walter Villa won the race to take his and Harley Davidson's first world title

125cc

GER/Nürburgring
- Fritz Reitmaier (GER) gave Maico the last of their five Grand Prix victories

CZE/Brno
- Kent Andersson retained the 125cc World Championship with a dominant win for Yamaha, finishing more than half a minute ahead of the second rider across the line

50cc

SPA/Montjuich
- Henk van Kessel (NED, Kreidler) took the sixth win of a dominant season in the 50cc class. He had to wait for the boycotted Belgian GP of 1979 for his only other victory

1974 WORLD CHAMPIONSHIP

500cc

Six best results were counted

Pos	Rider	Nat	Machine	FRA	GER	AUT	ITA	GBR	NED	BEL	SWE	FIN	CZE	Nett	Gross
1	Phil Read	GBR	MV Agusta	15	-	-	10	-	10	15	12	15	15	82	(92)
2	Gianfranco Bonera	ITA	MV Agusta	10	-	12	15	-	8	1	8	12	12	69	(78)
3	Tepi Lansivuori	FIN	Yamaha	8	-	-	12	-	12	-	15	10	10	67	
4	Giacomo Agostini	ITA	Yamaha	-	-	15	-	-	15	12	-	-	5	47	
5	Jack Findlay	AUS	Suzuki	-	-	8	8	-	-	6	-	8	4	34	
6	Barry Sheene	GBR	Suzuki	12	-	10	-	-	-	-	-	-	8	30	
7	Dieter Braun	GER	Yamaha	-	-	6	-	-	-	10	-	-	6	22	
8	Pentti Korhonen	FIN	Yamaha	-	-	-	-	-	4	-	10	6	2	22	
9	Billie Nelson	GBR	Yamaha	5	-	4	3	4	-	-	5	-	-	21	
10	Charlie Williams	GBR	Yamaha	-	-	-	-	12	6	-	-	-	-	18	
11	John Williams	GBR	Yamaha	4	-	3	-	-	1	4	1	5	-	18	
12	Helmut Kassner	GER	Yamaha	-	12	-	-	5	-	-	-	-	-	17	
13	Karl Auer	AUT	Yamaha	-	-	5	-	-	5	-	6	1	-	17	
14	Phil Carpenter	GBR	Yamaha	-	-	-	-	15	-	-	-	-	-	15	
14	Edmund Czihak	GER	Yamaha	-	15	-	-	-	-	-	-	-	-	15	
16	Michel Rougerie	FRA	Harley Davidson	6	-	-	-	-	-	5	-	-	3	14	
17	Werner Giger	SWI	Yamaha	-	-	-	4	-	2	-	4	3	-	13	
18	Walter Kaletsch	GER	Yamaha	-	10	-	-	-	-	-	-	-	-	10	
18	Tony Rutter	GBR	Yamaha	-	-	-	-	10	-	-	-	-	-	10	
20	Christian Leon	FRA	Kawasaki	-	-	-	2	-	-	3	-	4	-	9	
21	Billy Guthrie	GBR	Yamaha	-	-	-	-	8	-	-	-	-	-	8	
21	Udo Kochanski	GER	Konig	-	8	-	-	-	-	-	-	-	-	8	
21	Patrick Pons	FRA	Yamaha	-	-	-	-	-	-	8	-	-	-	8	
24	Paul Cott	GBR	Yamaha	-	-	-	-	6	-	-	-	-	-	6	
24	Roberto Gallina	ITA	Yamaha	-	-	-	6	-	-	-	-	-	-	6	
26	Victor Palomo	SPA	Yamaha	-	-	-	-	-	3	-	3	-	-	6	
27	Alex George	GBR	Yamaha		-	-	5	-	-	-	-	-	-	5	
28	Chas Mortimer	GBR	Yamaha	3	-	-	-	-	-	-	-	-	1	4	
29	Paul Eickelberg	GER	Konig	-	-	2	-	-	-	2	-	-	-	4	
30	Peter McKinley	GBR	Yamaha	-	-	-	-	3	-	-	-	-	-	3	
31	Philippe Coulon	SWI	Yamaha	-	-	-	-	-	-	-	-	2	-	2	
31	Selwyn Griffiths	GBR	Matchless	-	-	-	-	2	-	-	-	-	-	2	
31	Tom Herron	GBR	Yamaha	-	-	-	-	-	-	-	2	-	-	2	
31	Ramon Jimenez	FRA	Yamaha	2	-	-	-	-	-	-	-	-	-	2	
35	Geoff Barry	GBR	Matchless	-	-	-	-	1	-	-	-	-	-	1	
35	Jean-Paul Boinet	FRA	Yamaha	-	-	1	-	-	-	-	-	-	-	1	
35	Philippe Gerard	FRA	Yamaha	1	-	-	-	-	-	-	-	-	-	1	

Scoring system – 15, 12, 10, 8, 6, 5, 4, 3, 2, 1

MV'S LAST TITLE

Read's second 500cc title was the last for the MV Agusta factory in any class. Over the next two seasons Read and Ago did win two more races each, to take MV's total of GP victories in all classes to 275 on the way to six 125 titles, four in the 250s, ten 350 crowns and 18 wins in the 500cc class. The only MV racer that could actually be bought was a 125; all other MVs were by definition works bikes. The driving force behind this staggering achievement for a small specialist company was the autocratic Count Domenico Agusta, who decided every detail, be it road or race bike, at MV.

The MV 500 started off as a four in 1950, became a triple in 1966, then reverted to four cylinders for its final championship season. The original four was made competitive by Les Graham and then perfected by John Surtees, but MV's masterpiece was arguably the 350cc triple built for and around Giacomo Agostini and first raced in 1966. In the face of the rapidly advancing two-

350cc

Six best results were counted

Pos	Rider	Nat	Machine	Nett
1	Giacomo Agostini	ITA	Yamaha	75
2	Dieter Braun	GER	Yamaha	62
3	Patrick Pons	FRA	Yamaha	47
4	John Dodds	AUS	Yamaha	31
5	Chas Mortimer	GBR	Yamaha	29
6	Tepi Lansivuori	FIN	Yamaha	27
7	Pentti Korhonen	FIN	Yamaha	25
7	Michel Rougerie	FRA	Harley Davidson	25
9	Victor Palomo	SPA	Yamaha	24
10	Billie Nelson	GBR	Yamaha	22

250cc

Six best results were counted

Pos	Rider	Nat	Machine	Nett
1	Walter Villa	ITA	Harley Davidson	77
2	Dieter Braun	GER	Yamaha	58
3	Patrick Pons	FRA	Yamaha	50
4	Takazumi Katayama	JPN	Yamaha	43
5	Bruno Kneubuhler	SWI	Yamaha	43
6	Chas Mortimer	GBR	Yamaha	41
7	John Dodds	AUS	Yamaha	38
8	Kent Andersson	SWE	Yamaha	34
9	Michel Rougerie	FRA	Harley Davidson	21
10	Mick Grant	GBR	Yamaha	18
10	Pentti Korhonen	FIN	Yamaha	18

125cc

Six best results were counted

Pos	Rider	Nat	Machine	Nett	Gross
1	Kent Andersson	SWE	Yamaha	87	(117)
2	Bruno Kneubuhler	SWI	Yamaha	63	(68)
3	Angel Nieto	SPA	Derbi	60	
4	Otello Buscherini	ITA	Malanca	60	
5	Henk van Kessel	NED	Bridgestone	30	
6	Thierry Tchernine	FRA	Yamaha	25	
7	Harald Bartol	AUT	Suzuki	23	
8	Leif Gustafsson	SWE	Maico	23	
9	Benjamin Grau	SPA	Derbi	21	
10	Gert Bender	GER	Bender	20	

50cc

Six best results were counted

Pos	Rider	Nat	Machine	Nett	Gross
1	Henk van Kessel	NED	Kreidler	90	(114)
2	Herbert Rittberger	GER	Kreidler	65	(68)
3	Julien van Zeebroeck	BEL	Kreidler	59	(61)
4	Gerhard Thurow	GER	Kreidler	57	
5	Rudi Kunz	GER	Kreidler	52	(60)
6	Ulrich Graf	SWI	Kreidler	44	(49)
7	Jan Bruins	NED	Jamathi	27	
8	Otello Buscherini	ITA	Malanca	26	
9	Stefan Dorflinger	SWI	Kreidler	25	
10	Jan Huberts	NED	Kreidler	25	

strokes MV fielded a new 350-four in 1973, and this was the basis of the final four.

Agostini always credits the mechanics who were with him all through his MV career: Magni, Mazza, Carrano, Casteli and Rosolino – the 'Holy Five' – as vital elements of his success. Between them, and in the last years Fiorenzo Fanali, they understood every tiny nuance of their bikes' behaviour. They were the men who coaxed the final fractions of horsepower out of the 500cc four-stroke engine and kept it competitive longer than should have been possible. Don't forget, Honda arrived back in the 500 class with a four-stroke, the NR, in 1979, just three years after Ago gave MV its final victories in both the 350 and 500cc classes. They were nowhere near competitive, despite the almost unlimited resources thrown at the project.

As is often the way, the MV company did not survive as an independent entity long after the death of Count Domenico. It was Agusta's passionate obsession, coupled with the skill of one of the greatest riders and the accumulated knowledge of the Holy Five – just seven men – that made MV a legend.

OTHER MV AGUSTA RECORDS AND MILESTONES

- Last manufacturer to win a GP in the 500cc class with a four-stroke
- Last manufacturer to win a GP in the 350cc class with a four-stroke
- Last manufacturer to win the 500cc world title with a four-stroke
- Last manufacturer to win the 350cc world title with a four-stroke
- Won more 500cc constructors' titles than any other manufacturer
- Won more 350cc constructors' title than any other manufacturer
- Won 17 successive 500cc riders' championships between 1958 and 1974
- Won 8 successive 500cc constructors' titles between 1958 and 1965

MV AGUSTA STATISTICS

	Total	500cc	350cc	250cc	125cc
Grand Prix wins	275	139	76	26	34
Riders' World Championships	38	18	10	4	6
Constructors' World Championships	37	16	9	5	7

1975

Giacomo Agostini won the last of his 15 crowns; it was also the first 500cc crown for Yamaha and the first for a two-stroke

A two-stroke finally won the 500cc title thanks to a vengeful Giacomo Agostini and the reed-valve four-cylinder monoshock Yamaha, now in its third and final iteration as the OW26. The four-stroke rearguard was led by defending champion Phil Read, riding as well as ever on the MV. Crucially, Ago had strong back-up in the form of Hideo Kanaya, whereas the second MV was first in the hands of Armando Toracca (ITA) and then ridden by old hand Gianfranco Bonera. Neither managed a rostrum finish.

The surprise package was the square-four Suzuki RG500 (XR14), ridden by Barry Sheene (from round three onwards, after he'd recovered from his Daytona spill) and Tepi Lansivuori, plus John Newbold (GBR) for Assen and Spa, and Stan Woods in Germany and Italy. Initially the RGs were fast but fragile; the five-week gap between Imola and Assen gave the factory time to make significant improvements.

There was a Grand Prix in that time but it was the British round, at the Isle of Man TT, and the Suzuki, Yamaha and MV factory teams didn't race there. Their absence gifted Mick Grant (GBR) the win on a Kawasaki H1R, against limited competition – his fastest lap was 102.9mph (in less than ideal conditions); he clocked up 109.8mph in the non-championship Classic race, breaking Mike Hailwood's long-standing absolute lap record set in 1967.

Agostini won four races, Read just two, but although the Englishman notched up more points he lost the title as only the best six results counted. The RG's first win in the top class – and Sheene's – came at Assen, when Barry bamboozled Agostini by feinting to one side, then going the other way at the final corner of the final lap.

A new star appeared in the 350cc class. Johnny Cecotto (VEN, Yamaha) took the title aged 19 to become the youngest World Champion. Agostini started the year as the only Yamaha rider with a monoshock chassis (although factory test rider rider Kanaya sometimes appeared with one), but all supported riders had one by the end of the season. This was the bike that would become the TZ model C.

ABOVE Giacomo Agostini and the 500cc Yamaha at Spa. (*Henk Keulemans*)

RIGHT The shape of things to come, the four-cylinder across-the-frame, water-cooled, reed-valve Yamaha OW26 motor. (*Henk Keulemans*)

THE 1975 SEASON

500cc

AUT/Salzburgring

- Barry Sheene was banned from taking part in the race on medical grounds (the aftermath of injuries from his Daytona crash) after being allowed to practise and qualify in sixth place
- Hideo Kanaya became the first Japanese rider to win a 500cc GP
- Having won the earlier 350cc race, Kanaya became the only Japanese rider to take two GP victories on the same day

GBR/Isle of Man TT

- Mick Grant (GBR) gave Kawasaki their second and final victory in the 500cc class

NED/Assen

- Barry Sheene's first win in the 500cc class; also the first win for the four-cylinder RG500 Suzuki
- Sheene passed Agostini on the sprint to the line to win the race – the only occasion in 500cc GP history that the first two riders were credited with the same time

SWE/Anderstorp

- Sheene was followed home by Phil Read and John Williams – the last occasion that British riders filled the top three places in an overseas Grand Prix

CZE/Brno

- Phil Read took the last of his 52 Grand Prix victories
- Giacomo Agostini finished second in the final race of the year to take his 15th world title

350cc

FRA/Paul Ricard

- Johnny Cecotto repeated his victory in the earlier 250cc race, setting a record that still stands of being the youngest rider to win two GP races on the same day

AUT/Salzburgring

- Factory Yamaha rider Hideo Kanaya became the first Japanese rider to win a 350cc GP
- South African Jon Ekerold finished second in his first ever GP, riding a Yamaha

CZE/Brno

- Aged 19, Johnny Cecotto became the youngest World Champion despite breaking down while leading the race. His only challenger, veteran Giacomo Agostini, also suffered mechanical failure

250cc

FRA/Paul Ricard

- Johnny Cecotto won on his Grand Prix debut to become the youngest ever rider to win a GP

FIN/Imatra

- Michel Rougerie's win, on a Harley Davidson, was the first victory in the 250cc class by a French rider
- Despite crashing out of the race on the first lap, Walter Villa retained the 250cc title after Cecotto, his only challenger, failed to take the win

125cc

BEL/Spa-Francorchamps

- Italian Paolo Pileri took the victory, to become the first rider to take a world title riding a Morbidelli

50cc

SWE/Anderstorp

- Angel Nieto (Kreidler) won the 50cc world title for the fourth time, with a second-place finish

1975 WORLD CHAMPIONSHIP

500cc

Six best results were counted

Pos	Rider	Nat	Machine	FRA	AUT	GER	ITA	GBR	NED	BEL	SWE	FIN	CZE	Nett	Gross
1	Giacomo Agostini	ITA	Yamaha	15	-	15	15	-	12	-	-	15	12	84	
2	Phil Read	GBR	MV Agusta	10	10	12	12	-	10	15	12	-	15	76	(96)
3	Hideo Kanaya	JPN	Yamaha	12	15	8	10	-	-	-	-	-	-	45	
4	Tepi Lansivuori	FIN	Suzuki	-	12	10	-	-	6	-	-	12	-	40	
5	John Williams	GBR	Yamaha	-	-	-	-	12	4	6	10	-	-	32	
6	Barry Sheene	GBR	Suzuki	-	-	-	-	-	15	-	15	-	-	30	
7	Alex George	GBR	Yamaha	2	2	3	5	-	-	8	-	-	10	30	
8	John Newbold	GBR	Suzuki	-	-	-	4	-	8	12	-	-	-	24	
9	Armando Toracca	ITA	MV Agusta	8	8	-	8	-	-	-	-	-	-	24	
10	Jack Findlay	AUS	Yamaha	-	-	1	-	-	-	10	2	10	-	23	
11	Chas Mortimer	GBR	Yamaha	-	-	-	-	10	-	-	-	8	5	23	
12	Karl Auer	AUT	Yamaha	3	4	-	-	-	2	-	-	-	8	17	
13	Dieter Braun	GER	Yamaha	-	5	5	-	-	-	-	6	-	-	16	
14	Mick Grant	GBR	Kawasaki	-	-	-	-	15	-	-	-	-	-	15	
15	Gianfranco Bonera	ITA	MV Agusta	-	-	-	-	-	5	-	8	-	-	13	
16	Stan Woods	GBR	Suzuki	-	-	6	6	-	-	-	-	-	-	12	
17	Horst Lahfeld	GER	Konig	-	6	-	-	-	-	-	-	5	-	11	
18	Christian Leon	FRA	Konig	-	-	4	-	-	-	5	-	-	-	9	
19	Billy Guthrie	GBR	Yamaha	-	-	-	-	8	-	-	-	-	-	8	
20	Olivier Chevallier	FRA	Yamaha	-	-	-	-	-	-	-	-	-	6	6	
20	Steve Ellis	GBR	Yamaha	-	-	-	-	-	-	-	-	6	-	6	
20	Patrick Pons	FRA	Yamaha	6	-	-	-	-	-	-	-	-	-	6	
20	Steve Tonkin	GBR	Yamaha	-	-	-	-	6	-	-	-	-	-	6	
24	Thierry Tchernine	FRA	Yamaha	-	1	-	3	-	-	2	-	-	-	6	
25	Geoff Barry	GBR	Yamsel	-	-	-	-	5	-	-	-	-	-	5	
25	Pentti Korhonen	FIN	Yamaha	-	-	-	-	-	-	-	5	-	-	5	
25	Peter McKinley	GBR	Yamaha	5	-	-	-	-	-	-	-	-	-	5	
28	Marcel Ankone	NED	Suzuki	-	-	-	-	-	-	-	-	-	4	4	
28	Gerard Choukroun	FRA	Yamaha	-	-	-	-	-	-	-	4	-	-	4	
28	Alan North	RSA	Harley Davidson	-	-	-	-	-	-	4	-	-	-	4	
28	Michel Rougerie	FRA	Harley Davidson	4	-	-	-	-	-	-	-	-	-	4	
28	Thierry van der Veken	BEL	Yamaha	-	-	-	-	-	-	-	-	4	-	4	
28	Charlie Williams	GBR	Yamaha	-	-	-	-	4	-	-	-	-	-	4	
34	Johnny Bengtson	SWE	Yamaha	-	-	-	-	-	-	-	-	3	-	3	
34	Hans Braumandl	AUT	Yamaha	-	-	-	-	-	-	-	-	-	3	3	
34	Edmar Ferreira	BRA	Yamaha	-	-	-	-	-	-	-	3	-	-	3	
34	Tom Herron	GBR	Yamaha	-	3	-	-	-	-	-	-	-	-	3	
34	Francis Hollebecq	BEL	Yamaha	-	-	-	-	-	-	3	-	-	-	3	
34	Tony Rutter	GBR	Yamaha	-	-	-	-	3	-	-	-	-	-	3	
34	Hans Stadelmann	SWI	Yamaha	-	-	-	-	-	3	-	-	-	-	3	
41	Adu Celso-Santos	BRA	Yamaha	-	-	2	-	-	-	-	-	-	-	2	
41	Bernard Fau	FRA	Yamaha	-	-	-	2	-	-	-	-	-	-	2	
41	Bjorn Hasli	NOR	Yamaha	-	-	-	-	-	-	-	-	2	-	2	
41	Helmut Kassner	GER	Yamaha	-	-	-	-	2	-	-	-	-	-	2	
41	Borge Nielsen	DEN	Yamaha	-	-	-	-	-	-	-	-	-	2	2	
46	Jean-Francois Baldé	FRA	Yamaha	-	-	-	-	-	-	1	-	-	-	1	
46	Seppo Kangasniemi	FIN	Yamaha	-	-	-	-	-	-	-	-	1	-	1	
46	Ruedi Keller	SWI	Yamaha	-	-	-	1	-	-	-	-	-	-	1	
46	Les Kenny	AUS	Yamaha	-	-	-	-	1	-	-	-	-	-	1	
46	Pekka Nurmi	FIN	Yamaha	-	-	-	-	-	-	-	1	-	-	1	
46	Anssi Resko	FIN	Yamaha	-	-	-	-	-	-	-	-	-	1	1	
46	Kjell Solberg	NOR	Yamaha	1	-	-	-	-	-	-	-	-	-	1	
46	Piet van der Wal	NED	Yamaha	-	-	-	-	-	1	-	-	-	-	1	

Scoring system – 15, 12, 10, 8, 6, 5, 4, 3, 2, 1

350cc

Six best results were counted

Pos	Rider	Nat	Machine	Nett	
1	Johnny Cecotto	VEN	Yamaha	78	
2	Giacomo Agostini	ITA	Yamaha	59	
3	Pentti Korhonen	FIN	Yamaha	48	(49)
4	Dieter Braun	GER	Yamaha	47	
5	Patrick Pons	FRA	Yamaha	32	
6	Chas Mortimer	GBR	Yamaha	31	
7	Gerard Choukroun	FRA	Yamaha	28	
8	Otello Buscherini	ITA	Yamaha	27	
9	Tom Herron	GBR	Yamaha	26	
10	Hideo Kanaya	JPN	Yamaha	25	

250cc

Six best results were counted

Pos	Rider	Nat	Machine	Nett	
1	Walter Villa	ITA	Harley Davidson	85	
2	Michel Rougerie	FRA	Harley Davidson	76	(91)
3	Dieter Braun	GER	Yamaha	56	(62)
4	Johnny Cecotto	VEN	Yamaha	54	
5	Patrick Pons	FRA	Yamaha	48	(63)
6	Chas Mortimer	GBR	Yamaha	46	(47)
7	Otello Buscherini	ITA	Yamaha	40	
8	Leif Gustafsson	SWE	Yamaha	33	(34)
9	Bruno Kneubuhler	SWI	Yamaha	22	
10	Tapio Virtanen	FIN	Yamaha/MZ	20	

125cc

Six best results were counted

Pos	Rider	Nat	Machine	Nett	Gross
1	Paolo Pileri	ITA	Morbidelli	90	(115)
2	Pierpaolo Bianchi	ITA	Morbidelli	72	(80)
3	Kent Andersson	SWE	Yamaha	67	(83)
4	Leif Gustafsson	SWE	Yamaha	57	(72)
5	Eugenio Lazzarini	ITA	Piovaticci	47	(51)
6	Bruno Kneubuhler	SWI	Yamaha	43	(51)
7	Henk van Kessel	NED	Condor-AGV	38	
8	Harald Bartol	AUT	Suzuki	21	
9	Johann Zemsauer	AUT	Rotax	21	
10	Pierluigi Conforti	ITA	Morbidelli/Malanca	18	

50cc

Five best results were counted

Pos	Rider	Nat	Machine	Nett	Gross
1	Angel Nieto	SPA	Kreidler	75	(114)
2	Eugenio Lazzarini	ITA	Piovaticci	61	(79)
3	Julien van Zeebroeck	BEL	Kreidler	43	
4	Rudi Kunz	GER	Kreidler	37	(39)
5	Herbert Rittberger	GER	Kreidler	31	
6	Stefan Dorflinger	SWI	Kreidler	31	
7	Nico Polane	NED	Kreidler	28	
8	Gerhard Thurow	GER	Kreidler	21	
9	Hans Hummel	AUT	Kreidler	20	
10	Claudio Lusuardi	ITA	Derbi	16	

STROKERS TAKE THE LAST STRONGHOLD

The 1975 season is now regarded as the start of the modern era, when multi-cylinder water-cooled two-strokes finally overcame the air-cooled four-stroke MV Agustas. However, they needed the help of the points-scoring system to overcome the reliability of the MV. Read only failed to score once, in Finland, thanks to an engine failure, while Ago was stopped by seizures in Austria and Belgium (he also had a DNF in Sweden thanks to a puncture). The Suzuki, in its second year, was still prone to misfires and niggling vibration-induced failures, yet such was the pace of development that the factory supplied most of the grid with RGs the following season. Yamaha's TZ250/350C did the same for their classes.

Here was the triumph of mass production over the hand-built MVs that had relied on knowledge accumulated by a handful of dedicated technicians over many years to extract the best from their aging design. This mirrored the road-bike sector. It is no surprise that Honda could build a multi-cylinder DOHC 750cc engine given their racing history; the really clever thing was that they could mass produce it on an industrial scale far greater than MV, Benelli or Gilera could dream of.

The first company to score points and get on the rostrum with a stroker was DKW in the mid-1950s. In the later part of the decade MZ appeared from the other side of the Berlin Wall, getting their first rostrum and victory in 1958 (in the 125 and 250 classes, respectively). After lead rider Ernst Degner defected and went to Suzuki he won the first two-stroke title, the 50cc World Championship, in 1962. New Zealand racer Hugh Anderson won Suzuki the 125 title in 1963, and a year later Phil Read and Yamaha took the first quarter-litre crown with a two-stroke. Honda and MV then fought a four-stroke rearguard in the 350 and 500cc classes for the best part of a decade, until Giacomo Agostini left MV for Yamaha and promptly won the 1974 350cc championship. One more season and the two-strokes had triumphed. They would be unbeatable. It took the biggest change ever in Grand Prix regulations, the advent of MotoGP in 2002, to enable a four-stroke to win again.

1976

Barry Sheene led Suzuki's domination of the 500 GPs with the RG500 square-four as the four-strokes scored their last victories until the advent of MotoGP

This was the year when Barry Sheene transcended his celebrity status and over-the-counter bikes led the way. Sheene won his and Suzuki's first title with three races to spare and declined to race in Finland, Czechoslovakia and West Germany for financial reasons. There really was only one other true works motorcycle on the grid, an MV Agusta, and then only for three races. It was in the hands of Giacomo Agostini, reunited with the Italian factory out of necessity. After the second race of the year he did what nearly all the field had done and switched to Suzuki, albeit returning to MV to win the final race of the year.

The Suzuki factory had manufactured a batch of RG500s and every ambitious privateer had one. Factory efforts were then scaled back, as they put resources into development of the GS street-bike range, but three special RGs with a new bore and stroke, the classic 54x54mm, went to the UK for the importer, Heron, to run their own team with sponsorship from Texaco and Forward Trust. The intention was for them to be shared among team riders Sheene, John Newbold and John Williams, but Barry corralled the lot. The two Johns rode the previous year's bikes, with about 5kg (11lb) more weight and a narrower power band.

Yamaha did not field an official team, but Johnny Cecotto got hold of Agostini's bikes from the previous year and finished second in the first race only three seconds behind Sheene. However, the Yamaha was no longer competitive and after too many crashes caused by over-riding the Venezuelan parked the 500 and concentrated on the 350cc class.

The impact of the Suzuki customer bikes can be gauged from a look at the final points table. The top 12 were all on Suzukis – although Ago, in seventh, had of course raced an MV as well. The first non-Suzuki rider was Tom Herron, in 13th, and 15 of his 17 points came from the TT, an event that was again boycotted by the top riders. Herron (GBR) was given a race on Williams's Heron Suzuki in Finland but failed to finish – so maybe the top non-Suzuki rider was actually the Austrian Yamaha privateer Karl Auer in 14th!

ABOVE Sheene crosses the line in Sweden to become World Champion for the first time. (*Henk Keulemans*)

RIGHT Ago and MV's last win in the 350s – a demolition job on the TZs, Yamahas and Harley Davidsons at Assen. (*Henk Keulemans*)

THE 1976 SEASON

500cc

FRA/Le Mans
- Barry Sheene won the opening race of the year. He was followed home by Johnny Cecotto and Marco Lucchinelli (ITA), both making their debut on four-cylinder machines
- This was the youngest premier-class podium at that time – a record that stood until the opening race of 2008

AUT/Salzburgring
- Sheene took victory from Lucchinelli and Phil Read in the first ever all-Suzuki podium in the 500cc class

ITA-NAZ/Mugello
- On the first GP at the Mugello circuit, Barry Sheene won a 500cc race in which the top nine riders were all Suzuki mounted

GBR/Isle of Man TT
- Tom Herron won the final 500cc championship race to be held on the famous Mountain circuit, after John Williams (GBR) broke down with less than a mile to go when leading by over four minutes
- Herron's win was the last in the 500cc class by a twin-cylinder machine

NED/Assen
- Pat Hennen finished second to become the first American rider to stand on a 500cc podium outside the USA

BEL/Spa-Francorchamps
- Phil Read left the circuit after Friday's practice to bring to an end a 15-year Grand Prix career
- John Williams took his one and only 500cc GP victory

SWE/Anderstorp
- Barry Sheene clinched his first 500cc title, and the first for Suzuki, with a win

FIN/Imatra
- Pat Hennen became the first American rider to win a World Championship Grand Prix

CZE/Brno
- John Newbold took his one and only 500cc GP victory
- Newbold became the fourth different British rider to win a race in the 500cc class in 1976. In the following 32 years only one British rider – Barry Sheene – clocked up any wins in the premier class

350cc

FRA/Le Mans
- Walter Villa's first win in the 350cc class was also the first for Harley Davidson

ITA-NAZ/Mugello
- Franco Uncini (ITA) finished in second place – his first podium appearance in Grand Prix racing

YUG/Opatija
- Olivier Chevallier gave France its first victory in the 350cc class since 1954

NED/Assen
- Giacomo Agostini gave MV Agusta its final victory in the 350cc class and also the last for a four-stroke machine

GER/Nürburgring
- Walter Villa won the 350cc title for the first time with a victory over his closest rival, Johnny Cecotto

SPA/Montjuich
- South African Kork Ballington took his first GP victory on the final occasion the World Championships visited the historic Montjuich circuit

250cc

FRA/Le Mans
- Walter Villa won despite crashing out while leading and restarting without losing the lead

YUG/Opatija
- Former 125 and 250cc champion Dieter Braun took the last of his 14 GP victories

CZE/Brno
- With another convincing victory Walter Villa became the first rider to win three consecutive 250cc titles

125cc

GER/Nürburgring
- German Anton Mang scored his first Grand Prix victory riding a Morbidelli
- Even though he failed to score points after crashing, Pierpaolo Bianchi (ITA) won the 125cc title for the first time

50cc

ITA-NAZ/Mugello
- Angel Nieto gave Bultaco their first victory in the 50cc class

GER/Nürburgring
- Nieto retained his world title with victory in Germany

1976 WORLD CHAMPIONSHIP

500cc

Three best results from the first five rounds were counted plus three best scores from remaining rounds

Pos	Rider	Nat	Machine	FRA	AUT	ITA	GBR	NED	BEL	SWE	FIN	CZE	GER	Nett	Gross
1	Barry Sheene	GBR	Suzuki	15	15	15		15	12	15	-	-	-	72	(87)
2	Tepi Lansivuori	FIN	Suzuki	8	-	8	-	-	6	8	12	12	-	48	(54)
3	Pat Hennen	USA	Suzuki	-	-	6	-	12	3	-	15	-	10	46	
4	Marco Lucchinelli	ITA	Suzuki	10	12	-	-	-	-	-	6	-	12	40	
5	John Newbold	GBR	Suzuki	-	-	-	-	-	2	1	8	15	8	31	(34)
6	Philippe Coulon	SWI	Suzuki	-	-	3	-	-	-	5	10	10	-	28	
7	Giacomo Agostini	ITA	MV/Suzuki	6	5	-	-	-	-	-	-	-	15	26	
8	Jack Findlay	AUS	Suzuki	-	3	-	-	6	-	12	4	-	-	25	
9	John Williams	GBR	Suzuki	-	-	-	4	5	15	-	-	-	-	24	
10	Phil Read	GBR	Suzuki	-	10	12	-	-	-	-	-	-	-	22	
11	Marcel Ankone	NED	Suzuki	-	-	5	-	-	10	-	-	-	6	21	
12	Stu Avant	NZE	Suzuki	4	6	4	-	-	-	6	-	-	-	20	
13	Tom Herron	GBR	Yamaha	-	-	-	15	-	-	2	-	-	-	17	
14	Chas Mortimer	GBR	Suzuki	-	-	-	-	-	4	10	-	2	2	16	(18)
15	Michel Rougerie	FRA	Yamaha/Suzuki	-	8	-	-	-	8	-	-	-	-	16	
16	Karl Auer	AUT	Yamaha	2	2	-	-	-	-	3	1	8	-	16	
17	Dieter Braun	GER	Suzuki	3	-	2	-	-	5	-	5	-	-	15	
18	Victor Palomo	SPA	Yamaha	5	4	-	-	-	-	4	-	-	-	13	
19	Johnny Cecotto	VEN	Yamaha	12	-	-	-	-	-	-	-	-	-	12	
19	Ian Richards	GBR	Yamaha	-	-	-	12	-	-	-	-	-	-	12	
21	Virginio Ferrari	ITA	Suzuki	-		10	-	-	-	-	-	-	-	10	
21	Billy Guthrie	GBR	Yamaha	-	-	-	10	-	-	-	-	-	-	10	
21	Wil Hartog	NED	Suzuki	-	-	-	-	10	-	-	-	-	-	10	
24	Alex George	GBR	Yamaha	-	1	-	-	8	-	-	-	-	-	9	
25	Boet van Dulmen	NED	Yamaha/Suzuki	1	-	-	-	-	-	-	-	3	5	9	
26	Takazumi Katayama	JPN	Yamaha	-	-	-	8	-	-	-	-	-	-	8	
27	Roger Nicholls	GBR	Yamaha	-	-	-	6	-	-	-	-	-	-	6	
27	Max Wiener	AUT	Yamaha	-	-	-	-	-	-	-	-	6	-	6	
29	Jon Ekerold	RSA	Yamaha	-	-	-	5	-	-	-	-	-	-	5	
29	Olivier Chevallier	FRA	Yamaha	-	-	-	-	-	-	-	-	5	-	5	
31	Bernard Fau	FRA	Yamaha	-	-	-	-	4	-	-	-	-	-	4	
31	Bernd Tugenthal	GER	Yamaha	-	-	-	-	-	-	-	-	4	-	4	
31	Alan North	RSA	Suzuki	-	-	-	-	-	-	-	-	-	4	4	
34	Gordon Pantall	GBR	Yamaha	-	-	-	3	-	-	-	-	-	-	3	
34	Rob Bron	NED	Yamaha	-	-	-	-	3	-	-	-	-	-	3	
34	Christian Estrosi	FRA	Suzuki	-	-	-	-	-	-	-	3	-	-	3	
34	Christian Bourgeois	FRA	Yamaha	-	-	-	-	-	-	-	-	-	3	3	
38	Helmut Kassner	GER	Suzuki	-	-	-	-	2	1	-	-	-	-	3	
39	John Weeden	GBR	Yamaha	-	-	-	2	-	-	-	-	-	-	2	
39	Pekka Nurmi	FIN	Yamaha	-	-	-	-	-	-	-	2	-	-	2	
41	Borge Nielsen	DEN	Yamaha	-	-	1	-	-	-	-	-	-	-	1	
41	Bill Smith	GBR	Yamaha	-	-	-	1	-	-	-	-	-	-	1	
41	Dave Potter	GBR	Yamaha	-	-	-	-	1	-	-	-	-	-	1	
41	Edmar Ferreira	BRA	Yamaha	-	-	-	-	-	-	-	-	1	-	1	
41	Egid Schwemmer	GER	Nava	-	-	-	-	-	-	-	-	-	1	1	

Scoring system – 15, 12, 10, 8, 6, 5, 4, 3, 2, 1

350cc

Pos	Rider	Nat	Machine	Nett	Gross
1	Walter Villa	ITA	Harley Davidson	76	81
2	Johnny Cecotto	VEN	Yamaha	65	
3	Chas Mortimer	GBR	Yamaha	54	
4	Tom Herron	GBR	Yamaha	41	45
5	John Dodds	AUS	Yamaha	34	
6	Victor Palomo	SPA	Yamaha	29	32
7	Takazumi Katayama	JPN	Yamaha	28	29
8	Bruno Kneubuhler	SWI	Yamaha	28	30
9	Olivier Chevallier	FRA	Yamaha	27	
10	Franco Uncini	ITA	Yamaha	27	

250cc

Pos	Rider	Nat	Machine	Nett	Gross
1	Walter Villa	ITA	Harley Davidson	90	117
2	Takazumi Katayama	JPN	Yamaha	73	87
3	Gianfranco Bonera	ITA	Harley Davidson	61	77
4	Tom Herron	GBR	Yamaha	47	52
5	Pentti Korhonen	FIN	Yamaha	47	55
6	Dieter Braun	GER	Yamaha	42	50
7	Chas Mortimer	GBR	Yamaha	31	
8	Bruno Kneubuhler	SWI	Yamaha	29	
9	Olivier Chevallier	FRA	Yamaha	25	
10	Victor Palomo	SPA	Yamaha	25	28

125cc

Pos	Rider	Nat	Machine	Nett	Gross
1	Pierpaolo Bianchi	ITA	Morbidelli	90	105
2	Angel Nieto	SPA	Bultaco	67	
3	Paolo Pileri	ITA	Morbidelli	64	74
4	Henk van Kessel	NED	Condor-AGV	46	
5	Anton Mang	GER	Morbidelli	32	
6	Jean-Louis Guignabodet	FRA	Morbidelli	27	31
7	Eugenio Lazzarini	ITA	Morbidelli	26	
8	Gert Bender	GER	Bender	25	
9	Stefan Dorflinger	SWI	Morbidelli	23	
10	Julien van Zeebroeck	BEL	Morbidelli	18	

50cc

Pos	Rider	Nat	Machine	Nett	Gross
1	Angel Nieto	SPA	Bultaco	85	97
2	Herbert Rittberger	GER	Kreidler	76	92
3	Ulrich Graf	SWI	Kreidler	69	80
4	Eugenio Lazzarini	ITA	Morbidelli	53	61
5	Rudolf Kunz	GER	Kreidler	34	39
6	Julien van Zeebroeck	BEL	Kreidler	26	
7	Stefan Dorflinger	SWI	Kreidler	25	
8	Rolf Blatter	SWI	Kreidler	25	26
9	Hans Hummel	AUT	Kreidler	20	23
10	Pierre Audry	FRA	ABF	15	

THE LAST HURRAH

Although Agostini parked his 500 MV after a couple of GPs and, like the rest of the grid, bought an RG500 Suzuki, he kept the four-stroke in reserve. At the final round of the 500cc championship, held on the old Nürburgring, he used both bikes in practice but the MV for the race. Ago admitted to some 'sleight of hand' in this matter, but he made the choice because the four-stroke suited the track and conditions better – not, as the romantics would have us believe, because of the fans' reaction to the MV. Ago led from the start but really pulled away when the rain came. He had over a minute over the rest going into the last lap and won by 52 seconds. The MV, a bike developed for and around Ago, made its power more predictably and was easier to use around the 'Ring in good conditions than the disc-valve Suzukis, never mind in the wet. The victory was a triumph of experience and Ago's legendary attention to detail, and it is remembered not just because it was the final four-stroke win in the top class until the advent of MotoGP, but also because it was the last of Agostini's 122 Grand Prix wins. However, it should be noted that it was achieved in the absence of Barry Sheene, who had already wrapped up the title.

For a real swansong go back to the 350 race at Assen. Ago campaigned the smaller MV throughout the season, after two years on TZ350s, against a field of strokers including the Yamahas of Cecotto, Takazumi Katayama and Chas Mortimer, the Morbidelli of Dieter Braun and the Harley Davidsons of eventual (double) champion Walter Villa and Gianfranco Bonera. The MV broke in every race except one. That was the Dutch TT where, on a sweltering afternoon, Ago led every lap, and won by over 24 seconds. It was the last 350 class win for a four-stroke, for MV, and for the man himself. Many would argue that this was a greater achievement than his win at the Nürburgring later in the year.

GIACOMO AGOSTINI STATISTICS

- His total of 15 world titles is better than any other rider, Angel Nieto (13) being the next most successful
- 122 GP victories – the most successful racer of all time
- 8 premier-class titles; Valentino Rossi, with 6, is the next most successful
- 7 350cc titles, beating Jim Redman (4)
- 68 race wins in the premier class – only Rossi has won more
- 54 race wins in the 350cc class – more than any other rider
- 20 successive 500cc GP race victories during the 1968 and '69 seasons – an all-time record
- Only rider to win 500cc GP races and the 500 title on both two-stroke and four-stroke machines
- Only rider to win the 350cc title on two-stroke and four-stroke bikes
- Last rider to win both a 500cc GP and a 350cc GP on a four-stroke
- Last rider to win a 350cc world title on a four-stroke
- First rider to win both the 350cc and 500cc titles on a two-stroke
- Achieved a perfect season of 10 500cc GP wins from 10 races in 1968
- In 1970 he won 19 GP races (10 x 500cc, 9 x 350cc) to share the record for most GP wins in a single season with Mike Hailwood

1977

Defending a title is supposed to be more difficult than winning it in the first place; nobody told Barry Sheene

Barry Sheene retained his 500cc title comfortably and, despite Yamaha fielding a new generation straight four without reed valves, he was never beaten by one in a direct fight. Indeed, the World Champion was very rarely beaten at all. Sheene and his Suzuki won six out of the nine races in which they competed, boycotting the Austrian event along with the other big names. He was beaten by Wil Hartog (NED, Suzuki) in Holland, and finished down the field in Finland when his motor overheated, but that was enough to win the title so Barry didn't go to Czechoslovakia. Then overheating stopped him again at Silverstone, now the venue for the British round.

Yamaha fielded Johnny Cecotto, Steve Baker (USA) and Giacomo Agostini on their new bikes. The American newcomer was the most impressive of the trio, and although he didn't win a race he finished second overall. Cecotto took two race victories, but the start of his season was ruined by injury. The three Yamaha men shared the top six championship positions with the Texaco Heron Suzuki teamsters Sheene, Pat Hennen and new recruit Steve Parrish (GBR). Everyone from seventh down to 30th was riding a Suzuki RG500 at the end of the season.

This would be Agostini's last season as a rider. With just two rostrums on the 500 and one on the 350 Yamaha he decided to hang up his leathers. One notable first was Takazumi Katayama's 350cc championship, the first world title for a Japanese rider. Amazingly, it would be another 26 years before Tetsuya Harada became Japan's second World Champion. The success of Hennen and Baker was a sign of what was about to come from over the Atlantic, initially in the shape of Kenny Roberts.

For the first time scores from all races counted towards the World Championship a situation that pertains to this day with the sole exception of 1991.

ABOVE Sheene and the Suzuki RG500, an unbeatable combination in '77. (*Henk Keulemans*)

RIGHT Instant national hero: Wil Hartog on top of the rostrum at Assen after becoming the first Dutchman to win a 500cc GP. (*Henk Keulemans*)

THE 1977 SEASON

500cc

VEN/San Carlos

- Barry Sheene opened his title defence with a victory at the first ever Venezuelan Grand Prix
- American Steve Baker finished second on his GP debut riding the factory Yamaha

AUT/Salzburgring

- All the top riders boycotted the 500cc race after an accident in the 350cc race raised serious issues regarding safety

NED/Assen

- At his home Grand Prix Wil Hartog scored the first victory for Holland in the 500cc class

BEL/Spa-Francorchamps

- Barry Sheene won the fastest Grand Prix race of all time, setting the quickest lap ever at an average of more than 137mph (220km/h)

FIN/Imatra

- A sixth-place finish after suffering overheating problems was enough to give Sheene his second world title
- Johnny Cecotto took his first win in the 500cc class and the first win of the year for the Yamaha 500cc machine

CZE/Brno

- Cecotto scored another dominant win from pole, and set a new lap record. Earlier in the day he'd won the 350cc race by almost a full minute after starting from pole, and he set a new lap record

GBR/Silverstone

- Pat Hennen took the win, the first to be held on the British mainland, from Steve Baker – the first ever one-two result in GP racing for the USA

350cc

AUT/Salzburgring

- The race was stopped after an accident in which Swiss rider Hans Stadelmann lost his life and several other competitors received serious injuries, including Patrick Fernandez, Dieter Braun and Johnny Cecotto

GER/Hockenheim

- Takazumi Katayama gave the new three-cylinder Yamaha its first victory

FIN/Imatra

- Katayama's victory here made him the first Japanese rider to win a world title

GBR/Silverstone

- Kork Ballington won the 350cc race after taking the 250cc event earlier in the day – his first double victory

250cc

GER/Hockenheim

- Christian Sarron (FRA) took his first victory in GP racing in front of Akihiro Kiyohara, giving the in-line twin-cylinder Kawasaki its first podium finish

YUG/Opatija

- Mario Lega (ITA) scored his one and only Grand Prix victory, and the first win for Morbidelli in the 250cc class

NED/Assen

- Britain's Mick Grant gave Kawasaki their first victory in the 250cc GP class

CZE/Brno

- Third place was enough to give Mario Lega the world title – the first in the 250cc class for a Morbidelli rider

125cc

VEN/San Carlos

- Ivan Palazzese (Morbidelli) started the race even though, at 15, he was below the minimum age limit – and he finished on the podium in his home race

SWE/Anderstorp

- Pierpaolo Bianchi (Morbidelli) finished second to retain his 125cc world title

50cc

YUG/Opatija

- Ulrich Graf (SWI), the winner here a year earlier, lost his life after crashing due to a punctured rear tyre

SWE/Anderstorp

- Ricardo Tormo (SPA) scored his first Grand Prix victory riding the factory Bultaco
- Angel Nieto finished second behind his team-mate to clinch his sixth and final 50cc title

1977 WORLD CHAMPIONSHIP

500cc

All races were counted

Pos	Rider	Nat	Machine	VEN	AUT	GER	ITA	FRA	NED	BEL	SWE	FIN	CZE	GBR	Total
1	Barry Sheene	GBR	Suzuki	15	-	15	15	15	12	15	15	5	-	-	107
2	Steve Baker	USA	Yamaha	12	-	10	8	10	6	12	10	-	-	12	80
3	Pat Hennen	USA	Suzuki	10	-	12	-	1	10	10	1	-	8	15	67
4	Johnny Cecotto	VEN	Yamaha	8	-	-	-	-	-	-	12	15	15	-	50
5	Steve Parrish	GBR	Suzuki	2	-	8	-	5	-	6	8	6	4	-	39
6	Giacomo Agostini	ITA	Yamaha	-	-	-	6	12	-	3	2	-	12	2	37
7	Gianfranco Bonera	ITA	Suzuki	-	-	-	-	8	-	-	5	10	6	8	37
8	Philippe Coulon	SWI	Suzuki	6	-	6	5	6	8	5	-	-	-	-	36
9	Tepi Lansivuori	FIN	Suzuki	-	-	-	-	4	4	8	-	4	5	10	35
10	Wil Hartog	NED	Suzuki	-	-	5	-	-	15	4	6	-	-	-	30
11	Marco Lucchinelli	ITA	Suzuki	4	-	4	-	-	5	-	-	12	-	-	25
12	Virginio Ferrari	ITA	Suzuki	5	-	-	12	3	1	-	-	-	-	-	21
13	Michel Rougerie	FRA	Suzuki	-	-	-	-	-	3	-	-	8	10	-	21
14	Armando Toracca	ITA	Suzuki	-	-	-	10	2	2	-	4	3	-	-	21
15	Max Wiener	AUT	Suzuki	-	12	2	-	-	-	-	-	-	3	3	20
16	Jack Findlay	AUS	Suzuki	-	15	-	-	-	-	2	-	-	-	-	17
17	Alex George	GBR	Suzuki	-	10	-	-	-	-	-	-	-	-	5	15
18	Helmut Kassner	GER	Suzuki	-	8	-	-	-	-	-	-	-	1	-	9
19	Franz Heller	GER	Suzuki	-	6	-	-	-	-	-	-	-	-	-	6
19	Steve Wright	GBR	Suzuki	-	-	-	-	-	-	-	-	-	-	6	6
21	Christian Estrosi	FRA	Suzuki	3	-	-	3	-	-	-	-	-	-	-	6
22	Michael Schmid	AUT	Suzuki	-	5	-	-	-	-	-	-	-	-	-	5
23	Derek Chatterton	GBR	Suzuki	-	-	-	-	-	-	-	-	-	-	4	4
23	John Newbold	GBR	Suzuki	-	-	-	4	-	-	-	-	-	-	-	4
25	Anton Mang	GER	Suzuki	-	-	3	1	-	-	-	-	-	-	-	4
25	John Williams	GBR	Suzuki	-	-	-	-	-	-	1	3	-	-	-	4
27	Boet van Dulmen	NED	Suzuki	-	-	1	2	-	-	-	-	-	-	-	3
28	Jean-Philippe Orban	BEL	Suzuki	-	-	-	-	-	-	-	-	2	-	-	2
28	Franz Rau	GER	Suzuki	-	-	-	-	-	-	-	-	-	2	-	2
30	Karl Auer	AUT	Yamaha	-	-	-	-	-	-	-	-	1	-	-	1
30	Alan North	RSA	Suzuki	1	-	-	-	-	-	-	-	-	-	-	1
30	Kevin Wrettom	GBR	Yamaha	-	-	-	-	-	-	-	-	-	-	1	1

Scoring system – 15, 12, 10, 8, 6, 5, 4, 3, 2, 1

350cc

Pos	Rider	Nat	Machine	Total
1	Takazumi Katayama	JPN	Yamaha	95
2	Tom Herron	GBR	Yamaha	56
3	Jon Ekerold	RSA	Yamaha	54
4	Michel Rougerie	FRA	Yamaha	50
5	Kork Ballington	RSA	Yamaha	46
6	Olivier Chevallier	FRA	Yamaha	39
7	Christian Sarron	FRA	Yamaha	38
8	Patrick Fernandez	FRA	Yamaha	34
9	Johnny Cecotto	VEN	Yamaha	30
10	Alan North	RSA	Yamaha	30

250cc

Pos	Rider	Nat	Machine	Total
1	Mario Lega	ITA	Morbidelli	85
2	Franco Uncini	ITA	Harley Davidson	72
3	Walter Villa	ITA	Harley Davidson	67
4	Takazumi Katayama	JPN	Yamaha	58
5	Tom Herron	GBR	Yamaha	54
6	Kork Ballington	RSA	Yamaha	49
7	Alan North	RSA	Yamaha	43
8	Mick Grant	GBR	Kawasaki	42
9	Jon Ekerold	RSA	Yamaha	42
10	Patrick Fernandez	FRA	Yamaha	28

125cc

Pos	Rider	Nat	Machine	Total
1	Pierpaolo Bianchi	ITA	Morbidelli	131
2	Eugenio Lazzarini	ITA	Morbidelli	105
3	Angel Nieto	SPA	Bultaco	80
4	Jean-Louis Guignabodet	FRA	Morbidelli	62
5	Anton Mang	GER	Morbidelli	55
6	Gert Bender	GER	Bender	38
7	Harald Bartol	AUT	Morbidelli	32
8	Hans Muller	SWI	Morbidelli	32
9	Stefan Dorflinger	SWI	Morbidelli	32
10	Pierluigi Conforti	ITA	Morbidelli	30

50cc

Pos	Rider	Nat	Machine	Total
1	Angel Nieto	SPA	Bultaco	87
2	Eugenio Lazzarini	ITA	Kreidler	72
3	Ricardo Tormo	SPA	Bultaco	69
4	Herbert Rittberger	GER	Kreidler	53
5	Patrick Plisson	FRA	ABF	26
6	Stefan Dorflinger	SWI	Kreidler	24
7	Jean-Louis Guignabodet	FRA	Morbidelli	14
8	Hans Hummel	AUT	Kreidler	11
9	Julien van Zeebroeck	BEL	Kreidler	10
10	Ramon Gali	SPA	Derbi	10

THE FASTEST EVER

Barry Sheene won the Belgian Grand Prix at Spa-Francorchamps on his Suzuki RG500 at an average speed of 135.07mph (217.37km/h). There has never been a faster World Championship race. It was held on the 8.75-mile (14.12-km) version of the circuit that was shrunk to a 4.32-mile (6.95-km) track two years later. For comparison, in 2008 the fastest MotoGP race of the year was at Phillip Island, with Casey Stoner (AUS, Ducati) winning at 109.36mph (176.00km/h).

Spa was the last of the old-style road circuits, laid out in the days when engine technology was giving riders plenty of horsepower but chassis, brakes and tyres had hardly moved on from the pioneer days. Look at maps of tracks like the Sachsenring, parts of the old Brno road circuit, Dundrod (home of the Ulster GP), Monza before the chicanes, and even the Isle of Man Mountain circuit. What they have in common is fast, long straights and sweeping or interlinked corners that don't require much in the way of braking. In the late 1970s Spa-Francorchamps still had the Masta straight at the highest part of the course, with its 130mph (209km/h) kink. The only place riders dropped below 100mph was for the La Source hairpin that ended the lap. Eugenio Lazzarini (ITA, Kreidler) won the 50cc race earlier in the day at over 102mph (164km/h), which gives a pretty good indication of what was required to win at the old Spa.

This was not a trouble-free race for Sheene. His rev-counter bracket was repaired with duct tape after the warm-up lap, and in the early laps he was involved in a six-man group and after that in a lap-record-shattering dice with Michel Rougerie (FRA, Suzuki). On the very last lap fuel starvation nearly stopped Barry – he was down to 60mph (97km/h) at one point – but he still won by ten seconds from Steve Baker.

RIGHT The start of the fastest race in Grand Prix history, the 1977 Belgian 500cc race at Spa-Francorchamps. (*Henk Keulemans*)

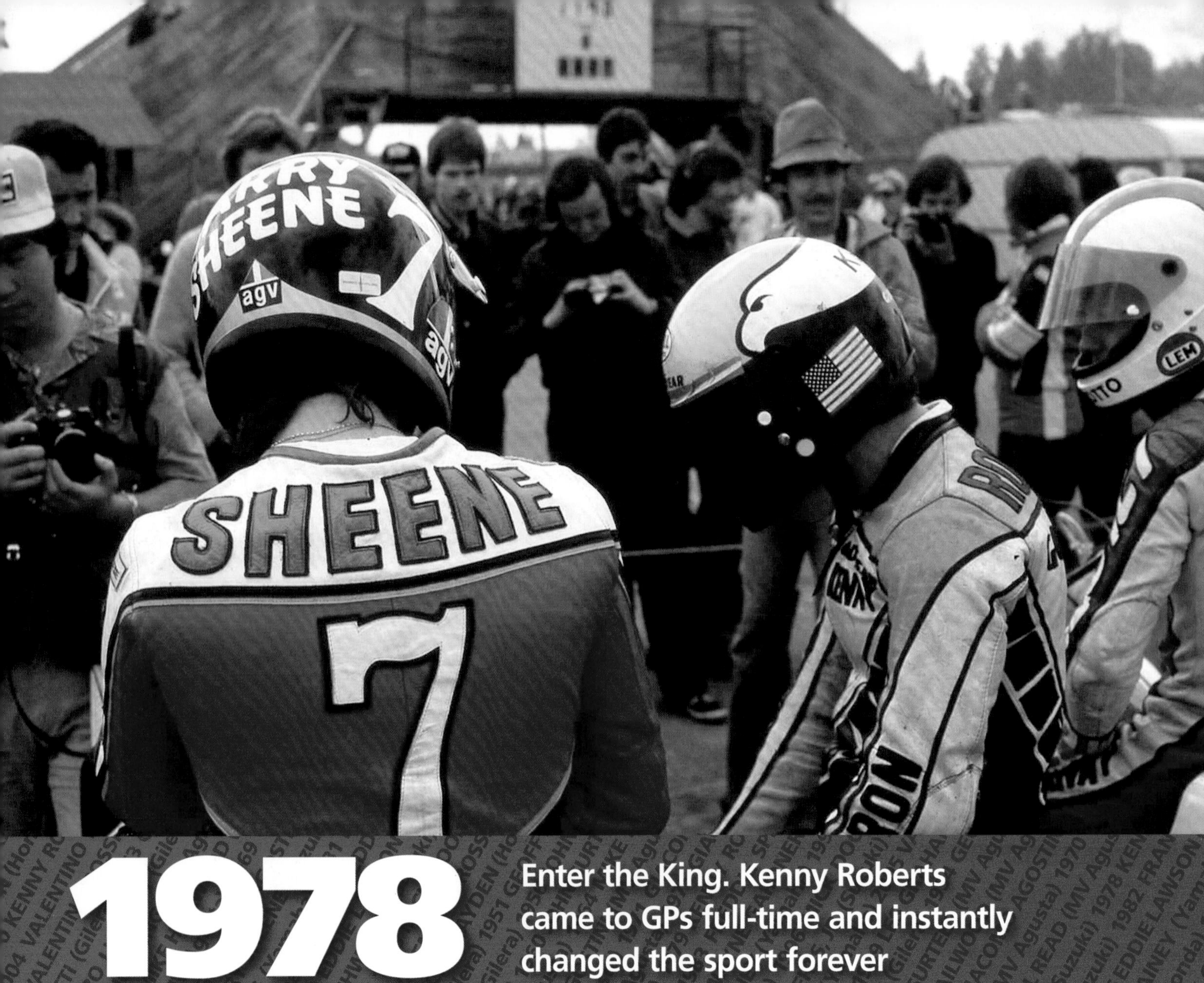

1978

Enter the King. Kenny Roberts came to GPs full-time and instantly changed the sport forever

This was the year when Yamaha finally got it right. The OW35 got the power-valve variable-height exhaust-port system, and American Kenny Roberts was brought in to partner Johnny Cecotto and Takazumi Katayama on the factory bikes, although they all ran in different colours. Actually, Kenny's team wasn't really a full works effort – the other riders got parts first – so the Yamaha America effort would probably be called a 'satellite' team today. Roberts was the only rider to use Goodyear tyres, which is normally a handicap in this situation, and he also had just one bike. No-one dreamt he could win the title at his first attempt, but Kenny put together three back-to-back wins in the first half of the season, along the way dealing mortal psychological blows to the opposition.

Suzuki also had a new bike, the XR22 stepped-cylinder version of the RG500, with the rear pair of cylinders higher than the front. Barry Sheene and Pat Hennen were retained in the Heron team, while the Italian importer ran Steve Baker who had, unaccountably, not been re-signed by Yamaha. When Hennen suffered career-ending injuries at the Isle of Man TT, right after setting the first sub-20-minute lap, Wil Hartog and later Michel Rougerie were drafted in to try and take points off Roberts. For the last race of the year Virginio Ferrari (ITA) also got an XR22, to help Suzuki take the Manufacturers' Championship.

Sheene was off-colour up until Assen, blaming a virus picked up in Venezuela.

In the 250 and 350cc classes Kork Ballington did the double on the almost unbeatable Kawasaki. In the 350s Ballington or his team-mate Gregg Hansford (AUS) won all but two races, and in the 250s they won all except four. However, one of those races was won by another Kawasaki rider, Anton Mang (GER), and the two victories went to Kenny Roberts, who quit the class after six rounds because, he claimed, of Yamaha's indifference. The turning point was Spa, where the bike broke, at which point the American was just three points behind Ballington and two in front of Hansford.

ABOVE Sheene, Roberts and Cecotto – the big three of '78. (*Henk Keulemans*)

RIGHT All attitude and American brashness, Kenny Roberts in the Nürburgring paddock after clinching his first world title. (*Henk Keulemans*)

THE **1978** SEASON

500cc

VEN/San Carlos

- Barry Sheene won the opening race of the season for the third successive year

SPA/Jarama

- Pat Hennen took the race victory in front of fellow-countryman Kenny Roberts, who finished on the podium for the first time in the 500cc class

AUT/Salzburgring

- Kenny Roberts took just three races to win in the 500cc class for the first time

FRA/Nogaro

- Roberts won his second successive race to lead the World Championship for the first time

NED/Assen

- Johnny Cecotto took the last of his three victories in the 500cc class

BEL/Spa-Francorchamps

- Wil Hartog won the last 500cc race to be held at the original Spa circuit – the last time that a GP race was run at more than 130mph (209km/h)

SWE/Karlskoga

- The circuit hosted its first GP event, and Barry Sheene won for the first time since the opening race of the year

GBR/Silverstone

- The race saw most riders come in to change wheels when rain started to fall. Kenny Roberts finally took the victory from Steve Manship (GBR, Suzuki), one of the few riders to start the race on intermediates and not come into the pits

GER/Nürburgring

- Virginio Ferrari took his maiden Grand Prix victory
- Kenny Roberts finished third to become America's first World Champion

350cc

AUT/Salzburgring

- Kork Ballington gave Kawasaki their first GP victory in the 350cc class

FRA/Nogaro

- Gregg Hansford backed up his win in the earlier 250cc race with victory in the 350cc event – the first rider to win two GP races on the same day riding Kawasaki machinery

GBR/Silverstone

- Ballington won the race to clinch his first world title

125cc

VEN/San Carlos

- After swapping from Morbidelli to Minarelli, Pierpaolo Bianchi won the season's first race, in defence of his crown, giving his new employers their first 125cc GP win

SPA/Jarama

- Italian Eugenio Lazzarini repeated his victory of the earlier 50cc race – his first double GP win

BEL/Spa-Francorchamps

- Angel Nieto swapped from the Bultaco to the Minarelli factory machine, to take his first podium of the year

FIN/Imatra

- Lazzarini effectively clinched the 125cc world title by finishing second when his only challenger, Bianchi, crashed into the woods and broke both legs

250cc

VEN/San Carlos

- Kenny Roberts took his first GP victory on his debut as a full-time Grand Prix rider

SPA/Jarama

- Gregg Hansford won for the first time in only his third GP start

GBR/Silverstone

- Anton Mang won for the first time in the 250cc class

YUG/Rijeka

- The 250cc title battle between Kawasaki team-mates Ballington and Hansford went to the final race of the year at the new circuit of Rijeka. The South African finished third to become double 250/350cc World Champion
- Hansford took the victory from Mang and Ballington – the first all-Kawasaki podium in the 250cc class

50cc

CZE/Brno

- Ricardo Tormo took the win to clinch his first 50cc world title

1978 WORLD CHAMPIONSHIP

500cc

Pos	Rider	Nat	Machine	VEN	SPA	AUT	FRA	ITA	NED	BEL	SWE	FIN	GBR	GER	Total
1	Kenny Roberts	USA	Yamaha	-	12	15	15	15	12	12	4	-	15	10	110
2	Barry Sheene	GBR	Suzuki	15	6	10	10	6	10	10	15	-	10	8	100
3	Johnny Cecotto	VEN	Yamaha	-	8	12	-	-	15	-	5	10	4	12	66
4	Wil Hartog	NED	Suzuki	-	2	4	6	5	6	15	12	15	-	-	65
5	Takazumi Katayama	JPN	Yamaha	-	10	-	-	-	8	5	10	12	2	6	53
6	Pat Hennen	USA	Yamaha	12	15	-	12	12	-	-	-	-	-	-	51
7	Steve Baker	USA	Suzuki	10	5	-	-	8	2	-	8	5	-	4	42
8	Tepi Lansivuori	FIN	Suzuki	-	4	6	-	4	-	6	3	8	6	2	39
9	Marco Lucchinelli	ITA	Suzuki	-	-	8	-	10	-	4	-	-	8	-	30
10	Michel Rougerie	FRA	Suzuki	-	-	5	-	-	5	8	-	-	-	5	23
11	Virginio Ferrari	ITA	Suzuki	-	-	-	-	-	-	-	6	-	1	15	22
12	Steve Parrish	GBR	Suzuki	8	1	-	4	-	1	-	-	6	-	-	20
13	Boet van Dulmen	NED	Suzuki	-	-	3	-	2	3	-	-	4	-	3	15
14	Steve Manship	GBR	Suzuki	-	-	-	-	-	-	-	-	-	12	-	12
15	Christian Estrosi	FRA	Suzuki	-	3	-	8	-	-	-	-	-	-	-	11
16	Graziano Rossi	ITA	Suzuki	-	-	-	5	-	-	-	-	2	-	-	7
17	John Newbold	GBR	Suzuki	-	-	-	-	-	4	-	-	-	3	-	7
18	Roberto Pietri	VEN	Yamaha	6	-	-	-	-	-	-	-	-	-	-	6
19	Gianni Rolando	ITA	Suzuki	-	-	-	-	1	-	-	-	-	5	-	6
20	Gerhard Vogt	GER	Yamaha	5	-	-	-	-	-	-	-	-	-	-	5
21	Philippe Coulon	SWI	Suzuki	-	-	-	-	3	-	-	2	-	-	-	5
22	Leandro Becheroni	ITA	Suzuki	4	-	-	-	-	-	-	-	-	-	-	4
23	Alex George	GBR	Suzuki	-	-	-	-	-	-	3	1	-	-	-	4
23	Jurgen Steiner	GER	Suzuki	-	-	-	-	-	-	-	-	3	-	1	4
25	Jean-Philippe Orban	BEL	Suzuki	-	-	-	3	-	-	-	-	-	-	-	3
26	Gianfranco Bonera	ITA	Suzuki	-	-	2	-	-	-	-	-	-	-	-	2
26	Carlo Perugini	ITA	Suzuki	-	-	-	2	-	-	-	-	-	-	-	2
26	Tom Herron	GBR	Suzuki	-	-	-	-	-	-	2	-	-	-	-	2
29	Bruno Kneubuhler	SWI	Suzuki	-	-	1	-	-	-	-	-	1	-	-	2
30	Kenny Blake	AUS	Yamaha	-	-	-	1	-	-	-	-	-	-	-	1
30	Dennis Ireland	NZE	Suzuki	-	-	-	-	-	-	1	-	-	-	-	1

Scoring system – 15, 12, 10, 8, 6, 5, 4, 3, 2, 1

350cc

Pos	Rider	Nat	Machine	Total
1	Kork Ballington	RSA	Kawasaki	134
2	Takazumi Katayama	JPN	Yamaha	77
3	Gregg Hansford	AUS	Kawasaki	76
4	Jon Ekerold	RSA	Yamaha	64
5	Tom Herron	GBR	Yamaha	50
6	Michel Rougerie	FRA	Yamaha	47
7	Gianfranco Bonera	ITA	Yamaha	37
8	Patrick Fernandez	FRA	Yamaha	36
9	Vic Soussan	AUS	Yamaha	34
10	Olivier Chevallier	FRA	Yamaha	27

250cc

Pos	Rider	Nat	Machine	Total
1	Kork Ballington	RSA	Kawasaki	124
2	Gregg Hansford	AUS	Kawasaki	118
3	Patrick Fernandez	FRA	Yamaha	55
4	Kenny Roberts	USA	Yamaha	54
5	Anton Mang	GER	Kawasaki	52
6	Tom Herron	GBR	Yamaha	48
7	Mario Lega	ITA	Morbidelli	44
8	Franco Uncini	ITA	Yamaha	42
9	Jon Ekerold	RSA	Yamaha	40
10	Paolo Pileri	ITA	Morbidelli	35

125cc

Pos	Rider	Nat	Machine	Total
1	Eugenio Lazzarini	ITA	MBA	114
2	Angel Nieto	SPA	Bultaco/Minarelli	88
3	Pierpaolo Bianchi	ITA	Minarelli	70
4	Harald Bartol	AUT	Morbidelli	68
5	Thierry Espie	FRA	Motobecane	62
6	Maurizio Massimiani	ITA	Morbidelli	56
7	Hans Muller	SWI	Morbidelli	48
8	Per-Edward Carlson	SWE	Morbidelli	46
9	Jean-Louis Guignabodet	FRA	Bender/Morbidelli	42
10	Clive Horton	GBR	Morbidelli	25

50cc

Pos	Rider	Nat	Machine	Total
1	Ricardo Tormo	SPA	Bultaco	99
2	Eugenio Lazzarini	ITA	Kreidler	64
3	Patrick Plisson	FRA	ABF	48
4	Wolfgang Muller	GER	Kreidler	28
5	Rolf Blatter	SWI	Kreidler	25
6	Stefan Dorflinger	SWI	Kreidler	24
7	Claudio Lusuardi	ITA	Bultaco	20
8	Peter Looijensteijn	NED	Kreidler	14
9	Ingo Emmerich	GER	Kreidler	14
10	Aldo Pero	ITA	Kreidler	13

THE KING

It is impossible to overstate the effect Kenny Roberts has had on Grand Prix motorcycle racing. He has been a champion as both rider and team owner, a unique achievement in itself, but he has also been a constructor. Along the way he has been credited with everything from being the first racer to get his knee down, the first to adopt the hang-off riding style, and the first deliberately to use rear-wheel steering. He didn't actually do any of these first, but he did completely revolutionise the way in which motorcycle racers were treated and GPs were run.

It was also very obvious that he didn't care whom he upset. He was a central player in the World Series scheme that threatened to break motorcycle racing away from FIM control. The plans never came to fruition, but the shock waves the idea generated hastened the end of races on deadly circuits and the exploitation of riders by greedy organisers. Roberts clearly saw the Catch 22 situation: every racer wants to be the best and that means being World Champion. However, to be a champion riders had to subject themselves to humiliation at the hands of organisers, and at tracks where capital punishment was the reward for a mistake on a motorcycle. Kenny did not like this, so he did something about it.

For the record, Kenny says it was by watching Jarno Saarinen (at Ontario in 1973) that he figured out that shifting his weight around would help him in corners. As for rear-wheel steering, Roberts says he learned from a Goodyear contact that American ace Cal Rayborn set his bikes up to push the front in slow corners and slide the rear in fast ones. That's what Kenny did in the States, and that's what he brought to Europe.

RIGHT Under the bubble with both wheels well off the ground: Roberts at the Finnish GP. (*Henk Keulemans*)

1979

Kenny Roberts retained his title despite injury and reduced support from Yamaha

Kenny Roberts defended his title with a motorcycle that was, to all intents and purposes, the same as the one on which he'd ended the 1978 season. The OW45 did have a new design of power valve and the only serious weakness – rear suspension that ran out of damping half-way through a race – was addressed. Roberts had a horrible crash while testing in Japan that resulted in him missing the first race while he recovered from back injury and an operation to remove his spleen. The only other OW45 went to Cecotto, but a broken knee at the second round put the Venezuelan out until Assen.

Suzuki gave three works bikes to the Heron team for Barry Sheene, the recalled Steve Parrish, and experienced privateer and TT ace Tom Herron. The Ulsterman would become the first Suzuki factory rider to be killed when he crashed at the non-championship North West 200. There were also factory bikes for Wil Hartog and Virginio Ferrari. All the top privateers were once more on RG500 Suzukis, and for the first time one of them won a race: Boet van Dulmen (NED) triumphed in Finland.

Despite his injuries and the lack of support, Roberts was able to win the second race of the year and then three of the next four races to establish a slim lead over Virginio Ferrari. Kenny's final win of the season came after an epic dice with Sheene on the old high-speed Silverstone. Fortunately, the BBC filmed it and it still crops up on the sort of programme that has 'Greatest' in its title. The American won by a wheel after Sheene was baulked by George Fogarty (Carl's dad) on the penultimate lap: Barry tried to ride round the outside of Roberts and set a new lap record, but it wasn't enough. Team members will still tell you it was Sheene's best ride for Suzuki.

There were no team orders imposed at Suzuki – it would have been difficult, as their top men rode for different teams – and their chances were blunted by injury to Hartog and two breakdowns for Ferrari in the Scandinavian races. The title was decided at the last round, when Ferrari crashed trying to make up ground after running off track while disputing the lead with Sheene.

ABOVE Roberts and the Yamaha on the gas at Assen, in the colours of the American importer. (*Henk Keulemans*)

RIGHT Mr Soichiro Honda himself came to Silverstone to support his team's re-entry into GPs. (*Henk Keulemans*)

THE **1979** SEASON

500cc

VEN/San Carlos

- Barry Sheene took victory in the season's opening race for the fourth successive year
- Kenny Roberts didn't go to Venezuela because of injuries received in a testing crash in Japan

BEL/Spa-Francorchamps

- Dennis Ireland (NZE, Suzuki) won a race boycotted by the leading riders on safety grounds, specifically the slippy nature of newly laid track

FIN/Imatra

- Dutchman Boet van Dulmen took his one and only GP victory, riding a Suzuki
- Randy Mamola (USA, Suzuki) finished second in only his third start in the 500cc class to become the youngest rider to stand on the podium in the premier class – a record he still holds

GBR/Silverstone

- Kenny Roberts and Barry Sheene battled all the way to the finish and were separated by just 0.03s as they crossed the line. For this era, when timing was done only to the nearest one-hundredth of a second, this was the closest ever finish
- Honda debuted their NR500 in the hands of Mick Grant and Takazumi Katayama. Grant crashed at the first corner and Katayama completed a couple of laps before stopping with engine failure

FRA/Le Mans

- Kenny Roberts finished third to retain his world title

250cc

VEN/San Carlos

- Walter Villa took the last of his 24 Grand Prix victories and his only one on a Yamaha. The rest were on Harley Davidsons
- Nineteen-year-old Randy Mamola, riding a Yamaha, finished fifth on his Grand Prix debut

YUG/Rijeka

- Graziano Rossi (ITA, Morbidelli) took his first Grand Prix victory

GBR/Silverstone

- Rossi crashed out of the lead with just three corners to go, leaving Ballington to win the race and retain the 250cc title

125cc

NED/Assen

- Angel Nieto (Minarelli) took the last in a sequence of 11 successive victories going back to the Finnish GP the previous year – still the record for the longest run of wins in the 125cc class, although it was equalled by Fausto Gresini (ITA, Garelli) in 1986–7

FIN/Imatra

- Nieto did not race in Finland due to a broken leg sustained in a non-championship event, but still took the world title because his closest challenger, Thierry Espié (FRA, Motobecane), was also unable to race due to injury
- Reigning 50cc champion Ricardo Tormo won for the first time in the 125cc class. This was also the last win in the class for Bultaco

CZE/Brno

- Guy Bertin (FRA) won a GP for the first time and also became the first rider to claim victory on a Motobecane

350cc

VEN/San Carlos

- Carlos Lavado (Yamaha) took his first Grand Prix victory, at home in Venezuela

CZE/Brno

- Kork Ballington won for Kawasaki and became double World Champion for the second year in succession

50cc

FRA/Le Mans

- Eugenio Lazzarini clinched his first 50cc title to add to his 125cc crown by winning the final race of the year, with his closest challenger Rolf Blatter (SWI) finishing third; both were Kreidler mounted

YOUNGEST RIDERS TO SCORE A PREMIER-CLASS GRAND PRIX PODIUM

	Rider	Age	Race
1	Randy Mamola	19 years 260 days	FIN/Imatra/1979
2	Norick Abe	20 years 10 days	BRA/Jacarepagua/1995
3	Mike Hailwood	20 years 77 days	GBR/Isle of Man TT/1960
4	Johnny Cecotto	20 years 91 days	FRA/Le Mans/1976
5	Freddie Spencer	20 years 98 days	ARG/Buenos Aires/1982
6	Dani Pedrosa	20 years 178 days	SPA/Jerez/2006
7	Casey Stoner	20 years 196 days	TUR/Istanbul Park/2006
8	Gary Hocking	20 years 293 days	GER/Nürburgring/1958
9	Jorge Lorenzo	20 years 310 days	QAT/Losail/2008
10	Takuma Aoki	21 years 58 days	JPN/Suzuka/1995

1979 WORLD CHAMPIONSHIP

500cc

Pos	Rider	Nat	Machine	VEN	AUT	GER	ITA	SPA	YUG	NED	BEL	SWE	FIN	GBR	FRA	Total
1	Kenny Roberts	USA	Yamaha	-	15	12	15	15	15	3	-	8	5	15	10	113
2	Virginio Ferrari	ITA	Suzuki	12	12	10	12	8	12	15	-	-	-	8	-	89
3	Barry Sheene	GBR	Suzuki	15	-	-	8	-	-	12	-	15	10	12	15	87
4	Wil Hartog	NED	Suzuki	-	10	15	-	12	8	10	-	-	1	10	-	66
5	Franco Uncini	ITA	Suzuki	8	5	5	-	6	10	5	-	-	-	4	8	51
6	Boet van Dulmen	NED	Suzuki	-	-	-	-	5	6	8	-	10	15	6	-	50
7	Jack Middelburg	NED	Suzuki	-	-	4	4	4	-	4	-	12	8	-	-	36
8	Randy Mamola	USA	Suzuki	-	-	-	-	-	-	-	-	5	12	-	12	29
9	Philippe Coulon	SWI	Suzuki	-	-	6	3	3	-	6	-	-	3	3	5	29
10	Tom Herron	GBR	Suzuki	10	8	-	10	-	-	-	-	-	-	-	-	28
11	Christian Sarron	FRA	Yamaha	4	-	3	-	-	4	2	-	2	6	5	-	26
12	Steve Parrish	GBR	Suzuki	-	4	2	-	-	2	1	-	6	-	-	4	19
13	Mike Baldwin	USA	Suzuki	-	-	1	6	10	-	-	-	-	-	-	-	17
14	Dennis Ireland	NZE	Suzuki	1	-	-	-	-	-	-	15	-	-	-	-	16
15	Michel Rougerie	FRA	Suzuki	6	-	-	-	2	5	-	-	-	-	-	3	16
16	Bernard Fau	FRA	Suzuki	-	-	8	5	-	-	-	-	-	-	-	-	13
17	Kenny Blake	AUS	Yamaha	-	-	-	-	-	-	-	12	-	-	-	-	12
18	Marco Lucchinelli	ITA	Suzuki	-	2	-	-	1	-	-	-	4	2	2	-	11
19	Gary Lingham	GBR	Suzuki	-	-	-	-	-	-	-	10	-	-	-	-	10
20	Johnny Cecotto	VEN	Yamaha	-	-	-	-	-	-	-	-	-	4	-	6	10
21	Gustav Reiner	GER	Suzuki	-	-	-	-	-	-	-	8	-	-	-	-	8
22	Henk de Vries	NED	Suzuki	-	-	-	-	-	-	-	6	-	-	-	-	6
22	Hiroyuki Kawasaki	JPN	Suzuki	-	6	-	-	-	-	-	-	-	-	-	-	6
24	Gerhard Vogt	GER	Suzuki	3	-	-	-	-	-	-	3	-	-	-	-	6
25	Josef Hage	GER	Suzuki	-	-	-	-	-	-	-	5	-	-	-	-	5
25	Roberto Pietri	VEN	Suzuki	5	-	-	-	-	-	-	-	-	-	-	-	5
27	Jacky Matagne	BEL	Suzuki	-	-	-	-	-	-	-	4	-	-	-	-	4
28	Max Wiener	AUT	Suzuki	-	3	-	-	-	1	-	-	-	-	-	-	4
29	Carlo Perugini	ITA	Suzuki	-	-	-	-	-	3	-	-	-	-	-	-	3
29	Ikujiro Takaï	JAP	Yamaha	-	-	-	-	-	-	-	-	3	-	-	-	3
31	Guy Cooremans	BEL	Suzuki	-	-	-	-	-	-	-	2	-	-	-	-	2
31	Sergio Pellandini	SWI	Suzuki	2	-	-	-	-	-	-	-	-	-	-	-	2
31	Graziano Rossi	ITA	Morbidelli	-	-	-	2	-	-	-	-	-	-	-	-	2
31	John Woodley	NZE	Suzuki	-	-	-	-	-	-	-	-	-	-	-	2	2
35	Mick Grant	GBR	Suzuki	-	1	-	-	-	-	-	-	-	-	-	-	1
35	Dieter Heinen	BEL	Yamaha	-	-	-	-	-	-	-	1	-	-	-	-	1
35	John Newbold	GBR	Suzuki	-	-	-	-	-	-	-	-	-	-	1	-	1
35	Giovanni Pelletier	ITA	Suzuki	-	-	-	1	-	-	-	-	-	-	-	-	1
35	Seppo Rossi	FIN	Suzuki	-	-	-	-	-	-	-	-	1	-	-	-	1
35	Peter Sjöström	SWE	Suzuki	-	-	-	-	-	-	-	-	-	-	-	1	1

Scoring system – 15, 12, 10, 8, 6, 5, 4, 3, 2, 1

350cc

Pos	Rider	Nat	Machine	Total
1	Kork Ballington	RSA	Kawasaki	99
2	Patrick Fernandez	FRA	Yamaha	90
3	Gregg Hansford	AUS	Kawasaki	77
4	Anton Mang	GER	Kawasaki	63
5	Michel Frutschi	SWI	Yamaha	47
6	Roland Freymond	SWI	Yamaha	38
7	Walter Villa	ITA	Yamaha	38
8	Jon Ekerold	RSA	Yamaha	34
9	Sadao Asami	JPN	Yamaha	27
10	Jeff Sayle	AUS	Yamaha	24

250cc

Pos	Rider	Nat	Machine	Total
1	Kork Ballington	RSA	Kawasaki	141
2	Gregg Hansford	AUS	Kawasaki	81
3	Graziano Rossi	ITA	Morbidelli	67
4	Randy Mamola	USA	Yamaha	64
5	Patrick Fernandez	FRA	Yamaha	63
6	Anton Mang	GER	Kawasaki	56
7	Walter Villa	ITA	Yamaha	39
8	Jean-François Baldé	FRA	Kawasaki	29
9	Edi Stollinger	AUT	Kawasaki	28
10	Roland Freymond	SWI	Yamaha	22

125cc

Pos	Rider	Nat	Machine	Total
1	Angel Nieto	SPA	Minarelli	120
2	Maurizio Massimiani	ITA	MBA	53
3	Hans Muller	SWI	MBA	50
4	Thierry Espie	FRA	Motobecane	48
5	Gert Bender	GER	Bender	47
6	Guy Bertin	FRA	Morbidelli	40
7	Ricardo Tormo	SPA	Bultaco	39
8	Harald Bartol	AUT	Morbidelli	36
8	Bruno Kneubuhler	SWI	Morbidelli	36
10	Pierpaolo Bianchi	ITA	Minarelli	35

50cc

Pos	Rider	Nat	Machine	Total
1	Eugenio Lazzarini	ITA	Kreidler	75
2	Rolf Blatter	SWI	Kreidler	62
3	Patrick Plisson	FRA	ABF	32
4	Gerhard Waibel	GER	Kreidler	31
5	Peter Looijensteijn	NED	Kreidler	30
6	Hagen Klein	GER	Kreidler	26
7	Henk van Kessel	NED	Kreidler	23
8	Jacques Hutteau	FRA	ABF	22
9	Ingo Emmerich	GER	Kreidler	19
10	Stefan Dorflinger	SWI	Kreidler	18

OVAL PISTON

There haven't been many bigger surprises than Honda's decision to return to Grand Prix racing with a four-stroke. The NR500 was, without a doubt, the most radical motorcycle ever built, the result of giving young engineers a blank sheet of paper. Why? Mr Honda really didn't like two-strokes.

But how could they achieve enough power to be competitive with the strokers? The answer was frankly outrageous: regulations demanded no more than four cylinders so Honda effectively built a V8, then siamesed the bores. Each oval piston had two connecting rods, each cylinder eight valves and two spark plugs. The cycle parts were just as advanced. Yamaha were still running their straight four, Suzuki a square four. The frame was an aluminium monocoque at a time when steel tubes were still the norm. The forks were outer upper tube (upside down), with 16-inch wheels and rear suspension rising-rate linkage years before they became the norm; Sheene's Suzuki still used twin rear shock absorbers and 18-inch wheels. The NR even had side-mounted radiators to avoid feeding warm air to the carbs ten years before it became common practice. Next to the opposition, the NR500 looked tiny.

Some Honda managers had counselled caution and asked for a parallel two-stroke programme, or at least some shakedown races at national level. The top men felt they wouldn't learn quickly enough that way. Of course, such a radical machine was a racing nightmare. It needed to run at 7000rpm to start – unfortunately push starts were still in force. The motor sounded like it stopped dead when the throttle was closed, so it is fair to assume that there was next to no flywheel. Riders Mick Grant and Takazumi Katayama had dreadful problems even qualifying.

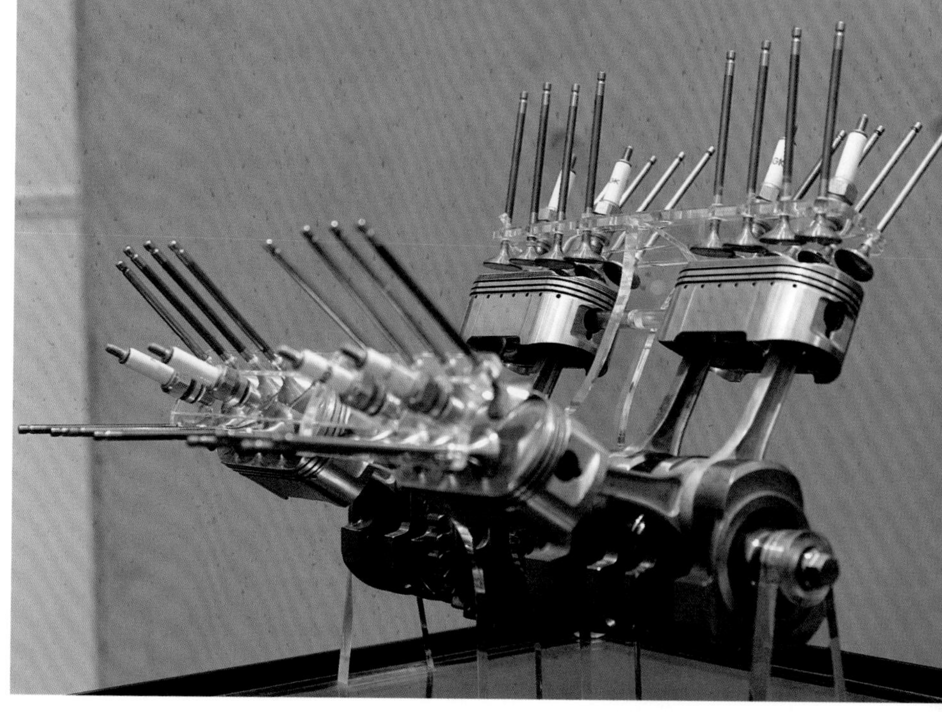

ABOVE This is what the fuss was all about: oval pistons, each with two con rods, two spark plugs and eight valves. (*Henk Keulemans*)

Seeing the world's largest motorcycle company suffering such public humiliation engendered much amusement, and the NR never scored a World Championship point. The first NR may have been a racing failure, but it is also probably the most misunderstood racer ever. Many top Honda men, including the current president, Takeo Fukui, started their careers on the project. Remember that the NR was Honda's first V4. Without the several hundred patents and the knowledge gained in four years of racing, would the RVF, RC30 and, indeed, the NSR have been such elegant designs?

1980

Roberts and Yamaha made it a hat-trick of titles but the story of the year was a privateer's triumph in the 350 class

Kenny Roberts made it three in a row thanks to early season form which saw him win the first three of just eight rounds – both the Venezuelan and Austrian events were cancelled. The American now had a choice of aluminium or steel frames but otherwise the bike was little changed. When the Suzukis got up to speed mid-season Yamaha reversed the outer cylinders of the engine to give all the exhaust pipes straight runs.

The factory also sold a Roberts Replica, the TZ500G. It differed from the factory bike in that the power valves were mechanically, not electrically, operated. One of these bikes did win – courtesy of Jack Middelburg, at home in Holland – but his machine was really a Nico Bakker chassis with RG Suzuki forks, and no-one else got one on the rostrum. The Cagiva that appeared at the last round, ridden by Virginio Ferrari, was built around a TZ500 bottom end.

Heron Suzuki had two new riders after Barry Sheene left to run a private Yamaha with Akai sponsorship – 20-year-old Randy Mamola and New Zealander Graeme Crosby. Graeme would win at Daytona on a Superbike, on the Isle of Man riding a 500 and in the Suzuka 8 Hours on an endurance machine before scoring his first GP rostrum at the final race of the year. Despite the problems of the previous season, when the Suzuki challenge had no clear leader, the factory again supplied full works bikes to their Dutch and Italian teams. Wil Hartog returned, while the Olio Nava Fiat team had two new riders: Graziano Rossi and Marco Lucchinelli. All the Suzuki riders had problems with their new rising-rate suspension systems at the start of the year, and Roberts took full advantage.

Honda also returned late in the season with a much simplified version of their oval-piston NR500 in a conventional steel tube frame engineered by UK specialist Maxton. The NR wasn't the only unconventional bike on the grid. Kawasaki fielded Kork Ballington on a rotary-valve square four housed in an aluminium monococque chassis, the KR500. It was very long, very heavy, but it was reliable.

ABOVE The final showdown: Jon Ekerold and Anton Mang duel on the Nürburgring with no-one else in sight. (*Henk Keulemans*)

RIGHT Jack Middelburg (NED) looking slightly shell-shocked after winnng the 500cc GP at Assen. It was the first of his two wins. (*Henk Keulemans*)

THE 1980 SEASON

500cc

ITA-NAZ/Misano
- Suzuki's Graziano Rossi finished on the podium for the first time in the 500cc class. (His only other podium on a 500cc machine was at the Dutch TT later in the year)

NED/Assen
- Jack Middelburg took his first GP victory at home in Holland, and became the only rider to win on a privateer four-cylinder Yamaha. This was also the last win in the class for a bike using an in-line four-cylinder engine layout

BEL/Zolder
- This was the only time that a Belgian GP was held at any circuit other than Spa-Francorchamps
- Randy Mamola became the youngest rider to win a 500cc race. Since then only three younger riders have won in the premier class: Freddie Spencer, Norick Abe and Dani Pedrosa
- Eighteen-year-old American Freddie Spencer made his GP debut on a private Yamaha tuned by Erv Kanemoto, but was forced to retire after a start-line shunt knocked a fuel line loose

GBR/Silverstone
- French rider Patrick Pons lost his life after crashing and being run over by a following rider

GER/Nürburgring
- Marco Lucchinelli took his first GP win more than four years after finishing on the podium on his 500cc debut
- Kenny Roberts retained his world title by finishing fourth, one place in front of closest challenger Randy Mamola

350cc

GER/Nürburgring
- Jon Ekerold came out on top of a winner-takes-all showdown with Anton Mang.
- Ekerold's winning speed on the Bimota Yamaha would have put him fourth in the 500cc race, in front of Kenny Roberts
- Former World Champion Johnny Cecotto finished third in his last appearance at a Grand Prix event, retiring from motorcycle racing at just 24 years of age

250cc

NED/Assen
- Venezuelan Carlos Lavado won for the first time in the 250cc class riding a Yamaha – the only non-Kawasaki win in the 250cc class in 1980

FIN/Imatra
- Anton Mang won his first world title by finishing second to his closest rival, Kork Ballington

125cc

GBR/Silverstone
- Loris Reggiani (ITA, Minarelli) took his first Grand Prix victory

CZE/Brno
- Pierpaolo Bianchi (MBA) finished in fifth but it was enough to secure his third world title after his closest challenger Angel Nieto (Minarelli) suffered mechanical problems and did not finish the race

50cc

BEL/Zolder
- More than seven years after making his GP debut Stefan Dorflinger (SWI, Kreidler) took his first victory

GER/Nürburgring
- Dorflinger repeated his Belgian win but missed out on the world title by just two points when Eugenio Lazzarini (Iprem) finished second to retain the title

1980 WORLD CHAMPIONSHIP

500cc

Pos	Rider	Nat	Machine	ITA	SPA	FRA	NED	BEL	FIN	GBR	GER	Total
1	Kenny Roberts	USA	Yamaha	15	15	15	-	10	12	12	8	87
2	Randy Mamola	USA	Suzuki	-	10	12	6	15	8	15	6	72
3	Marco Lucchinelli	ITA	Suzuki	-	12	10	-	12	-	10	15	59
4	Franco Uncini	ITA	Suzuki	12	4	-	10	5	10	5	4	50
5	Graziano Rossi	ITA	Suzuki	10	-	8	12	-	-	8	-	38
6	Wil Hartog	NED	Suzuki	-	-	-	-	6	15	-	10	31
7	Johnny Cecotto	VEN	Yamaha	8	5	2	5	-	-	6	5	31
8	Graeme Crosby	NZE	Suzuki	-	-	6	3	8	-	-	12	29
9	Jack Middelburg	NED	Yamaha	-	-	-	15	-	-	2	3	20
10	Takazumi Katayama	JPN	Suzuki	5	8	5	-	-	-	-	-	18
11	Carlo Perugini	ITA	Suzuki	6	1	-	-	4	4	-	2	17
12	Kork Ballington	RSA	Kawasaki	-	-	3	-	-	6	4	-	13
13	Philippe Coulon	SWI	Suzuki	2	3	-	-	-	3	3	-	11
14	Boet van Dulmen	NED	Yamaha	-	-	-	8	2	-	-	-	10
15	Barry Sheene	GBR	Yamaha	4	6	-	-	-	-	-	-	10
16	Patrick Pons	FRA	Yamaha	-	-	1	1	3	5	-	-	10
17	Patrick Fernandez	FRA	Yamaha	-	-	-	4	-	-	-	-	4
17	Michel Rougerie	FRA	Suzuki	-	-	4	-	-	-	-	-	4
19	Christian Estrosi	FRA	Suzuki	3	-	-	-	-	-	-	-	3
20	Sadao Asami	JPN	Yamaha	-	-	-	-	-	2	-	-	2
20	Michel Frutschi	SWI	Yamaha	-	2	-	-	-	-	-	-	2
20	Henk de Vries	NED	Suzuki	-	-	-	2	-	-	-	-	2
23	Bernard Fau	FRA	Suzuki	-	-	-	-	1	-	-	-	1
23	Sergio Pellandini	ITA	Suzuki	1	-	-	-	-	-	-	-	1
23	Dave Potter	GBR	Yamaha	-	-	-	-	-	-	1	-	1
23	Gustav Reiner	GER	Suzuki	-	-	-	-	-	-	-	1	1
23	Raymond Roche	FRA	Yamaha	-	-	-	-	-	1	-	-	1

Scoring system – 15, 12, 10, 8, 6, 5, 4, 3, 2, 1

350cc

Pos	Rider	Nat	Machine	Total
1	Jon Ekerold	RSA	Yamaha	63
2	Anton Mang	GER	Kawasaki	60
3	Jean-François Baldé	FRA	Kawasaki	38
4	Johnny Cecotto	VEN	Yamaha	37
5	Jeff Sayle	AUS	Yamaha	25
6	Eric Saul	FRA	Yamaha	24
7	Jacques Cornu	SWI	Yamaha	21
8	Massimo Matteoni	ITA	Yamaha	19
9	Walter Villa	ITA	Yamaha	16
10	Patrick Fernandez	FRA	Yamaha	12

250cc

Pos	Rider	Nat	Machine	Total
1	Anton Mang	GER	Kawasaki	128
2	Kork Ballington	RSA	Kawasaki	87
3	Jean-François Baldé	FRA	Kawasaki	59
4	Thierry Espie	FRA	Yamaha	53
5	Roland Freymond	SWI	Morbidelli	46
6	Carlos Lavado	VEN	Yamaha	29
7	Gianpaolo Marchetti	ITA	Yamaha/MBA	28
8	Jacques Cornu	SWI	Yamaha	26
9	Eric Saul	FRA	Yamaha	24
10	Patrick Fernandez	FRA	Yamaha	16

125cc

Pos	Rider	Nat	Machine	Total
1	Pierpaolo Bianchi	ITA	MBA	90
2	Guy Bertin	FRA	Motobecane	81
3	Angel Nieto	SPA	Minarelli	78
4	Bruno Kneubuhler	SWI	MBA	68
5	Hans Muller	SWI	MBA	64
6	Loris Reggiani	ITA	Minarelli	63
7	Ivan Palazzese	VEN	MBA	28
8	Maurizio Massimiani	ITA	Minarelli	20
9	Peter Looijensteijn	NED	MBA	18
10	Barry Smith	AUS	MBA	17

50cc

Pos	Rider	Nat	Machine	Total
1	Eugenio Lazzarini	ITA	Kreilder/Iprem	74
2	Stefan Dorflinger	SWI	Kreidler	72
3	Hans Hummel	AUT	Kreidler	37
4	Ricardo Tormo	SPA	Kreidler	36
5	Henk van Kessel	NED	Kreidler	31
6	Hans Spaan	NED	Kreidler	24
7	Theo Timmer	NED	Bultaco	19
8	Yves Dupont	FRA	ABF	18
9	Jacques Hutteau	FRA	ABF	18
10	Wolfgang Muller	GER	Kreidler/Protos	15

THE LAST PRIVATEER CHAMPION

Grand Prix motorcycle racing has changed enormously since 1980. The breakaway World Series never happened, but over the winter of 1979–80 the threat of it achieved a significantly improved deal for riders. However, most of the paddock still travelled in rusty vans, worked out of awnings and relied on appearance and prize money to get to the next race. It was a tough life, and the toughest racer of the lot was South African Jon Ekerold.

Ekerold was an archetypal privateer, riding a 350 Yamaha in a Bimota frame with no help from the factory. There was plenty of opposition from other TZ riders, notably Johnny Cecotto, but the 350 class (and the 250s) had been dominated for the last two seasons by the tandem-twin Kawasakis of Kork Ballington and Gregg Hansford. The South African was double champion in 1978 and 1979, but now he dropped the 350 in favour of the 500, while Aussie Hansford missed all but the last race of the season. Germany's Anton Mang and Frenchman Jean-François Baldé became Kawasaki's main men.

The 350 season turned into a fight between Ekerold and Mang. There were only six rounds, the South African winning the second and third, the German the fourth and fifth, and they went into the last round level on points. That race was on the old 14.19-mile (22.84-km) Nürburgring, in the last year the Nordschleife was used for a Grand Prix. It is difficult to imagine a more dramatic conclusion to a World Championship: put simply, the man who finished first would win the title.

Jon Ekerold blazed to the front from the start, but Mang worked his way into second and the pair pulled away from the pack. It seems incredible now, but they were one-and-a-half minutes in front of third-placed Cecotto at the flag. On the last lap Ekerold risked all, setting a new lap record that would have put him second on the grid for the 500 race, and beating his rival by 1.25s. There has never been a more dramatic or heroic finale to a World Championship.

LEFT Jon Ekerold and all his worldly possessions in the Silverstone pitlane. (*Henk Keulemans*)

1981

Suzuki seized the 500 title back from Yamaha thanks to Marco Lucchinelli and Roberto Gallina's Italian Nava team

Yamaha finally had to admit their across-the-frame four had reached the end of its development life. It had been winning races since 1973 but disc-valve induction was now being used by every other factory in GPs, so Yamaha gave Kenny Roberts a new square four with disc-valves and an aluminium frame, the OW54. It was powerful but underdeveloped and caused Roberts problems both with abrupt power delivery and handling. This was also the last year that Kenny, or anyone else, used Goodyear tyres in GPs. A revised chassis appeared for the French GP, along with a second square four for Barry Sheene from the French round onwards. Barry immediately went well on it and won the last race of the year. There were TZ500s as well, the model J, for privateers, and seven replicas of the 1980 bike complete with aluminium frames for senior men like Sheene, Boet van Dulmen and Christian Sarron, the most successful of whom was Dutch rider van Dulmen, with two third places.

Despite all this effort by Yamaha, it was Suzuki who won the title with their factory bike and Suzuki who supplied the best privateers. Randy Mamola and Graeme Crosby stayed with the Heron team, now with Ingersoll sponsorship, with Japanese test rider Hiroyuki Kawasaki appearing for the first few races. The Italian Nava team had just one rider, Marco Lucchinelli, as did the Dutch squad, who kept Wil Hartog. All were on XR35 square fours with conventional steel chassis. The exception was Mamola who got a square-section aluminium chassis which he raced from the Belgian GP onwards.

Dutch privateer Jack Middelburg gave the RG500 Suzuki what many consider its finest moment when he beat Roberts in a straight fight on the fearsomely fast old Silverstone circuit. Kork Ballington continued with the Kawasaki, which had lost some weight but was still too long and too heavy. He did get it on the rostrum twice, the only top-three finishes the KR500 ever managed. Kawasaki had no such problems in the 350 and 250cc classes where Anton Mang put together a season of utter domination.

ABOVE 'Lucky' Lucchinelli on his way to winning the Finnish GP on the closed roads of Imatra. (*Henk Keulemans*)

RIGHT Anton Mang and Kawasaki on their way to the 250/350 championship double. (*Henk Keulemans*)

THE **1981** SEASON

500cc

AUT/Salzburgring
- Randy Mamola won the opening race of the 500cc title chase in front of team-mate Crosby and Suzuki factory test rider Hiroyuki Kawasaki

GER/Hockenheim
- Kenny Roberts won on the square-four Yamaha for the first time
- After finishing the race in 14th, Wil Hartog decided to retire from GP racing

ITA-NAZ/Monza
- Roberts won for the second successive weekend, on the first GP visit to Monza since the tragic events of 1973

FRA/Paul Ricard
- Marco Lucchinelli took his first win of the year

NED/Assen
- Kork Ballington finished third to give the Kawasaki square-four machine its first podium

RSM/Imola
- Kenny Roberts failed to start the race due to a bout of food poisoning

GBR/Silverstone
- Pole-man Graeme Crosby crashed on the third lap, causing second-fastest qualifier Barry Sheene and World Championship leader Marco Lucchinelli to fall as well
- Jack Middelburg became the last ever true privateer to win in the 500cc class
- Freddie Spencer was aboard the Honda NR500 and got it up to fifth place before suffering mechanical failure

FIN/Imatra
- Marco Lucchinelli won the final 500cc GP race to be held at the Imatra circuit

SWE/Anderstorp
- Barry Sheene scored the last of his 19 race victories in the 500cc class – the last time that a British rider won in the premier class
- Ninth place was enough to give Marco Lucchinelli the world title when his closest challenger, Randy Mamola, failed to score points in a race run in changing weather conditions

350cc

ARG/Buenos Aires
- Jon Ekerold began the defence of his world title by winning the opening race of the year, as GPs returned to Argentina for the first time since 1963

YUG/Rijeka
- Frenchman Michel Rougerie lost his life after crashing on the second lap and being hit by another rider

GBR/Silverstone
- Anton Mang won the race, and with it the 350cc title for the first time
- Mang's closest challenger, Jon Ekerold, was unable to compete at Silverstone due to injuries sustained in a non-championship event

250cc

GER/Hockenheim
- Eddie Lawson (USA) made his Grand Prix debut riding a Kawasaki

ITA-NAZ/Monza
- Eric Saul (Yamaha) crossed the line first but was disqualified for failing to take his place on the grid at the proper time. The disqualification was later overturned, and the Frenchman reinstated as the winner

FIN/Imatra
- Anton Mang clinched his second world title of the year with a comfortable win

CZE/Brno
- Mang made it ten wins in the 250cc class in 1981, to equal the record set by Mike Hailwood in 1966

125cc

YUG/Rijeka
- Loris Reggiani (Minarelli) took his second 125cc GP victory from Pierpaolo Bianchi (MBA), with the riders so close as they crossed the finishing line they were awarded the same time

GBR/Silverstone
- Angel Nieto made it four 125cc championships with a victory at Silverstone, the second time he'd taken the title on a Minarelli

50cc

NED/Assen
- World Championship leader Stefan Dorflinger (Kreidler) crashed out of the race and broke his ankle, ending his title challenge

RSM/Imola
- Ricardo Tormo regained the 50cc world title with his sixth successive GP victory of the season

CZE/Brno
- Theo Timmer gives Bultaco the last of its 26 GP victories

1981 WORLD CHAMPIONSHIP

500cc

Pos	Rider	Nat	Machine	AUT	GER	ITA	FRA	YUG	NED	BEL	RSM	GBR	FIN	SWE	Total
1	Marco Lucchinelli	ITA	Suzuki	-	10	6	15	12	15	15	15	-	15	2	105
2	Randy Mamola	USA	Suzuki	15	12	-	12	15	-	10	8	10	12	-	94
3	Kenny Roberts	USA	Yamaha	-	15	15	6	10	-	12	-	12	4	-	74
4	Barry Sheene	GBR	Yamaha	8	5	12	8	6	-	8	12	-	-	15	72
5	Graeme Crosby	NZE	Suzuki	12	-	10	10	8	-	4	10	-	6	6	68
6	Boet van Dulmen	NED	Yamaha	6	8	8	3	4	12	6	-	5	-	12	64
7	Jack Middelburg	NED	Suzuki	3	3	4	2	-	6	5	4	15	8	10	60
8	Kork Ballington	RSA	Kawasaki	5	-	-	4	-	10	-	6	-	10	8	43
9	Marc Fontan	FRA	Yamaha	-	2	-	1	-	-	3	3	6	5	5	25
10	Hiroyuki Kawasaki	JPN	Suzuki	10	4	-	5	-	-	-	-	-	-	-	19
11	Bernard Fau	FRA	Suzuki	-	-	-	-	-	4	1	-	8	-	1	14
11	Guido Paci	ITA	Yamaha	-	-	5	-	2	2	-	5	-	-	-	14
13	Franco Uncini	ITA	Suzuki	4	1	3	-	-	-	-	-	-	-	4	12
14	Willem Zoet	NED	Suzuki	-	-	-	-	-	8	2	-	-	-	-	10
15	Seppo Rossi	FIN	Suzuki	-	-	-	-	3	-	-	-	-	3	3	9
16	Giovanni Pelletier	ITA	Suzuki	1	-	-	-	5	-	-	2	-	-	-	8
17	Michel Frutschi	SWI	Yamaha	-	6	-	-	-	-	-	-	-	-	-	6
18	Dave Potter	GBR	Yamaha	-	-	-	-	-	5	-	-	-	-	-	5
19	Stu Avant	NZE	Suzuki	-	-	-	-	-	-	-	-	4	-	-	4
20	Sergio Pellandini	SWI	Suzuki	-	-	1	-	-	3	-	-	-	-	-	4
21	Ikujiro Takai	JPN	Yamaha	-	-	-	-	-	-	-	-	3	-	-	3
22	Steve Parrish	GBR	Yamaha	-	-	-	-	-	-	-	-	2	1	-	3
23	Franck Gross	FRA	Suzuki	-	-	-	-	-	-	-	-	-	2	-	2
23	Wil Hartog	NED	Suzuki	2	-	-	-	-	-	-	-	-	-	-	2
23	Christian Sarron	FRA	Yamaha	-	-	2	-	-	-	-	-	-	-	-	2
26	Sadao Asami	JPN	Yamaha	-	-	-	-	-	1	-	-	-	-	-	1
26	Chris Guy	GBR	Suzuki	-	-	-	-	-	-	-	-	1	-	-	1
26	Keith Huewen	GBR	Suzuki	-	-	-	-	-	-	-	1	-	-	-	1
26	Kimmo Kopra	FIN	Suzuki	-	-	-	-	1	-	-	-	-	-	-	1

Scoring system – 15, 12, 10, 8, 6, 5, 4, 3, 2, 1

350cc

Pos	Rider	Nat	Machine	Total
1	Anton Mang	GER	Kawasaki	103
2	Jon Ekerold	RSA	Yamaha	52
3	Jean-François Baldé	FRA	Kawasaki	49
4	Patrick Fernandez	FRA	Yamaha	46
5	Carlos Lavado	VEN	Yamaha	41
6	Keith Huewen	GBR	Yamaha	29
7	Thierry Espie	FRA	Yamaha	24
8	Jacques Cornu	SWI	Yamaha	20
9	Eric Saul	FRA	Yamaha	18
10	Graeme McGregor	AUS	Yamaha	14

250cc

Pos	Rider	Nat	Machine	Total
1	Anton Mang	GER	Kawasaki	160
2	Jean-François Baldé	FRA	Kawasaki	95
3	Roland Freymond	SWI	Ad Majora	72
4	Carlos Lavado	VEN	Yamaha	56
5	Patrick Fernandez	FRA	Yamaha	43
6	Jean-Francois Guignabodet	FRA	Kawasaki	36
7	Jean-Louis Tournadre	FRA	Yamaha	34
8	Martin Wimmer	GER	Yamaha	33
9	Didier de Radigues	BEL	Yamaha	26
10	Richard Schlachter	USA	Yamaha	25

Pos	Rider	Nat	Machine	Total
125cc				
1	Angel Nieto	SPA	Minarelli	140
2	Loris Reggiani	ITA	Minarelli	95
3	Pierpaolo Bianchi	ITA	MBA	84
4	Hans Muller	SWI	MBA	58
5	Jacques Bolle	FRA	Motobecane	55
6	Guy Bertin	FRA	Sanvenero	40
7	Ivan Palazzese	VEN	MBA	37
8	Ricardo Tormo	SPA	Sanvenero	36
9	Maurizio Vitali	ITA	MBA	36
10	Hugo Vignetti	ARG	MBA	30

Pos	Rider	Nat	Machine	Total
50cc				
1	Ricardo Tormo	SPA	Bultaco	90
2	Theo Timmer	NED	Bultaco	65
3	Stefan Dorflinger	SWI	Kreidler	51
4	Hans Hummel	AUT	Sachs	43
5	Hagen Klein	GER	Kreidler	40
6	Rolf Blatter	SWI	Kreidler	39
7	Henk van Kessel	NED	Kreidler	36
8	Giuseppe Ascareggi	ITA	Minarelli	28
9	Claudio Lusuardi	ITA	Villa	23
10	George Looijensteyn	NED	Kreidler	21

THE DUTCH TRIUMVIRATE

Jack Middelburg's win at Silverstone was the last Grand Prix victory of the eight won by a trio of exceptional Dutch riders between 1977 and 1981. Wil Hartog, Boet van Dulmen and Middelburg all won 500cc GPs and were regular winners at internationals all over Europe. And they weren't just popular at home; foreign fans knew that if any of them turned up for one of the regular big-paying meetings then they weren't there just to pick up the start money.

The most successful, with five wins, was Wil Hartog, who was also the only one to be a true works rider. Tall, stylish and instantly recognisable in his white leathers topped with a helmet in national colours, he sparked what amounted to countrywide rejoicing when he became the first Dutchman to win a top-class race at Assen in 1977. Wil was also third in that epic Silverstone confrontation between Sheene and Roberts in 1979. His speech from the rostrum tells us a lot about him: 'The best men won, I could not have any faster gone.'

Van Dulmen's win came in Finland in 1979. All the top men were there – Mamola, Roberts, Sheene, Cecotto – but the Dutch rider beat them using a customer RG500 on a drying track with a narrow dry line. Despite his tough-guy demeanour, van Dulmen was reckoned to be one of the safest and most consistent riders of the era, a fact that may have had something to do with the number of closed-roads circuits on which Dutch riders then began their racing.

Jack Middelburg won two races, yet never received the support his talent deserved. He was always on the brink of retiring, and more than once was kept on track by Dutch fans having a whip round. Twice a triple champion at home (350, 500 and 750cc in 1977 and '78), he was the one of the trio who had a tendency to crash through trying too hard. He knew he had to take risks to be competitive with the factory riders so he did, knowingly and in cold blood. His nickname 'Jumping Jack' came from a succession of unpleasant leg injuries and consequent limp. Middelburg lost his life when he crashed leading a Dutch national championship race on a closed-roads circuit at Tolbert, early in 1984.

BELOW The last true privateer winner of a 500cc GP – Jack Middelburg on his RG500 Suzuki at Silverstone. (*Henk Keulemans*)

1982

Roberto Gallina's Suzuki squad won again, this time with Franco Uncini in the saddle of their RG500

The 1982 season was almost a carbon copy of '81, the only real indication of changing times being the use of two old road circuits, Imatra and Brno, for the last time. The Roberto Gallina-managed Italian Suzuki team put out one rider on a very well-sorted motorcycle, which ran even more perfectly than the previous year, although there was a different colour scheme for their new sponsor and a change of rider. Marco Lucchinelli took his number-one plate and joined Honda's new two-stroke team, leaving Franco Uncini to take advantage of the opposition's disarray. Uncini's team-mate was Loris Reggiani.

The UK-based Suzuki team kept Randy Mamola, but Graeme Crosby was pushed out and joined Giacomo Agostini's new Marlboro Yamaha team alongside Graziano Rossi. Another experienced Italian, Virgino Ferrari, became Mamola's team-mate. Yamaha's much-improved OW60 square four also went to Kenny Roberts (the factory's entry), Barry Sheene and Marc Fontan (FRA). Kawasaki persevered for one final year with their now plate-frame square four, ridden as ever by Kork Ballington.

Honda gave up on their quixotic NR four-stroke and, swallowing corporate pride, came in with a full-on two-stroke effort with three riders: Lucchinelli, Takazumi Katayama and wonder kid Freddie Spencer. The bike was almost as out of step with current practice as the NR – a small, lightweight, reed-valve triple – but it was good enough to be third first time out and first in only its seventh GP.

Roberts, now on Dunlops, switched to Yamaha's V4, the OW61, early in the season. It was far from ready and, by common consent, the worst bike the factory ever built. Yamaha's hopes looked to rest with Sheene, riding as well as he'd ever done. Yamaha were impressed enough to hand him a V4 for the British GP, but the crash that produced the most famous X-ray in the sport ended Sheene's season. Ironically, Roberts's season also ended the same weekend, when he crashed in the first corner of the race. Uncini won to effectively clinch the title, then failed to score another point in the season's remaining three rounds.

ABOVE Franco Uncini leads the man he was to deprive of the number-one plate, Marco Luccinelli, in Sweden. (*Henk Keulemans*)

RIGHT The wreckage of Barry Sheene's V4 Yamaha after his Silverstone crash. (*Henk Keulemans*)

THE **1982** SEASON

500cc

ARG/Buenos Aires
- Freddie Spencer finished third first time out on the three-cylinder two-stroke Honda

AUT/Salzburgring
- Franco Uncini took his first 500cc Grand Prix victory

FRA/Nogaro
- Michel Frutschi (SWI, Sanvenero) won a race that was boycotted by the top riders due to safety reasons and general concerns about the condition of the track and paddock

SPA/Jarama
- Angel Nieto's one and only GP start in the 500cc class was on a Honda
- Kenny Roberts gave the V4 Yamaha its first win

BEL/Spa-Francorchamps
- Freddie Spencer produced Honda's first Grand Prix victory with a two-stroke machine, in the process becoming the youngest rider ever to win in the premier class – a record that he still holds

GBR/Silverstone
- Barry Sheene suffered a huge practice accident that ended his season
- Kenny Roberts crashed at the first corner of the race, suffering injury that kept him out of 1982's remaining GPs

SWE/Anderstorp
- Franco Uncini broke down while leading the race but still became champion; his nearest challengers, Roberts and Sheene, had been sidelined by injuries

GER/Hockenheim
- Randy Mamola won from fellow-Suzuki riders Ferrari and Reggiani – the last all-Suzuki podium in the premier class

250cc

FRA/Nogaro
- Jean-Louis Tournadre (FRA, Yamaha) took his only Grand Prix victory
- As with the 500cc class, this race was boycotted by a number of top riders including Carlos Lavado and Anton Mang

FIN/Imatra
- Christian Sarron took his second GP victory five years after his first win

GER/Hockenheim
- Mang won the final race of the year, but a fourth-place finish for Tournadre was enough to give him the world title by a single point

350cc

FIN/Imatra
- Championship leader Jean-François Baldé (Kawasaki) was unable to start after crashing in the earlier 250cc race and breaking his foot

GER/Hockenheim
- Anton Mang finished second to clinch the final 350cc world title after his closest challenger Didier de Radigues (BEL, Yamaha) suffered mechanical problems and could only finish down in 12th place

125cc

ARG/Buenos Aires
- Angel Nieto won the race to give Garelli their first ever GP victory

SWE/Anderstorp
- Venezuelan Ivan Palazzese (MBA) won his first Grand Prix.
- Sixth place was good enough for Angel Nieto to clinch the 125cc title for the fifth time

50cc

NED/Assen
- Stefan Dorflinger completed a clean sweep of wins in the opening three races of the year
- This was the last of Kreidler's 68 wins in the 50cc class, making them the most successful manufacturer in the smallest class of GP racing

RSM/Mugello
- Dorflinger finished second to Eugenio Lazzarini (Garelli) to clinch his first world title

1982 WORLD CHAMPIONSHIP

500cc

Pos	Rider	Nat	Machine	ARG	AUT	FRA	SPA	ITA	NED	BEL	YUG	GBR	SWE	RSM	GER	Total
1	Franco Uncini	ITA	Suzuki	8	15	-	10	15	15	10	15	15	-	-	-	103
2	Graeme Crosby	NZE	Yamaha	-	8	-	8	10	8	-	12	10	10	10	-	76
3	Freddie Spencer	USA	Honda	10	-	-	-	12	-	15	8	12	-	15	-	72
4	Kenny Roberts	USA	Yamaha	15	10	-	15	8	12	8	-	-	-	-	-	68
5	Barry Sheene	GBR	Yamaha	12	12	-	12	-	10	12	10	-	-	-	-	68
6	Randy Mamola	USA	Suzuki	-	4	-	-	-	6	6	4	6	12	12	15	65
7	Takazumi Katayama	JPN	Honda	5	2	-	5	4	3	-	6	-	15	-	8	48
8	Marco Lucchinelli	ITA	Honda	6	-	-	6	6	-	5	3	-	6	5	6	43
9	Kork Ballington	RSA	Kawasaki	3	-	-	2	5	4	3	1	4	5	4	-	31
10	Marc Fontan	FRA	Yamaha	4	-	-	4	2	2	1	-	3	8	-	5	29
11	Virginio Ferrari	ITA	Suzuki	-	-	-	-	-	-	-	-	5	-	8	12	25
12	Boet van Dulmen	NED	Suzuki	-	6	-	-	-	5	4	-	-	4	-	4	23
13	Loris Reggiani	ITA	Suzuki	1	-	-	-	-	-	-	2	8	-	-	10	21
14	Michel Frutschi	SWI	Sanvenero	-	-	15	-	-	-	2	-	-	-	-	-	17
15	Sergio Pellandini	SWI	Suzuki	-	-	8	-	-	-	-	-	-	2	2	3	15
16	Jack Middelburg	NED	Suzuki	2	-	-	-	-	-	-	5	-	-	6	-	13
17	Franck Gross	FRA	Suzuki	-	-	12	-	-	-	-	-	-	-	-	-	12
18	Steve Parrish	GBR	Yamaha	-	-	10	-	-	-	-	-	-	1	-	-	11
19	Leandro Becheroni	ITA	Suzuki	-	3	-	-	3	-	-	-	2	-	3	-	11
20	Guido Paci	ITA	Yamaha	-	-	5	1	-	-	-	-	-	-	1	-	7
21	Stu Avant	NZE	Suzuki	-	-	6	-	-	-	-	-	-	-	-	-	6
22	Philippe Coulon	SWI	Suzuki	-	-	1	-	-	-	-	-	-	3	-	2	6
23	Seppo Rossi	FIN	Suzuki	-	5	-	-	-	-	-	-	-	-	-	-	5
24	Philippe Robinet	FRA	Suzuki	-	-	4	-	-	-	-	-	-	-	-	-	4
25	Chris Guy	GBR	Suzuki	-	-	3	-	-	-	-	-	1	-	-	-	4
26	Victor Palomo	SPA	Suzuki	-	-	-	3	-	-	-	-	-	-	-	-	3
27	Andreas Hofmann	SWI	Suzuki	-	1	2	-	-	-	-	-	-	-	-	-	3
28	Jon Ekerold	RSA	Cagiva	-	-	-	-	-	-	-	-	-	-	-	1	1
28	Raymond Roche	FRA	Suzuki	-	-	-	-	-	1	-	-	-	-	-	-	1
28	Peter Sjostrom	SWE	Suzuki	-	-	-	-	1	-	-	-	-	-	-	-	1

Scoring system – 15, 12, 10, 8, 6, 5, 4, 3, 2, 1

350cc

Pos	Rider	Nat	Machine	Total
1	Anton Mang	GER	Kawasaki	81
2	Didier de Radigues	BEL	Chevallier	64
3	Jean-François Baldé	FRA	Kawasaki	59
4	Eric Saul	FRA	Chevallier	52
5	Carlos Lavado	VEN	Yamaha	36
6	Alan North	RSA	Yamaha	31
7	Jacques Cornu	SWI	Yamaha	31
8	Christian Sarron	FRA	Yamaha	28
9	Patrick Fernandez	FRA	Yamaha/Bartol	21
10	Gustav Reiner	GER	Yamaha	19

250cc

Pos	Rider	Nat	Machine	Total
1	Jean-Louis Tournadre	FRA	Yamaha	118
2	Anton Mang	GER	Kawasaki	117
3	Roland Freymond	SWI	MBA	72
4	Martin Wimmer	GER	Yamaha	48
5	Carlos Lavado	VEN	Yamaha	39
6	Didier de Radigues	BEL	Yamaha	38
7	Paolo Ferretti	ITA	MBA	34
8	Jean-Louis Guignabodet	FRA	Kawasaki	30
9	Jeff Sayle	AUS	Armstrong	27
10	Christian Sarron	FRA	Yamaha	26

125cc

Pos	Rider	Nat	Machine	Total
1	Angel Nieto	SPA	Garelli	111
2	Eugenio Lazzarini	ITA	Garelli	95
3	Ivan Palazzese	VEN	MBA	75
4	Pierpaolo Bianchi	ITA	Sanvenero	59
5	Ricardo Tormo	SPA	Sanvenero	58
6	August Auinger	AUT	MBA	55
7	Pier Luigi Aldrovandi	ITA	MBA	52
8	Hans Muller	SWI	MBA	49
9	Jean-Claude Selini	FRA	MBA	39
10	Johnny Wickstrom	FIN	MBA	33

50cc

Pos	Rider	Nat	Machine	Total
1	Stefan Dorflinger	SWI	Kreidler	81
2	Eugenio Lazzarini	ITA	Garelli	69
3	Claudio Lusuardi	ITA	Villa	43
4	Ricardo Tormo	SPA	Bultaco	40
5	Giuseppe Ascareggi	ITA	Minarelli	38
6	Hans Hummel	AUT	Sachs	19
7	Theo Timmer	NED	Bultaco	15
8	Massimo de Lorenzi	ITA	Minarelli	14
9	Hans Spaan	NED	Kreidler	12
10	Hagen Klein	GER	Massa-Real	10

GOODBYE TO THE 350S

The final GP of the year, at Hockenheim, also saw the end of the 350cc class, but it was a good day for German fans: Anton Mang had lost his 250 title earlier in the day but retained his 350 crown with a second place. He was beaten by another German, local hero Manfred Herweh, who hadn't scored a Grand Prix point before finishing seventh in the 250cc race earlier that day. There was actually precious little in the way of mourning for the 350cc class – although, of course, there were privateers who lost some earnings potential – because the 250 and 350cc races were now almost indistinguishable from each other. Machinery was identical save for different coloured backgrounds for the racing numbers and a set of slightly bigger-bore cylinders. At Silverstone the race speeds of the two classes differed by less than 0.2mph.

The history of the class shows how GPs changed over time and riders started to specialise as opposed to riding a different bike in every class – the first 500cc World Champion, Les Graham, for instance, rode 125s at the same meetings as he competed with his 500. A rider's choice of class was obviously influenced by the machinery available. Manx Nortons were made as 350s as well as 500s, and if you rode an MV Agusta in the 500 class you also got a 350. This changed considerably from 1976 onwards when privateer riders concentrated on the 500cc class with an RG Suzuki, and the 350cc class was dominated by Yamaha and Kawasaki riders doubling up with the 250cc class. It is interesting to note that from 1976 onwards no rider who finished in the top four of the 500cc championship also finished in the 350cc top four. In every year from 1956 to 1975 at least one of the top four riders in the 500cc class also finished in the top four in the 350cc class, while from 1956 to 1973 the winner of the 500cc title always finished in the top four of the 350cc class.

If there was ever an iconic machine in the 350 class it was surely the three-cylinder MV Agusta that was developed for and by Giacomo Agostini, as is shown in the tables. After the four-stroke era, a 350 became merely an over-bored 250.

350CC STATISTICS: MANUFACTURERS AND GP WINS

Wins	Manufacturer
76	MV Agusta
67	Yamaha
35	Honda
28	Kawasaki
24	Moto Guzzi
20	Norton
10	Velocette
4	AJS
4	Gilera
4	Harley Davidson
4	Jawa
3	Chevallier
1	MZ
1	Yamsel

RIDERS WITH MOST WINS IN THE 350CC CLASS

Riders	Wins
1. Giacomo Agostini	54
2. Jim Redman	21
3. Mike Hailwood	16
4. John Surtees	15
5. Kork Ballington	14

BELOW The greatest rider/machine combination in 350cc history – Giacomo Agostini and the three-cylinder MV Agusta. (*Elwyn Roberts Collection*)

1983

American riders filled the top-four places of the 500cc championship on three different makes of motorcycle

This pivotal year saw the balance of power shifting decisively away from Suzuki and the American invasion gathering momentum. Suzuki's RG500 was reaching the end of its development, with only Randy Mamola getting on the rostrum. Mamola and reigning World Champion Franco Uncini were the factory riders, although they were run by different teams; customers, including Barry Sheene, back after three years on a Yamaha, had a miserable time.

The privateers who could afford it were turning to Honda RS500s, over-the-counter versions of the factory's NS500 triple – now sporting ATAC, Honda's variable-geometry exhaust-port system. There were four factory bikes: Freddie Spencer, Takazumi Katayama and Marco Lucchinelli all returned, and were joined by British racer Ron Haslam.

Yamaha's new OW70 was the first generation of the line of V4s that would go on to dominate the 500cc class right up until the advent of MotoGP. The disc-valve motor was housed in an aluminium chassis that was obviously not the conventional double cradle that a Manx Norton rider would have recognised. Fabricated spars ran either side of the top of the motor in a straight line from steering head to swingarm pivot with vestigial frame members running to engine mountings. Ohlins suspension was used for the first time. Kenny Roberts was joined by Eddie Lawson (USA). Marlboro sponsorship moved from Agostini's team, which folded and Ago became the team's figurehead.

Aluminium frames were now ubiquitous. Honda and Suzuki ran Michelin tyres; the factory Yamahas stuck with Dunlop.

It was a year of epic confrontation between Roberts and Spencer, the battle effectively decided at the penultimate round in Sweden when the Honda rider went inside Roberts at the end of the back straight. Both men ran off track but Spencer regained it much more quickly and won. All Freddie had to do at the last round was follow Kenny home to be champion. Roberts won the race – his last – but Spencer won the crown. That passing manoeuvre in Sweden is still a matter of dispute.

ABOVE Freddie Spencer and Kenny Roberts moments before the start of their final showdown in Sweden. (*Henk Keulemans*)

RIGHT Kenny and Freddie stayed civil. Roberts later admitted he'd underestimated his rival. (*Henk Keulemans*)

THE 1983 SEASON

500cc

RSA/Kyalami
- Freddie Spencer won the opening race of the championship – the first Grand Prix event to be held on the African continent
- Eddie Lawson finished eighth on his debut in a 500cc GP

FRA/Le Mans
- Michel Frutschi (Honda), the winner of the boycotted French GP in 1982, died from injuries suffered in a crash on lap six
- Freddie Spencer was followed home by team-mates Marco Lucchinelli and Ron Haslam – the first ever all Honda podium in the 500cc class

ITA-NAZ/Monza
- Spencer won from Randy Mamola and Eddie Lawson (his first rostrum finish) to make it the first all-American 500cc GP podium

AUT/Salzburgring
- Reigning 350cc champion Anton Mang made his first race appearance of the year after missing the early races due to a skiing injury

NED/Assen
- Reigning World Champion Franco Uncini suffered injuries that ended his season when he crashed on lap two and was hit by rookie GP rider Wayne Gardner (AUS, Honda)

GBR/Silverstone
- The race was run in two parts, the first stopped due to an accident in which both '82 Senior TT winner Norman Brown (GBR) and Peter Huber (SWI) lost their lives

SWE/Anderstorp
- Freddie Spencer took victory after a race-long battle with Kenny Roberts that climaxed on the last lap when both riders ran off the track while fighting for the win

RSM/Imola
- Spencer became the youngest ever 500cc World Champion when he finished second behind his closest rival Roberts and just two points ahead of him in the final table
- Kenny Roberts was the winner on his last appearance in a 500cc Grand Prix

250cc

FRA/Le Mans
- After qualifying down in 31st place on the grid, 18-year-old Alan Carter (GBR, Yamaha) became the youngest GP winner in any class, holding the record as youngest 250cc victor until 2004 when Dani Pedrosa took the record

AUT/Salzburgring
- A first 250cc GP win for German Manfred Herweh, riding a Real with a Rotax engine. The race was run in two parts after being stopped due to rain

GBR/Silverstone
- Jacques Bolle (FRA) gave the Pernod machine its single win in GPs in a race where just 0.4s covered the first five riders across the line – the closest top five of all time in the 250cc class
- Carlos Lavado (Yamaha) finished fourth to take his first 250cc world title

125cc

BEL/Spa-Francorchamps
- Ex-World Champion Eugenio Lazzarini (Garelli) took his only win of the year in the 125cc class – the last of his 27 GP victories

GBR/Silverstone
- Angel Nieto clinched his sixth world title (and his third for Garelli) in the 125cc class

50cc

RSM/Imola
- Stefan Dorflinger finished second to retain the world title for Kreidler, and became the last ever 50cc World Champion
- Ricardo Tormo (Garelli) took the last of his 19 Grand Prix wins in the final 50cc championship race

YOUNGEST RIDERS TO WIN A MOTOGP/500CC GRAND PRIX

	Rider	Age	Race
1	Freddie Spencer	20 years 196 days	BEL/Spa-Francorchamps/1982
2	Norick Abe	20 years 227 days	JPN/Suzuka/1996
2	Dani Pedrosa	20 years 227 days	CHN/Shanghai/2006
4	Randy Mamola	20 years 239 days	BEL/Zolder/1980
5	Jorge Lorenzo	20 years 345 days	POR/Estoril/2008
6	Mike Hailwood	21 years 75 days	GBR/Isle of Man TT/1961
7	Valentino Rossi	21 years 144 days	GBR/Donington/2000
8	Casey Stoner	21 years 145 days	QAT/Losail/2007
9	Johnny Cecotto	21 years 187 days	FIN/Imatra/1977
10	Jorge Kissling	21 years 219 days	ARG/Buenos Aires/1961

1983 WORLD CHAMPIONSHIP

500cc

Pos	Rider	Nat	Machine	RSA	FRA	ITA	GER	SPA	AUT	YUG	NED	BEL	GBR	SWE	RSM	Total
1	Freddie Spencer	USA	Honda	15	15	15	8	15	-	15	10	12	12	15	12	144
2	Kenny Roberts	USA	Yamaha	12	8	-	15	12	15	8	15	15	15	12	15	142
3	Randy Mamola	USA	Suzuki	6	-	12	3	8	10	12	8	10	10	4	6	89
4	Eddie Lawson	USA	Yamaha	3	-	10	2	5	12	10	6	6	8	6	10	78
5	Takazumi Katayama	JPN	Honda	-	-	6	12	10	8	6	12	8	5	10	-	77
6	Marc Fontan	FRA	Yamaha	8	5	4	5	4	5	5	4	5	6	8	5	64
7	Marco Lucchinelli	ITA	Honda	2	12	1	10	-	4	2	-	4	-	5	8	48
8	Ron Haslam	GBR	Honda	10	10	-	-	-	-	-	-	3	4	2	2	31
9	Franco Uncini	ITA	Suzuki	5	-	8	6	6	6	-	-	-	-	-	-	31
10	Raymond Roche	FRA	Honda	4	-	5	4	-	-	-	2	-	-	3	4	22
11	Boet van Dulmen	NED	Suzuki	-	-	-	1	-	1	4	3	2	3	-	3	17
12	Jack Middelburg	NED	Honda	-	1	-	-	3	3	-	5	-	-	-	-	12
13	Sergio Pellandini	SWI	Suzuki	-	2	3	-	2	2	1	-	1	-	-	-	11
14	Barry Sheene	GBR	Suzuki	1	4	2	-	-	-	-	-	-	2	-	-	9
15	Keith Huewen	GBR	Suzuki	-	6	-	-	1	-	-	-	-	-	-	-	7
16	Guido Paci	ITA	Honda	-	3	-	-	-	-	-	-	-	-	-	-	3
16	Giovanni Pelletier	ITA	Honda	-	-	-	-	-	-	3	-	-	-	-	-	3
18	Anton Mang	GER	Suzuki	-	-	-	-	-	-	-	-	-	-	1	1	2
19	Paul Lewis	AUS	Suzuki	-	-	-	-	-	-	-	-	-	1	-	-	1
19	Mark Salle	GBR	Suzuki	-	-	-	-	-	-	-	1	-	-	-	-	1

Scoring system – 15, 12, 10, 8, 6, 5, 4, 3, 2, 1

250cc

Pos	Rider	Nat	Machine	Total
1	Carlos Lavado	VEN	Yamaha	100
2	Christian Sarron	FRA	Yamaha	73
3	Didier de Radigues	BEL	Chevallier	68
4	Herve Guilleux	FRA	Kawasaki	63
5	Thierry Espie	FRA	Chevallier	55
6	Martin Wimmer	GER	Yamaha	45
7	Manfred Herweh	GER	Real	40
8	Jean-François Baldé	FRA	Chevallier	32
9	Jacques Cornu	SWI	Yamaha	32
10	Jacques Bolle	FRA	Yamaha/Pernod	26

125cc

Pos	Rider	Nat	Machine	Total
1	Angel Nieto	SPA	Garelli	102
2	Bruno Kneubuhler	SWI	MBA	76
3	Eugenio Lazzarini	ITA	Garelli	67
4	Maurizio Vitali	ITA	MBA	59
5	Ricardo Tormo	SPA	MBA	52
6	Hans Muller	SWI	MBA	43
7	Johnny Wickstrom	FIN	MBA	42
8	Pierpaolo Bianchi	ITA	Sanvenero	40
9	Fausto Gresini	ITA	MBA/Garelli	37
10	August Auinger	AUT	MBA	30

50cc

Pos	Rider	Nat	Machine	Total
1	Stefan Dorflinger	SWI	Kreidler	81
2	Eugenio Lazzarini	ITA	Garelli	69
3	Claudio Lusuardi	ITA	Villa	38
4	Hans Spaan	NED	Kreidler	34
5	George Looijesteijn	NED	Kreidler	34
6	Hagen Klein	GER	FKN	33
7	Ricardo Tormo	SPA	Garelli	25
8	Reiner Kunz	GER	FKN	21
9	Gerhard Bauer	GER	Ziegler	20
10	Reiner Scheidhauer	GER	Kreidler	17
10	Theo Timmer	NED	Bultaco/Casal	17

TRIPLE CROWN

Honda won their first 500cc title with a motorcycle that was smaller, lighter and less powerful than the opposition. Yamaha's V4 was bigger and faster but turned slowly in comparison and it ate rear tyres. Roberts wasn't beaten just by Spencer's unexpected streak of ruthlessness in Sweden; he was beaten by a more usable motorcycle. It had happened before, when the Manx Norton and other British singles beat the four-cylinder Gileras in the late 1940s and early '50s, but once Gilera's engineers added some handling and suspension refinements to their massive power outputs the singles were lucky to finish on the same lap. There was, however, a narrow time window in which the more usable bike could triumph.

This was true for the NS500 in 1983, but it needed the genius of Freddie Spencer to take that advantage. The other Honda riders ended the season fifth, seventh and eighth respectively. The NS and RS triples would continue to win GPs, but not another title. Chassis and suspension advances and the development of the radial tyre helped tame the V4s but, as the boxing saying goes, a good big 'un will always beat a good little 'un.

However, when Kenny Roberts became a constructor the bike he built was a triple, designed to take advantage of the lower minimum weight limit compared to that for four-cylinder machines. Kenny's triples could do comparable lap times to the V4s on a clear racetrack, although they had to carry a lot more pace in the corners to make up for their significantly inferior acceleration and top speeds. If they lost momentum, usually by being baulked by a V4 in a corner, they didn't have the punch out of corners to keep up with the competition. Honda tried the same formula with their V-twin 500, as did Aprilia. There was the occasional pole position or rostrum, but none of them ever won a race. The finest moment for the little bikes was probably Donington Park in 1997, when Brazilian Alex Barros put a customer Honda NSR500V on the rostrum.

LEFT There wasn't much eye contact on the Anderstorp rostrum. (*Henk Keulemans*)

BELOW The last champion of the 50cc class – Stefan Dorflinger (SWI) and the Kreidler. (*Henk Keulemans*)

1984

Eddie Lawson took his first world title for Yamaha as Honda got their first V4 design badly wrong

Kenny Roberts stopped riding and started managing, fronting the 250cc Yamaha team of Wayne Rainey (USA) and Britain's Alan Carter. Yamaha's men in the 500cc class were Eddie Lawson and Virginio Ferrari; the American got the new reed-valve OW76, a bike recognisable in every way as a modern racing machine. The French Yamaha importer pulled its team from 500s to concentrate on Christian Sarron's successful attack on the 250 title.

Honda gave champion Freddie Spencer their take on the V4, the first NSR500, the bike that became known as the 'upside down' V4. They too went the reed-valve V4 route with an aluminium frame, but located the petrol tank under the engine and ran the pipes over the top. This fitted cleverly with the contemporary wisdom that a low centre of gravity was the route to quick handling. It wasn't. By the end of the season it was realised that its mass centralisation low polar moments of inertia were the critical properties. The NSR was so unwieldy that Spencer got his triple out of mothballs for two races. It wasn't the bike that lost him the title, though, but missing five races through injury. Only Spencer got the NSR. The other Honda riders were on triples, Ron Haslam the factory rider on an NS, while Takazumi Katayama missed most of the season through injury. The stand-out customer bike rider was Raymond Roche (FRA), who got some factory support later in the year in an attempt to stop Lawson's march to the title.

Suzuki riders were headed by Barry Sheene, but the factory had ceased development of the RG500 so Sheene had an old Mamola motor put in a chassis built by Harris Performance. Barry was the only Suzuki rider to get on the rostrum all season – in South Africa, in the wet. Having proved the people who said he was past it conclusively wrong, Barry retired from bike racing at the end of the year.

Randy Mamola failed to agree terms with Suzuki and sat out the first two races of the year until he got a deal from Honda. He then won three races, one of them on the absent Spencer's NSR, to finish second in the championship for the third time in five years.

ABOVE Eddie Lawson's Yamaha leads Randy Mamola's Honda; they finished first and second in the championship. (*Henk Keulemans*)

RIGHT Lawson dominated the season with his trademark ruthless efficiency. (*Henk Keulemans*)

THE 1984 SEASON

500cc

RSA/Kyalami

- Reigning World Champion (and pole-position qualifier) Freddie Spencer missed the race due to injuries suffered in a practice crash caused by the rear wheel of his Honda collapsing
- Eddie Lawson won his first Grand Prix
- Barry Sheene finished on the podium for the last time in his career and also set the fastest lap of the race while moving through the field after a bad start

ITA-NAZ/Misano

- Freddie Spencer gave the V4 Honda NSR500 its first GP victory

SPA/Jarama

- Spencer missed the race after suffering injuries in a non-championship outing at Donington
- Randy Mamola finished second on his first appearance of the year, riding a Honda

GER/Nürburgring

- After the first day of practice Spencer reverted to the three-cylinder machine from 1983 to set pole and win the race

NED/Assen

- Freddie Spencer retired from the race with mechanical problems while leading
- Randy Mamola won for the first time on the three-cylinder Honda following a tremendous battle with similarly mounted Raymond Roche

BEL/Spa-Francorchamps

- Spencer won on his final appearance of the year – he was injured in a non-championship race at Laguna Seca before the next GP and sat out the rest of the season

GBR/Silverstone

- Randy Mamola won first time out on the V4 Honda

SWE/Anderstorp

- Eddie Lawson won and took his first world title

RSM/Mugello

- Barry Sheene retired on lap ten – his final appearance in a Grand Prix

250cc

ITA-NAZ/Misano

- Wayne Rainey finished on the podium in only his second GP start, riding for Kenny Roberts's Yamaha team

SPA/Jarama

- Sito Pons (Honda) had his first Grand Prix win at home in Spain

AUT/Salzburgring

- Christian Sarron took his first victory of the year and the lead in the championship

FRA/Paul Ricard

- Anton Mang's sole win of 1984 – and the only one of his 42 victories on a Yamaha

SWE/Anderstorp

- German Manfred Herweh (Rotax) won the race, which featured the closest 250cc top ten of all time, just 12.57s covering the ten riders
- Second place behind closest challenger Herweh was enough to give Christian Sarron the world title

125cc

GBR/Silverstone

- Angel Nieto (Garelli) made it six victories from six races to take his 13th and last world title

SWE/Anderstorp

- Fausto Gresini (ITA, Garelli) had his first Grand Prix win

80cc

ITA-NAZ/Misano

- Italian Pierpaolo Bianchi (Casal) had the honour of winning the first 80cc Grand Prix race
- This was the last GP start for ex-World Champion Ricardo Tormo, whose career was ended before the next race when he suffered a serious accident while testing the Derbi factory bike on public roads

AUT/Salzburgring

- Stefan Dorflinger gave Zundapp their first Grand Prix victory

NED/Assen

- Jorge 'Aspar' Martinez (SPA, Derbi) took his first Grand Prix win

RSM/Mugello

- Stefan Dorflinger's fifth place was enough to secure the first 80cc World Championship title

1984 WORLD CHAMPIONSHIP

500cc

Pos	Rider	Nat	Machine	RSA	ITA	SPA	AUT	GER	FRA	YUG	NED	BEL	GBR	SWE	RSM	Total
1	Eddie Lawson	USA	Yamaha	15	12	15	15	12	12	8	10	8	12	15	8	142
2	Randy Mamola	USA	Honda	-	-	12	10	10	10	12	15	12	15	-	15	111
3	Raymond Roche	FRA	Honda	12	10	10	5	6	-	10	12	10	-	12	12	99
4	Freddie Spencer	USA	Honda	-	15	-	12	15	15	15	-	15	-	-	-	87
5	Ron Haslam	GBR	Honda	-	5	8	8	8	8	6	8	6	10	-	10	77
6	Barry Sheene	GBR	Suzuki	10	-	4	1	1	6	4	-	2	6	-	-	34
7	Wayne Gardner	AUS	Honda	-	8	-	-	-	-	-	6	4	5	10	-	33
8	Boet van Dulmen	NED	Suzuki	4	4	6	3	2	-	-	-	-	-	4	2	25
9	Didier de Radigues	BEL	Chevallier	8	-	-	-	-	5	5	-	-	-	-	6	24
10	Virginio Ferrari	ITA	Yamaha	-	3	-	-	4	-	2	-	-	8	5	-	22
11	Rob McElnea	GBR	Suzuki	-	-	-	6	-	-	-	-	-	4	6	5	21
12	Sergio Pellandini	SWI	Suzuki	6	-	-	2	-	2	3	-	3	-	-	-	16
13	Takazumi Katayama	JPN	Honda	-	-	-	-	-	-	-	3	-	3	8	-	14
14	Franco Uncini	ITA	Suzuki	-	6	-	-	5	-	-	-	-	-	-	3	14
15	Reinhold Roth	GER	Honda	-	2	3	4	-	3	-	2	-	-	-	-	14
16	Tadahiko Taira	JPN	Yamaha	-	-	-	-	-	-	-	5	5	-	-	-	10
17	Massimo Broccoli	ITA	Honda	5	1	-	-	-	4	-	-	-	-	-	-	10
17	Gustav Reiner	GER	Honda	-	-	5	-	-	-	-	4	1	-	-	-	10
19	Keith Huewen	GBR	Honda	-	-	1	-	3	-	-	-	-	-	2	-	6
20	Leandro Becheroni	ITA	Suzuki	-	-	-	-	-	-	-	-	-	-	-	4	4
21	Christian le Liard	FRA	Chevallier	3	-	-	-	-	-	-	-	-	1	-	-	4
21	Wolfgang von Muralt	SWI	Suzuki	-	-	-	-	-	1	-	-	-	-	3	-	4
23	Fabio Biliotti	ITA	Honda	-	-	2	-	-	-	-	-	-	-	-	-	2
23	Chris Guy	GBR	Honda	2	-	-	-	-	-	-	-	-	-	-	-	2
23	Roger Marshall	GBR	Honda	-	-	-	-	-	-	-	-	-	2	-	-	2
26	Eero Hyvarinen	FIN	Suzuki	-	-	-	-	-	-	-	1	-	-	1	-	2
27	Armando Errico	ITA	Suzuki	-	-	-	-	-	-	-	-	-	-	-	1	1
27	Brett Hudson	RSA	Suzuki	1	-	-	-	-	-	-	-	-	-	-	-	1
27	Herve Moineau	FRA	Cagiva	-	-	-	-	-	-	1	-	-	-	-	-	1

Scoring system – 15, 12, 10, 8, 6, 5, 4, 3, 2, 1

250cc

Pos	Rider	Nat	Machine	Total
1	Christian Sarron	FRA	Yamaha	109
2	Manfred Herweh	GER	Rotax	100
3	Carlos Lavado	VEN	Yamaha	77
4	Sito Pons	SPA	Kobas	66
5	Anton Mang	GER	Yamaha	61
6	Jacques Cornu	SWI	Yamaha	60
7	Martin Wimmer	GER	Yamaha	47
8	Wayne Rainey	USA	Yamaha	29
9	Alan Carter	GBR	Yamaha	25
10	Jean-François Baldé	FRA	Pernod	25

125cc

Pos	Rider	Nat	Machine	Total
1	Angel Nieto	SPA	Garelli	90
2	Eugenio Lazzarini	ITA	Garelli	78
3	Fausto Gresini	ITA	MBA/Garelli	51
4	Maurizio Vitali	ITA	MBA	45
5	August Auinger	AUT	MBA	41
6	Jean-Claude Selini	FRA	MBA	33
7	Stefano Caracchi	ITA	MBA	29
8	Luca Cadalora	ITA	MBA	27
9	Hans Muller	SWI	MBA	27
10	Bruno Kneubuhler	SWI	MBA	27

80cc

Pos	Rider	Nat	Machine	Total
1	Stefan Dorflinger	SWI	Zundapp	82
2	Hubert Abold	GER	Zundapp	75
3	Pierpaolo Bianchi	ITA	Casal	68
4	Jorge Martinez	SPA	Derbi	62
5	Gerhard Waibel	GER	Real	61
6	Hans Spaan	NED	Kreidler	47
7	Willem Heykoop	NED	Casal	29
8	Hans Muller	SWI	Sachs	18
9	George Looijesteijn	NED	Casal	16
10	Theo Timmer	NED	Casal	13

LEFT Evolution of the 500cc class gave us this: the two-stroke V4 with crankcase reed-valve induction in a twin-spar aluminium chassis. (*Henk Keulemans*)

RIGHT The view the rest got of Lawson. (*Henk Keulemans*)

THE BLUEPRINT

This was the year the design of the machine that dominated the rest of the 500cc formula's time was finalised. A V4 has obvious advantages compared to an in-line four – low frontal area, reduced width, shorter and therefore stiffer crankshaft(s) – but it had to wait for water cooling to be practicable. That overcame problems due to the front pair of cylinders masking the rear two. Designers could now site all the carburettors in the V between the cylinder pairs and feed them from one airbox. Packaging the exhausts was also easier.

Everyone except Suzuki was now using reed-valve induction and aluminium twin-spar frames. Early use of the lightweight metal tended to replicate steel designs, usually with disastrous results. It was Spanish engineer Antonio Cobas who found the solution. He looked to the aerospace industry, specifically the use of aluminium fabrications in the wing spars of airliners, and came up with a box-section U-shaped chassis. The closed end of the U held the steering head, the open ends embraced the swingarm pivot. Extra strength was imparted to the arms of the U by large-diameter, thin-walled tubular inserts running across each one – just like the load-bearing members of an airframe. The factories replaced Cobas's sheet-metal fabrications with extrusions and castings but the principle remained the same.

The only significant difference between Honda and the rest was that HRC, as averse to internal friction as ever, went with a single crankshaft as opposed to the twin-crank layouts of Yamaha and Suzuki. From now until the end of the 500cc formula the reed-valve V4 two-stroke in what Yamaha christened the Deltabox chassis with rising-rate linkage rear suspension would dominate GPs.

Seventeen-inch wheels were now used on all the fours – Dunlop tyres on Yamaha, Michelin on the others – and the final part of the jigsaw was the Michelin radial tyre. Spencer was the first to win with a rear radial, Mamola the first with radials front and rear.

1985

Freddie Spencer doubled up in the 500 and 250cc classes, a unique achievement in the modern era

This time Honda built their V4 NSR500 with the petrol tank in the normal place. It worked and worked well. There was only one of them, for Freddie Spencer, with again a squadron of triples for Randy Mamola, Ron Haslam and Aussie Wayne Gardner. Wayne had ridden a few GPs in 1984, in between his British Championship commitments, but he now became a full-time Grand Prix rider. Like Haslam, he used Dunlops while Mamola and Spencer were on Michelin radials. This was the first year that Rothmans sponsored factory Hondas in both the 500 and 250 classes. Belgian rider Didier de Radigues also got a works NS triple run under the banner of the Elf team.

Yamaha retained Eddie Lawson and brought in Raymond Roche as his team-mate in the factory set-up. However, the tough man from Toulon, who had terrorised the factory bikes on an RS Honda the previous season on his way to third overall, had a dreadful year after crashing out of two of the first four races. To add insult to injury, his fellow-countryman and reigning 250 World Champion Christian Sarron also got a Yamaha V4, entered by the French Yamaha importer Sonauto, on which he not only finished third overall but won a race. The Yamaha, now called the OW81, was little changed, the most significant difference from '84 being the switch to Michelin tyres as the French company's radials now became standard fitment front (16in) and rear (17in).

Suzuki tried one more time with RG500s for Roberto Gallina's team, ridden by Franco Uncini and Sito Pons. The company's UK importer, Heron, tried a different approach with the now outgunned RG500. They housed their square-four motor in a composite chassis for Rob McElnea (GBR). However, it wasn't the most radical bike on the grid – that accolade belonged to the Elf2, which used a Honda triple motor with a swingarm bolted on either end. It looked like no motorcycle ever seen before – no telescopic forks, no frame in the conventional sense of the word – and was ridden at the start of the year by Christian le Liard (FRA) and then by Pierre-Etienne Samin (FRA).

ABOVE Spencer on the 500 V4 rides around the outside of Freddie Spencer on the 250 V-twin. (*Henk Keulemans*)

RIGHT Spencer with his race engineer and strong right hand, Erv Kanemoto. (*Henk Keulemans*)

THE **1985** SEASON

500cc

GER/Hockenheim

- Reigning 250cc champion Christian Sarron took his one and only 500cc victory, the first French victory in the class since Pierre Monneret (Gilera) won the 1954 French GP at Reims

ITA-NAZ/Mugello

- Freddie Spencer became the first rider since Jarno Saarinen in 1973 to win both the 250 and 500cc GP races on the same day

AUT/Salzburgring

- Spencer beat Eddie Lawson by just 0.03s in a two-part race that was interrupted by rain

NED/Assen

- Freddie Spencer was knocked off by Christian Sarron on the first lap, and the race was won in wet conditions by Randy Mamola – the final victory in the 500cc class by a three-cylinder machine

FRA/Le Mans

- Spencer achieved his fourth 250/500cc double of the year, the last occasion on which a rider won both races on the same day

SWE/Anderstorp

- Freddie Spencer started from pole for the ninth successive race and won from closest rival Eddie Lawson to clinch the 500cc title for the second time
- This was the last time Spencer finished a race on the podium

250cc

RSA/Kyalami

- Freddie Spencer won first time out in the 250cc class, giving Honda its first win in the class with a two-stroke machine

AUT/Salzburgring

- Spencer took the win from Anton Mang and Fausto Ricci (ITA), the first all-Honda podium in the 250cc class since the Ulster GP of 1962

GBR/Silverstone

- Freddie Spencer finished fourth to clinch the world title. He did not compete again in the 250cc class
- Anton Mang, Spencer's closest challenger, won from Reinhold Roth (Romer) and Manfred Herweh (Real) – the last time that all three podium places in a GP race have been occupied by German riders
- Mang's victory made him the only rider to have won in the 250cc class on machines from three different Japanese manufacturers (Kawasaki, Yamaha and Honda)

125cc

SPA/Jarama

- Pierpaolo Bianchi (MBA) won the first race of the year and led the World Championship until the final round

RSM/Misano

- Starting the final race of the year with a five-point deficit, Fausto Gresini (Garelli) took his first world title, winning after Bianchi suffered mechanical failure in the closing stages of the race while lying second

80cc

GER/Hockenheim

- Stefan Dorflinger gave Krauser their first Grand Prix victory

FRA/Le Mans

- Angel Nieto (Derbi) took the last of his 90 Grand Prix victories, 16 years after his first win
- Dorflinger's second-place finish was enough to clinch his fourth successive title in the smallest class of GP racing

1985 WORLD CHAMPIONSHIP

500cc

Pos	Rider	Nat	Machine	RSA	SPA	GER	ITA	AUT	YUG	NED	BEL	FRA	GBR	SWE	RSM	Total
1	Freddie Spencer	USA	Honda	12	15	12	15	15	12	-	15	15	15	15	-	141
2	Eddie Lawson	USA	Yamaha	15	12	8	12	12	15	-	12	8	12	12	15	133
3	Christian Sarron	FRA	Yamaha	5	10	15	6	10	6	-	10	-	10	8	-	80
4	Wayne Gardner	AUS	Honda	10	8	5	10	-	10	10	8	-	-	-	12	73
5	Ron Haslam	GBR	Honda	8	3	10	5	-	8	12	5	6	-	10	6	73
6	Randy Mamola	USA	Honda	6	-	3	8	8	-	15	-	10	6	6	10	72
7	Raymond Roche	FRA	Yamaha	-	6	-	4	1	5	-	6	12	5	3	8	50
8	Didier de Radigues	BEL	Honda	4	5	6	1	5	4	5	4	-	8	5	-	47
9	Rob McElnea	GBR	Suzuki	-	-	4	2	6	3	4	-	-	-	-	1	20
10	Boet van Dulmen	NED	Honda	-	-	1	-	3	-	8	2	-	4	-	-	18
11	Mike Baldwin	USA	Honda	2	4	-	-	4	-	-	-	1	-	4	3	18
12	Pierre-Etienne Samin	FRA	Honda	-	-	-	-	-	-	6	-	5	-	-	-	11
13	Sito Pons	SPA	Suzuki	3	2	2	-	-	-	-	-	4	-	-	-	11
14	Gustav Reiner	GER	Honda	-	-	-	-	-	2	-	1	3	-	-	4	10
15	Franco Uncini	ITA	Suzuki	-	-	-	3	-	-	-	-	-	-	-	5	8
16	Fabio Biliotti	ITA	Honda	-	1	-	-	-	-	-	-	2	-	-	2	5
17	Roger Burnett	GBR	Honda	-	-	-	-	-	-	-	-	-	3	-	-	3
17	Takazumi Katayama	JPN	Honda	-	-	1	-	-	-	-	3	-	-	-	-	3
17	Mile Pajic	NED	Honda	-	-	-	-	-	-	3	-	-	-	-	-	3
20	Thierry Espie	FRA	Chevallier	1	-	-	-	-	-	-	-	-	-	2	-	3
21	Neil Robinson	GBR	Suzuki	-	-	-	-	-	-	-	-	-	2	-	-	2
21	Tadahiko Taira	JPN	Yamaha	-	-	-	-	2	-	-	-	-	-	-	-	2
21	Henk van der Mark	NED	Honda	-	-	-	-	-	-	2	-	-	-	-	-	2
24	Paul Lewis	AUS	Honda	-	-	-	-	-	-	-	-	-	1	-	-	1
24	Massimo Messere	ITA	Suzuki	-	-	-	-	-	-	-	-	-	-	1	-	1
24	Dave Petersen	ZIM	Honda	-	-	-	-	-	1	-	-	-	-	-	-	1
24	Rob Punt	NED	Suzuki	-	-	-	-	-	-	1	-	-	-	-	-	1

Scoring system – 15, 12, 10, 8, 6, 5, 4, 3, 2, 1

250cc

Pos	Rider	Nat	Machine	Total
1	Freddie Spencer	USA	Honda	127
2	Anton Mang	GER	Honda	124
3	Carlos Lavado	VEN	Yamaha	94
4	Martin Wimmer	GER	Yamaha	69
5	Fausto Ricci	ITA	Honda	50
6	Loris Reggiani	ITA	Aprilia	44
7	Alan Carter	GBR	Honda	32
8	Manfred Herweh	GER	Rotax	31
9	Reinhold Roth	GER	Yamaha	29
10	Jacques Cornu	SWI	Honda	25

125cc

Pos	Rider	Nat	Machine	Total
1	Fausto Gresini	ITA	Garelli	109
2	Pierpaolo Bianchi	ITA	MBA	99
3	August Auinger	AUT	MBA	78
4	Ezio Gianola	ITA	Garelli	77
5	Bruno Kneubuhler	SWI	LCR	58
6	Domenico Brigaglia	ITA	MBA	45
7	Jean-Claude Selini	FRA	MBA	36
8	Jussi Hautaniemi	FIN	MBA	26
9	Lucio Pietroniro	BEL	MBA	25
10	Olivier Liegeois	BEL	KLS	23

80cc

Pos	Rider	Nat	Machine	Total
1	Stefan Dorflinger	SWI	Krauser	86
2	Jorge Martinez	SPA	Derbi	67
3	Gerd Kafka	AUT	Seel	48
4	Manuel Herreros	SPA	Derbi	45
5	Gerhard Waibel	GER	Seel	35
6	Ian McConnachie	GBR	Krauser	33
7	Theo Timmer	NED	Huvo	21
8	Henk van Kessel	NED	Huvo	18
9	Angel Nieto	SPA	Derbi	15
10	Paul Rimmelzwaan	NED	Harmsen	15

OPPOSITE Randy Mamola (2) leads the 500s off the grid at Spa with Gardner (7) and Haslam (5) in close attendance. Local hero de Radigues (9) and eventual winner Spencer (4) are also prominent. (*Henk Keulemans*)

FREDDIE SPENCER'S RESULTS AND STATISTICS, 1983–5

	Starts	Wins	Podiums	Poles
500cc	30	18	26	22
250cc	10	7	8	6
Total	40	25	34	28

FREDDIE DOUBLES UP

When Freddie Spencer and his race engineer Erv Kanemoto decided to contest not just the 500cc championship but also the 250cc class, Honda built them what was effectively half an NSR500, known as the RS250R-W, to fight the Yamahas of '83 World Champion Carlos Lavado and Martin Wimmer (GER). Consider what Spencer took on that year: he was single-handedly developing both the 500 and the 250 as well as Michelin radials for both bikes. In the big class he had to deal with the previous year's title winner, Eddie Lawson, and in the smaller one not just the never-say-die Lavado but also multi-champion Anton Mang on a particularly well-prepared customer Honda.

It took Spencer just two races to win on the 500, while he was victorious with the 250 on its first outing, though beaten in the next two rounds. He then put on a sustained exhibition of riding that it is hard to overpraise, winning both races next time out at Mugello and following up that double with another at the Salzburgring. In the 250s he won the next four races as well, then settled for fourth in the pouring rain at Silverstone to win the title. Freddie then parked the 250 to concentrate on the 500. After his double-double he was beaten by Lawson in Rijeka and then skittled at Assen, but he won the next four 500 races, doubling up again in both France and Belgium, before skipping the final race.

It was a superhuman effort, and with hindsight it looks as if it was all too much. Freddie retired from the first 500cc race of the following season while leading and never won another race. He raced on, retired, made a comeback and 'finally' retired in 1988 before making ill-fated comebacks again in both 1989 and '93. Spencer's overall career statistics are impressive enough: 20 500cc wins plus seven in the 250s is a total few riders achieve. To rack up all but two of those victories in just three years is staggering (his other 500 wins were at Spa and Mugello in 1982). He is still the youngest ever 500 champion and many people (including the authors of this book) would argue that he was the most naturally gifted rider in modern GP history. What is indisputable is that he is the only man ever to have won the two most prestigious titles in Grand Prix racing, the 250 and 500cc, in the same year.

1986

Yamaha wrested the title back from Honda with impressive mechanical reliability and Eddie Lawson at his best

There were more V4s than ever before on the grid. For the first time Honda fielded two, one for Freddie Spencer and one for Wayne Gardner. Spencer suffered badly enough from carpal tunnel syndrome to pull out of the first race of the year while leading. He missed the next two races, came to Austria but failed to score, and then did not reappear all year. Japanese test rider Shunji Yatsushiro rode the V4 for three races before Raymond Roche parked his Honda NS500 triple and took over. But the '86 NSR was Spencer's bike and no-one else could get the best out of it. Ron Haslam took over the Elf, now in its third incarnation.

By contrast Yamaha fielded five V4s, their approach being made clear by the dropping of the 'OW' designation used for full factory bikes and the adoption of the YZR500 nomenclature that had a close relationship to the company's street-bike range. Eddie Lawson led the Marlboro-sponsored factory team, still managed by Giacomo Agostini, with Rob McElnea as his new team-mate. Christian Sarron stayed on the Sonauto machine and a new Yamaha team appeared managed by Kenny Roberts with Lucky Strike sponsorship. Naturally the riders were also American: Randy Mamola and Mike Baldwin. The bike had only detail changes from the previous year but was now versatile enough to suit all its riders, and it was completely reliable: none of the five riders failed to finish a race because of mechanical problems. It took Lawson just one race to start winning, after which he won another three on the bounce and ended the season with seven wins out of eleven races. The only time Eddie wasn't on the rostrum was when he fell on the first lap at Assen.

Suzuki's teams were still waiting for their own V4 but both Gallina and Heron squads raced reed-valve versions of the old square four. Pier-Francesco Chili (ITA) of the Gallina team was the top Suzuki scorer, while the British operation gave 500cc GP debuts to Scot Niall Mackenzie and Kevin Schwantz (USA).

Juan Garriga (SPA) gave the Italian Cagiva company their most promising season since they'd come to the 500cc class in 1982 with their own Yamaha-like V4.

ABOVE Eddie Lawson and the Yamaha YZR500 – a clinically efficient combination. (*Henk Keulemans*)

RIGHT Ian McConnachie (Krauser) on his way to winning the 80cc race at Silverstone and becoming the only British rider to win a race there. (*Henk Keulemans*)

THE 1986 SEASON

500cc

SPA/Jarama

- After leading the early part of the race Freddie Spencer retired on lap 15 with tendonitis. He did not reappear until the Austrian GP in June
- Wayne Gardner took his first Grand Prix win
- American Mike Baldwin made a podium appearance on his debut on the factory Yamaha

ITA-NAZ/Monza

- Eddie Lawson won from fellow-countrymen Randy Mamola and Baldwin, the first time that all the podium finishers were on V4 Yamahas

AUT/Salzburgring

- Freddie Spencer qualified fifth but finished down in 16th after calling into the pits with steering-damper problems. Ongoing wrist problems meant he did not appear again all year

NED/Assen

- Kevin Schwantz made his GP debut on the square-four Suzuki, qualifying in 12th but failing to finish

BEL/Spa-Francorchamps

- Randy Mamola was victorious, becoming the only rider to have won 500cc GP races on machines from three different Japanese manufacturers – Suzuki, Honda and Yamaha

GBR/Silverstone

- Wayne Gardner won the 500cc race at Silverstone, the circuit used for ten years for the British GP. Donington Park would be the venue in 1987

SWE/Anderstorp

- Eddie Lawson won the race from his closest challenger, Wayne Gardner, to clinch his second 500cc world title

250cc

SPA/Jarama

- Carlos Lavado (Yamaha) was lucky to win after crashing on the opening lap: he got a second chance when the race was stopped and restarted because of a start-line incident

GBR/Silverstone

- Dominique Sarron (FRA, Honda), brother of 1984 champion Christian, won his first GP

RSM/Misano

- Tadahiko Taira (JPN, Yamaha) took his only Grand Prix victory after making a terrible start and being down in 22nd place at the end of the first lap

SWE/Anderstorp

- Lavado won the race from closest challenger Sito Pons (Honda) to regain the world title he'd won in 1983

125cc

GER/Nürburgring

- Luca Cadalora (ITA, Garelli) won a Grand Prix for the first time

RSM/Misano

- August Auinger (Bartol) took the last of his five GP victories, the last time an Austrian won a solo World Championship race

GER-BW/Hockenheim

- Angel Nieto (Ducados) made his last championship appearance more than 21 years after his 1965 debut at the Spanish GP
- Luca Cadalora finished second behind his closest challenger, Fausto Gresini (Garelli), to clinch his first world title

80cc

GBR/Silverstone

- Ian McConnachie (Krauser) became the first British rider to win in the 80cc class. This was the only home win across all solo classes during the ten years that the GPs were held at Silverstone

RSM/Misano

- Pierpaolo Bianchi took the last of his 27 Grand Prix victories ten years after his first win in Austria in 1976
- Jorge Martinez (Derbi) finished second to win his first world title

1986 WORLD CHAMPIONSHIP

500cc

Pos	Rider	Nat	Machine	SPA	ITA	GER	AUT	YUG	NED	BEL	FRA	GBR	SWE	RSM	Total
1	Eddie Lawson	USA	Yamaha	12	15	15	15	15	-	12	15	10	15	15	139
2	Wayne Gardner	AUS	Honda	15	-	12	12	10	15	8	6	15	12	12	117
3	Randy Mamola	USA	Yamaha	8	12	5	10	12	12	15	12	6	3	10	105
4	Mike Baldwin	USA	Yamaha	10	10	10	6	6	10	-	8	-	10	8	78
5	Rob McElnea	GBR	Yamaha	4	-	8	5	8	8	6	5	8	8	-	60
6	Christian Sarron	FRA	Yamaha	6	8	-	8	5	6	10	10	-	-	5	58
7	Didier de Radigues	BEL	Chevallier	-	6	6	-	-	2	4	3	12	5	4	42
8	Raymond Roche	FRA	Honda	5	-	4	-	4	5	-	-	5	6	6	35
9	Ron Haslam	GBR	Elf-Honda	1	-	3	-	-	4	-	4	2	2	2	18
10	Pier-Francesco Chili	ITA	Suzuki	-	4	-	2	-	-	5	-	-	-	-	11
10	Niall Mackenzie	GBR	Suzuki	-	-	-	-	-	-	-	-	4	4	3	11
12	Boet van Dulmen	NED	Honda	-	5	-	1	-	-	2	-	-	-	-	8
13	Shunji Yatsushiro	JPN	Honda	-	-	-	4	3	-	-	-	-	-	-	7
14	Fabio Biliotti	ITA	Honda	2	3	-	-	-	-	-	-	-	-	-	5
14	Gustav Reiner	GER	Honda	-	-	2	3	-	-	-	-	-	-	-	5
16	Dave Petersen	ZIM	Suzuki	-	-	1	-	2	-	-	2	-	-	-	5
17	Juan Garriga	SPA	Cagiva	3	-	-	-	-	1	-	-	-	-	-	4
17	Paul Lewis	AUS	Suzuki	-	2	-	-	1	-	-	1	-	-	-	4
19	Roger Burnett	GBR	Honda	-	-	-	-	-	3	-	-	-	-	-	3
19	Kenny Irons	GBR	Yamaha	-	-	-	-	-	-	-	-	3	-	-	3
19	Mile Pajic	NED	Honda	-	-	-	-	-	-	3	-	-	-	-	3
22	Kevin Schwantz	USA	Suzuki	-	-	-	-	-	-	1	-	-	-	1	2
22	Wolfgang von Muralt	SWI	Suzuki	-	-	-	-	-	-	-	-	1	1	-	2
24	Marco Papa	ITA	Honda	-	1	-	-	-	-	-	-	-	-	-	1

Scoring system – 15, 12, 10, 8, 6, 5, 4, 3, 2, 1

250cc

Pos	Rider	Nat	Machine	Total
1	Carlos Lavado	VEN	Yamaha	114
2	Sito Pons	SPA	Honda	108
3	Dominique Sarron	FRA	Honda	72
4	Anton Mang	GER	Honda	65
5	Jean-François Baldé	FRA	Honda	63
6	Martin Wimmer	GER	Yamaha	56
7	Jacques Cornu	SWI	Honda	32
8	Fausto Ricci	ITA	Honda	30
9	Tadahiko Taira	JPN	Yamaha	28
10	Donnie McLeod	GBR	Armstrong	27

125cc

Pos	Rider	Nat	Machine	Total
1	Luca Cadalora	ITA	Garelli	122
2	Fausto Gresini	ITA	Garelli	114
3	Domenico Brigaglia	ITA	MBA	80
4	August Auinger	AUT	Bartol	60
5	Ezio Gianola	ITA	MBA	57
6	Bruno Kneubuhler	SWI	LCR	54
7	Lucio Pietroniro	BEL	MBA	37
8	Pierpaolo Bianchi	ITA	Seel MBA	34
9	Johnny Wickstrom	FIN	Tunturi	33
10	Willy Perez	ARG	Zanella	26

80cc

Pos	Rider	Nat	Machine	Total
1	Jorge Martinez	SPA	Derbi	94
2	Manuel Herreros	SPA	Derbi	85
3	Stefan Dorflinger	SWI	Krauser	82
4	Hans Spaan	NED	Huvo	57
5	Gerhard Waibel	GER	Real	51
6	Ian McConnachie	GBR	Krauser	50
7	Angel Nieto	SPA	Derbi	45
8	Pierpaolo Bianchi	ITA	Seel	44
9	Josef Fischer	AUT	Krauser	13
10	Gerd Kafka	AUT	Krauser	9

LEFT Luca Cadalora won his first world title in the colours of Team Italia, a well-financed team set up by the Italian federation to bring on young talent. It worked. *(Henk Keulemans)*

KING OF THE TIDDLERS

Angle Nieto, who retired at the end of the 1986 season, was for years the undisputed master of the 50 (later 80) and 125cc classes. He was also one of Spain's best-known and most popular sportsmen, with a public profile only exceeded by the galacticos of Real Madrid football club. Nieto was also one of the country's best-paid sportsmen – something the newly arrived American and Australian stars of the 500cc class never really understood. At Spanish GPs Angel's races were the main event, with thousands of fans heading for the exits when the 500s came out.

Nieto became Spain's first World Champion when he won the 50cc crown on a Derbi in 1969, going on to win 12 more titles while riding for Kreidler, Bultaco, Minarelli and Garelli. This was the era of Spanish protectionism, when foreign motorcycles were excluded from the market, and as a result Spanish riders were not on the shopping list for the big Japanese companies. Although Nieto won domestic championships in every capacity class from 50cc to 750cc, he never got the chance to move up to 250 GPs until too late in his career. He did ride in a 500 GP once, at Jarama in 1982, but that was because King Juan Carlos of Spain made it known he thought it would be a good idea, so an extra factory Honda was magically made available. That fact on its own gives some idea of Nieto's standing at home.

In his younger days Nieto had a deserved reputation for toughness and a quick temper, machinery that had let him down being abandoned without a backward glance as he headed for his Bentley. He dominated his opponents with a mix of blinding speed and ruthless psychological warfare. Nowadays he is an expert MotoGP commentator for Spain's biggest TV network, and anything but an extrovert presence. Just don't tell him he won 13 world titles; his legendary superstition lingers on. That's why the statue on the inside of the corner that bears his name at Jerez is inscribed with the figures '12+1'.

RIGHT Angel Nieto, the second most successful racer in GP history, retired after winning 12 titles. Here he is astride the 50cc Derbi in 1972. *(Henk Keulemans)*

1987

Wayne Gardner became Australia's first 500cc World Champion as he forced the recalcitrant Honda V4 to bend to his will

Yamaha didn't change anything for 1987. The riders and teams remained the same: Lawson and McElnea for Marlboro and Agostini; Mamola and Baldwin for Lucky Strike and Roberts; and Sarron for Sonauto and Gauloises. The only significant change was that Kenny Roberts's team switched to Dunlops. Honda, in contrast, did not rest on their laurels. The NSR got a complete revamp, with the direction of crank rotation reversed and the angle of the V between the banks of cylinders opened out so that the carburettors could be housed there. Apart from the single crankshaft there was now little to distinguish the Honda from the Yamaha.

The difference turned out to be Wayne Gardner. The Aussie arm-wrestled the still far from perfect Honda into submission to become his country's first 500cc World Champion. As in the previous year, Freddie Spencer was supposed to head the Honda challenge but a pre-season injury followed by knee damage put him out until the ninth round. Typically, Freddie immediately went into the lead at Donington Park but retired with a mysterious mechanical malady. He scored points next time out but for a variety of ever more bizarre reasons only rode twice more all year, finishing 11th at Brno and retiring at Misano.

The only man who could win on the Honda was Gardner. Niall Mackenzie rode one, as did Ron Haslam before the Elf team put the V4 into their own chassis. Pier-Francesco Chili impressed on a Honda NS triple.

Cagiva had a new narrow-angle V4 and enough money to employ Raymond Roche as well as Didier de Radigues. Suzuki hired Kenny Irons (GBR) as their lone full-time rider on the new XR75 reed-valve V4, but Kevin Schwantz also rode it on occasions. The discovery of the year was Kevin Magee (AUS) who raced a Yamaha in Japan, Holland and Spain, qualifying on the front row at Assen and getting on the rostrum in Jarama.

In the 125s Honda fielded a single, the RS125, in preparation for the regulation change that would limit the class to one pot. Ezio Gianola (ITA) spent the year riding the wheels off it against the Garelli twins.

ABOVE Wayne Gardner – the only rider not to be intimidated by the Honda V4. (*Henk Keulemans*)

RIGHT Anton Mang won his third 250cc title. (*Henk Keulemans*)

THE **1987** SEASON

500cc

JPN/Suzuka

- At the first Grand Prix to be held in Japan in 20 years Niall Mackenzie (GBR) qualified on pole on his debut on the factory Honda but crashed on the last lap while lying third
- Factory test rider Takumi Ito (JPN) finished third in the first race for the new Suzuki V4
- Reigning World Champion Eddie Lawson started the race on intermediate tyres hoping that the track would dry but came in to change to wets before finally retiring

SPA/Jerez

- Wayne Gardner took his first win of the year on the first visit by the GP circus to the Jerez circuit
- Kevin Schwantz made his debut on the V4 Suzuki and finished fifth – his best result of the year

GER/Hockenheim

- Eddie Lawson took his first victory of the year after Gardner's Honda faltered when he was leading by nine seconds

FRA/Le Mans

- Pier-Francesco Chili finished second in wet conditions, giving the three-cylinder Honda its last podium finish in a non-boycotted GP

CZE/Brno

- Wayne Gardner won the first 500cc GP race to be held at the new purpose-built Brno circuit

BRA/Goiania

- Gardner took his seventh win of the year to become the first Australian 500cc World Champion

ARG/Buenos Aires

- Wayne Gardner finished third, the only rider in the top class to score in every one of the 15 rounds
- Eddie Lawson won the race but Randy Mamola finished second to take second place in the championship from Lawson by a single point
- This was the fourth time that Mamola had been runner-up in the 500cc World Championship

250cc

JPN/Suzuka

- Reigning World Champion Carlos Lavado was unable to start due to injuries suffered in a pre-season crash
- Wild-card rider Masaru Kobayashi (JPN, Honda), using Bridgestone tyres, won on his Grand Prix debut

FRA/Le Mans

- Honda-mounted Reinhold Roth took his first Grand Prix victory

RSM/Misano

- Loris Reggiani (ITA) gave the Aprilia factory their first GP victory

POR/Jarama

- Anton Mang won his eighth race of the year to claim the 250cc title for the third time

ARG/Buenos Aires

- Sito Pons won the final race of the year to finish equal on points with Reinhold Roth for second place in the final table; the German got runner-up spot on a tie-break
- The top five riders in the championship were all on Hondas

125cc

FRA/Le Mans

- Ezio Gianola finished second in the wet at Le Mans to give the single-cylinder Honda its first podium finish

RSM/Misano

- Fausto Gresini (Garelli) took his tenth victory of the year to set a new record for most victories in a single season in the 125cc class
- This record stood until 1997 when it was broken by Valentino Rossi

POR/Jarama

- Gresini failed in his attempt to win all 11 races when he crashed on lap ten, the win going to Paolo Casoli (ITA, AGV)

80cc

SPA/Jerez

- Reigning champion Jorge Martinez (Derbi) won from fellow-Spaniard Alex Criville (Derbi) on the 17-year-old rider's GP debut

GBR/Donington

- Jorge Martinez won his sixth race out of the first seven GPs of the year to retain his world title with three races to spare

CLUTCH STARTS INTRODUCED FOR ALL CLASSES

All World Championship racing up until the 1987 Japanese GP at Suzuka had commenced with push starts, but these were now deemed both old fashioned and unsafe. Although that moment of silent drama between the flag dropping and engines bursting into life was lost, riders in particular welcomed the change.

1987 WORLD CHAMPIONSHIP

500cc

Pos	Rider	Nat	Machine	JPN	SPA	GER	ITA	AUT	YUG	NED	FRA	GBR	SWE	CZE	RSM	POR	BRA	ARG	Total
1	Wayne Gardner	AUS	Honda	12	15	1	15	15	15	12	8	12	15	15	10	8	15	10	178
2	Randy Mamola	USA	Yamaha	15	5	12	-	12	12	10	15	10	10	8	15	12	10	12	158
3	Eddie Lawson	USA	Yamaha	-	12	15	12	-	10	15	-	15	12	12	12	15	12	15	157
4	Ron Haslam	GBR	Honda/Elf	6	10	10	6	8	8	6	6	4	5	-	-	2	-	1	72
5	Niall Mackenzie	GBR	Honda	-	8	4	1	10	-	-	4	6	6	6	4	5	3	4	61
6	Tadahiko Taira	JPN	Yamaha	5	4	8	5	2	4	-	-	3	-	10	8	-	4	3	56
7	Christian Sarron	FRA	Yamaha	-	-	-	10	5	-	-	10	8	-	4	3	6	6	-	52
8	Pier-Francesco Chili	ITA	Honda	8	-	5	4	1	5	2	12	-	-	2	-	4	2	2	47
9	Shunji Yatsushiro	JPN	Honda	-	3	-	-	4	3	-	3	-	-	5	6	3	5	8	40
10	Rob McElnea	GBR	Yamaha	-	-	6	8	6	-	8	-	-	8	3	-	-	-	-	39
11	Roger Burnett	GBR	Honda	3	2	3	-	3	-	4	1	2	1	1	5	-	-	-	25
12	Didier de Radigues	BEL	Cagiva	-	-	-	-	-	-	5	-	5	3	-	-	-	8	-	21
13	Raymond Roche	FRA	Cagiva	1	-	-	2	-	6	-	-	-	-	-	-	-	-	6	15
14	Kenny Irons	GBR	Suzuki	-	-	-	-	-	1	3	5	1	2	-	-	-	-	-	12
15	Kevin Magee	AUS	Yamaha	-	-	-	-	-	-	1	-	-	-	-	-	10	-	-	11
16	Kevin Schwantz	USA	Suzuki	-	6	-	3	-	-	-	2	-	-	-	-	-	-	-	11
17	Takumi Ito	JPN	Suzuki	10	-	-	-	-	-	-	-	-	-	-	-	-	-	-	10
18	Mike Baldwin	USA	Yamaha	-	-	-	-	-	-	-	-	-	-	-	-	-	1	5	6
19	Gustav Reiner	GER	Honda	-	-	2	-	-	-	-	-	-	-	-	2	1	-	-	5
20	Hiroyuki Kawasaki	JPN	Yamaha	4	-	-	-	-	-	-	-	-	-	-	-	-	-	-	4
20	Freddie Spencer	USA	Honda	-	-	-	-	-	-	-	-	-	4	-	-	-	-	-	4
22	Richard Scott	NZE	Yamaha	-	1	-	-	-	2	-	-	-	-	-	-	-	-	-	3
23	Shinji Katayama	JPN	Yamaha	2	-	-	-	-	-	-	-	-	-	-	-	-	-	-	2
24	Marco Gentile	SWI	Fior	-	-	-	-	-	-	-	-	-	-	-	1	-	-	-	1

Scoring system – 15, 12, 10, 8, 6, 5, 4, 3, 2, 1

250cc

Pos	Rider	Nat	Machine	Total
1	Anton Mang	GER	Honda	136
2	Reinhold Roth	GER	Honda	108
3	Sito Pons	SPA	Honda	108
4	Dominique Sarron	FRA	Honda	97
5	Carlos Cardus	SPA	Honda	70
6	Loris Reggiani	ITA	Aprilia	68
7	Luca Cadalora	ITA	Yamaha	63
8	Martin Wimmer	GER	Yamaha	61
9	Jacques Cornu	SWI	Honda	50
10	Carlos Lavado	VEN	Yamaha	46

125cc

Pos	Rider	Nat	Machine	Total
1	Fausto Gresini	ITA	Garelli	150
2	Bruno Casanova	ITA	Garelli	88
3	Paolo Casoli	ITA	AGV	61
4	Domenico Brigaglia	ITA	AGV	58
5	August Auinger	AUT	MBA	54
6	Ezio Gianola	ITA	Honda	45
7	Pierpaolo Bianchi	ITA	MBA	43
8	Andres Marin Sanchez	SPA	Ducados	40
9	Lucio Pietroniro	BEL	MBA	32
10	Mike Leitner	AUT	MBA	32

80cc

Pos	Rider	Nat	Machine	Total
1	Jorge Martinez	SPA	Derbi	129
2	Manuel Herreros	SPA	Derbi	86
3	Gerhard Waibel	GER	Krauser	82
4	Stefan Dorflinger	SWI	Krauser	75
5	Ian McConnachie	GBR	Krauser	53
6	Jorg Seel	GER	Seel	38
7	Hubert Abold	GER	Krauser	33
8	Luis Reyes	SPA	Autisa	31
9	Josef Fischer	AUT	Krauser	19
10	Julian Miralles	SPA	Derbi	18

LEFT Rejoicing in Misano as Loris Reggiani wins Aprilia's first GP. (*Henk Keulemans*)

RIGHT Wayne Gardner – the epitome of the never-give-up Aussie sportsman. (*Henk Keulemans*)

THE AUSTRALIAN WAY

Wayne Gardner was Australia's first premier-class World Champion. His career route from domestic Superbike racing to the All-Japan Championship and thence to GPs (in Wayne's case via the British Championship too) would be the blueprint for his compatriots Kevin Magee and Daryl Beattie, and later Mick Doohan.

Australia's first GP winner, on a Norton, had been Ken Kavanagh who won the 1952 350cc Ulster GP held at the Clady circuit. The following year he won the 500cc Ulster race at Dundrod, also on a Norton, to become the first Aussie winner in the top class. Keith Campbell (Moto Guzzi) became Australia's first World Champion when he won the 1957 350cc title, while Tom Phillis was the country's first 125cc winner, at Montjuich Park, Spain, in 1961, on his way to the World Championship. This was also Honda's first GP win. Phillis, uncle of World Superbike star Robbie, also won 250 races that year. Barry Smith (Derbi) made it an Aussie winner in every solo class when he won the 50cc race at the 1968 Isle of Man TT.

The other World Champion before Gardner was Kel Carruthers, winner of the 250cc title in 1969 on a Benelli. He went on to assist Kenny Roberts's arrival into GPs and his winning of those three 500cc world titles.

After Gardner came two other men from the same mould, Mick Doohan and Casey Stoner. It's never easy to beat an Aussie.

1988

Honda got their sums wrong again; Lawson and Yamaha took advantage again

The previous season's two promising newcomers, Kevin Schwantz and Kevin Magee, arrived in GPs full time. Along with another stellar new boy, Wayne Rainey (USA), Magee rode for Roberts's Lucky Strike Yamaha team. Agostini's Marlboro Yamaha operation retained Eddie Lawson and partnered him with Didier de Radigues. Rob McElnea left to join Schwantz at Suzuki (now with Pepsi sponsorship) on the now competitive V4. For the first time the French Yamaha team had a second rider, Patrick Igoa (FRA), alongside Christian Sarron.

Honda expected Freddie Spencer to return, and so did he. However, an old wrist injury prevented him riding and he decided to retire. Instead, Shunji Yatsushiro was drafted in to ride alongside Gardner in the factory team. Niall Mackenzie and Pier-Francesco Chili were on satellite bikes for different teams and HRC continued to provide engines for Elf's experimental machine, again piloted by Ron Haslam.

Only the Roberts team was not on Michelins, staying loyal to Dunlop. Cagiva retained Raymond Roche, signed Randy Mamola, and made it three tyre manufacturers in the top class by starting a partnership with Pirelli. It was a good enough combination for Mamola to get third place in the rain at Spa, the Cagiva factory's first rostrum.

The Honda was a brute, massively powerful but fatally compromised by the Honda engineers rediscovering their obsession with a low centre of gravity, which only produced massive wheelspin. Modifications masterminded by Jerry Burgess in mid-season got Gardner competitive, but a piston failure while leading on the last lap of an epic French GP ended his chances. Lawson and the YZR500's consistency won them their third title.

Another great champion retired before the end of the season. Anton Mang had already made the decision to call it quits at the end of the year, but a crash at the first corner of the Yugoslav GP hastened his decision. The 250 class turned into a classic confrontation between two Spaniards, Sito Pons (Honda) and Juan Garriga (Yamaha).

ABOVE Eddie Lawson in solitary splendour at Spa. (*Henk Keulemans*)

RIGHT Derbi won both the 125cc and 80cc classes; this is Jorge 'Aspar' Martinez's 80. (*Henk Keulemans*)

THE **1988** SEASON

500cc

JPN/Suzuka
- Kevin Schwantz's first GP win, and also the first victory for the V4 Suzuki

USA/Laguna Seca
- Grand Prix racing returned to America for the first time since Daytona hosted the event in 1965
- Wayne Rainey qualified on pole in only his second start in the 500cc class

SPA/Jarama
- Kevin Magee (Yamaha), making just his sixth start, qualified on pole and won the race, but it was his only victory in GP racing

NED/Assen
- Christian Sarron (Yamaha) grabbed pole to complete a unique family double with his younger brother Dominique (Honda), on pole in the 250cc class
- Reigning champion Wayne Gardner took his first victory of the year

BEL/Spa-Francorchamps
- In a race run in mixed weather conditions, Randy Mamola finished third – the first podium for the Cagiva factory

FRA/Paul Ricard
- After an epic battle the top three riders (Lawson, Sarron and Schwantz) crossed the line separated by just 0.46s, the first time in the 500cc class that the three podium finishers were covered by less than half a second

GBR/Donington
- Wayne Rainey took his first GP victory with a dominant performance, leading from start to finish. It was the first time carbon fibre brakes were used in a race

CZE/Brno
- In spite of main challenger Gardner winning the race, second place was enough for Eddie Lawson to clinch the 500cc title for the third time

BRA/Goiania
- Lawson took the last of his 26 GP wins riding Yamaha machinery – the most successful Yamaha rider of all time in the 500cc class

250cc

JPN/Suzuka
- Anton Mang opened the defence of his title with a race victory, the last of his 42 Grand Prix wins

USA/Laguna Seca
- Just two weeks after making his GP debut in Japan, 20-year-old John Kocinski (USA, Yamaha) qualified on pole and finished the race in fourth
- Victory went to Jim Filice (USA), a replacement rider for Honda's injured factory rider Masahiro Shimizu (JPN)

POR/Jerez
- Juan Garriga won his first GP, to move to within one point of fellow-Spaniard and rival, Sito Pons, at the top of the championship table

GER/Nürburgring
- Luca Cadalora (Yamaha) took his first win in the 250cc class at the same circuit where he'd scored his initial 125cc win just two years earlier

AUT/Salzburgring
- At the age of 35, Jacques Cornu (SWI, Honda) won his first GP, more than ten years after making his debut

BRA/Goiania
- Pons finished third to clinch the title from Garriga after a season-long battle in which the two Spaniards had not been separated by more than ten points since the fourth race of the year

125cc

SPA/Jarama
- Jorge Martinez (Derbi) took his first 125cc GP victory in the first race of the year

GER/Nürburgring
- Ezio Gianola gave Honda their first 125cc GP win since 1966

ITA-NAZ/Imola
- Martinez won both the 125 and 80cc races at Imola – the first of four double victories for 'Aspar' during 1988

FRA/Paul Ricard
- Taru Rinne (FIN) became the first female to score World Championship points when she rode her Honda into 14th place

SWE/Anderstorp
- Martinez won the race from closest challenger Gianola to take the title

CZE/Brno
- Jorge Martinez's final 125/80cc double win of the year – and the last time that a rider won two GPs in one day

80cc

SPA/Jarama
- Ex-champion Stefan Dorflinger (Krauser) won the opening race of the year, the last of his 18 GP victories

YUG/Rijeka
- Jorge Martinez clinched his third 80cc world title with a victory for Derbi

1988 WORLD CHAMPIONSHIP

500cc

Pos	Rider	Nat	Machine	JPN	USA	SPA	POR	ITA	GER	AUT	NED	BEL	YUG	FRA	GBR	SWE	CZE	BRA	Total
1	Eddie Lawson	USA	Yamaha	15	20	17	20	20	13	20	17	17	6	20	10	20	17	20	252
2	Wayne Gardner	AUS	Honda	17	17	15	11	17	8	-	20	20	20	13	17	17	20	17	229
3	Wayne Rainey	USA	Yamaha	10	13	10	17	15	17	15	9	11	15	11	20	11	15	-	189
4	Christian Sarron	FRA	Yamaha	8	10	13	13	-	15	-	15	-	17	17	15	15	-	11	149
5	Kevin Magee	AUS	Yamaha	9	-	20	15	11	11	10	13	-	11	7	11	10	-	10	138
6	Niall Mackenzie	GBR	Honda	13	15	11	9	5	7	-	11	5	-	-	13	13	10	13	125
7	Didier de Radigues	BEL	Yamaha	7	8	8	10	-	9	17	4	13	10	9	9	9	-	7	120
8	Kevin Schwantz	USA	Suzuki	20	11	-	-	13	20	13	8	-	-	15	-	4	-	15	119
9	Pier-Francesco Chili	ITA	Honda	2	-	9	-	10	10	11	10	8	5	8	8	7	13	9	110
10	Rob McElnea	GBR	Suzuki	-	7	4	8	4	5	7	6	10	8	5	-	3	8	8	83
11	Ron Haslam	GBR	Elf-Honda	4	9	6	-	-	-	8	3	9	7	6	2	5	9	-	68
12	Randy Mamola	USA	Cagiva	-	-	-	-	9	-	-	-	15	13	10	5	6	-	-	58
13	Shunji Yatsushiro	JPN	Honda	6	-	7	-	8	6	9	5	7	9	-	-	-	-	-	57
14	Patrick Igoa	FRA	Yamaha	3	-	-	-	1	4	6	7	6	4	-	-	-	7	6	44
15	Tadahiko Taira	JPN	Yamaha	11	-	-	-	6	-	-	-	-	-	-	6	2	11	-	36
16	Alessandro Valesi	ITA	Honda	-	5	3	6	3	-	-	-	4	-	2	-	-	3	-	26
17	Marco Papa	ITA	Honda	-	-	-	7	-	2	-	2	2	-	-	-	-	4	-	17
18	Roger Burnett	GBR	Honda	-	-	-	-	-	-	-	-	-	-	-	7	8	-	-	15
19	Mike Baldwin	USA	Honda	-	6	-	-	-	-	-	-	-	2	3	3	-	-	-	14
20	Raymond Roche	FRA	Cagiva	-	-	5	-	7	-	-	-	-	-	-	-	1	-	-	13
21	Fabio Barchitta	RSM	Honda	-	-	-	-	-	-	-	-	-	-	1	-	-	6	5	12
22	Bruno Kneubuhler	SWI	Honda	-	-	1	2	-	-	4	-	-	1	-	-	-	1	-	9
23	Donnie McLeod	GBR	Honda	-	-	-	-	-	-	-	-	3	3	-	-	-	-	3	9
24	Marco Gentile	SWI	Fior	-	-	-	-	2	-	-	1	-	-	-	-	-	5	-	8
25	Daniel Amatriain	SPA	Honda	-	-	2	5	-	-	-	-	-	-	-	-	-	-	-	7
26	Hikaru Miyagi	JPN	Honda	5	-	-	-	-	-	-	-	-	-	-	-	-	-	-	5
26	Gustav Reiner	GER	Honda	-	-	-	-	-	-	5	-	-	-	-	-	-	-	-	5
28	Mal Campbell	AUS	Elf-Honda	-	-	-	-	-	-	-	-	-	-	4	-	-	-	-	4
28	Norihiku Fujiwara	JPN	Yamaha	-	-	-	-	-	-	-	-	-	-	-	4	-	-	-	4
28	Steve Manley	GBR	Suzuki	-	-	-	4	-	-	-	-	-	-	-	-	-	-	-	4
28	Fernando Gonzales	SPA	Honda	-	-	-	-	-	-	-	-	-	-	-	-	-	-	4	4
32	Fabio Biliotti	ITA	Honda	-	-	-	-	-	-	3	-	-	-	-	1	-	-	-	4
33	Rachel Nicotte	FRA	Honda	-	-	-	3	-	-	-	-	-	-	-	-	-	-	-	3
33	Peter Schleef	GER	Honda	-	-	-	-	-	3	-	-	-	-	-	-	-	-	-	3
35	Massimo Broccoli	ITA	Cagiva	-	-	-	-	-	-	2	-	-	-	-	-	-	-	-	2
35	Peter Linden	SWE	Honda	-	-	-	-	-	-	-	-	-	-	-	-	-	2	-	2
37	Cees Doorakkers	NED	Honda	-	-	-	1	-	-	-	-	1	-	-	-	-	-	-	1
37	Maarten Duyzers	NED	Honda	-	-	-	-	-	-	-	-	-	-	-	-	-	-	-	1
37	Manfred Fischer	GER	Honda	-	-	-	-	-	-	1	-	-	-	-	-	-	-	-	1
37	Osamu Hiwatashi	JPN	Suzuki	1	-	-	-	-	-	-	-	-	-	-	-	-	-	-	1
37	Michael Rudroff	GER	Honda	-	-	-	-	-	1	-	-	-	-	-	-	-	-	-	1

Scoring system – 20, 17, 15, 13, 11, 10, 9, 8, 7, 6, 5, 4, 3, 2, 1

250cc

Pos	Rider	Nat	Machine	Total
1	Sito Pons	SPA	Honda	231
2	Juan Garriga	SPA	Yamaha	221
3	Jacques Cornu	SWI	Honda	166
4	Dominique Sarron	FRA	Honda	158
5	Reinhold Roth	GER	Honda	158
6	Luca Cadalora	ITA	Yamaha	136
7	Jean-Philippe Ruggia	FRA	Yamaha	104
8	Anton Mang	GER	Honda	87
9	Carlos Cardus	SPA	Honda	71
10	Masahiro Shimizu	JPN	Honda	68

125cc

Pos	Rider	Nat	Machine	Total
1	Jorge Martinez	SPA	Derbi	197
2	Ezio Gianola	ITA	Honda	168
3	Hans Spaan	NED	Honda	110
4	Julian Miralles	SPA	Honda	104
5	Domenico Brigaglia	ITA	Rotax	69
6	Gastone Grassetti	ITA	Honda	66
7	Adi Stadler	GER	Honda	63
8	Stefan Prein	GER	Honda	59
9	Lucio Pietroniro	BEL	Honda	56
10	Gerhard Waibel	GER	Honda	52

80cc

Pos	Rider	Nat	Machine	Total
1	Jorge Martinez	SPA	Derbi	137
2	Alex Criville	SPA	Derbi	90
3	Stefan Dorflinger	SWI	Krauser	77
4	Manuel Herreros	SPA	Derbi	69
5	Peter Ottl	GER	Krauser	65
6	Bogdan Nikolov	BUL	Krauser	55
7	Karoly Juhasz	HUN	Krauser	54
8	Jos van Dongen	NED	Casal	47
9	Giuseppe Ascareggi	ITA	BBFT	46
10	Gabriele Gnani	ITA	Gnani	36

HI-TECH

There were three notable technical innovations in 1988. The 'gull-wing' swingarm appeared on both the Yamaha and Cagiva 500s to give exhaust pipes a more efficient run. The same factories also experimented with Ohlins 'upside down' forks, more properly known as 'outer upper tube', and by mid-season they were preferred to the conventional design.

The other advance was carbon brakes, used for the first time by Wayne Rainey at Donington Park for his maiden victory. It wasn't the stopping power that let him open up an astonishing lead on the first lap, it was the fact that the discs were nearly 1.5kg lighter than the usual steel rotors and the consequent reduction in gyroscopic effect (actually moment of inertia) made his 500 Yamaha steer 'like a 250' down through Craner Curves. Ron Haslam had tested carbon brakes on the hub-centre-steered Elf, but never raced with them. Rainey tested them for the first time in Donington qualifying and immediately went over a second quicker than with steel discs. His first words after coming in from his initial experience of carbon brakes were: 'Can I race it? I've got to race it!' He then reported that the first time he'd flicked the bike into the left-hander at Craner, as normal, he nearly ran up the inside kerb. Interestingly, Rainey didn't report a major improvement in stopping power, but he was never a manic braker. His team-mate Kevin Magee, definitely a demon on the stoppers, said after he used them for the first time that it was like throwing out the proverbial anchor.

Where did this technology come from? The answer, of course, was the aviation industry, where carbon had been used for years to stop jumbos because, as well as being light, carbon fibre has a high coefficient of friction but needs to be hot. Generating heat is not a problem when stopping a 747 with 400 people on board – everything gets hot very quickly – and the cold brake problem can be solved by using massive clamping forces. Car racers were onto carbon brakes quickly, using complex ducting and shrouds to keep the rotors at 400 degrees, their minimum working temperature. As a happy by-product, the drastic reduction in unsprung weight also enabled tyre and suspension designers to push their ideas forward. AP Lockheed's breakthrough was to get consistent performance out of their material at much lower temperatures and cope with the vast amounts of extra heat generated.

1989

Eddie Lawson moved to Honda and became the first man to win back-to-back titles on different makes of motorcycle

Over the winter break the number-one plate migrated from Yamaha to Honda when, to universal surprise, Eddie Lawson left the company he'd been with throughout his GP career to ride a satellite Honda. He had Erv Kanemoto as his engineer and, vitally, they had the freedom to do what they wanted to the bike. Lawson rode in Rothmans colours but was not part of the factory team, which consisted of Wayne Gardner and new tough Aussie Mick Doohan. Pier-Francesco Chili (on Pirellis) and Dominique Sarron were on satellite bikes, while American dirt-track legend Bubba Shobert received an '88-spec Honda.

Lawson's defection threw the official Yamaha team into chaos. Manager Giacomo Agostini summoned Freddie Spencer out of retirement and signed Niall Mackenzie as his team-mate, but still prefers not to talk about Spencer. Kenny Roberts again fielded Wayne Rainey and Kevin Magee, Christian Sarron was still backed by Sonauto, and Alessandro Valesi (ITA) got the previous year's bike. At Suzuki Kevin Schwantz was joined by Ron Haslam, with Randy Mamola kept on by Cagiva.

Sito Pons retained his World Championship in the 250s, with Spaniards winning both titles in the smaller classes as well. Unusually, neither was won by 'Aspar' Martinez, who was beaten by Alex Criville (JJ Cobas) in the 125s and by his Derbi team-mate Manuel Herreros in the last ever 80cc championship.

Injury and worse played a big part in the year, especially in the USA. Gardner broke his leg badly, then a horrible slowing-down lap collision severely damaged Magee's ankle and left Shobert with head injuries which would prevent him racing again. British rider Rob McElnea took over the American's Honda.

Safety at GP circuits had most definitely improved in recent years, but the appalling response of the organisers to the death of Ivan Palazzese at Hockenheim showed that there was still a lot of work to do. This was confirmed by such incidents as the thrice-started Belgian GP and the riders' strike at Misano.

ABOVE The 1989 NSR was one of the most vicious racing motorcycles ever built; it took the combined genius of Lawson and race engineer Erv Kanemoto to tame it. (*Henk Keulemans*)

RIGHT Alex Criville became the youngest ever World Champion to date on the 125 Cobas. Since then, seven younger men have won world titles. (*Author's Collection*)

THE 1989 SEASON

500cc

JPN/Suzuka

- Kevin Schwantz, starting his first full-time GP season for Suzuki, won from great rival Rainey (Yamaha) after a race-long battle. Defending champion Eddie Lawson took the last podium slot on his debut on a Honda
- Mick Doohan (AUS, Honda), making his Grand Prix debut, qualified sixth but failed to finish the race after his crankshaft broke

AUS/Phillip Island

- Home hero Wayne Gardner took the win on the first visit to Australia for a Grand Prix event

USA/Laguna Seca

- Bubba Shobert suffered career-ending injuries after a collision with Kevin Magee on the slowing-down lap

SPA/Jerez

- Eddie Lawson took his first victory on a Honda

ITA-NAZ/Misano

- After the race had been stopped due to rain the leading riders refused to restart due to safety concerns. Honda-mounted Pier-Francesco Chili won on Pirelli tyres

GER/Hockenheim

- Mick Doohan finished third – the best result of his first season in GP racing

BEL/Spa-Francorchamps

- After the race was stopped and restarted twice Lawson was declared the winner, but half points were awarded because it was decided the second restart was not allowed under FIM rules
- John Kocinski (Yamaha), making his debut in the 500cc class as a wild card, finished in fourth place

GBR/Donington

- Luca Cadalora finished eighth on his debut in the 500cc class, riding the factory Yamaha vacated by Freddie Spencer when he parted company with the team

SWE/Anderstorp

- Championship leader Wayne Rainey crashed out with two laps to go while fighting for the win with Eddie Lawson

BRA/Goiania

- Lawson finished second to become the first rider to win back-to-back 500cc titles on bikes from two different manufacturers

250cc

JPN/Suzuka

- Wild-card rider John Kocinski (Yamaha) took his first win in just his fifth GP start

USA/Laguna Seca

- Kocinski made it two wins in two races as a wild card

GER/Hockenheim

- Twice a winner in the 125cc class, Ivan Palazzese (VEN) lost his life in a first-lap crash

GBR/Donington

- Sito Pons retained his title with three races remaining

CZE/Brno

- Reinhold Roth beat Masahiro Shimizu by just 0.001s – the closest finish in the 250cc class since the introduction of electronic timing

125cc

AUS/Phillip Island

- Alex Criville (JJ Cobas) took his first Grand Prix victory to become the youngest winner in the 125cc class, breaking a record set 30 years earlier by Mike Hailwood

GER/Hockenheim

- After qualifying in second place on the grid and battling for the lead early in the race Taru Rinne (FIN, Honda) finished seventh to set a new record for best GP result by a female rider

FRA/Le Mans

- Reigning champion Jorge Martinez (Derbi) took his only 125cc win of the year
- Having already been victorious in the earlier 80cc race in Italy, 'Aspar' was the last rider to win in two different GP classes in a single season

CZE/Brno

- Alex Criville won the final race of the year from closest challenger Hans Spaan (NED, Honda) to become the first teenager to win a World Championship title

80cc

NED/Assen

- Peter Ottl (GER, Krauser) won his third successive race to go equal on points at the top of the table with Spanish rider Manuel Herreros (Derbi) with one race remaining

CZE/Brno

- Herri Torrentegui (SPA, Krauser) won the last ever 80cc race
- Manuel Herreros finished second to clinch the title without having won a race

1989 WORLD CHAMPIONSHIP

500cc

Pos	Rider	Nat	Machine	JPN	AUS	USA	SPA	ITA	GER	AUT	YUG	NED	BEL	FRA	GBR	SWE	CZE	BRA	Total
1	Eddie Lawson	USA	Honda	15	11	15	20	-	17	17	15	17	10	20	17	20	17	17	228
2	Wayne Rainey	USA	Yamaha	17	17	20	17	-	20	15	17	20	7.5	15	15	-	15	15	210.5
3	Christian Sarron	FRA	Yamaha	9	15	10	13	-	11	13	11	15	6.5	13	11	17	13	8	165.5
4	Kevin Schwantz	USA	Suzuki	20	-	17	-	-	-	20	20	-	8.5	17	20	-	20	20	162.5
5	Kevin Magee	AUS	Yamaha	11	13	13	-	-	9	11	13	13	4.5	11	10	11	9	10	138.5
6	Pier-Francesco Chili	ITA	Honda	-	-	9	10	20	13	10	7	11	5	10	7	9	11	-	122
7	Niall Mackenzie	GBR	Yamaha	10	-	11	15	-	-	-	4	8	3	9	13	13	10	7	103
8	Ron Haslam	GBR	Suzuki	4	9	-	9	-	-	9	8	9	-	-	9	10	8	11	86
9	Mick Doohan	AUS	Honda	-	8	8	-	-	15	8	10	7	4	8	-	-	-	13	81
10	Wayne Gardner	AUS	Honda	13	20	-	-	-	-	-	-	10	-	-	-	15	-	9	67
11	Rob McElnea	GBR	Honda	-	-	-	-	-	6	5	5	6	2.5	7	6	7	4	4	52.5
12	Simon Buckmaster	GBR	Honda	-	4	3	3	17	2	3	2	-	0.5	2	1	4	-	2	43.5
13	Alessandro Valesi	ITA	Yamaha	-	5	5	6	-	3	4	-	4	-	3	-	5	2	3	40
14	Tadahiko Taira	JPN	Yamaha	8	10	-	8	-	-	-	-	-	-	-	-	6	7	-	39
15	Dominique Sarron	FRA	Honda	-	6	6	7	-	8	6	6	-	-	-	-	-	-	-	39
16	Freddie Spencer	USA	Yamaha	2	-	-	11	-	7	7	-	3	3.5	-	-	-	-	-	33.5
17	Marco Gentile	SWI	Fior	-	3	4	4	13	-	2	-	2	2	-	3	-	-	-	33
18	Randy Mamola	USA	Cagiva	-	-	-	-	-	4	-	9	5	-	5	-	-	5	5	33
19	Adrien Morillas	FRA	Honda	-	-	-	-	-	-	-	-	-	-	6	-	8	6	6	26
20	Michael Rudroff	GER	Honda	-	1	1	-	15	-	-	1	-	-	-	-	-	-	-	18
21	Norihiku Fujiwara	JPN	Yamaha	7	-	-	-	-	10	-	-	-	-	-	-	-	-	-	17
22	Bubba Shobert	USA	Honda	5	-	7	-	-	-	-	-	-	-	-	-	-	-	-	12
23	Sepp Doppler	AUT	Honda	-	-	-	-	11	-	-	-	-	-	-	-	-	-	-	11
24	Alois Meyer	GER	Honda	-	-	-	-	10	-	-	-	-	-	-	-	-	-	-	10
25	Romolo Balbi	ITA	Honda	-	-	-	-	9	-	-	-	-	-	-	-	-	-	-	9
26	Luca Cadalora	ITA	Yamaha	-	-	-	-	-	-	-	-	-	-	-	8	-	-	-	8
26	Fernando Gonzales	SPA	Honda	-	-	-	-	8	-	-	-	-	-	-	-	-	-	-	8
28	Niggi Schmassman	SWI	Honda	-	2	-	-	6	-	-	-	-	-	-	-	-	-	-	8
29	Massimo Broccoli	ITA	Cagiva	-	-	-	5	-	-	-	3	-	-	-	-	-	-	-	8
30	Michael Dowson	AUS	Yamaha	-	7	-	-	-	-	-	-	-	-	-	-	-	-	-	7
30	Andreas Leuthe	GER	Suzuki	-	-	-	-	7	-	-	-	-	-	-	-	-	-	-	7
32	Shinichi Itoh	JPN	Honda	6	-	-	-	-	-	-	-	-	-	-	-	-	-	-	6
33	Fabio Biliotti	ITA	Honda	-	-	-	-	-	-	-	-	-	-	1	2	3	-	-	6
34	Bruno Kneubuhler	SWI	Honda	-	-	2	-	-	1	1	-	-	-	-	-	2	-	-	6
35	John Kocinski	USA	Yamaha	-	-	-	-	-	-	-	-	-	5.5	-	-	-	-	-	5.5
36	Ernst Gschwender	GER	Suzuki	-	-	-	-	-	5	-	-	-	-	-	-	-	-	-	5
36	Fred Merkel	USA	Honda	-	-	-	-	-	-	-	-	-	-	-	5	-	-	-	5
38	Roger Burnett	GBR	Honda	-	-	-	-	-	-	-	-	-	-	-	4	-	-	-	4
38	Thierry Crine	FRA	Suzuki	-	-	-	-	-	-	-	-	-	-	4	-	-	-	-	4
40	Juan Lopez Mella	SPA	Honda	-	-	-	2	-	-	-	-	-	-	-	-	1	-	1	4
41	Alberto Rota	ITA	Yamaha	-	-	-	-	-	-	-	-	-	-	-	-	-	3	-	3
41	Shunji Yatsushiro	JPN	Honda	3	-	-	-	-	-	-	-	-	-	-	-	-	-	-	3
43	Cees Doorakkers	NED	Honda	-	-	-	-	-	-	-	-	1	1.5	-	-	-	-	-	2.5
44	Eddie Laycock	IRL	Honda	-	-	-	1	-	-	-	-	-	1	-	-	-	-	-	2
45	Peter Linden	SWE	Honda	-	-	-	-	-	-	-	-	-	-	-	-	-	1	-	1
45	Kunio Machii	JPN	Yamaha	1	-	-	-	-	-	-	-	-	-	-	-	-	-	-	1

Scoring system – 20, 17, 15, 13, 11, 10, 9, 8, 7, 6, 5, 4, 3, 2, 1

250cc

Pos	Rider	Nat	Machine	Total
1	Sito Pons	SPA	Honda	262
2	Reinhold Roth	GER	Honda	190
3	Jacques Cornu	SWI	Honda	187
4	Carlos Cardus	SPA	Honda	162
5	Luca Cadalora	ITA	Yamaha	127
6	Masahiro Shimizu	JPN	Honda	116
7	Jean-Philippe Ruggia	FRA	Yamaha	110
8	Juan Garriga	SPA	Yamaha	98
9	Helmut Bradl	GER	Honda	88
10	Martin Wimmer	GER	Aprilia	62

125cc

Pos	Rider	Nat	Machine	Total
1	Alex Criville	SPA	Cobas	166
2	Hans Spaan	NED	Honda	152
3	Ezio Gianola	ITA	Honda	138
4	Hisashi Unemoto	JPN	Honda	104
5	Fausto Gresini	ITA	Aprilia	102
6	Koji Takada	JPN	Honda	99
7	Stefan Prein	GER	Honda	92
8	Julian Miralles	SPA	Derbi	90
9	Jorge Martinez	SPA	Derbi	72
10	Allan Scott	USA	Honda	54

80cc

Pos	Rider	Nat	Machine	Total
1	Manuel Herreros	SPA	Derbi	92
2	Stefan Dorflinger	SWI	Krauser	80
3	Peter Ottl	GER	Krauser	75
4	Herri Torontegui	SPA	Krauser	75
5	Gabriele Gnani	ITA	Gnani	45
6	Paolo Pileri	ITA	Krauser	41
7	Bogdan Nikolov	BUL	Krauser	40
8	Jorge Martinez	SPA	Derbi	35
9	Jaime Mariano	SPA	Casal	33
10	Jorg Seel	GER	Seel	32

EDDIE LAWSON'S RESULTS AND STATISTICS, 500cc

Starts	Wins	Podiums	Poles
127	31	78	18

Debut RSA/Kyalami/1983
First win RSA/Kyalami/1984
Last win HUN/Hungaroring/1992

LAWSON MAKES HISTORY

It is difficult to justify Lawson's 'Steady Eddie' nickname. It's true that in the Yamaha years a stopwatch was necessary to tell if he was going fast, so smooth was his riding. The Honda didn't allow him that option, though, so he modified his style – and all this while fighting for supremacy with Rainey, Schwantz and Gardner. Only two men had previously won the championship on different makes of motorcycle: Geoff Duke on Norton and Gilera, Giacomo Agostini on MV Agusta and Yamaha. Neither of them equalled what Eddie Lawson achieved by winning back-to-back titles on different bikes.

This was also Lawson's fourth title, putting him level with great British stars Geoff Duke, John Surtees and Mike Hailwood. At the time only Agostini had racked up more titles, but subsequently Mick Doohan and Valentino Rossi would exceed that mark.

The hallmark of Lawson's riding was ruthless efficiency and a studied indifference to what anyone thought about him. The first aspect of his character was shown by the way he and Kanemoto's small team worked through myriad chassis and suspension modifications as the season turned into a fight between Lawson and Rainey that would effectively be resolved when the Yamaha man crashed coming onto the back straight in Sweden with two rounds remaining. Wayne and Eddie were, of course, dicing for the lead at the time. The second could be seen at any press conference or riders' meeting: Lawson had once told his colleagues that he would do the opposite of whatever they decided. Then, as if to maintain his reputation for contrariness, at the end of the '89 season Eddie promptly left Honda to rejoin Yamaha. A year later he would move on again, this time to Cagiva, and in 1991 he gave the Italian company their first GP win.

1990

Wayne Rainey took over where the injured Lawson left off, with a clinical demolition of the opposition

Having moved 12 months previously from Yamaha to Honda, Eddie Lawson promptly moved right back again. This time, though, he joined Kenny Roberts's operation. Wayne Rainey was the other factory Yamaha rider. Christian Sarron was joined in the French Yamaha team by Jean-Philippe Ruggia, and Juan Garriga came up from 250s in a one-man team.

Honda also recruited a Spaniard from the 250s to ride a satellite bike – double champion Sito Pons – and Pier-Francesco Chili kept his satellite V4. The factory team was cut back to the two Aussies, Wayne Gardner and Mick Doohan. At Suzuki, Kevin Schwantz was joined by Kevin Magee, but a serious head injury sustained at Laguna Seca put the Australian out for the season and Niall Mackenzie was recalled from the wilderness of a privateer 250 ride. Cagiva had three riders: Randy Mamola, Ron Haslam and class rookie Alex Barros (BRA).

The Roberts team, now christened Marlboro Yamaha, became the dominating presence in the paddock and Wayne Rainey duly won his first title with a near-perfect season. The only time he finished off the rostrum was when he had to retire from the Hungarian GP with a front-brake problem, and by then he was already World Champion.

As in '89, injuries played their part. While Rainey avoided them, Lawson was sidelined for the first half of the year with a crushed heel, Doohan started the year hurt, Gardner missed races, and Schwantz and Mamola both rode with injuries, while the abiding image of the season was Doohan and Chili's synchronised highside at the Nürburgring. Things got so bad there were only 16 starters and nine finishers at the mid-season Yugoslav GP – and the last four of them were off-the-pace privateers.

Fortunately the 125 and 250 championships threw up new stars. Yamaha-mounted John Kocinski won the bigger class after a tough fight with Carlos Cardus (SPA, Honda), and Loris Capirossi (ITA, Honda) won the 125s, along the way becoming the youngest GP winner and the youngest World Champion.

ABOVE Wayne Rainey and Eddie Lawson: the newly formed Marlboro Yamaha team. (*Henk Keulemans*)

RIGHT Loris Capirossi – still the youngest ever World Champion. (*Henk Keulemans*)

THE 1990 SEASON

500cc

JPN/Suzuka

- Sito Pons finished fifth on his debut in the 500cc class – at that time the best result by a Spanish rider in the 500cc class at a GP held outside Spain

USA/Laguna Seca

- Reigning champion Eddie Lawson suffered a crushed right heel when his front brake failed in Friday qualifying. He missed six races
- Kevin Magee crashed on the second lap and suffered head injuries that ended his season

YUG/Rijeka

- Wayne Rainey won the 500cc race at the last ever Yugoslavian GP

BEL/Spa-Francorchamps

- The last time the circuit held a Grand Prix. Spa had been in continuous use as a GP venue since 1949, the first year of the World Championships, apart from 1980 when Zolder held the Belgian GP. Only Assen has hosted more GP events

HUN/Hungaroring

- Mick Doohan scored his first GP victory on the championship's first visit to Hungary for a GP event
- Wayne Rainey had his only non-score of the year, ending a run of 15 successive podium finishes going back to the 1989 Czech GP

CZE/Brno

- Rainey won the race to clinch his first world title

AUS/Phillip Island

- Wayne Gardner won by less than a second from team-mate Mick Doohan – the first occasion on which Australian riders finished first and second in the 500cc class
- Former 250cc World Champion Christian Sarron made his last GP appearance, bringing to an end a 15-year Grand Prix career

250cc

GER/Nürburgring

- Wilco Zeelenberg (Honda) became the only Dutch rider to win a 250cc GP race

YUG/Rijeka

- The race ended short of full distance after an accident to Reinhold Roth that ended the German's racing career

HUN/Hungaroring

- John Kocinski took the victory, to move to just five points behind championship leader Carlos Cardus with one round remaining

AUS/Phillip Island

- John Kocinski clinched the world title with a win at the final race of the year after Cardus retired late in the race with a broken gear lever
- Kocinski's victory in Australia was the last win for the USA in the 250cc class

125cc

GBR/Donington

- Loris Capirossi's first victory made him the youngest rider ever to win a GP at that time

CZE/Brno

- Hans Spaan took his fifth victory of the year – the last Grand Prix victory by a Dutch rider

AUS/Phillip Island

- Loris Capirossi won the final race of the year, and the title, after championship leader Stefan Prein (GER) retired on lap seven with mechanical problems

YOUNGEST RIDERS TO WIN A WORLD TITLE

	Rider	Age	Class	Year
1	Loris Capirossi (ITA)	17 years 165 days	125cc	1990
2	Dani Pedrosa (SPA)	18 years 13 days	125cc	2003
3	Valentino Rossi (ITA)	18 years 196 days	125cc	1997
4	Andrea Dovizioso (ITA)	18 years 201 days	125cc	2004
5	Manuel Poggiali (RSM)	18 years 262 days	125cc	2001
6	Thomas Luthi (SWI)	19 years 61 days	125cc	2005
7	Haruchika Aoki (JPN)	19 years 173 days	125cc	1995
8	Alex Criville (SPA)	19 years 176 days	125cc	1989
9	Jorge Lorenzo (SPA)	19 years 178 days	250cc	2006
10	Johnny Cecotto (VEN)	19 years 211 days	350cc	1975

1990 WORLD CHAMPIONSHIP

500cc

Pos	Rider	Nat	Machine	JPN	USA	SPA	ITA	GER	AUT	YUG	NED	BEL	FRA	GBR	SWE	CZE	HUN	AUS	Total
1	Wayne Rainey	USA	Yamaha	20	20	17	20	17	17	20	17	20	15	17	20	20	-	15	255
2	Kevin Schwantz	USA	Suzuki	15	-	15	17	20	20	17	20	9	20	20	-	-	15	-	188
3	Mick Doohan	AUS	Honda	-	17	13	15	-	15	13	13	10	13	13	13	7	20	17	179
4	Niall Mackenzie	GBR	Suzuki	-	-	8	11	15	11	15	11	4	10	11	11	13	9	11	140
5	Wayne Gardner	AUS	Honda	17	-	20	13	-	-	-	-	6	17	-	15	17	13	20	138
6	Juan Garriga	SPA	Yamaha	6	10	7	8	9	7	-	10	7	8	9	8	11	11	10	121
7	Eddie Lawson	USA	Yamaha	-	-	-	-	-	-	-	15	15	11	15	17	15	17	13	118
8	Jean-Philippe Ruggia	FRA	Yamaha	8	11	6	-	10	8	11	5	17	-	7	9	8	10	-	110
9	Christian Sarron	FRA	Yamaha	-	13	9	-	13	9	-	9	13	-	8	-	10	-	-	84
10	Sito Pons	SPA	Honda	11	-	10	10	11	10	-	-	-	-	-	-	9	6	9	76
11	Pier-Francesco Chili	ITA	Honda	9	15	11	-	-	13	-	8	-	-	-	-	-	-	7	63
12	Alex Barros	BRA	Cagiva	-	8	-	-	8	5	-	6	11	-	5	7	-	7	-	57
13	Randy Mamola	USA	Cagiva	-	9	-	9	7	6	-	-	-	9	10	-	5	-	-	55
14	Marco Papa	ITA	Honda	-	-	-	7	5	3	10	2	-	7	3	5	3	4	6	55
15	Ron Haslam	GBR	Cagiva	-	-	-	-	-	4	-	7	8	6	6	6	4	5	-	46
16	Cees Doorakkers	NED	Honda	-	-	3	2	6	2	9	3	1	4	1	4	-	-	4	39
17	Eddie Laycock	IRL	Honda	-	-	5	-	-	-	-	4	3	5	4	-	2	2	5	30
18	Carl Fogarty	GBR	Honda	-	-	-	-	-	-	-	-	-	-	-	10	6	8	-	24
19	Niggi Schmassman	SWI	Honda	-	6	4	3	3	-	7	-	-	-	-	-	-	-	-	23
20	Peter Linden	SWE	Honda	-	7	-	4	1	-	-	-	-	-	-	3	-	-	-	15
21	Kevin Magee	AUS	Suzuki	13	-	-	-	-	-	-	-	-	-	-	-	-	-	-	13
22	Karl Truchsess	AUT	Honda	-	-	-	-	-	1	8	1	2	-	-	-	-	-	-	12
23	Tadahiko Taira	JPN	Yamaha	10	-	-	-	-	-	-	-	-	-	-	-	-	-	-	10
24	Peter Goddard	AUS	Yamaha	-	-	-	-	-	-	-	-	-	-	-	-	-	-	8	8
25	Andreas Leuthe	GER	Honda	-	-	2	-	4	-	-	-	-	-	2	-	-	-	-	8
26	Shinichi Itoh	JPN	Honda	7	-	-	-	-	-	-	-	-	-	-	-	-	-	-	7
27	Romolo Balbi	ITA	Honda	-	-	-	6	-	-	-	-	-	-	-	-	-	-	-	6
28	Norihiko Fujiwara	JPN	Yamaha	-	-	-	-	-	-	-	-	5	-	-	-	-	-	-	5
28	Hikaru Miyagi	JPN	Honda	5	-	-	-	-	-	-	-	-	-	-	-	-	-	-	5
28	Michele Valdo	ITA	Honda	-	-	-	5	-	-	-	-	-	-	-	-	-	-	-	5
31	Shinji Katayama	JPN	Yamaha	4	-	-	-	-	-	-	-	-	-	-	-	-	-	-	4
32	Rachel Nicotte	FRA	Plaisir	-	-	-	-	-	-	-	-	-	-	-	-	1	3	-	4
33	Osamu Hiwatashi	JPN	Suzuki	3	-	-	-	-	-	-	-	-	-	-	-	-	-	-	3
34	Hansjorg Butz	GER	Honda	-	-	1	-	2	-	-	-	-	-	-	-	-	-	-	3
35	Vittorio Scatola	ITA	Paton	-	-	-	1	-	-	-	-	-	-	-	-	-	-	-	1
35	Martin Trosch	GER	Honda	-	-	-	-	-	-	-	-	-	-	-	-	-	1	-	1

Scoring system – 20, 17, 15, 13, 11, 10, 9, 8, 7, 6, 5, 4, 3, 2, 1

250cc

Pos	Rider	Nat	Machine	Total
1	John Kocinski	USA	Yamaha	223
2	Carlos Cardus	SPA	Honda	208
3	Luca Cadalora	ITA	Yamaha	184
4	Helmut Bradl	GER	Honda	150
5	Wilco Zeelenberg	NED	Honda	127
6	Martin Wimmer	GER	Aprilia	118
7	Masahiro Shimizu	JPN	Honda	100
8	Jochen Schmid	GER	Honda	92
9	Jacques Cornu	SWI	Honda	86
10	Dominique Sarron	FRA	Honda	78

125cc

Pos	Rider	Nat	Machine	Total
1	Loris Capirossi	ITA	Honda	182
2	Hans Spaan	NED	Honda	173
3	Stefan Prein	GER	Honda	169
4	Doriano Romboni	ITA	Honda	130
5	Dirk Raudies	GER	Honda	113
6	Jorge Martinez	SPA	Cobas	105
7	Fausto Gresini	ITA	Honda	102
8	Bruno Casanova	ITA	Honda	97
9	Alessandro Gramigni	ITA	Aprilia	84
10	Heinz Luthi	SWI	Honda	78

LORIS CAPIROSSI

Loris Capirossi emerged from a pack of Honda RS125 riders to beat '89 runner-up, Dutchman Hans Spaan, at the last round of the year and become the youngest ever World Champion. He had already become the youngest winner at the British GP. Winning a world title in a debut season would be reason enough to earn a place in the history books, but Loris was still gracing the paddock 20 years later. Along the way he retained his 125 title, added a 250 World Championship and then won 500cc/MotoGP races on three different makes of motorcycle. At the time of writing it is possible he could make that four.

The win at Brno in 2006 on the Ducati made Loris's winning career the longest in Grand Prix history. His first win, the British 125 race in 1990, had come 16 years and 15 days earlier, breaking the record of Angel Nieto whose winning career in the smaller classes started with the 50cc GP of East Germany in 1969 and ended with the 80cc race at the 1985 French GP. The gap between those two races is exactly a week shorter than between Loris's first and his win in Brno.

If Loris wins again in MotoGP he will also have the longest winning career in the top class. His first 500cc win was the Australian race in 1996, 10 years and 338 days before his last win, in Japan in 2007. Giacomo Agostini, Phil Read and Alex Barros all have longer gaps between their first and last 500cc/MotoGP wins, with the Brazilian holding the record with 11 years and 204 days between Jarama 1993 and Estoril 2005.

LORIS CAPIROSSI'S ACHIEVEMENTS

- By the end of 2008 he had made 282 Grand Prix starts – more than any other rider in GP history
- He has taken part in 37.9 per cent of the 743 Grand Prix events staged since the start of the World Championship series back in 1949
- He has finished in a points-scoring position a record 231 times
- 2009 is his 20th year as a full-time GP rider – equalling the record of Angel Nieto
- He has won GP races on seven different motorcycles: 125cc Honda, 250cc Honda, 250cc Aprilia, 500cc Yamaha, 500cc Honda, 990cc Ducati and 800cc Ducati
- He is one of only two riders who have won on 500cc two-stroke, 990cc four-stroke and 800cc four-stroke; the other is Valentino Rossi
- During his career he has competed at 41 different Grand Prix circuits
- He still holds the record set in 1990 of being the youngest ever rider to win a World Championship, at the age of 17 years 165 days

BELOW Loris leads the 125s. (*Henk Keulemans*)

1991

Wayne Rainey retained his title in the face of strong challenges from Mick Doohan and the mercurial Kevin Schwantz

Eddie Lawson swapped bikes for the third year in a row, leaving Yamaha to replace Randy Mamola at perennial under-achievers Cagiva. Alex Barros kept his ride with the Italian team, which had been expected to stop racing until Eddie signed. Honda reduced their commitment to three bikes: the factory Rothmans team of Aussies Wayne Gardner and Mick Doohan plus Sito Pons, who got a second year on a satellite bike.

Wayne Rainey was back on a Roberts Yamaha to defend his title, with 250 champion John Kocinski as his new team-mate. The Roberts team also put Doug Chandler (USA) on a third Yamaha, run in factory rather than sponsor's colours. The French Yamaha team promoted Christian Sarron to a management role, so Jean-Philippe Ruggia became their leading rider with back-up from veteran all-rounder Adrien Morillas (FRA). Niall Mackenzie would ride a third Sonauto Yamaha later in the season. Juan Garriga also got a second year on a satellite bike. Suzuki had, rather surprisingly, decided not to re-employ Mackenzie, who had finished fourth overall in 1990, choosing instead to field Belgian Didier de Radigues alongside Kevin Schwantz. Kevin Magee recovered from his terrible Laguna Seca crash the previous year to ride the first two races for Suzuki, then discovered he hadn't got a contract. He rode in the last race of the year, in Malaysia, for Roberts Yamaha as team-mate to Chandler.

There was another Yamaha on the grid, though, and a very significant one. Team Millar's rider Eddie Laycock (IRL) had a V4 leased from the factory, not operated under the aegis of a national importer, a first for a private team. This was by way of a test to see if a complicated beast like a YZR500 could be entrusted to a private team. The experiment was a success. Laycock racked up enough points to finish twelfth overall and it might have been even better if he had not damaged his shoulder when he crashed at Assen while lying seventh.

This season was the last time a points-scoring system which did not count all rounds was used: riders dropped their worst two scores of the year.

ABOVE The 'Evil Empire': Kenny Roberts' Marlboro Yamaha team of Wayne Rainey and John Kocinski. (*Henk Keulemans*)

RIGHT New star Noboru Ueda leads double 125 champion Fausto Gresini. 'Nobby' was the spearhead of a Japanese invasion of the class. (*Henk Keulemans*)

THE 1991 SEASON

500cc

JPN/Suzuka
- The rules were changed, with the minimum weight rising from 115 to 130kg
- Kevin Schwantz won the opening race of the year after a tremendous battle, the first four riders covered by just over half a second at the flag – the closest ever top four in a 500cc GP at that time

AUS/Eastern Creek
- Wayne Rainey won the first 500cc GP race to be held at the New South Wales circuit

USA/Laguna Seca
- Rainey made it three wins in a row at Laguna Seca

SPA/Jerez
- Mick Doohan took his first win of the year to head the World Championship table for the first time in his career
- Juan Garriga finished fourth at his home GP – the best result by a Spanish rider in the 500cc class for 20 years

ITA/Misano
- Eddie Lawson finished third, giving Cagiva their first ever dry weather podium finish

GER/Hockenheim
- After a race-long battle Schwantz crossed the line just 0.016s ahead of Rainey in the closest ever finish between the two great rivals

NED/Assen
- In winning the Dutch TT Kevin Schwantz set a lap record which was not bettered until the track was remodelled in 2002

GBR/Donington
- Ron Haslam finished 12th on the rotary-engined Norton, the last points-scoring finish for the manufacturer that won the first 500cc GP race back in 1949

FRA-VdM/Le Mans
- Wayne Rainey finished third to retain the world title with one race remaining, in the process becoming the last rider to win the 500cc crown using Dunlop tyres

MAL/Shah Alam
- New champion Rainey and fellow-American Kevin Schwantz both missed the final race of the year after suffering injuries in pre-race testing
- John Kocinski took his maiden 500cc win on the first occasion that a Grand Prix event had been held in Malaysia

250cc

JPN/Suzuka
- Luca Cadalora won first time out on a Honda, and maintained his championship lead throughout the year

SPA/Jerez
- Helmut Bradl (GER, Honda) scored his first GP victory

NED/Assen
- Pier-Francesco Chili won for the first time on a 250, giving Aprilia only their second class win and their first victory for four years

FRA-VdM/Le Mans
- Luca Cadalora finished third to win the 250cc world title for the first time

125cc

JPN/Suzuka
- Newcomer Noboru Ueda (JPN, Honda) qualified on pole and won the race – the last time that a GP was won by a rider making his Grand Prix debut

SPA/Jerez
- Ueda made it two wins from three races in his first ever GP in Europe

CZE/Brno
- Alessandro Gramigni (ITA) scored his first GP victory and the first victory for Aprilia in the 125cc class
- Loris Capirossi finished second to retain the 125cc world title

1991 WORLD CHAMPIONSHIP

500cc

500cc – thirteen best results were counted

Pos	Rider	Nat	Machine	JPN	AUS	USA	SPA	ITA	GER	AUT	EUR	NED	FRA	GBR	RSM	CZE	VdM	MAL	Nett	Gross
1	Wayne Rainey	USA	Yamaha	15	20	20	15	7	17	17	20	17	20	17	20	20	15	-	233	240
2	Mick Doohan	AUS	Honda	17	17	17	20	20	15	20	17	-	17	15	15	17	17	15	224	239
3	Kevin Schwantz	USA	Suzuki	20	11	15	-	9	20	15	13	20	13	20	7	11	20	-	204	
4	John Kocinski	USA	Yamaha	13	15	-	17	17	-	7	11	10	-	13	10	15	13	20	161	
5	Wayne Gardner	AUS	Honda	11	13	9	9	-	11	13	15	15	6	11	13	13	11	17	161	167
6	Eddie Lawson	USA	Cagiva	10	10	11	10	15	13	11	-	13	15	10	-	8	-	-	126	
7	Juan Garriga	SPA	Yamaha	9	-	8	13	8	9	10	10	4	5	7	9	10	10	13	121	125
8	Didier de Radigues	BEL	Suzuki	2	6	6	8	-	10	8	6	11	9	8	8	9	8	8	105	107
9	Doug Chandler	USA	Yamaha	5	4	-	6	10	7	9	7	5	10	-	7	6	9	-	85	
10	Jean-Philippe Ruggia	FRA	Honda	-	9	13	11	11	-	-	9	8	11	-	6	-	-	-	78	
11	Adrien Morillas	FRA	Yamaha	4	7	7	7	-	8	-	8	7	8	-	-	-	6	9	71	
12	Eddie Laycock	IRL	Yamaha	-	3	3	5	6	6	6	4	-	-	5	5	5	5	4	57	
13	Alex Barros	BRA	Cagiva	6	8	10	-	13	-	-	-	9	-	-	-	-	-	-	46	
14	Sito Pons	SPA	Honda	8	-	-	-	-	-	-	5	6	7	-	-	7	7	-	40	
15	Cees Doorakkers	NED	Honda	-	2	2	3	4	5	-	3	3	4	2	3	3	-	6	40	
16	Marco Papa	ITA	Honda	-	-	-	4	5	-	4	-	-	3	6	4	-	3	7	36	
17	Niall Mackenzie	GBR	Yamaha	-	-	-	-	-	-	-	-	-	-	9	11	-	4	10	34	
18	Michael Rudroff	GER	Honda	-	-	-	1	1	4	5	2	2	2	3	2	4	-	-	26	
19	Kevin Magee	AUS	Suz/Yam	3	5	-	-	-	-	-	-	-	-	-	-	-	-	11	19	
20	Hans Becker	GER	Yamaha	-	-	-	2	-	3	-	-	-	-	-	1	2	-	5	13	
21	Kenichiro Iwahashi	JPN	Honda	7	-	-	-	-	-	-	-	-	-	-	-	-	-	-	7	
22	Simon Buckmaster	GBR	Suzuki	-	-	-	-	2	2	-	-	-	-	-	-	1	1	-	6	
23	Rich Oliver	USA	Yamaha	-	-	5	-	-	-	-	-	-	-	-	-	-	-	-	5	
24	Niggi Schmassman	SWI	Honda	-	-	1	-	-	-	-	1	1	-	-	-	-	-	2	5	
25	Ron Haslam	GBR	Norton	-	-	-	-	-	-	-	-	-	-	4	-	-	-	-	4	
25	Robbie Petersen	USA	Yamaha	-	-	4	-	-	-	-	-	-	-	-	-	-	-	-	4	
27	Sepp Doppler	AUT	Yamaha	-	-	-	-	-	-	-	-	-	1	-	-	-	-	3	4	
28	Romolo Balbi	ITA	Honda	-	-	-	-	3	-	-	-	-	-	-	-	-	-	-	3	
29	Andreas Leuthe	GER	Suzuki	-	-	-	-	-	-	-	-	-	-	1	-	-	2	-	3	
30	Peter Goddard	AUS	Yamaha	1	-	-	-	-	-	-	-	-	-	-	-	-	-	-	1	
30	Steve Spray	GBR	Roton	-	1	-	-	-	-	-	-	-	-	-	-	-	-	-	1	

Scoring system – 20, 17, 15, 13, 11, 10, 9, 8, 7, 6, 5, 4, 3, 2, 1

250cc

250cc – thirteen best results were counted

Pos	Rider	Nat	Machine	Total	Gross
1	Luca Cadalora	ITA	Honda	237	259
2	Helmut Bradl	GER	Honda	220	228
3	Carlos Cardus	SPA	Honda	205	225
4	Wilco Zeelenberg	NED	Honda	158	
5	Masahiro Shimizu	JPN	Honda	142	
6	Loris Reggiani	ITA	Aprilia	128	
7	Pier-Francesco Chili	ITA	Aprilia	107	
8	Jochen Schmid	GER	Honda	96	
9	Martin Wimmer	GER	Suzuki	89	
10	Paolo Casoli	ITA	Yamaha	65	

125cc

125cc – eleven best results were counted

Pos	Rider	Nat	Machine	Total	Gross
1	Loris Capirossi	ITA	Honda	200	225
2	Fausto Gresini	ITA	Honda	181	191
3	Ralf Waldmann	GER	Honda	141	
4	Gabriele Debbia	ITA	Aprilia	111	
5	Noboru Ueda	JPN	Honda	105	
6	Jorge Martinez	SPA	Cobas/Honda	99	
7	Alessandro Gramigni	ITA	Aprilia	90	
8	Dirk Raudies	GER	Honda	81	
9	Peter Ottl	GER	Rotax	67	
10	Noboyuki Wakai	JPN	Honda	60	

TELEVISION COVERAGE

You couldn't guarantee to see a GP on TV before 1988. Up until then, individual promoters kept the TV rights for their rounds and no broadcaster was likely to negotiate with a dozen of them to be able to show the whole series. Clearly this situation was holding back the progress of the series, so in 1988, just as the digital TV revolution got into its stride, a joint venture between IRTA, the teams' association, and ROPA, the promoters, bought the TV rights to GPs from the sport's governing body, the FIM, and formed a company called MotoMedia.

MotoMedia was charged with 'guaranteeing as wide a retransmission of all GPs as possible,' according to FIM records. MotoMedia was set up as a management company, which sought offers to produce the TV pictures for a world feed. The best offer came from F1 supremo Bernie Ecclestone's company ISC. A four-year deal was signed and the FIM stood to benefit by a minimum US$800,000 per year. Responsibility for producing the TV feed actually still lay with the local national federation, but ISC could take charge of production if that was how the federation wanted to work. Some national federations had not wanted to take on the responsibility for the TV feed, and the 1989 German GP only got to air because MotoMedia stumped up 50,000 Deutschmarks on the Saturday morning of race weekend. There was also considerable internal stress within the FIM over the organisation's representation within MotoMedia. This was also a time when relations between IRTA and the FIM were seriously strained over matters of money and safety as well as the management of TV rights.

Early in 1990 the FIM decided it did not want to extend the contract with MotoMedia, and it also requested an increased share of any profits. The FIM did get an increase, to a third of net income with a minimum of US$266,667. Rumours surfaced that ISC had sold on the TV rights to a company owned by Silvio Berlusconi. They weren't true.

The FIM now wanted to negotiate the rights for 1993–97 for a minimum of US$18 million. After bad experiences with other series, it wanted bank guarantees from the seven companies who made offers. The seven were also invited to make second offers of over $20 million. The Spanish company Dorna bid $30 million and was invited to make a presentation in December 1990. The contract was signed in February 1991, but subsequent events saw it cancelled in December.

There were initial difficulties, not least with communication. Following on from other issues – calendar, money, safety – this was enough to provoke IRTA/ROPA, with Ecclestone, into planning their own series – much as World Series had been mooted in the early '80s. IRTA signed up their last team, Yamaha, at the Malaysian GP and told Ecclestone their plans could be put into action. But it didn't happen quite like that.

Instead Bernie Ecclestone revived his original Brabham company, rechristened it Two Wheel Promotions, and obtained all the commercial rights to GPs from the FIM. Dorna were then leased the TV rights. Frustrated by having to negotiate with several parties rather than issue edicts as he was wont to in F1, Ecclestone sold a controlling share in TWP to Dorna in 1993.

This convoluted political process resolved itself with Dorna entrenched as both TV and commercial rights holder, and IRTA contracted by them to provide the teams, run the events and police the paddock – the situation that pertains to this day.

ABOVE Carmelo Ezpeleta, CEO of Dorna; Francesco Zerbi, Deputy President of the FIM during the time GP TV rights were such a thorny issu, and President from 1995-2005; and the man he succeeded, Jos Vaessen, FIM President from 1989 to 1995 when relations with teams and promoters were at their most difficult (*Henk Keulemans*)

1992

Wayne Rainey made it three in a row, but only after Mick Doohan broke his leg and saw a 53-point lead disappear

Wayne Rainey emulated team-manager Kenny Roberts by winning his third consecutive championship for Yamaha in a year when injury affected nearly all the top contenders. John Kocinksi was again Rainey's team-mate, while Randy Mamola had the third Roberts bike. Juan Garriga was back for a third year on a satellite Yamaha, while the French squad kept Niall Mackenzie, who had guested for them in '91, and brought in Miguel DuHamel (CAN).

Mick Doohan and Wayne Gardner stayed as Honda's works riders while Sito Pons handed the leased NSR to 1989 125 champ Alex Criville and went into team-management. Kevin Schwantz was again Suzuki's lead rider, although fellow-American Doug Chandler would prove to be the first team-mate capable of outperforming the Texan. Cagiva kept both their riders, Eddie Lawson and Alex Barros, but brought in a new team-manager – none other than Giacomo Agostini.

The experiment of the previous season with Team Millar had demonstrated that it was possible for private teams to run V4s, so Yamaha now made engines available to privateers by way of French and English chassis builders ROC and Harris Performance. This enabled over a dozen privateers to get on the grid, the best of whom was Peter Goddard (AUS), the reigning All-Japan Champion, on a bike run by Bob McLean's WCM team.

Rainey started the year hurt, then missed two races in the middle of the season after a crash in Germany. Gardner broke his leg at the first round in Japan, Schwantz his hand at the third race, in Malaysia, and then everyone fell off at Assen. Mick Doohan's crash, actually his second of the weekend, didn't look too bad but his right leg went under the bike when it hit the kerbing and he fractured the tibia and fibula. It looked a relatively simple case, but then infection set in and Mick came terribly close to losing the leg. He was 53 points in front of the field – 65 in front of Rainey – before the Dutch race, with six of 13 races remaining, having won five races and finished second twice. Doohan returned for the last two races, a ghostly presence, but couldn't prevent Rainey winning the championship again.

ABOVE Mick Doohan is carried into Assen's medical centre with what started as a relatively straightforward fracture but soon became a nightmare. (*Henk Keulemans*)

RIGHT Doohan returns with Dr Costa in close attendance. (*Henk Keulemans*)

THE **1992** SEASON

500cc

JPN/Suzuka
- Mick Doohan won the opening race of the year from Doug Chandler, having his first ride on the Suzuki, with team-mate Kevin Schwantz third
- Wayne Gardner fell early in the race, remounted and then fell again on lap 19 when up to sixth, breaking his leg and missing the next five races

AUS/Eastern Creek
- Daryl Beattie (AUS, Honda) made his GP debut as a wild card and finished third

MAL/Shah Alam
- Alex Criville finished third in only his third start on a 500cc Honda, the first podium finish by a Spanish rider in the premier class

SPA/Jerez
- Mick Doohan became the first rider since Giacomo Agostini in 1972 to win the opening four races of the year

GER/Hockenheim
- Wayne Rainey crashed in practice and suffered injuries that caused him to retire from the race and miss the Dutch TT

NED/Assen
- Mick Doohan crashed in qualifying and missed the next four races
- Alex Criville became the first Spanish rider to win a 500cc Grand Prix
- Cagiva's Alex Barros had his first podium with a third-place finish

HUN/Hungaroring
- In mixed weather conditions Eddie Lawson gave the Cagiva factory their first GP victory
- Randy Mamola took the last of his 54 podium finishes in the 500cc class, 13 years after finishing on the podium for the first time

GBR/Donington
- Wayne Gardner won the last of his 18 GPs just days after announcing he was retiring from World Championship racing at the end of the year

BRA/Interlagos
- Mick Doohan returned from injury, still far from fully fit, and finished out of the points in 12th

RSA/Kyalami
- Wayne Rainey arrived at the final race of the year just two points behind Mick Doohan. The Aussie finished down in sixth while Rainey finished third to take his third successive title

125cc

SPA/Jerez
- Alessandro Gramigni missed the Spanish GP after breaking his leg in a road-bike crash

GER/Hockenheim
- Bruno Casanova (ITA, Aprilia) took his only GP victory in a tight race
- Sixth-place finisher Dirk Raudies (GER, Honda) was just 0.883s behind the winner – the first time that the top six riders in a full-length 125cc GP were covered by less than a second

BRA/Interlagos
- Dirk Raudies took his first Grand Prix victory

RSA/Kylami
- Third at the final race of the year was enough to clinch the world title for Alessandro Gramigni – the first Aprilia rider to win a World Championship

250cc

MAL/Shah Alam
- For the second successive year Luca Cadalora opened the year with three successive victories

ITA/Mugello
- Max Biaggi (ITA, Aprilia) finished third to make his first appearance on a Grand Prix podium
- Cadalora took the win from fellow-Italians Loris Reggiani and Max Biaggi – the first all-Italian podium in the 250cc class since 1977

GER/Hockenheim
- Pier-Francesco Chili won from Biaggi and Reggiani – the first ever all-Aprilia podium in GP racing

GBR/Donington
- Fourth place was enough to give Luca Cadalora his second successive 250cc title

RSA/Kyalami
- Max Biaggi scored his first GP victory at the final race of the year

1992 WORLD CHAMPIONSHIP

500cc

500cc – all races were counted

Pos	Rider	Nat	Machine	JPN	AUS	MAL	SPA	ITA	EUR	GER	NED	HUN	FRA	GBR	BRA	RSA	Total
1	Wayne Rainey	USA	Yamaha	-	15	15	15	-	20	-	-	8	20	15	20	12	140
2	Mick Doohan	AUS	Honda	20	20	20	20	15	15	20	-	-	-	-	-	6	136
3	John Kocinski	USA	Yamaha	-	-	-	8	12	8	8	15	4	12	-	15	20	102
4	Kevin Schwantz	USA	Suzuki	12	10	-	10	20	10	15	-	10	-	-	4	8	99
5	Doug Chandler	USA	Suzuki	15	8	8	1	10	12	3	-	15	-	-	12	10	94
6	Wayne Gardner	AUS	Honda	-	-	-	-	-	-	12	-	6	15	20	10	15	78
7	Juan Garriga	SPA	Yamaha	-	2	10	4	6	1	2	10	3	10	12	-	1	61
8	Alex Criville	SPA	Honda	-	4	12	-	3	-	10	20	-	-	-	6	4	59
9	Eddie Lawson	USA	Cagiva	-	6	-	-	-	6	6	-	20	8	10	-	-	56
10	Randy Mamola	USA	Yamaha	8	3	4	3	1	2	-	8	12	3	-	1	-	45
11	Niall Mackenzie	GBR	Yamaha	4	-	-	12	2	4	-	4	-	6	-	2	3	37
12	Miguel DuHamel	CAN	Yamaha	-	1	-	2	4	3	-	6	-	4	4	8	2	34
13	Alex Barros	BRA	Cagiva	-	-	-	-	8	-	4	12	2	-	-	3	-	29
14	Daryl Beattie	AUS	Honda	-	12	6	-	-	-	-	-	-	-	-	-	-	18
15	Peter Goddard	AUS	Yamaha	-	-	3	6	-	-	1	-	-	-	8	-	-	18
16	Shinichi Itoh	JPN	Honda	10	-	-	-	-	-	-	-	-	-	-	-	-	10
17	Keiiji Ohishi	JPN	Suzuki	6	-	-	-	-	-	-	-	-	-	-	-	-	6
17	Terry Rymer	GBR	Yamaha	-	-	-	-	-	-	-	-	-	-	6	-	-	6
19	Corrado Catalano	ITA	Yamaha	-	-	2	-	-	-	-	3	-	-	-	-	-	5
20	Eddie Laycock	IRL	Yamaha	-	-	1	-	-	-	-	2	1	-	-	-	-	4
21	Toshihiko Honma	JPN	Yamaha	3	-	-	-	-	-	-	-	-	-	-	-	-	3
21	Michael Rudroff	GER	Yamaha	-	-	-	-	-	-	-	-	-	-	3	-	-	3
23	Norihiko Fujiwara	JPN	Yamaha	2	-	-	-	-	-	-	-	-	-	-	-	-	2
23	Dominique Sarron	FRA	Yamaha	-	-	-	-	-	-	-	-	-	-	2	-	-	2
23	Jamie Whitham	GBR	Yamaha	-	-	-	-	-	-	-	-	-	2	-	-	-	2
26	Toshiyuki Arakaki	JPN	Yamaha	-	-	-	-	-	-	-	-	-	1	1	-	-	2
27	Kevin Mitchell	GBR	Yamaha	-	-	-	-	-	-	-	1	-	-	-	-	-	1
27	Satoshi Tsujimoto	JPN	Honda	1	-	-	-	-	-	-	-	-	-	-	-	-	1

Scoring system – 20, 15, 12, 10, 8, 6, 4, 3, 2, 1

250cc

250cc – all races were counted

Pos	Rider	Nat	Machine	Total
1	Luca Cadalora	ITA	Honda	203
2	Loris Reggiani	ITA	Aprilia	159
3	Pier-Francesco Chili	ITA	Aprilia	119
4	Helmut Bradl	GER	Honda	89
5	Max Biaggi	ITA	Aprilia	78
6	Alberto Puig	SPA	Aprilia	71
7	Jochen Schmid	GER	Yamaha	58
8	Carlos Cardus	SPA	Honda	48
9	Masahiro Shimizu	JPN	Honda	46
10	Doriano Romboni	ITA	Honda	43

125cc

125cc – all races were counted

Pos	Rider	Nat	Machine	Total
1	Alessandro Gramigni	ITA	Aprilia	134
2	Fausto Gresini	ITA	Honda	118
3	Ralf Waldmann	GER	Honda	112
4	Ezio Gianola	ITA	Honda	105
5	Bruno Casanova	ITA	Aprilia	96
6	Dirk Raudies	GER	Honda	91
7	Jorge Martinez	SPA	Honda	83
8	Gabriele Debbia	ITA	Honda	58
9	Noboru Ueda	JPN	Honda	57
10	Noboyuki Wakai	JPN	Honda	52

BIG BANG TAKES OVER

The Honda V4s sounded different, growling rather than shrieking. In the search for usability as opposed to outright power, HRC came up with a new engine in which all four cylinders fired within around 65–70 degrees of crank rotation – the 'big-bang' motor. For reasons no-one was able to explain satisfactorily for the next 15 years, this new firing order transformed the 500cc V4 two-stroke from a man-eater into a relative pussy cat. The out-of-balance forces generated necessitated strengthened transmission components and a power-sapping balance shaft, but lap times came down. The balance shaft also cured many of the problems Honda had suffered from due to the gyroscopic effect of their single-crankshaft design – all the other manufacturers used contra-rotating twin-crank engines which, as well as being simpler to produce and cheaper to maintain, cancelled out any gyro effects.

Power could be fed in earlier, tyres lasted longer and class rookies could get on the rostrum – as Alex Criville demonstrated in the third race of the year. That would have been almost unthinkable with a regular firing-order 'screamer' motor, or even the slightly softer version that fired two cylinders together at 180-degree intervals. Honda's innovation was so spectacularly successful that the other manufacturers were forced to follow suit as quickly as they could. There is no doubt that Doohan and the big-bang Honda NSR would have won their first title in 1992 but for the complications that followed Mick's Assen accident.

Even in the MotoGP era manufacturers continued to search for the optimal crankshaft phasing. A variety of big-bang and long-bang layouts were tried, without any theoretical justification; the stopwatch made its empirical judgement. Improbable theories about the rear tyre slipping and gripping were eventually overtaken by Maseo Furusawa of Yamaha's demonstration that torque flutter due to acceleration and deceleration of the crank, rods and pistons at small throttle openings can be significant on regular firing order motors.

The 1992 NSR500 looked very like the '91 model from the outside, but the rearrangement of its engine internals had a profound effect on racing. It just took a few years to work out why.

ABOVE & BELOW At last, the V4 was tamed thanks to 'big-bang' firing orders. (*Henk Keulemans*)

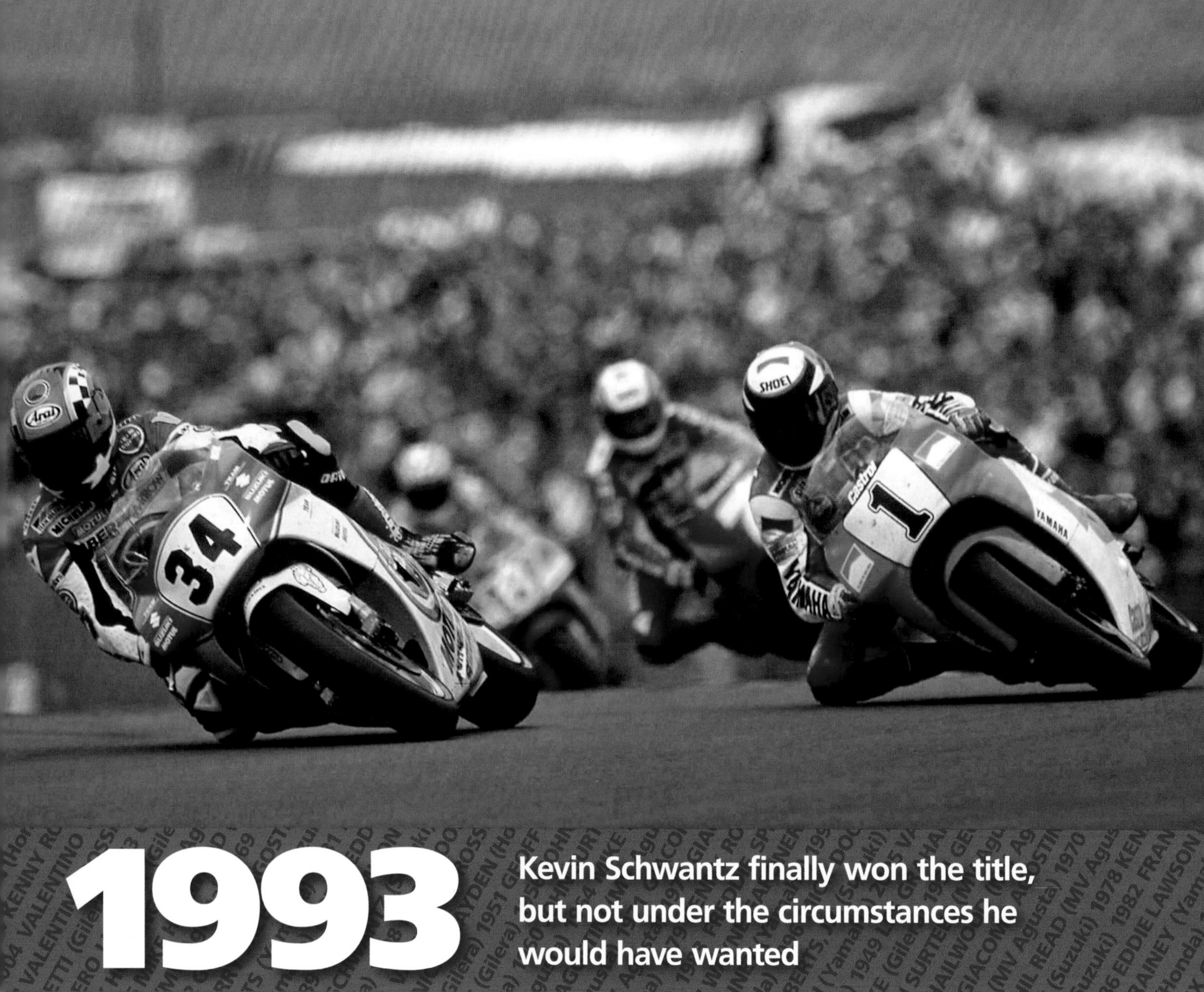

1993

Kevin Schwantz finally won the title, but not under the circumstances he would have wanted

Mick Doohan was back with Repsol Honda for the start of the season but was far from recovered from his leg injuries, and he also had to cope with the aftermath of a pre-season crash that broke his left wrist. He would have further operations to try and restore movement in his ankle, but in the meantime he pioneered a thumb-operated rear-brake system. Mick was joined by two new team-mates – Daryl Beattie, another product of the production line that took young Aussie hot-shots to GPs via the All-Japan Championship, and a second ex-A-J champ, Shinichi Itoh. The Japanese rider was charged with development of the fuel-injected NSR motor. Alex Criville continued on the lone satellite Honda.

Triple champion Wayne Rainey was joined by 125 and twice 250 champion Luca Cadalora, but the new Yamaha chassis proved too stiff and led to Rainey trying a ROC customer frame. The French Yamaha team bought Freddie Spencer out of retirement for a second and disastrous comeback, alongside Bernard Garcia. Another fast French youngster, José Kuhn, replaced Spencer later in the season. There was a veritable armada of ROC and Harris Yamahas, the fastest again being the WCM team's machine with Niall Mackenzie on board.

Cagiva had two new riders, Doug Chandler recruited from Yamaha and young Aussie Superbike hot-shot Matt Mladin. When the team brought John Kocinski in after his sacking by the 250 Suzuki team, the original riders were seriously undermined.

Suzuki found another partner for Kevin Schwantz in the shape of Alex Barros, the Brazilian rider who had impressed in his three years on the Cagiva. Schwantz took full advantage of the opposition's disarray, ripping into a 23-point lead after nine rounds – four of which he won – but next time out at Donington he was skittled by an errant Doohan. Rainey hit back at Brno, and then came Misano and the crash that ended Wayne Rainey's career. It also made Kevin Schwantz World Champion, but in a manner that fundamentally unsettled him and led directly to his retirement.

ABOVE Schwantz and Rainey in close combat, as they'd been since they raced each other on Superbikes in the American Championship. (*Henk Keulemans*)

THE **1993** SEASON

500cc

AUS/Eastern Creek
- In an all-American podium, Kevin Schwantz won the opening race of the year from great rival Wayne Rainey, with Doug Chandler in third, making his debut on the factory Cagiva

JPN/Suzuka
- Rainey won from Schwantz and Daryl Beattie, with just 0.287s covering all three riders – the closest ever podium in the 500cc class at that time

GER/Hockenheim
- In the final qualifying session Shinichi Itoh became the first rider to be officially timed at a speed of more than 200mph (322km/h) on his fuel-injected factory Honda
- Daryl Beattie took his first GP victory on his first visit to the Hockenheim circuit

RSM/Mugello
- Mick Doohan returned to the top of the podium for the first time since his crash at Assen more than a year before

GBR/Donington
- Luca Cadalora won for the first time in the 500cc class from team-mate Rainey after a first-lap collision eliminated Schwantz, Doohan and Barros
- Niall Mackenzie passed wild-card Carl Fogarty (GBR, Cagiva) on the last lap to take third place – the only podium finish achieved by a privateer ROC Yamaha

ITA/Misano
- Wayne Rainey crashed on lap ten while leading the race and suffered crippling injuries
- Kevin Schwantz finished third to take the lead in the championship standings and effectively win the title

USA/Laguna Seca
- Freddie Spencer crashed during qualifying, failed to make the race and never again rode in a Grand Prix
- On just his third appearance of the year in the 500cc class John Kocinski scored Cagiva's first ever dry-weather GP win

SPA-FIM/Jarama
- Alex Barros took his first Grand Prix win and became the seventh different winner of the year in the 500cc class

250cc

AUS/Eastern Creek
- Tetsuya Harada (JPN, Yamaha) won on his debut as a full-time GP rider in his first Grand Prix outside Japan
- John Kocinski was second, making his debut on the Suzuki, and Max Biaggi came third in his first ride on a Honda

MAL/Shah Alam
- Capirossi, Biaggi, Cardus and Ruggia were all given a one-minute penalty for anticipating the start
- Nobuatsu Aoki (JPN, Honda) scored his only GP victory, and was followed home by fellow-Japanese riders Harada and Tadayuki Okada (Honda) – the first all-Japanese podium in the 250cc class

SPA/Jerez
- Japanese rider Noboyuki Wakai (Suzuki) lost his life after a collision with a spectator crossing pitlane

AUT/Salzburgring
- Doriano Romboni (ITA, Honda) took his first victory in the 250cc class by just 0.05s from fellow-Italian Loris Capirossi after a tremendous race-long battle

NED/Assen
- Loris Capirossi took his first victory since moving up to the 250cc class at the start of 1992
- After finishing third, John Kocinski failed to attend the podium ceremony and subsequently split with the factory Suzuki team

SPA-EUR/Barcelona
- Max Biaggi took his only win of the year on board the factory Honda

GBR/Donington
- Frenchman Jean-Philippe Ruggia scored his first victory and became the first non-Italian to win a GP riding an Aprilia

USA/Laguna Seca
- Capirossi won and opened up a ten-point lead over Harada with one race to go

SPA-FIM/Jarama
- Tetsuya Harada was victorious, the first Japanese rider to become 250cc World Champion
- Loris Capirossi led early on, only to run off the circuit and finally finish fifth

125cc

SPA/Jerez
- After finishing second behind German rider Dirk Raudies at the opening three races of the year, Kazuto Sakata (JPN, Honda) took his first career victory

SPA-EUR/Barcelona
- Noboru Ueda took the win in a close race, with the fourth-place finisher just 0.224s behind the winner – the first time that less than a quarter of a second covered the top four finishers in the 125cc class

USA/Laguna Seca
- Dirk Raudies took his ninth win of the year at the first 125cc GP to be held at the Laguna Seca circuit, a record for most 125cc class wins in a single season by a Honda rider
- The victory gave Raudies a 22-point advantage over Kazuto Sakata going into the final race of the year

SPA-FIM/Jarama
- Dirk Raudies took a comfortable eighth-place finish to clinch the world title

1993 WORLD CHAMPIONSHIP

500cc

Pos	Rider	Nat	Machine	AUS	MAL	JPN	SPA	AUT	GER	NED	EUR	RSM	GBR	CZE	ITA	USA	FIM	Total
1	Kevin Schwantz	USA	Suzuki	25	16	20	25	25	20	25	16	20	-	11	16	13	16	248
2	Wayne Rainey	USA	Yamaha	20	25	25	20	16	11	11	25	16	20	25	-	-	-	214
3	Daryl Beattie	AUS	Honda	13	20	16	10	9	25	-	13	10	10	10	9	11	20	176
4	Mick Doohan	AUS	Honda	-	13	9	13	20	-	20	20	25	-	16	20	-	-	156
5	Luca Cadalora	ITA	Yamaha	8	-	-	11	11	8	9	1	11	25	20	25	16	-	145
6	Alex Barros	BRA	Suzuki	11	9	10	-	13	-	-	11	9	-	6	11	20	25	125
7	Shinichi Itoh	JPN	Honda	9	10	13	-	10	16	10	-	13	11	9	8	10	-	119
8	Alex Criville	SPA	Honda	10	11	11	16	-	3	16	-	-	-	8	10	9	13	117
9	Niall Mackenzie	GBR	Yamaha	6	8	3	9	5	7	8	10	8	16	-	7	8	8	103
10	Doug Chandler	USA	Cagiva	16	7	5	-	8	10	13	-	-	-	7	6	-	11	83
11	John Kocinski	USA	Cagiva	-	-	-	-	-	-	-	-	-	-	13	13	25	-	51
12	Juan Lopez Mella	SPA	Yamaha	-	3	-	8	3	2	-	9	-	9	2	4	6	-	46
13	Mat Mladin	AUS	Cagiva	7	6	-	-	6	9	-	-	7	-	-	-	-	10	45
14	Jose Kuhn	FRA	Yamaha	3	-	-	2	7	-	3	8	6	4	1	-	5	6	45
15	John Reynolds	GBR	Yamaha	-	4	-	-	2	-	6	-	-	7	4	5	7	7	42
16	Bernard Garcia	FRA	Yamaha	4	-	-	-	-	6	5	-	5	3	5	3	-	9	40
17	Renzo Colleoni	ITA	Yamaha	-	1	-	3	-	-	-	6	4	8	-	-	-	-	22
18	Laurent Naveau	BEL	Yamaha	5	5	-	-	4	4	1	-	-	1	-	-	1	-	21
19	Sean Emmett	GBR	Yamaha	-	2	1	7	-	-	-	4	-	-	-	-	3	2	19
20	Tsutomu Udagawa	JPN	Yamaha	2	-	2	6	1	5	2	-	-	-	-	-	-	-	18
21	Michael Rudroff	GER	Yamaha	-	-	-	-	-	3	4	-	-	6	3	1	-	-	17
22	Jeremy McWilliams	GBR	Yamaha	-	-	-	-	-	-	-	5	3	-	-	-	4	5	17
23	Carl Fogarty	GBR	Cagiva	-	-	-	-	-	-	-	-	-	13	-	-	-	-	13
24	Toshihiko Honma	JPN	Yamaha	-	-	8	-	-	-	-	-	-	-	-	-	-	-	8
25	Simon Crafar	NZE	Yamaha	-	-	-	-	-	-	7	-	-	-	-	-	-	-	7
25	Juan Garriga	SPA	Cagiva	-	-	-	-	-	-	-	7	-	-	-	-	-	-	7
25	Kevin Magee	AUS	Yamaha	-	-	7	-	-	-	-	-	-	-	-	-	-	-	7
28	Norihiko Fujiwara	JPN	Yamaha	-	-	6	-	-	-	-	-	-	-	-	-	-	-	6
29	Lucio Pedercini	ITA	Yamaha	-	-	-	4	-	-	-	-	1	-	-	-	-	1	6
30	Serge David	SWI	Yamaha	1	-	-	1	-	-	-	-	2	-	-	-	2	-	6
31	Corrado Catalano	ITA	Yamaha	-	-	-	5	-	-	-	-	-	-	-	-	-	-	5
31	James Haydon	GBR	Yamaha	-	-	-	-	-	-	-	-	-	5	-	-	-	-	5
33	Toshiyuki Arakaki	JPN	Yamaha	-	-	4	-	-	-	-	-	-	-	-	-	-	-	4
33	Andrew Stroud	NZE	Yamaha	-	-	-	-	-	-	-	-	-	-	-	-	-	4	4
35	Andreas Meklau	AUT	Yamaha	-	-	-	-	-	-	-	3	-	-	-	-	-	-	3
35	Kevin Mitchell	GBR	Yamaha	-	-	-	-	-	-	-	-	-	-	-	-	-	3	3
37	Cees Doorakkers	NED	Yamaha	-	-	-	-	-	-	-	2	-	-	-	-	-	-	2
37	Ron Haslam	GBR	Yamaha	-	-	-	-	-	-	-	-	-	2	-	-	-	-	2
37	Freddie Spencer	USA	Yamaha	-	-	-	-	-	-	-	-	-	-	-	2	-	-	2
40	Bruno Bonhuil	FRA	Yamaha	-	-	-	-	-	1	-	-	-	-	-	-	-	-	1

Scoring system – 25, 20, 16, 13, 11, 10, 9, 8, 7, 6, 5, 4, 3, 2, 1

OPPOSITE Rainey leads Luca Cadalora and Kevin Schwantz at Misano not long before the crash that put Wayne in a wheelchair. (*Henk Keulemans*)

250cc

Pos	Rider	Nat	Machine	Total
1	Tetsuya Harada	JPN	Yamaha	197
2	Loris Capirossi	ITA	Honda	193
3	Loris Reggiani	ITA	Aprilia	158
4	Max Biaggi	ITA	Honda	142
5	Doriano Romboni	ITA	Honda	139
6	Jean-Philippe Ruggia	FRA	Aprilia	129
7	Helmut Bradl	GER	Honda	126
8	Tadayuki Okada	JPN	Honda	120
9	Alberto Puig	SPA	Honda	106
10	Pier-Francesco Chili	ITA	Yamaha	106

125cc

Pos	Rider	Nat	Machine	Total
1	Dirk Raudies	GER	Honda	280
2	Kazuto Sakata	JPN	Honda	266
3	Takeshi Tsujimura	JPN	Honda	177
4	Ralf Waldmann	GER	Aprilia	160
5	Noboru Ueda	JPN	Honda	129
6	Akira Saito	JPN	Honda	117
7	Oliver Petrucciani	SWI	Aprilia	82
8	Jorge Martinez	SPA	Honda	74
9	Herri Torrontegui	SPA	Aprilia	65
10	Peter Ottl	GER	Aprilia	64

WAYNE RAINEY

The accident that paralysed Wayne Rainey happened at the first corner of the old Misano circuit while the three-times World Champion was leading the Italian GP and holding an 11-point lead over Kevin Schwantz in the standings. He crashed alone, tumbled through the gravel trap and came to rest with a broken back.

Wayne Rainey comes from Los Angeles and worked his way up from local dirt-track races to the national championship, then to road racing – first with the underdog Kawasaki team, then Honda in AMA Superbike racing, and finally to GPs with Yamaha. Kevin Schwantz is Texan, the son of a motorcycle dealer, who was talent-spotted by Suzuki very early on and fast-tracked to GPs. The pair were implacable enemies who brought their rivalry over to GPs from the AMA Superbike Championship, and they continued to find reasons to dislike each other. Rainey was a grafter, hard working and analytical; Schwantz seemed to get by on unadulterated natural talent. Their mutual dislike fuelled some great racing in the 500cc GP class in the early 1990s. Schwantz's own decision to retire came after a long 'plane conversation with Rainey at the start of 1995.

Despite his grievous injuries Rainey was back in the paddock at the start of the '94 season, taking over from Kenny Roberts as team-manager for the 250 Yamaha squad. No matter that it was too much too soon after his accident, Wayne persevered through his rehabilitation and then took over the 500 team when Kenny embarked on his project as a constructor. Eventually, though, Rainey had to admit he found the role unsatisfying and retired to what seems to be a happy family life. He has a powerful speedboat and has been known to race a very trick kart built for him by Eddie Lawson. Nowadays he is only seen once a year at a bike race, at Laguna Seca, which is close to his home – and where there is a section of the track named after him.

For the full, at times harrowing story of the two lives of a driven man get hold of a copy of *Wayne Rainey* by Michael Scott (Haynes, 1997). It is out of print but well worth the effort of tracking down.

1994

The combination of Mick Doohan and the Honda NSR500 won the first of their five titles in dominant fashion

The paddock looked very different in 1994: Wayne Rainey was back but in a wheelchair and as a team-manager; Honda had lost their works team's sponsor; and Kevin Schwantz was racing with number one on his Suzuki, not his customary 34.

Without Rothmans, Honda ran their three men – Doohan, Itoh and Criville – in strangely old-fashioned-looking corporate colours. The lone lease NSR went to Spaniard Alberto Puig in a satellite team run by Sito Pons. Mick duly marched almost unopposed to his first title, on the rostrum for every one of the 14 rounds and taking nine wins. Honda did have another highlight, though, in the stunning wild-card debut of Norifumi 'Norick' Abe at Suzuka. The reigning All-Japan 500cc champion was still only 18 and had the temerity to race with – and scare – Doohan and Schwantz before crashing out at high speed with only three laps to go. A star was born.

Yamaha, struggling to come to terms with what had happened to Wayne Raine, had yet to get their bike anywhere near right. Luca Cadalora was joined in the Roberts team by Daryl Beattie: neither had an enjoyable season, although Cadalora won two races and finished second overall. There was a veritable flood of ROC and Harris Yamahas, the quickest of which was again Mackenzie on the WCM team's ROC.

Cagiva stuck with Doug Chandler and retained John Kocinski full time, while Schwantz and Alex Barros stayed at Suzuki. However, Kevin injured himself in a pre-season mountain-bike crash, and then again when he damaged his wrist – always the wrist – at Assen and aggravated the injury when he crashed in France. More crashes followed at Donington and Brno, until a big highside coming out of Laguna Seca's Corkscrew ended his season. The opposition might have had their problems, but it's actually doubtful if anyone could have challenged Doohan and the now dominant Honda NSR.

Thankfully, spectators saw enthralling 250 season, with Max Biaggi on an Aprilia fighting a bevy of talented Honda riders. Aprilia also tried a 'super 250' twin, actually 380cc, in the 500 class.

ABOVE Mick Doohan won his first title by the astonishing margin of 143 points. (*Henk Keulemans*)

RIGHT Aprilia's new star Max Biaggi celebrates with team boss Carlo Pernat. (*Henk Keulemans*)

THE 1994 SEASON

500cc

AUS/Eastern Creek

- John Kocinski won the opening race of the year to become the only rider to have led the championship standings riding a Cagiva
- Kocinski's win in the 500cc race followed Aprilia victories for Max Biaggi in the 250cc class and Kazuto Sakata in 125s – this was the first time since the West German GP of 1976 that the three classes had been won by non-Japanese manufacturers

JPN/Suzuka

- Norick Abe (JPN, Honda) made his GP debut at 18 and fought for the lead, crashing with just three laps to go. This was Abe's only GP start on anything other than a Yamaha

SPA/Jerez

- Loris Reggiani gave the new Aprilia V-twin its debut in the 500cc class, qualifying a creditable seventh and finishing ninth

AUT/Salzburgring

- Mick Doohan won the 500cc race on the 22nd and final visit to the Austrian circuit for a GP event

GER/Hockenheim

- Mick Doohan won the last GP to be held at the Hockenheim circuit
- This was the last time a Grand Prix was completed at an average speed of more than 124mph/200km/h

GBR/Donington

- After suffering a huge highside crash in qualifying, Kevin Schwantz took the last of his 25 Grand Prix victories
- Norick Abe, having signed for Yamaha, was scheduled to make his overseas GP debut but was eliminated when he crashed in practice and broke a bone in his hand

CZE/Brno

- Mick Doohan won, and clinched his first world title with three races remaining

USA/Laguna Seca

- Luca Cadalora took the first win of the year for Yamaha and became the first non-American to win a 500cc GP at Laguna Seca

SPA-EUR/Barcelona

- John Kocinski's third-place finish was the final GP podium by a Cagiva rider

250cc

AUS/Eastern Creek

- Defending champion Tetsuya Harada crashed during qualifying and damaged his hand, missing the opening two races of the year
- On his first race since returning to Aprilia, Max Biaggi won from fellow-Italian young guns Doriano Romboni and Loris Capirossi

JPN/Suzuka

- Tadayuki Okada (Honda) scored his first Grand Prix victory

ARG/Buenos Aires

- Okada took his second win of the year to put himself just eight points behind championship leader Biaggi going into the final race

SPA-EUR/Barcelona

- Max Biaggi won to clinch his first world title, and the first in the 250cc class for Aprilia

125cc

AUS/Eastern Creek

- Kazuto Sakata won first time out riding an Aprilia

JPN/Suzuka

- Aged 18, Takeshi Tsujimura (Honda) became the youngest Japanese rider to win a Grand Prix – a record that he still held at the end of 2008
- Tsujimura was joined on the podium by fellow-Japanese riders Kazuto Sakata and Hideyuki Nakajyo (Honda) – the first all-Japanese podium in the 125cc class

ITA/Mugello

- Roberto Locatelli (ITA, Aprilia), making his debut as a wild-card rider, qualified on pole, the last time a rider has been on pole in his first GP race

ARG/Buenos Aires

- Jorge Martinez took the last of his 37 Grand Prix victories, and the only one riding a Yamaha. This was also the last of 47 wins in the 125cc class by Yamaha
- Kazuto Sakata's seventh place was enough to give him his first world title

SPA-EUR/Barcelona

- Fausto Gresini finished tenth in his final GP appearance, bringing to an end a 12-year Grand Prix career that brought him two world titles and 21 race victories

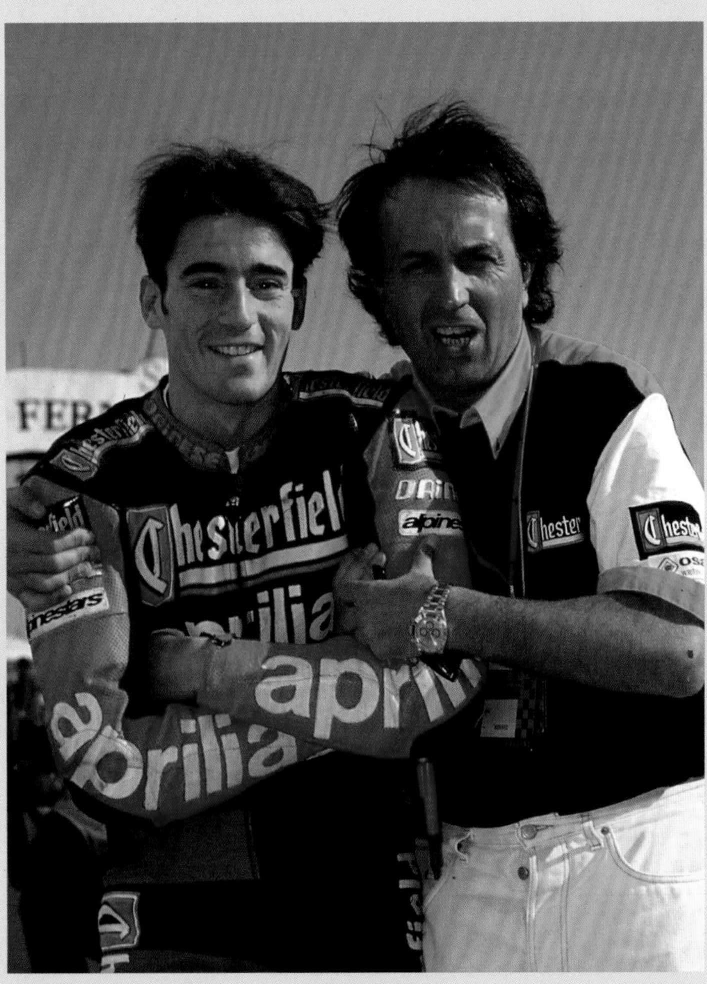

1994 WORLD CHAMPIONSHIP

500cc

Pos	Rider	Nat	Machine	AUS	MAL	JPN	SPA	AUT	GER	NED	ITA	FRA	GBR	CZE	USA	ARG	EUR	Total
1	Mick Doohan	AUS	Honda	16	25	20	25	25	25	25	25	25	20	25	16	25	20	317
2	Luca Cadalora	ITA	Yamaha	20	13	13	-	-	-	7	20	9	16	16	25	10	25	174
3	John Kocinski	USA	Cagiva	25	20	7	16	11	-	8	-	20	13	-	20	16	16	172
4	Kevin Schwantz	USA	Suzuki	13	10	25	20	20	20	11	16	-	25	9	-	-	-	169
5	Alberto Puig	SPA	Honda	9	11	8	10	10	16	13	13	13	9	11	9	11	9	152
6	Alex Criville	SPA	Honda	10	8	9	11	16	13	16	-	16	10	13	-	9	13	144
7	Shinichi Itoh	JPN	Honda	11	16	16	-	13	10	-	11	10	7	20	13	13	-	141
8	Alex Barros	BRA	Suzuki	8	9	11	13	9	11	20	9	11	-	8	8	8	10	134
9	Doug Chandler	USA	Cagiva	7	7	6	9	-	9	10	-	-	11	-	11	20	6	96
10	Niall Mackenzie	GBR	Yamaha	-	5	-	8	7	8	-	7	-	8	7	6	5	8	69
11	Bernard Garcia	FRA	Yamaha	5	-	5	-	-	7	6	8	-	5	5	4	4	7	56
12	Jeremy McWilliams	GBR	Yamaha	-	2	3	5	-	-	-	1	8	6	6	7	7	4	49
13	Daryl Beattie	AUS	Yamaha	-	6	-	-	8	-	9	10	-	-	-	-	-	11	44
14	John Reynolds	GBR	Yamaha	6	4	4	6	6	6	-	-	-	2	4	-	-	5	43
15	Sean Emmett	GBR	Yam/Suz	2	3	-	-	4	5	-	2	-	4	3	5	6	-	34
16	Juan Lopez Mella	SPA	Yam/Suz	3	-	1	3	-	4	-	6	6	-	-	-	-	3	25
17	Norick Abe	JPN	Yamaha	-	-	-	-	-	-	-	-	-	-	10	10	-	-	20
18	Laurent Naveau	BEL	Yamaha	-	-	2	-	1	2	4	-	-	3	-	3	2	2	19
19	Jean-Pierre Jeandat	FRA	Yamaha	-	-	-	2	3	-	5	5	-	-	-	2	-	-	17
20	Cristiano Migliorati	ITA	Yamaha	1	-	-	4	2	-	-	4	1	-	-	-	-	-	12
21	Marc Garcia	FRA	Yamaha	-	-	-	-	-	-	-	-	7	-	1	-	3	-	11
22	Toshihiko Honma	JPN	Yamaha	-	-	10	-	-	-	-	-	-	-	-	-	-	-	10
23	Jean Foray	FRA	Yamaha	-	-	-	-	-	-	1	-	5	-	2	-	-	-	8
24	Loris Reggiani	ITA	Aprilia	-	-	-	7	-	-	-	-	-	-	-	-	-	-	7
25	Bernard Haenggeli	SWI	Yamaha	-	-	-	-	-	-	-	3	4	-	-	-	-	-	7
26	Julian Miralles	SPA	Yamaha	-	-	-	1	-	3	3	-	-	-	-	-	-	-	7
27	Bruno Bonhuil	FRA	Yamaha	-	-	-	-	-	1	2	-	3	1	-	-	-	-	7
28	Herve Moineau	FRA	Yamaha	-	-	-	-	5	-	-	-	-	-	-	-	-	-	5
29	Scott Doohan	AUS	Yamaha	4	-	-	-	-	-	-	-	-	-	-	-	-	-	4
30	Udo Mark	GER	Yamaha	-	-	-	-	-	-	-	-	2	-	-	-	-	-	2
31	Lucio Pedercini	ITA	Yamaha	-	1	-	-	-	-	-	-	-	-	-	1	-	-	2
32	Neil Hodgson	GBR	Yamaha	-	-	-	-	-	-	-	-	-	-	-	-	1	-	1
32	Andrew Stroud	NZE	Yamaha	-	-	-	-	-	-	-	-	-	-	-	-	-	1	1

Scoring system – 25, 20, 16, 13, 11, 10, 9, 8, 7, 6, 5, 4, 3, 2, 1

250cc

Pos	Rider	Nat	Machine	Total
1	Max Biaggi	ITA	Aprilia	234
2	Tadayuki Okada	JPN	Honda	214
3	Loris Capirossi	ITA	Honda	199
4	Doriano Romboni	ITA	Honda	170
5	Ralf Waldmann	GER	Honda	156
6	Jean-Philippe Ruggia	FRA	Aprilia	149
7	Tetsuya Harada	JPN	Yamaha	109
8	Jean-Michel Bayle	FRA	Aprilia	105
9	Luis d'Antin	SPA	Honda	100
10	Nobuatsu Aoki	JPN	Honda	95

125cc

Pos	Rider	Nat	Machine	Total
1	Kazuto Sakata	JPN	Aprilia	224
2	Noboru Ueda	JPN	Honda	194
3	Takeshi Tsujimura	JPN	Honda	190
4	Dirk Raudies	GER	Honda	162
5	Peter Ottl	GER	Aprilia	160
6	Jorge Martinez	SPA	Yamaha	135
7	Stefano Perugini	ITA	Aprilia	106
8	Masaki Tokudome	JPN	Honda	87
9	Oliver Petrucciani	SWI	Aprilia	74
10	Herri Torrontegui	SPA	Aprilia	73

ITALY DOES THE DOUBLE

This was the first time Aprilia won both the 125 and 250 titles in the same season, a remarkable enough achievement for a company of any size but a minor miracle for a tiny factory that relied for its existence on selling scooters to fashion-conscious Italian youth. The Aprilia story started with Loris Reggiani and what was basically a Rotax motor in their own chassis. The combination was good enough for a rostrum in its first season, 1985, despite Reggiani suffering a couple of nasty injuries. Progress stalled the following season when Loris went to Honda, but in 1987 he was back and gave the factory its first Grand Prix victory in front of a raucous home crowd at Misano. This was in a field stuffed with factory Hondas ridden by aces like Anton Mang, Reinhold Roth and Sito Pons, and Yamahas with Luca Cadalora and Carlos Lavado on them. In 1988 Aprilia entered Corrado Catalano on a 125; he gave the factory their first podium in the class at the French GP.

Customer 250s were available in 1989 but only Germany's Martin Wimmer got one on the rostrum, in Austria. Next season Wimmer was on the rostrum twice, Didier de Radigues and Reggiani once. In '91 Reggiani and Chili rode the factory 250s, and 125s appeared for the first time in the hands of Gabriele Debbia and Alessandro Gramigni. The last named duly gave Aprilia their first world title in 1992 after stalling on the line at the last round and riding through the field to third place. The 250 crown eluded Reggiani, though, frustrated by the brilliance of Honda's Cadalora and Kanemoto. The next year it was Tetsuya Harada (JPN, Yamaha) and Loris Capirossi (ITA, Honda) who thwarted Loris. Then Max Biaggi joined the team, and 1994 saw the beginning of his run of three Aprilia-mounted championships (and one on a Honda, just to make a point); 1994 was also the year the 125 crown went to Kazuto Sakata, the first Japanese rider to win a world title on a European machine.

From the early 1990s onwards Aprilia were at least the equal of the Japanese companies in the smaller classes, and as Japan Inc's interest in two-strokes waned the Italian factory continued to develop their bikes and lease LE models (replicas of the previous season's works machines) to customer teams. After Aprilia was absorbed by the giant Piaggio group, other brand names such as Gilera and Derbi have been affixed to what are, in fact, Aprilias. Taking that into account, the only years since '93 when Aprilia has not provided a World Champion were 2004 and 2005, thanks to Spanish youngster Dani Pedrosa taking the 250 title in both years, and Andrea Dovizioso (ITA) and Thomas Luthi (SWI), the respective 125 champions.

ABOVE Max Biaggi won five GPs in 1994. (*Henk Keulemans*)

BELOW Biaggi's 250 nose-to-nose with Kazuto Sakata's 125, the bikes that achieved Aprilia's first double. (*Henk Keulemans*)

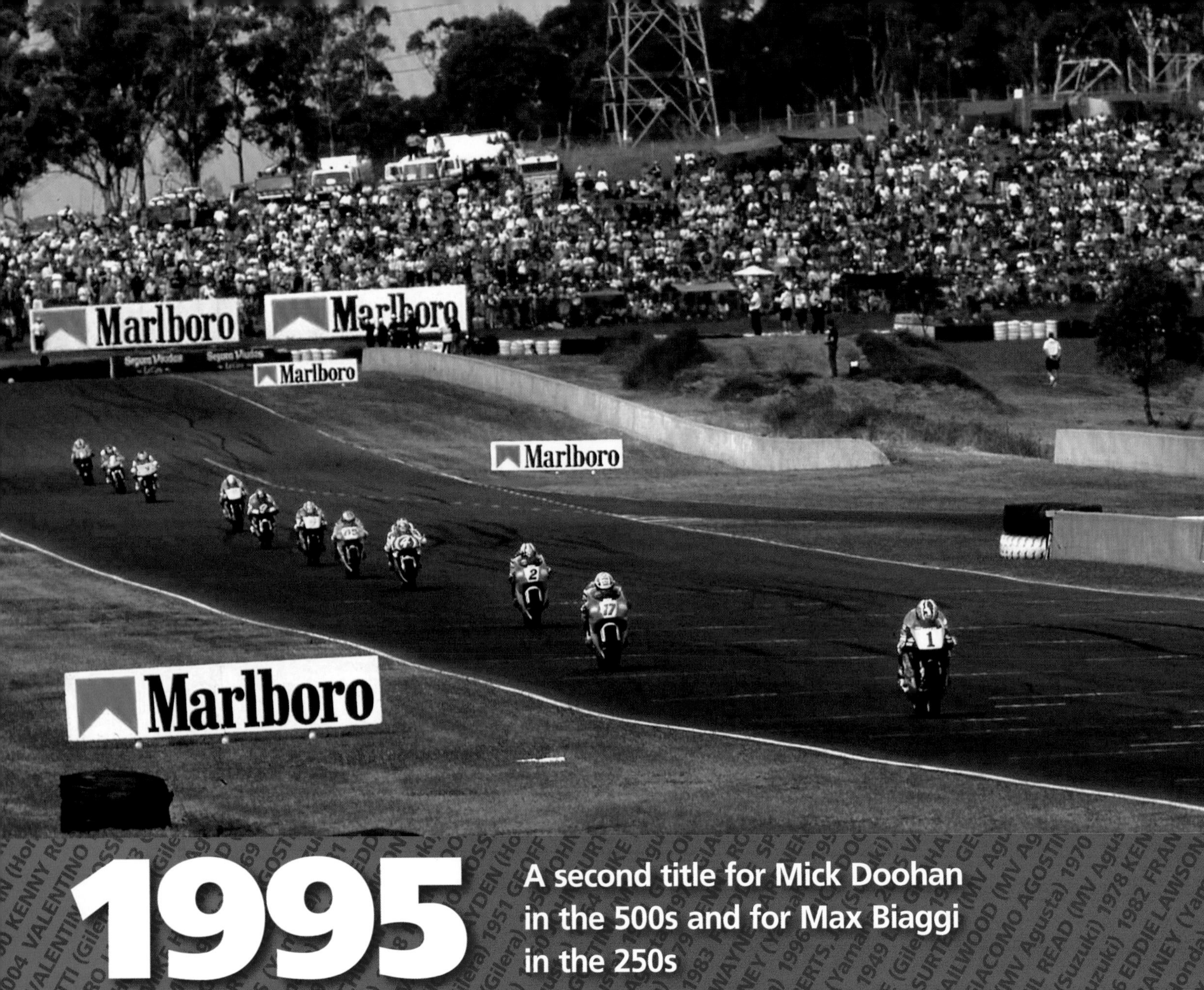

1995 A second title for Mick Doohan in the 500s and for Max Biaggi in the 250s

Mick Doohan backed-up his first title by again dominating the season, despite throwing away the lead on the last lap of the third round, then crashing while leading the next two races. His crash at Jerez handed the championship lead to Daryl Beattie, now Suzuki's lead rider after the retirement of Kevin Schwantz, but a run of four consecutive wins in the middle of the season put Doohan 15 points in front of Beattie, and he was never headed again. Britain's Sean Emmett had a couple of points-scoring outings on the Suzuki before the 1993 World Superbike Champion Scott Russell (USA) got the job full time.

Yamaha's challenge was led by Luca Cadalora, the Italian starting the season on Dunlops, with which he failed to come to terms, so Team Roberts got him onto Michelins, or sometimes even a cocktail of Michelin front and Dunlop rear. He won back-to-back races after Doohan's run of four. Cadalora's team-mate, and the only other full factory Yamaha rider, was Norick Abe. The squadron of other Yamahas in the results were ROC and Harris-framed privateer machines.

This was the first year of Repsol's sponsorship of the factory Honda team, as well as Doohan, with Alex Criville and Shinichi Itoh also running in the Spanish oil company's colours. Barros and Puig rode leased Hondas, as did class newcomer Loris Capirossi.

It was a promising year for Spanish riders. Alberto Puig had seemed to be an ordinary 250 rider, but in his second full season in 500s he looked far from ordinary. He won at home and looked a likely contender until he crashed in practice at Le Mans's ultra-fast first turn and broke his left leg very badly, putting himself out for the rest of the season. His replacement in the satellite Pons team, Carlos Checa, had also looked average in 250s but also took to 500s remarkably rapidly. In the final race of the year, the European GP at his home track, the Circuit de Catalunya, Checa came within five laps of winning the race, then crashed out after a heroic ride, gifting the victory to another Spaniard – and future 500cc World Champion – Alex Criville.

ABOVE Which way did he go? Mick Doohan leads the fist lap of the year at Eastern Creek. (*Henk Keulemans*)

RIGHT The two sides of Alberto Puig's season. He became the first Spaniard to win the 500cc Spanish GP but then he crashed at Le Mans and suffered terrible injury to his left leg. (*Henk Keulemans*)

THE 1995 SEASON

500cc

AUS/Eastern Creek
- Reigning champion Mick Doohan won the opening race of the year from fellow Australian Daryl Beattie

JAP/Suzuka
- Daryl Beattie won for the first time since joining the Suzuki factory team
- Wild-card rider Takumi Aoki finished third on his debut ride in a 500cc Grand Prix
- Takuma Aoki's (Honda) third place in the 500cc race followed Haruchika Aoki's (Honda) victory in the 125cc race and Nobuatsu Aoki's (Honda) second place in the 250cc race. The first time that three brothers finished on each of the three podiums at a Grand Prix

SPA/Jerez
- Alberto Puig (Honda) became the first Spanish rider to win a 500cc race on home soil
- With Puig winning and Alex Criville (Honda) finishing third this was the first time that two Spanish riders had finished on the podium in the 500cc class
- A seventh-place finish for Daryl Beattie was enough to take the lead in the championship standings after Mick Doohan had crashed out while leading on lap 21

ITA/Mugello
- Kevin Schwantz announced his retirement from Grand Prix racing. Along with Schwantz, the number 34 is retired. Schwantz was replaced in the Suzuki factory team by former World Superbike Champion Scott Russell
- Pier Francesco Chili finished tenth to score the last ever points in the 500cc class for the Cagiva factory

NED/Assen
- Championship leader Daryl Beattie missed the race after crashing during practice and breaking a collarbone

FRA/Le Mans
- Alberto Puig crashed during qualifying and suffered serious injuries that eliminated him from the remainder of the season. He was replaced by Carlos Checa from the British GP onwards

CZE/Brno
- Luca Cadalora gave Yamaha their first 500cc win of the year and then repeated the victory at the next race in Brazil

ARG/Buenos Aires
- Mick Doohan won to become the first Australian and first Honda rider to take back-to-back 500cc world titles

EUR/Catalunya
- Alex Criville became the second Spaniard to win on home soil during 1995. This was the first time that a country had two home winners in the 500cc class in the same year

EUR/Catalunya
- Loris Capirossi's first podium finish in his debut year in the 500cc class

250cc

JPN/Suzuka
- Race stopped after 12 of the scheduled 18 laps due to rain. Winner Ralf Waldmann (Honda) won after crashing while in the lead and restarting

SPA/Jerez
- Tetsuya Harada took his only victory of the year for Yamaha in the 250cc class

BRA/Jacarepagua
- After missing several races due to injuries suffered in a crash at the German GP, Doriano Romboni (Honda) took his fourth and last 250cc win
- Max Biaggi (Aprilia) finished second to retain the world title and become the youngest ever rider to win back-to-back titles in the 250cc class

ARG/Buenos Aires
- Former world motocross champion Jean-Michel Bayle (FRA, Aprilia) qualifies on pole but retires from the race after three laps with mechanical problems

EUR/Catalunya
- Max Biaggi won for the eighth time in 1995 and was on the podium for the 12th time from 13. This performance by Biaggi resulted in Aprilia taking their first 250cc constructors' title

125cc

AUS/Eastern Creek
- Haruchika Aoki (JPN, Honda) took his first Grand Prix victory just two days before his 19th birthday

MAL/Shah Alam
- Garry McCoy takes his first GP victory in a race stopped after 12 laps due to rain and for which half points were awarded

NED/Assen
- Former World Champion Dirk Raudies (Honda) took the last of his 14 Grand Prix victories

BRA/Jacarepagua
- Haruchika Aoki clinched the world title with two races to spare and became the youngest ever Japanese rider to win a world title

1995 WORLD CHAMPIONSHIP

500cc

Pos	Rider	Nat	Machine	AUS	MAL	JPN	SPA	GER	ITA	NED	FRA	GBR	CZE	BRA	ARG	EUR	Total
1	Mick Doohan	AUS	Honda	25	25	20	-	-	25	25	25	25	20	20	25	13	248
2	Daryl Beattie	AUS	Suzuki	20	20	25	9	25	20	-	16	20	16	13	20	11	215
3	Luca Cadalora	ITA	Yamaha	13	-	13	20	20	4	9	20	11	25	25	16	-	176
4	Alex Criville	SPA	Honda	16	16	-	16	13	11	20	-	16	10	10	13	25	166
5	Shinichi Itoh	JPN	Honda	6	9	-	8	16	13	8	13	10	11	6	7	20	127
6	Loris Capirossi	ITA	Honda	8	-	-	10	10	7	13	-	13	13	7	11	16	108
7	Alex Barros	BRA	Honda	10	10	-	11	9	9	11	11	-	7	8	8	10	104
8	Alberto Puig	SPA	Honda	9	11	11	25	11	16	16	-	-	-	-	-	-	99
9	Norick Abe	JPN	Yamaha	7	-	7	13	8	10	10	-	-	-	16	10	-	81
10	Loris Reggiani	ITA	Aprilia	5	8	6	-	7	8	7	-	-	9	-	-	9	59
11	Neil Hodgson	GBR	Yamaha	-	-	2	4	2	2	3	8	9	6	5	6	7	54
12	Juan Borja	SPA	Yamaha	-	7	9	7	6	-	6	-	8	4	-	5	-	52
13	Scott Russell	USA	Suzuki	-	-	-	-	-	5	4	10	-	5	11	-	8	43
14	Bernard Garcia	FRA	Yamaha	3	6	5	-	-	3	5	-	7	3	-	4	5	41
15	Kevin Schwantz	USA	Suzuki	11	13	10	-	-	-	-	-	-	-	-	-	-	34
16	Carlos Checa	SPA	Yamaha	-	-	-	-	-	-	-	-	-	8	9	9	-	26
17	Adrian Bosshard	SWI	Honda	1	-	1	-	4	-	1	5	6	1	1	1	-	21
18	Laurent Naveau	BEL	Yamaha	-	-	-	3	3	-	-	6	-	2	3	-	4	21
19	Jeremy McWilliams	GBR	Yamaha	-	2	-	5	-	-	-	9	-	-	4	-	-	20
20	Toshiyuki Arakaki	JPN	Yamaha	-	-	8	-	-	-	-	7	5	-	-	-	-	20
21	Cristiano Migliorati	ITA	Yamaha	2	4	-	6	5	-	-	-	-	-	-	-	-	17
22	Sean Emmett	GBR	Yamaha	4	-	3	-	-	-	-	-	3	-	2	2	3	17
23	Takuma Aoki	JPN	Honda	-	-	16	-	-	-	-	-	-	-	-	-	-	16
24	James Haydon	GBR	Yamaha	-	-	-	-	-	-	2	-	-	-	-	3	6	11
25	Frederic Protat	FRA	Yamaha	-	5	-	-	-	-	-	4	-	-	-	-	-	9
26	Mark Garcia	FRA	Yamaha	-	3	-	-	-	1	-	3	-	-	-	-	2	9
27	Pier-Francesco Chili	ITA	Cagiva	-	-	-	-	-	6	-	-	-	-	-	-	-	6
28	Bruno Bonhuil	FRA	Yamaha	-	-	-	1	-	-	-	-	4	-	-	-	-	5
28	Andrew Stroud	NZE	Yamaha	-	1	4	-	-	-	-	-	-	-	-	-	-	5
30	Eugene McManus	GBR	Yamaha	-	-	-	2	-	-	-	-	2	-	-	-	-	4
31	Bernard Hanggeli	SWI	Yamaha	-	-	-	-	-	-	-	2	-	-	-	-	-	2
32	Jean-Pierre Jeandat	FRA	Paton	-	-	-	-	1	-	-	-	-	-	-	-	-	1
32	Philippe Monneret	FRA	Yamaha	-	-	-	-	-	-	-	1	-	-	-	-	-	1
32	Lucio Pedercini	ITA	Yamaha	-	-	-	-	-	-	-	-	-	-	-	-	1	1
32	Chris Walker	GBR	Yamaha	-	-	-	-	-	-	-	-	1	-	-	-	-	1

Scoring system – 25, 20, 16, 13, 11, 10, 9, 8, 7, 6, 5, 4, 3, 2, 1

250cc

Pos	Rider	Nat	Machine	Total
1	Max Biaggi	ITA	Aprilia	283
2	Tetsuya Harada	JPN	Yamaha	220
3	Ralf Waldmann	GER	Honda	203
4	Tadayuki Okada	JPN	Honda	136
5	Jean-Philippe Ruggia	FRA	Honda	115
6	Nobuatsu Aoki	JPN	Honda	105
7	Luis d'Antin	SPA	Honda	88
8	Kenny Roberts Jnr	USA	Yamaha	82
9	Doriano Romboni	ITA	Honda	75
10	Olivier Jacque	FRA	Honda	66

125cc

Pos	Rider	Nat	Machine	Total
1	Haruchika Aoki	JPN	Honda	224
2	Kazuto Sakata	JPN	Aprilia	140
3	Emilio Alzamora	SPA	Honda	129
4	Akira Saito	JPN	Honda	127
5	Dirk Raudies	GER	Honda	124.5
6	Stefano Perugini	ITA	Aprilia	118
7	Masaki Tokudome	JPN	Aprilia	105.5
8	Tomomi Manako	JPN	Honda	102
9	Hideyuki Nakajyo	JPN	Honda	88
10	Peter Ottl	GER	Aprilia	76

NUMBER 34 SAYS GOODBYE

Was there ever a more naturally talented or spectacular racer than Kevin Schwantz? Or a braver one? Or a rider more popular with fans everywhere? The tall, skinny Texan was never given to over-analysing what he did; he just went fast and braked later than anyone else: 'See God, then back off.' His first full season was in 1988, so he was competing from the start with fellow-Americans Lawson, Rainey and Mamola, plus Aussies Gardner and Magee at the start, before young bloods Doohan and Kocinski came along. By any standards that constitutes a grid full of champions, yet none of them ever eclipsed Kevin.

Schwantz's Suzuki was always more sensitive to set up than the Honda and Yamaha, and Kevin got hurt with alarming frequency and came back from injury with even more alarming speed. These quick fixes took their inevitable toll on his ability to control a 500, and final realisation came at the third race of the '95 season. The Suzuka track and rainy conditions were both Schwantz favourites, but at a sodden Japanese GP he could only manage sixth, over 20 seconds behind winner and fellow-Suzuki rider, Daryl Beattie. Kevin didn't travel to the next two GPs, but he did turn up at Mugello to announce his retirement. He thought he might be given a hard time for quitting mid-season and was genuinely surprised by the standing ovation at his press conference. The injuries played a part in his decision but so, surely, did the absence of his career-long nemesis, Wayne Rainey. Why race if Wayne wasn't there to beat?

LEFT Kevin Schwantz – the fans' favourite and the inspiration for another generation of racers. (*Henk Keulemans*)

1996

Mick Doohan continued to build his legend with a third consecutive title, as did Max Biaggi in the 250s

It was a year in which the NSR Honda was little changed but the opposition got no closer to Mick Doohan who did have to work to beat a strong Alex Criville, again his Repsol Honda team-mate. There were two more Repsol Hondas, this time a new V-twin, the NSR500V, in the hands of Japanese duo Tadayuki Okada and Shinichi Itoh. It might have seemed like the same idea as Aprilia's twin but it wasn't that simple. Where Aprilia pumped up their 250, Honda built a brand-new bike to the full 500cc limit to take as much benefit as possible from the 30kg minimum weight advantage for twins. Okada promptly put it on pole first time out. Satellite team NSRs went to Alex Barros, Luca Cadalora and the Spanish Pons team, with Alberto Puig back from injury alongside the man who had replaced him after the accident, Carlos Checa.

Kenny Roberts and Wayne Rainey both managed factory Yamaha teams. The former ran Kenny Roberts Jnr, Jean-Michel Bayle (FRA) and Norick Abe; the latter two former World Champions, Loris Capirossi on a 500 and Tetsuya Harada on a 250.

Aprilia's 500 – or rather 410cc – V-twin project continued with Doriano Romboni replacing Loris Reggiani. Max Biaggi was the factory's only fully supported works 250cc rider. He fought off a squadron of factory Hondas for his third consecutive title. Suzuki stuck with very much the same machinery, and retained riders Aussie Daryl Beattie and American Scott Russell.

All but two 500cc races were won by Hondas, and one of them was the result of Criville's last-corner lunge in Australia, which took down both himself and Doohan to let in Capirossi. It could thus be argued that the only non-Repsol Honda winner in a straight fight was Norick Abe, who became the first Japanese winner of a Japanese GP. It was a reminder of that wild-card ride two years earlier when Abe burst on to the scene for the first time. However, that was but a sideshow to Doohan's majestic progress – and the immense irritation the persistent Criville's back-to-back wins provoked in the World Champion.

ABOVE Two triple champions together – Doohan and Biaggi. (*Henk Keulemans*)

RIGHT When Norick Abe won his home Grand Prix, it seemed that he would be the next big star. (*Henk Keulemans*)

THE **1996** SEASON

500cc

MAL/Shah Alam
- Tadayuki Okada qualified on pole on the debut outing for the new V-twin Honda. This was the first time that a twin-cylinder machine had been fastest qualifier in the 500cc class since Tony Rutter (GBR, Yamaha) at the 1975 TT races
- Luca Cadalora won first time out on a Honda in the 500cc class

INA/Sentul
- Mick Doohan won the 500cc race at the first ever Indonesian Grand Prix

JPN/Suzuka
- Norick Abe took his first victory, to become the second-youngest rider to win a 500cc GP after Freddie Spencer

SPA/Jerez
- Doohan was victorious after the crowd invaded the track on the last lap and local favourite Alex Criville crashed at the final corner while battling him for the win
- Tadayuki Okada became the first rider since 1979 to finish on the podium in the 500cc class with a twin-cylinder machine

AUT/A1-Ring
- Alex Criville beat team-mate Doohan for the first time in a straight fight to the flag

CZE/Brno
- After a race-long battle Criville took the win from Doohan by just two-thousandths of a second – the closest recorded finish in the 500cc class since the introduction of electronic timing

IMO/Imola
- Mick Doohan won the Imola GP, a race cut short by rain. This was the 500th race in the 500cc class

SPA-EUR/Catalunya
- Honda-mounted Carlos Checa took his first GP victory, and on home soil. This was the 100th win in the 500cc class for Honda
- Mick Doohan finished second to clinch his third successive world title

AUS/Eastern Creek
- Loris Capirossi took his first 500cc GP win after Criville collided with race leader Doohan at the final corner and both riders crashed out

250cc

INA/Sentul
- Testsuya Harada took his only GP win of the year on the Michelin-tyred factory Yamaha, the last time a 250cc GP was won by a rider not using Dunlops

GER/Nürburgring
- Max Biaggi finished fourth after being on the rostrum at the previous 17 races – the longest sequence of successive podium finishes in the 250cc class

RIO/Jacarepagua
- Olivier Jacque (FRA, Honda) scored his first Grand Prix victory

AUS/Eastern Creek
- Max Biaggi came to the final race of the year with a one-point advantage over nearest rival Ralf Waldmann. The two riders battled it out, but victory – and the title – finally went to the Italian

125cc

MAL/Shah Alam
- New regulations set a rider–bike combined minimum weight limit of 160kg

SPA/Jerez
- Fifth-placed Kazuto Sakata (Aprilia) finished just 0.224s behind the winner, fellow-Japanese Haruchika Aoki (Honda) – the first time that the first five riders in a GP have been covered by less than a quarter of a second

AUT/A1-Ring
- Aged 16, Ivan Goi (ITA, Honda) became the youngest GP winner

CZE/Brno
- Italian teenager Valentino Rossi took his first Grand Prix victory, riding an Aprilia

AUS/Eastern Creek
- Garry McCoy (Honda) won his home GP to create a new record of nine different winners in the 125cc class in a single season
- Haruchika Aoki finished second in the final race of the year to become the first Japanese rider to retain a world title

1996 WORLD CHAMPIONSHIP

500cc

Pos	Rider	Nat	Machine	MAL	INA	JPN	SPA	ITA	FRA	NED	GER	GBR	AUT	CZE	IMO	CAT	RIO	AUS	Total
1	Mick Doohan	AUS	Honda	11	25	10	25	25	25	25	20	25	20	20	25	20	25	8	309
2	Alex Criville	SPA	Honda	-	13	20	-	20	20	20	16	20	25	25	20	16	20	10	245
3	Luca Cadalora	ITA	Honda	25	10	-	20	16	10	-	25	7	13	-	10	13	10	9	168
4	Alex Barros	BRA	Honda	20	20	-	8	10	9	16	8	9	11	7	8	8	11	13	158
5	Norick Abe	JPN	Yamaha	8	7	25	-	5	13	10	10	16	16	5	11	6	16	-	148
6	Scott Russell	USA	Suzuki	13	9	16	-	-	11	13	13	11	10	16	9	5	7	-	133
7	Tadayuki Okada	JPN	Honda	-	-	13	16	9	-	3	9	13	5	9	16	11	8	20	132
8	Carlos Checa	SPA	Honda	16	11	6	6	-	-	5	-	4	9	8	5	25	13	16	124
9	Jean-Michel Bayle	FRA	Yamaha	10	8	8	9	11	-	8	6	-	7	10	13	-	9	11	110
10	Loris Capirossi	ITA	Yamaha	-	16	-	13	-	-	-	4	10	8	4	-	7	4	25	98
11	Alberto Puig	SPA	Honda	9	6	7	11	4	16	4	5	5	3	6	4	9	5	-	93
12	Shinichi Itoh	JPN	Honda	-	3	5	7	8	-	6	7	6	-	13	7	10	6	7	77
13	Kenny Roberts Jnr	USA	Yamaha	-	-	4	10	6	-	11	11	-	-	-	6	-	3	5	69
14	Juan Borja	SPA	Elf 500	6	-	-	5	-	-	7	-	8	6	-	-	-	2	-	34
15	Frederic Protat	FRA	Yamaha	7	2	-	3	1	8	1	2	2	-	2	-	3	-	3	32
16	Jeremy McWilliams	GBR	Yamaha	2	4	3	2	-	5	2	-	-	2	-	-	4	-	-	26
17	Lucio Pedercini	ITA	Yamaha	4	-	-	-	3	6	-	3	1	-	-	3	-	1	4	25
18	Daryl Beattie	AUS	Suzuki	-	-	11	-	13	-	-	-	-	-	-	-	-	-	-	24
19	Doriano Romboni	ITA	Aprilia	-	5	9	-	7	-	-	-	-	-	-	2	-	-	-	23
20	Terry Rymer	GBR	Suzuki	-	-	-	-	-	-	9	-	-	4	3	-	-	-	-	16
21	James Haydon	GBR	Yamaha	1	-	1	4	-	7	-	-	3	-	-	-	-	-	-	16
22	Sean Emmett	GBR	Yamaha	5	1	-	1	2	-	-	-	-	-	-	-	-	-	-	9
23	Peter Goddard	AUS	Suzuki	-	-	-	-	-	-	-	-	-	-	-	-	-	-	6	6
24	Eugene McManus	GBR	Yamaha	-	-	-	-	-	4	-	1	-	-	-	1	-	-	-	6
25	Toshiyuki Arakaki	JPN	Yamaha	-	-	2	-	-	1	-	-	-	-	-	-	-	-	1	4
26	Florian Ferracci	FRA	Yamaha	-	-	-	-	-	3	-	-	-	-	-	-	-	-	-	3
26	Laurent Naveau	BEL	Yamaha	3	-	-	-	-	-	-	-	-	-	-	-	-	-	-	3
28	Jean-Marc Deletang	FRA	Yamaha	-	-	-	-	-	2	-	-	-	-	-	-	-	-	-	2
28	Andrew Stroud	NZE	Yamaha	-	-	-	-	-	-	-	-	-	-	-	-	-	-	2	2
28	Paul Young	AUS	Yamaha	-	-	-	-	-	-	-	-	-	-	-	-	2	-	-	2
29	Chris Walker	GBR	Elf 500	-	-	-	-	-	-	-	-	-	1	-	-	1	-	-	2
32	Marcellino Lucchi	ITA	Aprilia	-	-	-	-	-	-	-	-	-	-	1	-	-	-	-	1

Scoring system – 25, 20, 16, 13, 11, 10, 9, 8, 7, 6, 5, 4, 3, 2, 1

250cc

Pos	Rider	Nat	Machine	Total
1	Max Biaggi	ITA	Aprilia	274
2	Ralf Waldmann	GER	Honda	268
3	Olivier Jacque	FRA	Honda	193
4	Jurgen Fuchs	GER	Honda	174
5	Tohru Ukawa	JPN	Honda	142
6	Luis d'Antin	SPA	Honda	138
7	Nobuatsu Aoki	JPN	Honda	105
8	Tetsuya Harada	JPN	Yamaha	104
9	Jean-Philippe Ruggia	FRA	Honda	91
10	Luca Boscoscuro	ITA	Aprilia	62

125cc

Pos	Rider	Nat	Machine	Total
1	Haruchika Aoki	JPN	Honda	220
2	Masaki Tokudome	JPN	Aprilia	193
3	Tomomi Manako	JPN	Honda	167
4	Emilio Alzamora	SPA	Honda	158
5	Jorge Martinez	SPA	Aprilia	131
6	Stefano Perugini	ITA	Aprilia	128
7	Noboru Ueda	JPN	Honda	126
8	Kazuto Sakata	JPN	Aprilia	113
9	Valentino Rossi	ITA	Aprilia	111
10	Ivan Goi	ITA	Honda	110

OPPOSITE RIGHT, TOP TO BOTTOM The three ages of sidecar: Hilerbrand and Grunwald's 1954 BMW (*Stuart Dent Archive*); Scheidegger and Robinson's 1966 kneeler BMW (*Henk Keulemans*); and Rolf Biland and Kurt Waltisperg's 1980 LCR Yamaha. (*Henk Keulemans*)

THREE WHEELS ON MY WAGON

This was the last year that the sidecars ran as a GP class. They'd been there since the start of the World Championships in 1949, for a couple of years with a 600cc capacity limit, when Norton singles raced pre-war Gilera fours. The outfits started to move away from their origins – a motorcycle with a third wheel bolted on – as early as 1954 when Eric Oliver (GBR, Norton Watsonian) raced a fully streamlined machine which he rode in a kneeling position.

Germany then took over as the sidecar specialists thanks to the BMW Rennsport boxer-twin motor, which could have been designed for the job. BMW engines won the championship every year from 1954 to 1974 with just two interruptions from the engineering genius that was Helmut Fath, who won in '68 and '71 with his own four-cylinder URS motor. (In the second of those title seasons Fath also prepared Phil Read's two-stroke Yamaha motor with which he won the 250cc World Championship.) Sidecar crews had adapted the Konig flat-four two-stroke powerboat engine in the early 1970s – at the same time as Kiwi Kim Newcombe was getting one on the rostrum in 500cc solo GPs. The BMWs held out until 1975 when the top nine crews in the championship were on either Konigs or Yamaha-powered outfits.

Third that year was Swiss driver Rolf Biland, who would dominate the three-wheelers for the next 20 years. His Yamaha-powered Seymaz outfit cut the last connection with the origin of sidecars, doing away with leading-link forks and using hub-centre steering. Sidecars were now a Formula 3 car with a corner cut off. The engines, Yamaha fours until the early '90s, migrated to the back of the outfit and the rider's position gradually became horizontal. Biland was so adept at getting round any technical regulations that in 1979 there were two separate sidecar GPs, B2A and B2B, because the Beo with which he won the '78 title was so radical – the driver used a steering wheel and the passenger didn't move! Before the Jerez chicane was opened up Biland qualified on it quicker than the 500s.

That's not to say the sidecars didn't provide good entertainment. In the late 1980s and early '90s Biland's battles with Steve Webster (GBR), Alain Michel (FRA) and Egbert Streuer (NED) were often the highlight of the day's racing. But the sidecar class never had mass appeal outside Germany and the UK, and it gradually withered away. None of which should detract from the amazing record of Rolf Biland.

MOST SIDECAR WINS (1949 TO 1996)

1	Rolf Biland(SWI)	81
2	Klaus Enders (GER)	27
3	Steve Webster (GBR)	23
4	Egbert Streuer (NED)	22
5	Alain Michel (FRA)	18

MOST SIDECAR WORLD TITLES (1949 TO 1996)

1	Rolf Biland (SWI)	7
2	Klaus Enders (GER)	6
3=	Max Deubel (GER)	4
3=	Eric Oliver (GBR)	4
3=	Steve Webster (GBR)	4

1997

The Honda steamroller, driven again by Mick Doohan, rolls to the top five places in the 500s; Max Biaggi joins Honda and wins the 250s for a fourth time

Another record-breaking year saw near-total domination by Mick Doohan. His fellow-Honda V4 riders all pressurised him at one time or another, but none of them could put together a consistent challenge. Of the Repsol men, Alex Criville and Tadayuki Okada were on V4s while the middle of the three Aoki brothers, Takuma, took over on the factory V-twin, with older brother Nobuatsu riding a '96-spec NSR in FCC-Technical Sports colours. The Movistar team of Sito Pons retained both Carlos Checa and Alberto Puig.

Suzuki's lead rider was Daryl Beattie but, still troubled by injury, he had a mediocre season and retired at the end of the year. Scott Russell was replaced by Anthony Gobert, a naturally talented rider, but when he failed a drug test Suzuki found themselves needing the services of another Australian, tester Peter Goddard.

Yamaha's effort was somewhat shaken by Kenny Roberts departing to build his own bikes and taking sponsor Marlboro with him, as well as riders Roberts Jnr and Frenchman Jean-Michel Bayle. When Loris Capirossi decided to go back to the 250 class Wayne Rainey had to cast around for another rider, and he signed Sete Gibernau (SPA) to partner Norick Abe. Yamaha's other team was essentially the squad that had taken Troy Corser to the World Superbike Championship in 1996. They partnered the Aussie with Luca Cadalora early in the season. After sponsorship dried up, the WCM team took over the team's bikes. Kenny Roberts's bikes were triples, allowed to be 15kg lighter than a four, badged as Modenas machines thanks to sponsorship from the giant Malaysian Proton automotive company. Aprilia's V-twin got a last run-out, with Doriano Romboni staying as the rider.

In the 250s, Max Biaggi left Aprilia in a huff with the intention of proving that it was the man not the bike who had taken the last three titles. All three classes now had 26 permanent entries who were contracted to ride at all GPs. Up to six wild card cards were selected by the FIM, IRTA and the local federation.

ABOVE Tady Okada leads Mick Doohan, Alex Criville and Takuma Aoki in a factory Honda procession. *(Henk Keulemans)*

RIGHT Jean-Michel Bayle about to set off on Kenny Roberts' Modenas triple. *(Henk Keulemans)*

THE 1997 SEASON

500cc

MAL/Shah Alam

- Mick Doohan opened his title defence with victory from fellow-Honda riders Alex Criville and 500cc debutant Nobuatsu Aoki

SPA/Jerez

- Alex Criville won the Spanish GP at Jerez for the first time

NED/Assen

- Criville crashed during the second qualifying session and suffered injuries that resulted in him missing five races
- Doriano Romboni's third place was the first podium finish for the V-twin Aprilia

IMO/Imola

- Mick Doohan was followed across the line by Nobuatsu Aoki and Takuma Aoki, the first time in the class that two Japanese riders finished together on the podium and only the second occasion that two brothers have shared a 500cc GP rostrum

GBR/Donington

- Alex Barros took third – the only podium finish achieved by a private V-twin Honda

INA/Sentul

- Tadayuki Okada won his first 500cc GP by passing team-mate Doohan at the last corner and crossing the line with an advantage of just 0.069s
- Mick Doohan's second place gave him a new record total for a single season of 340 points

AUS/Phillip Island

- Mick Doohan started from pole for the 12th time in 1997 – a record that still stands for most poles in one season in the premier class
- Doohan crashed out of his home GP on lap 17 when leading by eight seconds, the only race all year that he failed to finish on the podium. The crash ended a record sequence of 37 successive points-scoring races for the four-times World Champion
- Alex Criville gave Honda their 15th win of the season – a record for the number of premier-class wins in a single season by one manufacturer, which Honda themselves achieved again in 2003

250cc

MAL/Shah Alam

- Max Biaggi won on his first ride on a Honda since 1993. This was the 500th GP win by Italian riders across all solo classes

JPN/Suzuka

- Wild-card Japanese rider, 20-year-old Daijiro Kato, took his first victory in only his second GP start – and while still recovering from a serious car crash

NED/Assen

- Max Biaggi was shown the black flag during the race as punishment for missing a stop-and-go penalty for his team not clearing the grid at the correct time

INA/Sentul

- Biaggi took the victory, to go to the last round leading a three-way battle for the title with a six-point advantage over Tetsuya Harada and seven points clear of Ralf Waldmann

AUS/Phillip Island

- Waldmann won the final race of the year but Biaggi's second place was enough for the Italian to take his fourth successive title by two points

125cc

MAL/Shah Alam

- Valentino Rossi started his second year in the class with the second GP win of his career from experienced fellow-Aprilia rider Kazuto Sakata and Noboru Ueda (Honda)

JPN/Suzuka

- Ueda won his home race after qualifying on pole and then calling into the pits after the sighting lap to change his gearing and subsequently starting from the back of the grid
- Valentino Rossi crashed out of the race on the penultimate lap – his only non-finish of the year and one of only two occasions when he failed to finish on the podium

CZE/Brno

- Noboru Ueda won a race in which all points-scoring riders were covered by just 13.289s – the first time the top 15 riders in a Grand Prix have been covered by less than 15 seconds
- Valentino Rossi finished third to take his first world title

INA/Sentul

- Rossi won for the 11th time in 1997 – a record for most wins in a single season in the 125cc class
- Jorge Martinez finished third, in his final season of racing – and 14 years after first appearing on a Grand Prix podium

1997 WORLD CHAMPIONSHIP

500cc

Pos	Rider	Nat	Machine	MAL	JPN	SPA	ITA	AUT	FRA	NED	IMO	GER	RIO	GBR	CZE	CAT	INA	AUS	Total
1	Mick Doohan	AUS	Honda	25	25	20	25	25	25	25	25	25	25	25	25	25	20	-	340
2	Tadayuki Okada	JPN	Honda	6	16	16	-	20	16	4	11	20	20	20	-	10	25	13	197
3	Nobuatsu Aoki	JPN	Honda	16	11	11	16	13	-	13	20	13	13	13	16	11	13	-	179
4	Alex Criville	SPA	Honda	20	20	25	13	11	13	-	-	-	-	-	13	16	16	25	172
5	Takuma Aoki	JPN	Honda	11	13	13	-	-	11	-	16	16	-	6	10	9	9	20	134
6	Luca Cadalora	ITA	Yamaha	13	5	5	20	16	-	-	10	-	16	11	20	13	-	-	129
7	Norick Abe	JPN	Yamaha	8	9	9	9	7	9	6	9	-	11	7	11	4	11	16	126
8	Carlos Checa	SPA	Honda	10	10	-	-	10	20	20	13	-	-	-	-	20	10	6	119
9	Alex Barros	BRA	Honda	5	6	8	10	3	10	10	7	10	-	16	8	-	-	8	101
10	Doriano Romboni	ITA	Aprilia	-	-	10	5	6	5	16	-	11	9	9	-	6	6	5	88
11	Daryl Beattie	AUS	Suzuki	-	-	4	11	5	4	9	3	4	3	10	6	-	4	-	63
12	Alberto Puig	SPA	Honda	9	8	-	-	8	8	11	4	6	2	-	3	1	2	1	63
13	Sete Gibernau	SPA	Yamaha	7	-	7	7	-	3	-	5	9	-	-	-	-	8	10	56
14	Regis Laconi	FRA	Honda	4	4	6	6	-	-	-	-	-	7	-	9	5	-	11	52
15	Anthony Gobert	AUS	Suzuki	-	-	-	3	9	6	3	6	7	6	-	4	-	-	-	44
16	Kenny Roberts Jnr	USA	Modenas	-	-	-	-	-	-	8	-	-	-	5	7	8	7	2	37
17	Juan Borja	SPA	Elf 500	2	-	-	-	4	7	1	-	8	-	8	-	7	-	-	37
18	Jean-Michel Bayle	FRA	Modenas	-	2	3	8	2	-	-	8	-	8	-	-	-	-	-	31
19	Jurgen van den Goorbergh	NED	Honda	1	1	2	-	-	1	-	-	5	5	3	5	2	-	4	29
20	Jurgen Fuchs	GER	Elf 500	-	-	-	-	-	-	7	2	3	10	1	-	-	5	-	28
21	Kirk McCarthy	AUS	Yamaha	-	-	1	2	-	-	-	1	1	4	4	-	3	1	3	20
22	Peter Goddard	AUS	Suzuki	-	3	-	-	-	-	-	-	-	-	-	-	-	3	7	13
23	Troy Corser	AUS	Yamaha	3	-	-	4	-	2	2	-	-	-	-	-	-	-	-	11
24	Yukio Kagayama	JPN	Suzuki	-	-	-	-	-	-	-	-	-	-	-	-	-	-	9	9
25	Norihiko Fujiwara	JPN	Yamaha	-	7	-	-	-	-	-	-	-	-	-	-	-	-	-	7
26	Bernard Garcia	FRA	Honda	-	-	-	-	-	-	5	-	2	-	-	-	-	-	-	7
27	Laurent Naveau	BEL	Yamaha	-	-	-	-	1	-	-	-	-	-	-	2	-	-	-	3
28	Jason Vincent	GBR	Honda	-	-	-	-	-	-	-	-	-	-	2	-	-	-	-	2
29	Lucio Pedercini	ITA	Yamaha	-	-	-	1	-	-	-	-	-	1	-	-	-	-	-	2

Scoring system – 25, 20, 16, 13, 11, 10, 9, 8, 7, 6, 5, 4, 3, 2, 1

250cc

Pos	Rider	Nat	Machine	Total
1	Max Biaggi	ITA	Honda	250
2	Ralf Waldmann	GER	Honda	248
3	Tetsuya Harada	JPN	Aprilia	235
4	Olivier Jacque	FRA	Honda	201
5	Tohru Ukawa	JPN	Honda	173
6	Loris Capirossi	ITA	Aprilia	116
7	Takeshi Tsujimura	JPN	Honda	109
8	Haruchika Aoki	JPN	Honda	102
9	Stefano Perugini	ITA	Aprilia	85
10	Jeremy McWilliams	GBR	Honda	73

125cc

Pos	Rider	Nat	Machine	Total
1	Valentino Rossi	ITA	Aprilia	321
2	Noboru Ueda	JPN	Honda	238
3	Tomomi Manako	JPN	Honda	190
4	Kazuto Sakata	JPN	Aprilia	179
5	Masaki Tokudome	JPN	Aprilia	120
6	Jorge Martinez	SPA	Aprilia	119
7	Garry McCoy	AUS	Aprilia	109
8	Roberto Locatelli	ITA	Honda	97
9	Mirko Giansanti	ITA	Honda	83
10	Frederic Petit	FRA	Honda	83

REPSOL WHITEWASH

This was the year that the factory Honda team totally dominated the 500 class, with Mick Doohan winning 12 races to make it four crowns in a row. He failed to win just three times: in Spain an engine fault slowed him and Criville won; Okada beat him in the penultimate race in Indonesia; and in Australia Mick fell while leading his home race to hand Alex Criville his second win of the year. The Spanish rider had had a horrible accident in practice at Assen that threatened to end his career, so it was an impressive win under any circumstances.

The team also hogged pole position: Okada was fastest at the first three GPs, Doohan at all the rest. Takuma Aoki got in on the action too, putting the twin on the rostrum three times. The Repsol Honda team also monopolised the rostrum on four occasions. It wasn't just the Repsol team that dominated, though, it was Honda as a whole. NSR500 riders finished in the top four places in the championship, with Nobuatsu Aoki, a class rookie, third overall and his little brother Takuma fifth on the twin. It was the sort of domination that MV Agusta had enjoyed in the late 1950s, but then they didn't have any four-cylinder opposition. Biaggi's win in the 250 class gave Honda their first 250/500 double in eight years and meant the only championship the factory didn't get its hands on was the 125 – Valentino Rossi (Aprilia) won his first title.

LEFT Valentino Rossi celebrating his 125 title at Brno. (*Henk Keulemans*)

With hindsight this was probably Mick Doohan at his finest. He won by a massive points margin with four races to spare and all on the old 'screamer' engine to which he'd decided to revert. This was the last year of leaded petrol, so the bike was considerably more brutal than the now standard-issue big-bang motors that everyone else used. His team-mates tried it but didn't race it. Why did he go back to the vicious old technology? Doohan said it let him ride like he wanted. Mind you, a little later he also said that it was to mess with the opposition's heads. And Mick would most certainly have included his team-mates in that definition.

BELOW Repsol Honda's invincibles: Doohan, Criville, Okada and Aoki. (*Henk Keulemans*)

1998

Mick Doohan makes it five in a row as Honda dominate again; 500cc rookie Max Biaggi gets closest to Mighty Mick

After four straight championships in the 250cc class, Max Biaggi moved up to the premier class to ride a Honda NSR500 engineered by Erv Kanemoto. Mick Doohan, Alex Criville and Tadayuki Okada all stayed as the Repsol Honda V4 riders, while Sete Gibernau took over the factory V-twin from Takuma Aoki, who had been paralysed from the waist down in a testing crash. The other satellite Honda teams were Movistar Pons, which retained Carlos Checa – and they were also given American John Kocinski, back in GPs as a reward for his World Superbike Championship win – and Team Gresini with rider Alex Barros, but on a V4 rather than a V-twin.

Yamaha again had two teams. Wayne Rainey kept Norick Abe and brought in Jean-Michel Bayle, only for the Frenchman to become another victim of a pre-season crash. He was replaced first by Kyoji Nanba (JPN) and then by Luca Cadalora. WCM, running as Red Bull Yamaha, went with Simon Crafar (NZE) and Regis Laconi (FRA). The Red Bull Yamahas were the only V4s on Dunlops rather than Michelins.

Suzuki brought in Nobuatsu Aoki after his impressive debut, and his intended team-mate was another Japanese, Katsuaki Fujiwara, but he too was hurt in pre-season tests. The second bike was therefore ridden by Keiichi Kitagawa at the first round, and then by Yukio Kagayama, among others. Kenny Roberts's Team KR lost most of their sponsorship to Biaggi, and their rider Bayle to Rainey's Yamaha team. Kenny Jnr was retained and German Ralf Waldmann brought in; they were the other Dunlop team.

The wild-card regulation for the 500 class was opened up to allow for a second entry nominated by the GP Manufacturers' Association. The other major change was the introduction of lead-free petrol – 'green gas'.

Valentino Rossi moved up to the 250 class on a factory Aprilia. Along with the official factory team of Tetsuya Harada and Loris Capirossi they dominated a posse of Hondas on new twin-crank NSRs. Only Daijiro Kato, a wild card at Suzuka, could win on it.

ABOVE Mick Doohan led another Honda sweep of the top five places, but Max Biaggi did get to him just a little bit. (*Henk Keulemans*)

THE **1998** SEASON

500cc

JPN/Suzuka
- Max Biaggi became the first rider for 25 years to win on his debut in the 500cc class.
- Honda-mounted Biaggi was the first European rider ever to win a 500cc GP race in Japan
- Noriyuki Haga (JPN, Yamaha) finished third in his 500cc Grand Prix debut as a wild card

MAL/Johor
- Mick Doohan took his first win of the year on the only occasion the Johor circuit was used for a Grand Prix

ITA/Mugello
- Doohan won at Mugello for the sixth successive year

FRA/Paul Ricard
- Alex Criville took his second win of the year to become the first Spanish rider to lead the 500cc championship table

MAD/Jarama
- Carlos Checa scored the second of his premier-class victories, with fellow-Spaniard Sete Gibernau third on the V-twin Honda, taking his first GP podium, at the Madrid Grand Prix

NED/Assen
- Doohan's victory at the Dutch TT was the last in a record sequence of 22 successive wins in the 500cc class by Honda riders

GBR/Donington
- Kiwi Simon Crafar took his only Grand Prix victory – the only 500cc win of the year for Yamaha and also the last 500cc win for a rider using Dunlop tyres
- Mick Doohan's second place at Donington was his 89th podium finish – a new record for the 500cc class

GER/Sachsenring
- Doohan made it 50 Grand Prix victories on the World Championship's first visit to the new Sachsenring
- Mick's win in Germany was the 100th victory for the 500cc V4 NSR Honda

IMO/Imola
- After missing most of the season due to injury, Jean-Michel Bayle qualified on pole in only his second start of the year

CAT/Catalunya
- Max Biaggi crossed the finishing line in first place but was disqualified for first ignoring a stop-and-go flag and then the subsequent black flag

AUS/Phillip Island
- Mick Doohan won his home race to clinch his fifth successive 500cc world title

ARG/Buenos Aires
- Luca Cadalora rode an MuZ, his third different factory ride of the year, having already had outings as a replacement rider in the Suzuki team at Assen and for Yamaha at Paul Ricard and Jarama

250cc

JPN/Suzuka
- Wild-card rider Daijiro Kato (Honda) took victory for the second successive year, sharing the podium with two other Japanese wild cards, Shinya Nakano and Naoki Matsudo, both on Yamaha machinery
- Valentino Rossi, making his debut in the 250cc class, failed to finish after suffering mechanical problems with his Aprilia

SPA/Jerez
- Loris Capirossi won his first 250cc GP for four years and his first on the factory Aprilia
- Second was Loris's Aprilia team-mate, Valentino Rossi, appearing for the first time on a 250cc GP podium

ITA/Mugello
- At the age of 41, and 16 years after making his GP debut, wild-card rider and factory tester Marcellino Lucchi took his first GP win ahead of the three official Aprilia riders – Rossi, Tetsuya Harada and Capirossi

NED/Assen
- Valentino Rossi won for the first time in the 250cc class

ARG/Buenos Aires
- Team-mates Loris Capirossi and Tetsuya Harada arrived at the final race separated by just four points
- Capirossi collided with Harada at the final corner, causing the Japanese rider to crash, but Loris stayed on his machine to finish second and take the title. The Italian was then disqualified from the results, but later reinstated on appeal

125cc

ITA/Mugello
- Tomomi Manako won the 500th GP race in the 125cc class

MAD/Jarama
- Lucio Cecchinello (ITA, Honda) scored his first GP victory

NED/Assen
- Marco Melandri (ITA, Honda) became the youngest rider to win a Grand Prix – a record that stood until British rider Scott Redding's win at Donington ten years later

GER/Sachsenring
- Melandri became the youngest rider to qualify on pole for a Grand Prix

CAT/Catalunya
- The race ended with the rider in 15th place crossing the line just 5.025s behind race winner Tomomi Manako – the closest top 15 of all time in GP racing

AUS/Phillip Island
- Kazuto Sakata's fourth-place finish was enough to regain the world title he had previously won in 1994
- Sakata was initially disqualified from the results due to an irregular fuel sample, but was later reinstated on appeal

1998 WORLD CHAMPIONSHIP

500cc

Pos	Rider	Nat	Machine	JPN	MAL	SPA	ITA	FRA	MAD	NED	GBR	GER	CZE	IMO	CAT	AUS	ARG	Total
1	Mick Doohan	AUS	Honda	-	25	20	25	20	-	25	20	25	-	25	25	25	25	260
2	Max Biaggi	ITA	Honda	25	16	16	20	11	10	20	10	20	25	16	-	8	11	208
3	Alex Criville	SPA	Honda	13	13	25	16	25	11	10	13	16	20	20	-	16	-	198
4	Carlos Checa	SPA	Honda	8	20	13	13	16	25	11	-	-	9	6	10	-	8	139
5	Alex Barros	BRA	Honda	9	-	11	7	-	7	13	11	13	16	13	9	13	16	138
6	Norick Abe	JPN	Yamaha	2	-	10	10	9	20	-	16	-	11	10	16	11	13	128
7	Simon Crafar	NZE	Yamaha	7	-	3	9	7	8	16	25	-	5	5	11	20	3	119
8	Tadayuki Okada	JPN	Honda	20	-	9	-	-	-	8	-	-	13	9	20	7	20	106
9	Nobuatsu Aoki	JPN	Suzuki	10	-	8	8	8	13	9	9	6	4	7	5	10	4	101
10	Regis Laconi	FRA	Yamaha	-	-	2	6	5	9	7	8	11	7	4	8	9	10	86
11	Sete Gibernau	SPA	Honda	6	-	4	2	6	16	-	-	-	10	8	13	-	7	72
12	John Kocinski	USA	Honda	3	11	5	11	13	-	-	-	-	1	3	7	4	6	64
13	Kenny Roberts Jnr	USA	Modenas	5	5	7	-	3	-	4	-	10	6	2	6	6	5	59
14	Ralf Waldmann	GER	Modenas	-	7	6	5	4	6	-	-	9	3	1	4	-	1	46
15	Jurgen van den Goorbergh	NED	Honda	-	8	-	-	1	-	6	7	8	-	-	3	5	2	40
16	Jean-Michel Bayle	FRA	Yamaha	-	-	-	-	-	-	-	-	-	8	11	-	-	9	28
17	Garry McCoy	AUS	Honda	-	6	1	3	-	5	5	3	-	-	-	-	-	-	23
18	Kyoji Nanba	JPN	Yamaha	11	-	-	4	-	-	-	-	7	-	-	-	-	-	22
19	Matt Wait	USA	Honda	-	4	-	-	-	3	3	-	2	-	-	2	3	-	17
20	Noriyuki Haga	JPN	Yamaha	16	-	-	-	-	-	-	-	-	-	-	-	-	-	16
21	Scott Smart	GBR	Honda	-	-	-	-	-	4	2	6	-	-	-	1	1	-	14
22	Luca Cadalora	ITA	Yamaha	-	-	-	-	10	-	-	-	-	-	-	-	-	-	10
22	Yukio Kagayama	JPN	Suzuki	-	10	-	-	-	-	-	-	-	-	-	-	-	-	10
24	Bernard Garcia	FRA	Honda	-	-	-	-	-	-	1	5	4	-	-	-	-	-	10
25	Norihiko Fujiwara	JPN	Yamaha	-	9	-	-	-	-	-	-	-	-	-	-	-	-	9
26	Eskil Suter	SWI	MuZ	-	-	-	-	-	2	-	-	3	2	-	-	-	-	7
27	Gregorio Lavilla	SPA	Honda	-	-	-	-	-	-	-	-	5	-	-	-	-	-	5
28	John McGuinness	GBR	Honda	-	-	-	-	-	-	-	4	-	-	-	-	-	-	4
28	Doriano Romboni	ITA	MuZ	4	-	-	-	-	-	-	-	-	-	-	-	-	-	4
30	Sebastien Gimbert	FRA	Honda	-	3	-	1	-	-	-	-	-	-	-	-	-	-	4
31	Fernando Cristobal	SPA	Honda	-	-	-	-	-	1	-	2	1	-	-	-	-	-	4
32	Juan Borja	SPA	Honda	1	-	-	-	2	-	-	-	-	-	-	-	-	-	3
33	Mark Willis	AUS	Suzuki	-	-	-	-	-	-	-	-	-	-	-	-	2	-	2
34	Fabio Carpani	ITA	Honda	-	-	-	-	-	-	-	1	-	-	-	-	-	-	1

Scoring system – 25, 20, 16, 13, 11, 10, 9, 8, 7, 6, 5, 4, 3, 2, 1

250cc

Pos	Rider	Nat	Machine	Total
1	Loris Capirossi	ITA	Aprilia	224
2	Valentino Rossi	ITA	Aprilia	201
3	Tetsuya Harada	JPN	Aprilia	200
4	Tohru Ukawa	JPN	Honda	145
5	Olivier Jacque	FRA	Honda	112
6	Haruchika Aoki	JPN	Honda	112
7	Stefano Perugini	ITA	Honda	102
8	Takeshi Tsujimura	JPN	Yamaha	91
9	Jeremy McWilliams	GBR	Honda	87
10	Luis d'Antin	SPA	Yamaha	74

125cc

Pos	Rider	Nat	Machine	Total
1	Kazuto Sakata	JPN	Aprilia	229
2	Tomomi Manako	JPN	Honda	217
3	Marco Melandri	ITA	Honda	202
4	Masao Azuma	JPN	Honda	135
5	Lucio Cecchinello	ITA	Honda	130
6	Mirko Giansanti	ITA	Honda	113
7	Masaki Tokudome	JPN	Aprilia	97
8	Gianluigi Scalvini	ITA	Honda	89
9	Roberto Locatelli	ITA	Honda	87
10	Frederic Petit	FRA	Honda	78

BIAGGI WINS FIRST TIME OUT

The arrival of Max Biaggi was just what the 500 class needed. His win first time out was helped by circumstances, but it served to reignite Mick Doohan's enthusiasm for racing – or, rather, for beating Max.

The coming of 'green gas' had several effects. First, it necessitated lower compression ratios and therefore softened the power of both fours and twins. However, it only slowed down the twins and effectively removed any hope they had of being competitive, whereas flattening the peak power of the V4s meant more people could ride them nearer the limit. Max Biaggi broke Mick Doohan's Suzuka lap record by over a second at the first race of the year. Second, there were also worries about how the loss of the petrol-borne lead's lubricating properties would affect reliability.

The more user-friendly nature of the NSR500 certainly helped Biaggi to be instantly competitive. He started the race from pole and, as just mentioned, set the fastest lap of the race. Doohan ran off track early on, at the first corner, something that could only be interpreted as rider error, and then he had the crankshaft break on him while he was climbing back through the field. This was the first time Mick had been let down by his bike since he came to GPs. It is possible that the motor ingested some debris during its trip into the gravel trap, but with bulk seizures of 250 Aprilias in mind most mechanics worried about the new fuel.

Assisted by circumstance or not, it's a measure of Biaggi's feat in winning first time out on a 500 that it had last been achieved by Jarno Saarinen, 25 years earlier. Max only won one other race all season, at Brno, a track that suited his wheels-in-line style perfectly, but he was impeccably consistent and ended the year second overall. It also helped that the Italian brought his usual abrasive attitude up from the 250 class, and that turned out to be a major contributing reason for Mick Doohan to decide to keep racing for one more year.

RIDERS WHO HAVE SCORED ON THEIR 500CC DEBUT

Harold Daniell (GBR, Norton): GBR/Isle of Man TT/1949 (this was the first 500cc race counting towards the World Championship)

Geoff Duke (GBR, Norton): GBR/Isle of Man TT/1950

Jorge Kissling (ARG, Matchless): ARG/Buenos Aires/1961 (race not attended by most leading riders)

Jarno Saarinen (FIN, Yamaha): FRA/Paul Ricard/1973

Edmund Czihak (GER, Yamaha): GER/Nürburgring/1974 (race boycotted by top riders due to safety issues)

Max Biaggi (ITA, Honda): JPN/Suzuka/1998

BELOW Max Biaggi exultant after winning at Suzuka on his 500cc debut. (*Henk Keulemans*)

1999

The end of an era. Mick Doohan retires from racing after a bad crash, Alex Criville steps out from the shadow of the master

The Repsol Honda team started the year with a familiar line-up – Mick Doohan, Tadayuki Okada and Alex Criville on V4s, with Sete Gibernau again on the factory V-twin – but that all changed when Doohan fell in practice for the third race of the year and sustained a collection of injuries serious enough to persuade even this toughest of men it was time to retire. Gibernau inherited his V4 two races later and the Repsol V-twin was quietly shelved. There were two Honda satellite teams: the Pons squad with Alex Barros and Juan Borja (SPA), and the impecunious Kanemoto operation with John Kocinski as rider.

Yamaha lined up with two new men in the factory team, both recruited from satellite Honda squads: Max Biaggi and Carlos Checa. WCM (Red Bull Yamaha) opted to keep Regis Laconi and Simon Crafar, but the latter spectacularly failed to come to terms with a switch to Michelin tyres and was replaced by ex-125 winner Garry McCoy from Assen onwards. A new satellite team, run by Spanish ex-250 racer Luis d'Antin, got a year-old YZR500 to run Norick Abe.

Nobuatsu Aoki was retained by Suzuki, who also prised Kenny Roberts Jnr – assisted by technical guru Warren Willing – away from his dad's team. They were rewarded with their first wins since Beattie's successes in 1995. Both, note, involved beating Doohan fair and square.

Team KR re-employed Jean-Michel Bayle only to lose him to injury early in the year, a fate which seemed to befall everyone else they hired during the season. Aprilia brought back their V-twin after spending a year enlarging the engine to somewhere near 500cc and put Tetsuya Harada on it. It was the only factory bike on Dunlops.

After Roberts and Suzuki blitzed the first two races, Alex Criville stepped into the shoes of the absent Mick Doohan and showed his six years as the great man's understudy had not been wasted to win six races and become the first Spanish 500cc World Champion.

ABOVE Alex Criville, Spain's first 500cc World Champion. (*Henk Keulemans*)

RIGHT Mick Doohan's last race, the extremely wet Japanese GP at Twin Ring Motegi. (*Henk Keulemans*)

THE 1999 SEASON

500cc

MAL/Sepang
- Kenny Roberts Jnr took his first GP win on his debut with Suzuki

JPN/Motegi
- Roberts Jnr made it back-to-back victories with a win in the first 500cc GP to be held at the Twin-Ring Motegi circuit
- Mick Doohan finished second in the last of his 137 Grand Prix starts

SPA/Jerez
- Alex Criville took the 200th GP win by a Spanish rider

FRA/Paul Ricard
- John Kocinski finished second – his last podium finish in GP racing

ITA/Mugello
- Tetsuya Harada gave the V-twin Aprilia its first pole position

CAT/Catalunya
- Alex Criville became the first European rider to win four successive 500cc GP races since Agostini in 1972

CZE/Brno
- Tadayuki Okada won a race that was stopped and restarted when Jamie Whitham's crashed Modenas set light to some straw bales

VAL/Ricardo Tormo
- At the first Grand Prix of Valencia, Regis Laconi became only the third French rider to win a 500cc GP, joining Christian Sarron and Pierre Monneret
- With Yamaha team-mates Laconi and McCoy finishing first and third, and Suzuki rider Roberts second, this was the first 500cc podium without a Honda rider since the US GP of 1993

AUS/Phillip Island
- Just 0.124s covered the podium finishers – the closest top three of all time in the premier class

RIO/Jacarepagua
- Alex Criville became the first Spanish rider to win the 500cc World Championship, and the first European to take the title since Franco Uncini in 1982

250cc

MAL/Sepang
- Reigning World Champion Loris Capirossi won the opening race of the year after swapping from Aprilia to Honda machinery

JPN/Motegi
- Shinya Nakano (Yamaha) took his first GP win in just his fourth start

FRA/Paul Ricard
- Another Japanese rider, Tohru Ukawa (Honda), won for the first time after race leader Rossi's chain jumped the sprockets at the start of the last lap

ITA/Mugello
- Capirossi was black-flagged for dangerous riding at the start of the race when he caused an accident involving pole-man Marcellino Lucchi (Aprilia). Loris was also suspended from the following race

RSA/Welkom
- Valentino Rossi's victory was the 100th Grand Prix win for Aprilia

RIO/Jacarepagua
- A win for Valentino Rossi made him the youngest ever 250cc World Champion

125cc

MAL/Sepang
- Masao Azuma's win in Malaysia was the 100th Grand Prix victory for Japanese riders

FRA/Paul Ricard
- Italian Roberto Locatelli (Aprilia) scored his first victory

ITA/Mugello
- Gino Borsoi (ITA, Aprilia) in tenth place finished just 1.338s behind race winner Locatelli – the closest top-ten finish in any class of Grand Prix racing

CAT/Catalunya
- Arnaud Vincent (FRA, Aprilia) became the first French rider to win in the 125cc class since Jean-Claude Selini (MBA) in 1982

CZE/Brno
- Championship leader Masao Azuma (JPN, Honda) survived a spectacular practice accident without serious injury when he collided with a young deer

ARG/Buenos Aires
- Spain's Emilio Alzamora finished second behind closest challenger Marco Melandri, both riding Hondas, to take the title by a single point without having won a race

1999 WORLD CHAMPIONSHIP

500cc

Pos	Rider	Nat	Machine	MAL	JPN	SPA	FRA	ITA	CAT	NED	GBR	GER	CZE	IMO	VAL	AUS	RSA	RIO	ARG	Total
1	Alex Criville	SPA	Honda	16	13	25	25	25	25	-	25	20	20	25	-	11	16	10	11	267
2	Kenny Roberts Jnr	USA	Suzuki	25	25	3	-	11	10	20	8	25	16	10	20	6	-	16	25	220
3	Tadayuki Okada	JPN	Honda	11	1	13	7	16	20	25	20	-	25	13	13	25	13	9	-	211
4	Max Biaggi	ITA	Yamaha	-	7	20	-	20	-	11	13	-	13	16	9	20	25	20	20	194
5	Sete Gibernau	SPA	Honda	6	11	16	13	10	16	16	-	7	6	6	7	10	20	11	10	165
6	Norick Abe	JPN	Yamaha	-	16	11	10	-	-	10	10	16	-	5	10	-	7	25	16	136
7	Carlos Checa	SPA	Yamaha	20	10	6	11	9	9	-	-	13	-	-	11	13	10	-	13	125
8	John Kocinski	USA	Honda	-	-	10	20	8	7	9	7	11	2	8	8	7	6	3	9	115
9	Alex Barros	BRA	Honda	10	8	-	6	-	-	6	11	8	9	20	6	-	5	13	8	110
10	Tetsuya Harada	JPN	Aprilia	3	-	-	16	13	13	5	16	9	11	3	5	-	1	4	5	104
11	Regis Laconi	FRA	Yamaha	9	-	9	8	-	-	4	-	3	7	11	25	16	2	5	4	103
12	Juan Borja	SPA	Honda	8	5	7	9	7	11	8	9	6	4	-	-	-	11	-	7	92
13	Nobuatsu Aoki	JPN	Suzuki	7	6	-	-	-	5	13	-	-	10	9	4	8	9	7	-	78
14	Garry McCoy	AUS	Yamaha	-	-	-	-	-	-	1	-	5	8	7	16	9	8	8	3	65
15	Haruchika Aoki	JPN	Honda	1	-	4	3	5	6	7	-	10	3	4	-	5	4	1	1	54
16	Jurgen van den Goorbergh	NED	MuZ	-	-	5	-	-	8	3	-	4	5	2	-	4	3	-	6	40
17	Mick Doohan	AUS	Honda	13	20	-	-	-	-	-	-	-	-	-	-	-	-	-	-	33
18	Simon Crafar	NZE	Yamaha/MuZ	2	-	2	5	4	-	-	6	-	-	-	-	-	-	-	-	19
19	Sebastien Gimbert	FRA	Honda	-	-	-	4	3	2	2	-	2	-	-	3	-	-	-	-	16
20	Luca Cadalora	ITA	MuZ	-	-	8	-	6	-	-	-	-	-	-	-	-	-	-	-	14
21	Shinichi Itoh	JPN	Honda	-	9	-	-	-	-	-	-	-	-	-	-	-	-	-	-	9
22	Yukio Kagayama	JPN	Suzuki	5	4	-	-	-	-	-	-	-	-	-	-	-	-	-	-	9
23	David de Gea	SPA	Modenas	-	-	-	-	-	-	-	-	1	-	-	2	3	-	2	-	8
24	Markus Ober	GER	Honda	-	-	1	2	1	3	-	-	-	-	-	-	-	-	-	-	7
25	Anthony Gobert	AUS	MuZ	-	-	-	-	-	-	-	-	-	-	-	-	-	-	6	-	6
26	Jose Luis Cardoso	SPA	Honda	-	2	-	-	-	4	-	-	-	-	-	-	-	-	-	-	6
27	Michael Rutter	GBR	Honda	-	-	-	-	-	-	-	5	-	-	-	-	-	-	-	-	5
28	Jean-Michel Bayle	FRA	Modenas	4	-	-	-	-	-	-	-	-	-	-	-	-	-	-	-	4
29	Noriyasu Numata	JPN	MuZ	-	3	-	-	-	-	-	-	-	-	-	-	-	-	-	-	3
30	Mark Willis	AUS	BSL/Modenas	-	-	-	-	-	-	-	-	-	-	-	-	1	-	-	2	3
31	Mike Hale	USA	Modenas	-	-	-	-	-	-	-	-	-	1	1	1	-	-	-	-	3
32	Steve Martin	AUS	Honda	-	-	-	-	-	-	-	-	-	-	-	-	2	-	-	-	2
32	Jamie Whitham	GBR	Modenas	-	-	-	-	2	-	-	-	-	-	-	-	-	-	-	-	2

Scoring system – 25, 20, 16, 13, 11, 10, 9, 8, 7, 6, 5, 4, 3, 2, 1

250cc

Pos	Rider	Nat	Machine	Total
1	Valentino Rossi	ITA	Aprilia	309
2	Tohru Ukawa	JPN	Honda	261
3	Loris Capirossi	ITA	Honda	209
4	Shinya Nakano	JPN	Yamaha	207
5	Stefano Perugini	ITA	Honda	151
6	Ralf Waldmann	GER	Aprilia	131
7	Olivier Jacque	FRA	Yamaha	122
8	Franco Battaini	ITA	Aprilia	121
9	Sebastian Porto	ARG	Yamaha	98
10	Jeremy McWilliams	GBR	Aprilia	83

125cc

Pos	Rider	Nat	Machine	Total
1	Emilio Alzamora	SPA	Honda	227
2	Marco Melandri	ITA	Honda	226
3	Masao Azuma	JPN	Honda	190
4	Roberto Locatelli	ITA	Aprilia	173
5	Noboru Ueda	JPN	Honda	171
6	Gianluigi Scalvini	ITA	Aprilia	163
7	Arnaud Vincent	FRA	Aprilia	155
8	Simone Sanna	ITA	Honda	123
9	Lucio Cecchinello	ITA	Honda	108
10	Gino Borsoi	ITA	Aprilia	106

MICK DOOHAN

Ask Mick Doohan to name his finest race and the chances are he will pick one where he won by more than ten seconds from pole position and hardly saw an opponent. Champions are always fixated on winning, but Mick piled up wins and took five consecutive titles with a single-minded ferocity that intimidated not just the opposition but the rest of the paddock as well. He utterly dominated the 500cc class between 1994 and 1998 with a mixture of ruthless dedication and physical courage that few have equalled.

It is often claimed that he didn't have to beat men of the calibre of Rainey and Schwantz, but people who advance this argument should be forcibly reminded that Mick was 53 points in front of a field containing those two as well as Gardner, Lawson, Kocinski and Mamola when he broke his leg at Assen in 1992. That break nearly became amputation when infection set in. His recovery and premature comeback left him with severely restricted movement in his left ankle, so he adopted the thumb-operated rear brake. There were other injuries and some terrifying crashes, especially at the start of his career, but by what looked like sheer force of will he mastered the 500 Honda and, with the help of race engineer Jerry Burgess and his mainly Aussie crew, shaped the development of the ultimate two-stroke V4.

What engineers want from their rider is direction, and Mick always knew what he wanted and refused to waste time on distractions. Jerry Burgess took that approach on to his work with Rossi. It is also often said that Mick had the best bike. Well, if that is true, it is because he made it the best bike.

How good was he? Well only John Surtees, Giacomo Agostini and Valentino Rossi have dominated the top class for extended periods of time in the way Mick did. Not bad company.

ABOVE Halfway through the season Mick Doohan still needed crutches to get about; this picture was taken at Assen. (*Henk Keulemans*)

DOOHAN RESULTS AND STATISTICS

- **Mick Doohan won five successive titles – the only other riders to have achieved this feat are Agostini and Rossi**
- **Doohan won more 500cc races on a two-stroke than any other rider**
- **His 12 race victories in 1997 is an all-time record for wins in a season**
- **Mick Doohan made 95 podium appearances – more than any other rider in the 500cc class**
- **He achieved more race victories on Honda machinery than any other rider**
- **Doohan started from pole on 12 occasions in 1997 – a record for most poles in a single season in the premier class**
- **Of the 71 races Doohan started in his five championship-winning years he finished on the podium 61 times (86 per cent) and won 44 (62 per cent) of them**

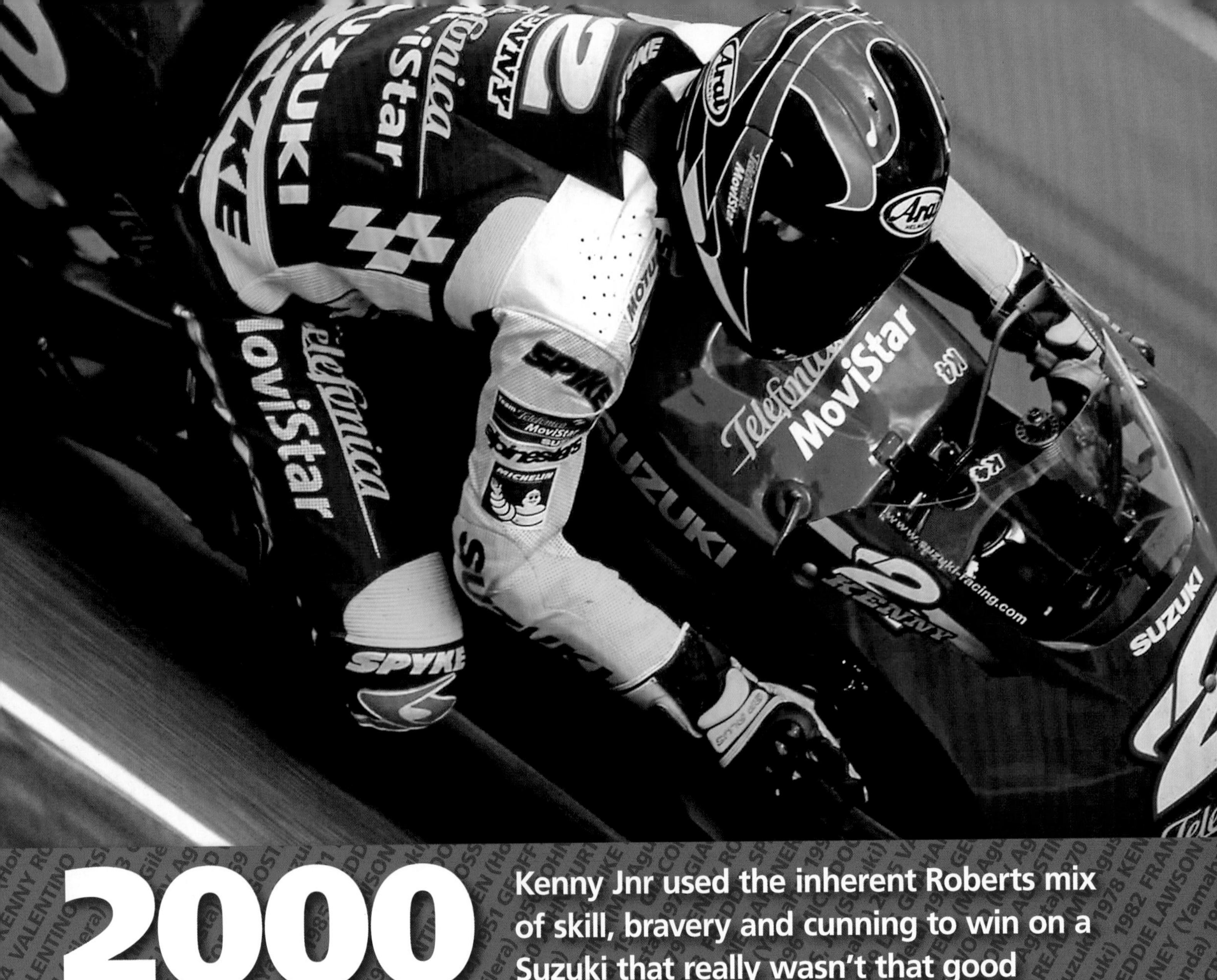

2000

Kenny Jnr used the inherent Roberts mix of skill, bravery and cunning to win on a Suzuki that really wasn't that good

For the first time since 1988 the season started without Mick Doohan. Alex Criville, Sete Gibernau and Tadayuki Okada all rode Hondas under the Repsol banner in the factory squad. Class newcomer Valentino Rossi was in a one-man team sponsored by Nastro Azzurro with machinery one notch down from the works boys, while Sito Pons's customer team ran Alex Barros and 500-class returnee Loris Capirossi.

Pons's old sponsor Telefonica moved to the Suzuki team, which retained Kenny Roberts Jnr and Nobuatsu Aoki. Yamaha again led with Max Biaggi and Carlos Checa in the factory squad and the satellite WCM team also went for continuity with Garry McCoy and Regis Laconi. Aprilia kept Tetsuya Harada on their twin and promoted British veteran Jeremy McWilliams from 250s. Team Roberts recruited young Spaniard David de Gea to ride their Modenas.

All the V4s were on Michelins. The Aprilias and the Modenas started the season on Dunlops but had moved over to Michelin by the middle of the year, leaving only under-resourced privateers and V-twin Hondas on the British rubber.

In the 250s Marco Melandri took over Rossi's factory ride at Aprilia and Daijiro Kato, a double GP winner as a wild card, came aboard for Honda. As in the 500 class, Yamaha kept their line-up from the previous season with Olivier Jacque and Shinya Nakano on the works bikes run by the French Tech 3 team.

Kenny Roberts Jnr won the title with a brilliant mix of brave riding, clever tactics and bloody mindedness – a Roberts family characteristic if ever there was one. There was no doubt that the Suzuki wasn't the best bike out there, but team and rider extracted the maximum from it, and occasionally from the rule book too. Their crafty approach to rain-interrupted races caused an unofficial revision of the system. The year was summed up by the way Kenny Jnr won the championship, scoring an underwhelming sixth in Brazil and then coming out the following week at Motegi to win by a distance on a track that wasn't supposed to suit the Suzuki.

ABOVE Kenny Jnr on his way to becoming the only son of a World Champion to himself become a World Champion. (*Henk Keulemans*)

RIGHT The 250 championship went down to the last yard of the last race between Yamaha team-mates Nakano and Jacque. Tech 3 team manager Hervé Poncheral (latterly President of IRTA) mugs for the camera before the decider in Australia. (*Henk Keulemans*)

THE 2000 SEASON

500cc

RSA/Welkom
- Garry McCoy won for the first time in the 500cc class after starting from ninth on the grid.
- McCoy's win was the last in a record streak of seven different winners in seven races going back to the Imola GP of 1999: Criville, Laconi, Okada, Biaggi, Abe, Roberts, McCoy
- Valentino Rossi made his debut in the class and crashed out on lap 13 after setting fastest lap

JPN/Suzuka
- Norick Abe was victorious after his countrymen Daijiro Kato and Youichi Ui had won in the smaller classes, the only occasion when Japanese riders have won all three classes at a GP event

SPA/Jerez
- Kenny Roberts won a two-part race in which Valentino Rossi claimed his first podium, finishing third

FRA/Le Mans
- Reigning champion Alex Criville won his only GP of the year

ITA/Mugello
- Loris Capirossi became the first Italian rider to win a 500cc GP at Mugello
- Capirossi's win made Honda the most successful manufacturer of all time in the 500cc class with 140 wins – one more than MV Agusta
- Jeremy McWilliams finished on the podium on the V-twin Aprilia – the first 500cc podium for a British rider since Niall Mackenzie finished third at the British GP at Donington Park in 1993

NED/Assen
- Alex Barros (Honda) won for the second time, almost seven years after the Brazilian won the final race of 1993 riding a Suzuki

GBR/Donington
- Valentino Rossi took a wet win – his first victory in the top class

CZE/Brno
- Max Biaggi became a record eighth different 500cc winner in a single season

VAL/Ricardo Tormo
- Garry McCoy ended a record 22-race streak of no rider taking back-to-back 500cc victories (he'd won the previous race in Portugal)

RIO/Jacarepagua
- Kenny Jnr's sixth-place finish was enough to give him the world title

AUS/Phillip Island
- Tenth-placed Nobuatsu Aoki (Suzuki) was just 12.5s behind winner Max Biaggi – the closest top ten of all time in a premier-class Grand Prix

250cc

GBR/Donington
- German Ralf Waldmann (Aprilia) took the last of his 20 GP victories, scoring more wins than any other rider not to have won a world title
- His win came after choosing full wet tyres and being 90 seconds behind the leader half-way through the race and before it started to rain

POR/Estoril
- Aprilia-mounted Marco Melandri finished third, to become the youngest rider ever to finish on the podium in the 250cc class

AUS/Phillip Island
- In one of the closest championship battles of all-time Olivier Jacque passed team-mate Shinya Nakano on the run to the flag to take the title by just 0.014s

125cc

NED/Assen
- Manuel Poggiali's third place finish is the San Marino rider's first podium finish

PAC/Motegi
- Roberto Locatelli won the first 'Pacific' GP race to clinch the world title

AUS/Phillip Island
- Locatelli started from pole for the ninth time to set a new record for most poles in one 125 season

2000 WORLD CHAMPIONSHIP

500cc

Pos	Rider	Nat	Machine	RSA	MAL	JPN	SPA	FRA	ITA	CAT	NED	GBR	GER	CZE	POR	VAL	RIO	PAC	AUS	Total
1	Kenny Roberts Jnr	USA	Suzuki	10	25	20	25	10	10	25	-	20	16	13	20	20	10	25	9	258
2	Valentino Rossi	ITA	Honda	-	-	5	16	16	4	16	10	25	20	20	16	-	25	20	16	209
3	Max Biaggi	ITA	Yamaha	-	13	-	-	-	7	11	13	7	13	25	13	16	11	16	25	170
4	Alex Barros	BRA	Honda	13	8	9	11	11	-	-	25	2	25	-	6	11	20	9	13	163
5	Garry McCoy	AUS	Yamaha	25	16	7	-	13	-	-	1	-	6	16	25	25	16	-	11	161
6	Carlos Checa	SPA	Yamaha	20	20	11	20	9	20	-	11	5	7	5	4	9	1	13	-	155
7	Loris Capirossi	ITA	Honda	16	-	4	10	8	25	10	16	13	10	11	3	-	-	8	20	154
8	Norick Abe	JPN	Yamaha	9	-	25	-	20	11	20	6	10	5	-	7	-	13	11	10	147
9	Alex Criville	SPA	Honda	11	-	10	13	25	-	-	20	9	-	9	10	-	5	10	-	122
10	Nobuatsu Aoki	JPN	Suzuki	8	11	13	9	5	13	13	3	-	3	8	-	13	4	7	6	116
11	Tadayuki Okada	JPN	Honda	-	10	16	6	2	8	1	5	6	11	6	9	7	7	6	7	107
12	Regis Laconi	FRA	Yamaha	7	7	2	8	7	9	3	8	4	9	3	11	10	8	5	5	106
13	Jurgen van den Goorbergh	NED	Honda	6	5	3	7	3	5	9	7	11	-	4	8	6	6	1	4	85
14	Jeremy McWilliams	GBR	Aprilia	-	6	8	-	4	16	4	-	16	-	7	5	-	-	2	8	76
15	Sete Gibernau	SPA	Honda	-	9	-	-	1	6	-	9	8	8	10	-	8	9	4	-	72
16	Tetsuya Harada	JPN	Aprilia	-	4	-	5	6	-	7	4	-	-	2	2	-	3	3	2	38
17	David de Gea	SPA	Modenas	1	2	1	4	-	-	8	2	-	-	-	-	5	-	-	-	23
18	Jose Luis Cardoso	SPA	Honda	5	3	-	-	-	3	-	-	-	4	-	-	4	-	-	-	19
19	Yoshiteru Konishi	JPN	Honda	3	-	-	3	-	1	6	-	-	-	-	-	2	-	-	1	16
20	Sebastien Legrelle	BEL	Honda	-	-	-	-	-	2	5	-	-	-	-	-	-	-	-	-	7
21	Akira Ryo	JPN	Suzuki	-	-	6	-	-	-	-	-	-	-	-	-	-	-	-	-	6
22	Sebastien Gimbert	FRA	Honda	4	1	-	-	-	-	-	-	-	-	-	-	-	-	-	-	5
23	Shane Norval	RSA	Honda	2	-	-	-	-	-	2	-	-	-	-	-	-	-	-	-	4
24	Tekkyu Kayoh	JPN	Honda	-	-	-	-	-	-	-	-	-	-	-	-	-	-	-	3	3
24	John McGuinness	GBR	Honda	-	-	-	-	-	-	-	-	3	-	-	-	-	-	-	-	3
24	David Tomas	SPA	Honda	-	-	-	-	-	-	-	-	-	-	-	-	3	-	-	-	3
27	Luca Cadalora	ITA	Modenas	-	-	-	-	-	-	-	-	-	2	1	-	-	-	-	-	3
27	Mark Willis	AUS	Modenas	-	-	-	-	-	-	-	-	-	-	-	1	-	2	-	-	3
29	Phil Giles	GBR	Honda	-	-	-	-	-	-	-	-	-	-	-	-	1	-	-	-	1
29	Anthony Gobert	AUS	Modenas	-	-	-	-	-	-	-	-	1	-	-	-	-	-	-	-	1
29	Paolo Tessari	ITA	Paton	-	-	-	-	-	-	-	-	-	1	-	-	-	-	-	-	1

Scoring system – 25, 20, 16, 13, 11, 10, 9, 8, 7, 6, 5, 4, 3, 2, 1

250cc

Pos	Rider	Nat	Machine	Total
1	Olivier Jacque	FRA	Yamaha	279
2	Shinya Nakano	JPN	Yamaha	272
3	Daijiro Kato	JPN	Honda	259
4	Tohru Ukawa	JPN	Honda	239
5	Marco Melandri	ITA	Aprilia	159
6	Anthony West	AUS	Honda	146
7	Ralf Waldmann	GER	Aprilia	143
8	Franco Battaini	ITA	Aprilia	96
9	Sebastian Porto	ARG	Yamaha	83
10	Naoki Matsudo	JPN	Yamaha	79

125cc

Pos	Rider	Nat	Machine	Total
1	Roberto Locatelli	ITA	Aprilia	230
2	Youichi Ui	JPN	Derbi	217
3	Emilio Alzamora	SPA	Honda	203
4	Masao Azuma	JPN	Honda	176
5	Noboru Ueda	JPN	Honda	153
6	Simone Sanna	ITA	Aprilia	132
7	Arnaud Vincent	FRA	Aprilia	132
8	Mirko Giansanti	ITA	Honda	129
9	Gino Borsoi	ITA	Aprilia	113
10	Ivan Goi	ITA	Honda	108

LIKE FATHER, LIKE SON

When Kenny Roberts Jnr became World Champion in 2000 he completed a unique family double. Kenny Snr had been the 500cc champion three times, from 1978–80 inclusive, so they became the only father and son both to have won world titles. Senior won two 250cc races as well as 22 in 500s (all on Yamahas), Junior won eight 500cc races, all with Suzuki. However, they are not the only Senior and Junior to have won Grands Prix.

The very first 125cc World Champion, Italian Nello Pagani, won in 1949 for Mondial and also rode a Gilera to second in the 500cc class. He won two 125 races (SWI, NED) and two 500 GPs (NED, ITA-NAZ) that year and went on to manage the MV Agusta team. His son Alberto won three 500cc GPs, one for Linto (ITA-NAZ/1969) and two on MVs (ITA-NAZ/1971, YUG/1972).

Les Graham was the very first 500cc World Champion, riding an AJS *Porcupine*. The British rider won once on a 125 MV (GBR/1953), once on a 350 AJS (SWI/1950), once on a 350 Velocette (SWI/1951), twice in his 500cc championship year (SWI, ULS) and once in 1950 on the AJS (SWI), then twice in 1952 on a 500 MV (ITA-NAZ, SPA). In 1967 his son Stuart won two GPs for Suzuki (50cc GBR, 125 cc FIN) and finished third in both championships. Stuart Graham also holds the unique distinction of have won the Isle of Man TT on both two and four wheels.

Thirteen-times World Champion Angel Nieto's son Pablo had a long 125cc career but won only one race (POR/2003).

Graziano Rossi won three 250cc GPs in 1979 (YUG, NED, SWE) on his way to third in the championship on a Morbidelli. He moved up to 500s and scored two rostrums in 1980 (ITA-NAZ, NED) on a Suzuki before injury forced his retirement. His son Valentino is also quite well known.

The most recent offspring of a GP winner is Germany's Stefan Bradl, winner of the 2008 125cc Czech GP. Dad Helmut competed exclusively in the 250cc class riding a Honda, making a total of 84 Grand Prix starts between 1986 and 1993. His best year was 1991 when he scored all of his five victories (SPA, GER, AUT, CZE, FRA-VdM) and finished second in the final championship standings behind Luca Cadalora.

ABOVE A little fatherly advice from Roberts Senior to Junior. (*Henk Keulemans*)

LEFT Graziano Rossi won three GPs but never a Championship – unlike his son Valentino. They are pictured here in 1997 after Rossi Junior won his first world title. (*Henk Keulemans*)

2001

One season to learn, then win the title at the second attempt; Rossi won the last ever 500cc championship in the same timescale he'd won in 125 and 250

The last year of the 500s saw Valentino Rossi as Honda's most favoured rider. He duly won the first three races of the year and was never headed in the points standings. The Italian again ran on his own in Nastro Azzurro's yellow colours while the notional works team shrunk to two with only Alex Criville being retained but joined by 250 ace Tohru Ukawa. The Pons satellite team retained Loris Capirossi and Alex Barros and gained West sponsorship. The last NSR went to Chris Walker (GBR) but he was gone by mid-season and the team did not see out the year.

Suzuki's defending champion Kenny Roberts Jnr was joined by Sete Gibernau, but even before the first race the American was warning that the bike was nowhere near being competitive: the previous year's victory had led to assumptions that it was actually better than it was. However, the Suzuki team-mates were responsible for the abiding images of the year. Sete won at Valencia, in the immediate aftermath of the attack on the Twin Towers, with 'I Love New York' written in tape on his leathers and carrying both the American and Spanish flags to the rostrum, where third-placed Roberts wore a New York Fire Department baseball hat.

Yamaha retained Max Biaggi and Carlos Checa for the factory team for a third season, Garry McCoy stayed with WCM and was joined by World Superbike ace Noriyuki Haga, and the d'Antin team went back up to two riders with Spaniard José Luis Cardoso joining Norick Abe. Team Roberts changed the name of their bike to Proton and brought in Dutch rider Jurgen van der Goorbergh. Two private teams, Sabre and Pulse, fielded V4s; the first was really a slightly updated old ROC Yamaha, the second the last incarnation of the Elf, MuZ and Swissauto projects. The Aprilia V-twin did not return.

There was also a shrinking of factory involvement in the 250 class. Yamaha handed their all-conquering 2000 bikes to the Petronas team, Honda gave works bike only to the Gresini team of Daijiro Kato and Emilio Alzamora, and Aprilia's favoured duo were old champion Tetsuya Harada and young gun Marco Melandri.

ABOVE Rossi harassed by Biaggi – the story of the season. (*Henk Keulemans*)

RIGHT Gilera returned to winning ways in the 125 class with Manuel Poggiali. (*Henk Keulemans*)

THE 2001 SEASON

500cc

JPN/Suzuka
- Valentino Rossi won the race to take the 500th GP victory for Honda

RSA/Welkom
- Rossi qualified on pole – his first on a 500cc machine

FRA/Le Mans
- Max Biaggi tookYamaha's first win of the year from pole position to end a run of three successive wins for Rossi

ITA/Mugello
- Alex Barros's only win of the year was in a race run in two parts after a rain interruption

CAT/Catalunya
- Rossi won from Biaggi, but an altercation on the way to the podium caused both riders to be reprimanded by the FIM

NED/Assen
- Max Biaggi won for the second time in 2001, in a race cut short by rain

GBR/Donington
- Norick Abe became the youngest rider to reach the milestone of 100 starts in the 500cc class
- Valentino Rossi gave Honda their 150th win in the 500cc class

GER/Sachsenring
- Max Biaggi, Carlos Checa and Shinya Nakano give Yamaha their last clean sweep of the podium places in the 500cc class

CZE/Brno
- Valentino Rossi became the first rider to win in all three classes at the purpose-built Brno circuit

VAL/Ricardo Tormo
- Sete Gibernau won his first Grand Prix and gave Suzuki their last win in the 500cc class

AUS/Phillip Island
- Valentino Rossi won the race to become the youngest rider to win world titles in three different classes
- One of the closest races of all time and the only time in the 500cc class that the eighth rider home was less than three seconds behind the winner

RIO/Jacarepagua
- Run in two parts after rain started to fall after just four laps, Rossi won the final 500cc GP by less than two-tenths of a second from Carlos Checa, who 'won' the second part of the race

250cc

JPN/Suzuka
- Daijiro Kato took victory and an early lead in the championship, which he held throughout the year

FRA/Le Mans
- Another victory for Kato made him the first rider since Mike Hailwood in 1966 to win the first four 250cc GPs of the year

ITA/Mugello
- By finishing 14th, Katja Poensgen became the first female rider to score points in the 250cc class

NED/Assen
- Jeremy McWilliams was the first British rider to win a 250cc GP since Alan Carter at the French GP of 1983

GER/Sachsenring
- Marco Melandri took his first win in the 250cc class to become the youngest rider to win in two classes of GP racing

PAC/Motegi
- Championship leader Kato crashed out of the 'Pacific' race, unable to avoid the fallen Melandri, and failed to score points for the first time in his GP career

MAL/Sepang
- Daijiro Kato took the win to clinch the world title

RIO/Jacarepagua
- Kato made it 11 victories in a year – a new record for wins in a single season in the 250cc class

125cc

FRA/Le Mans
- Manuel Poggiali won for the first time and gave Gilera their first victory in GP racing since John Hartle won the 500cc Dutch TT in 1963

ITA/Mugello
- Noboru Ueda took the last of his 13 GP victories in the 125cc class – more wins than any other rider in the class who had not also been World Champion

NED/Assen
- Toni Elias scored his first victory to become the youngest Spanish rider to win a Grand Prix

VAL/Ricardo Tormo
- Manuel Poggiali was followed home by Toni Elias and Dani Pedrosa – the first all-teenage podium in any class of GP racing

RIO/Jacarepagua
- Poggiali did enough by finishing fifth to become the first rider from San Marino to win a world title

2001 WORLD CHAMPIONSHIP

500cc

Pos	Rider	Nat	Machine	JPN	RSA	SPA	FRA	ITA	CAT	NED	GBR	GER	CZE	POR	VAL	PAC	AUS	MAL	RIO	Total
1	Valentino Rossi	ITA	Honda	25	25	25	16	-	25	20	25	9	25	25	5	25	25	25	25	325
2	Max Biaggi	ITA	Yamaha	16	8	5	25	16	20	25	20	25	6	11	6	-	20	-	16	219
3	Loris Capirossi	ITA	Honda	8	20	8	9	20	16	16	6	8	16	20	-	16	16	20	11	210
4	Alex Barros	BRA	Honda	10	7	10	8	25	-	13	16	11	7	-	20	20	13	9	13	182
5	Shinya Nakano	JPN	Yamaha	11	13	13	5	8	13	11	10	16	-	7	9	10	9	13	7	155
6	Carlos Checa	SPA	Yamaha	6	-	2	20	-	8	-	11	20	9	13	13	9	-	6	20	137
7	Norick Abe	JPN	Yamaha	13	11	20	13	7	10	-	-	13	13	-	8	13	3	3	10	137
8	Alex Criville	SPA	Honda	7	10	16	11	13	5	-	9	-	20	-	-	5	5	10	9	120
9	Sete Gibernau	SPA	Suzuki	-	6	6	7	10	11	9	5	6	8	-	25	7	7	8	4	119
10	Tohru Ukawa	JPN	Honda	-	16	11	-	9	9	8	-	-	11	-	10	11	11	11	-	107
11	Kenny Roberts Jnr	USA	Suzuki	9	9	9	10	-	-	10	8	7	-	10	16	8	1	-	-	97
12	Garry McCoy	AUS	Yamaha	20	-	7	-	-	-	-	-	5	10	16	4	4	-	16	6	88
13	Jurgen van den Goorbergh	NED	Proton	5	5	3	6	4	7	7	4	2	-	9	7	-	6	-	-	65
14	Noriyuki Haga	JPN	Yamaha	-	-	4	-	6	6	6	13	4	5	-	-	-	8	7	-	59
15	Olivier Jacque	FRA	Yamaha	-	-	-	-	-	4	5	7	10	4	8	11	-	10	-	-	59
16	Jose Luis Cardoso	SPA	Yamaha	-	3	-	3	5	2	4	-	3	3	6	-	3	-	5	8	45
17	Haruchika Aoki	JPN	Honda	4	4	-	-	11	1	2	-	-	2	5	-	-	2	-	2	33
18	Anthony West	AUS	Honda	-	2	1	-	-	-	1	2	1	-	4	3	2	4	4	3	27
19	Leon Haslam	GBR	Honda	3	-	-	-	-	-	3	-	-	-	-	-	1	-	1	5	13
20	Chris Walker	GBR	Honda	-	1	-	4	-	3	-	1	-	-	-	-	-	-	-	-	9
21	Yukio Kagayama	JPN	Suzuki	-	-	-	-	-	-	-	-	-	-	-	-	6	-	-	-	6
22	Johan Stigefelt	SWE	Sabre	-	-	-	-	-	-	-	-	-	1	3	2	-	-	-	-	6
23	Brendan Clarke	AUS	Honda	-	-	-	-	-	-	-	-	-	-	2	-	-	-	2	1	5
24	Barry Veneman	NED	Honda	-	-	-	2	-	-	-	-	-	-	1	1	-	-	-	-	4
25	Jay Vincent	GBR	Yamaha	-	-	-	-	-	-	-	3	-	-	-	-	-	-	-	-	3
25	Mark Willis	AUS	Pulse	-	-	-	-	3	-	-	-	-	-	-	-	-	-	-	-	3
27	Jarno Janssen	NED	Honda	-	-	-	1	-	-	-	-	-	-	-	-	-	-	-	-	1

Scoring system – 25, 20, 16, 13, 11, 10, 9, 8, 7, 6, 5, 4, 3, 2, 1

250cc

Pos	Rider	Nat	Machine	Total
1	Daijiro Kato	JPN	Honda	322
2	Tetsuya Harada	JPN	Aprilia	273
3	Marco Melandri	ITA	Aprilia	194
4	Roberto Rolfo	ITA	Aprilia	177
5	Fonsi Nieto	SPA	Aprilia	167
6	Jeremy McWilliams	GBR	Aprilia	141
7	Emilio Alzamora	SPA	Honda	136
8	Roberto Locatelli	ITA	Aprilia	134
9	Naoki Matsudo	JPN	Yamaha	112
10	Franco Battaini	ITA	Aprilia	75

125cc

Pos	Rider	Nat	Machine	Total
1	Manuel Poggiali	RSM	Gilera	241
2	Youichi Ui	JPN	Derbi	232
3	Toni Elias	SPA	Honda	217
4	Lucio Cecchinello	ITA	Aprilia	156
5	Masao Azuma	JPN	Honda	142
6	Gino Borsoi	ITA	Aprilia	130
7	Simone Sanna	ITA	Aprilia	125
8	Dani Pedrosa	SPA	Honda	100
9	Noboru Ueda	JPN	Honda	94
10	Arnaud Vincent	FRA	Honda	94

ROSSI WINS HONDA'S 500TH GP

Who writes Valentino Rossi's scripts? He had never even been on the rostrum at Suzuka, yet he won the first race of the 2001 season (his third career win in the 500 class) to give Honda their 500th Grand Prix win at their home circuit. HRC were desperate to pass this milestone at home with Honda Motor Company royalty in attendance, and it was made very clear to 125 rider Masao Azuma that he should win or not bother turning up for work on Monday morning. His demeanour when he just managed to beat off the challenges of Aprilia, Gilera and Derbi (the next Honda was eighth) was not the usual delight of a man who had just won his home Grand Prix. No such worries for the Big H in the 250 race. Kato's pole time was a second quicker than anyone else and he won by the best part of 20 seconds.

So the stage was set for Rossi and the final evolution of the racing 500cc motorcycle, Honda's NSR500 V4, and Valentino duly won the Japanese Grand Prix, chased home by four Yamahas. The only time he looked uncomfortable was when a company flag – here's one we prepared earlier – was thrust into his hand in a meticulously pre-planned 'spontaneous' gesture. Soichiro Honda himself would have nodded in approval at the circuit his company built hosting their 500th win thanks to their latest young champion on the best racing motorcycle to turn a wheel. Which is no doubt why current HRC staff were so keen on it happening as it did.

Honda's first win had come 39 years 11 months and 5 days earlier, at the first race of the 1961 season, when Aussie Tom Phillis won the 125cc Spanish Grand Prix on the Montjuich circuit in central Barcelona. Mr Honda had decided to go racing both to improve his company's products and to promote the company's name in overseas markets. In the late 1950s, when he announced his intention to compete in the Isle of Man, this ambition was seen as ludicrously optimistic if not downright crazy. Today it looks like just another piece of visionary thinking.

ABOVE Daijiro Kato, here with team manager Fausto Gresini, dominated the 250 class. (*Henk Keulemans*)

BELOW HRC management celebrate the 500th Honda GP win at Suzuka; the riders are Azuma, Kato and Rossi. (*Henk Keulemans*)

2002

Enter MotoGP: the biggest-ever upheaval in motorcycle Grand Prix technical regulations

The MotoGP era opened at Suzuka with just nine four-strokes on the grid of 22, and two of those were being ridden by wild cards (Shinichi Itoh on a Honda and Akira Ryo on a Suzuki). Valentino Rossi and Tohru Ukawa rode V5 Honda RC211Vs for the Repsol team, Max Biaggi and Carlos Checa were on across-the-frame four-cylinder M1 Yamahas, Kenny Roberts Jnr and Sete Gibernau were on V4 Suzukis and Regis Laconi was on the lone Aprilia triple.

There was general shock at the immediate and crushing superiority of the new bikes, which were undoubtedly helped by Michelin's new-generation S4 tyres. Suzuki jumped ship to Michelin after two races, leaving Aprilia the only factory team on Dunlops. Team KR and Jurgen van den Goorbergh's Kanemoto Honda were the only Bridgestone users.

Honda fielded two more V5s later in the year, first for Daijiro Kato at Brno and then for Alex Barros at Motegi. Both men immediately put the bikes on the rostrum, the Brazilian winning first time out. Barros's team-mate Loris Capirossi was passed over for the four-stroke as a hand injury sustained at Assen had kept him out of three races. Hondas won 14 of the 16 races, Biaggi taking the other two for Yamaha. Kawasaki entered the frame with their MotoGP machine as a wild card from Motegi onwards, Ducati paraded their Desmosedici before the final race of the season at Valencia, and Team KR promised to have their own four-stroke for the 2003 season.

The Honda was so superior to the opposition that Rossi clinched the title in Brazil with four races still to run. Ukawa beat him in South Africa, helped by a better tyre choice, and Biaggi won at Brno when Valentino's rear tyre broke up, but Max's win in Malaysia and Barros's in Valencia were achieved without outside help.

Dorna introduced their franchise system to give the five private teams – Tech 3, Roberts, Gresini, WCM and d'Antin – guaranteed long-term grid slots. The plan was to allow two more factories to join MotoGP but no more private teams, thus giving the privateers assets and long-term security.

ABOVE The first moments of MotoGP: 7 is Checa on a Yamaha M1, 72 is Itoh on a Honda V5, 65 is Capirossi on a Honda two-stroke, and 46 is Rossi on another V5. (*Henk Keulemans*)

RIGHT Past and present: the first MotoGP winner, the Honda RC211V (left), and the last 500 winner, the Honda NSR500 (right). (*Henk Keulemans*)

THE 2002 SEASON

MotoGP

JPN/Suzuka

- Valentino Rossi won the first MotoGP race from pole on a Honda with Ryo (Suzuki) second and Checa (Yamaha) third

RSA/Welkom

- Loris Capirossi was the first man to put a 500 on a MotoGP rostrum, coming third on a West-sponsored Honda

SPA/Jerez

- Daijiro Kato scored his first rostrum finish in the top class with second on a two-stroke Honda

FRA/Le Mans

- For the first time, all front-row qualifiers were on four-stroke machines

ITA/Mugello

- During practice Regis Laconi became the first man in MotoGP to break the 200mph barrier

GER/Sachsenring

- Oliver Jacque set pole position on a two-stroke Yamaha

CZE/Brno

- Max Biaggi became the first non-Honda rider to win under MotoGP regulations
- Daijiro Kato scored a rostrum finish in his first ride on a four-stroke

RIO/Jacarepagua

- Valentino Rossi took his second World Championship title with four races to spare

PAC/Motegi

- Alex Barros received a V5 Honda and won first time out, while team-mate Capirossi, angry at being passed over, scored the last ever rostrum finish by a two-stroke 500
- Kawasaki debuted their MotoGP bike in the hands of Akira Yanagawa

AUS/Phillip Island

- Jeremy McWilliams (Team KR Proton) led an all-two-stroke front row. It was the first pole in the premier class for Bridgestone tyres and the last for a two-stroke. It was also the only pole by the three-cylinder Roberts machine
- The other front-row men were Garry McCoy (Red Bull Yamaha), Nobuatsu Aoki (Team KR Proton) and Jurgen van der Goorbergh (Kanemoto Honda)

250cc

JPN/Suzuka

- Wild-card rider Osamu Miyazaki (Yamaha) won the opening 250cc race of the year in very wet conditions, followed home by another wild card, Daisaku Sakai (Honda). This was the last win in any class by a wild-card rider

SPA/Jerez

- Fonsi Nieto (Aprilia) took his first GP victory, and the first by a Spanish rider in the 250cc class since Carlos Cardus won at Brno in 1990
- Casey Stoner (AUS, Aprilia) finished sixth to become the youngest rider to score points in the 250cc class

CZE/Brno

- Marco Melandri's victory was the 100th successive GP win for Dunlop in the 250cc class

POR/Estoril

- Fonsi Nieto won in horrendously wet conditions after falling off and remounting

RIO/Jacarepagua

- Sebastian Porto became the first rider from Argentina to win a GP since 1962 – and he also made it the last GP victory for Yamaha in the 250cc class

AUS/Phillip Island

- Marco Melandri took the win to become the youngest rider to take the 250cc world title

125cc

SPA/Jerez

- Jorge Lorenzo (SPA, Derbi) became the youngest rider to take part in a GP race, aged just 15 years and 1 day, missing the first day of qualifying because he was too young to take part

CAT/Catalunya

- Jorge Lorenzo finished 14th to become the youngest ever point-scoring rider in GP racing

NED/Assen

- Dani Pedrosa took his first GP victory, the youngest Spanish winner in Grand Prix racing

VAL/Ricardo Tormo

- In finishing second Arnaud Vincent became the first French rider to win the 125cc world title

2002 WORLD CHAMPIONSHIP

MotoGP

Pos	Rider	Nat	Machine	JPN	RSA	SPA	FRA	ITA	CAT	NED	GBR	GER	CZE	POR	RIO	PAC	MAL	AUS	VAL	Total
1	Valentino Rossi	ITA	Honda	25	20	25	25	25	25	25	25	25	-	25	25	20	20	25	20	355
2	Max Biaggi	ITA	Yamaha	-	7	-	16	20	13	13	20	20	25	10	20	-	25	10	16	215
3	Tohru Ukawa	JPN	Honda	-	25	16	20	16	20	11	-	16	16	16	-	13	13	16	11	209
4	Alex Barros	BRA	Honda	10	-	11	8	11	11	20	16	-	7	11	13	25	16	20	25	204
5	Carlos Checa	SPA	Yamaha	16	11	-	-	13	16	16	-	13	11	20	-	11	9	5	-	141
6	Norick Abe	JPN	Yamaha	11	9	10	13	9	-	7	13	10	8	9	10	8	6	-	6	129
7	Daijiro Kato	JPN	Honda	6	13	20	-	-	8	4	9	-	20	-	-	-	11	13	13	117
8	Loris Capirossi	ITA	Honda	7	16	13	9	10	10	-	-	-	10	-	11	16	7	-	-	109
9	Kenny Roberts Jnr	USA	Suzuki	-	-	8	11	-	9	10	2	-	5	13	16	10	8	7	-	99
10	Olivier Jacque	FRA	Yamaha	-	10	5	-	7	7	2	11	-	6	-	9	9	-	8	7	81
11	Shinya Nakano	JPN	Yamaha	-	8	-	3	5	-	8	6	11	-	4	-	-	10	3	10	68
12	Nobuatsu Aoki	JPN	Proton	9	-	9	10	-	-	-	7	8	-	-	4	7	-	9	-	63
13	Jurgen van den Goorbergh	NED	Honda	-	5	4	1	2	-	6	1	4	4	-	7	3	3	11	9	60
14	Jeremy McWilliams	GBR	Proton	-	-	-	6	-	4	-	-	9	9	7	-	6	4	6	8	59
15	John Hopkins	USA	Yamaha	4	2	3	5	4	6	9	8	-	-	8	2	2	-	-	5	58
16	Sete Gibernau	SPA	Suzuki	-	-	7	4	-	-	-	10	-	13	-	8	-	2	4	3	51
17	Tetsuya Harada	JPN	Honda	5	4	6	-	6	3	3	5	-	1	6	3	1	-	2	2	47
18	Akira Ryo	JPN	Suzuki	20	-	-	-	-	5	1	3	5	2	-	-	-	5	-	-	41
19	Regis Laconi	FRA	Aprilia	8	1	2	7	8	2	-	-	-	-	-	-	5	-	-	-	33
20	Garry McCoy	AUS	Yamaha	-	6	1	-	-	-	-	4	7	3	5	6	-	1	-	-	33
21	Shinichi Itoh	JPN	Honda	13	-	-	-	-	-	-	-	-	-	-	-	-	-	-	-	13
22	Alex Hofmann	GER	Yamaha	-	-	-	-	-	-	5	-	6	-	-	-	-	-	-	-	11
23	Jose Luis Cardoso	SPA	Yamaha	-	-	-	-	-	-	-	-	3	-	-	5	-	-	1	-	9
24	Jean-Michel Bayle	FRA	Yamaha	-	-	-	2	3	-	-	-	-	-	-	-	-	-	-	-	5
25	Andrew Pitt	AUS	Kawasaki	-	-	-	-	-	-	-	-	-	-	-	-	-	-	-	4	4
25	Wataru Yoshikawa	JPN	Yamaha	-	-	-	-	-	-	-	-	-	-	-	-	4	-	-	-	4
27	Pere Riba	SPA	Yamaha	-	3	-	-	-	1	-	-	-	-	-	-	-	-	-	-	4

Scoring system – 25, 20, 16, 13, 11, 10, 9, 8, 7, 6, 5, 4, 3, 2, 1

250cc

Pos	Rider	Nat	Machine	Total
1	Marco Melandri	ITA	Aprilia	298
2	Fonsi Nieto	SPA	Aprilia	241
3	Roberto Rolfo	ITA	Honda	219
4	Toni Elias	SPA	Aprilia	178
5	Sebastian Porto	ARG	Yamaha	172
6	Franco Battaini	ITA	Aprilia	142
7	Emilio Alzamora	SPA	Honda	120
8	Roberto Locatelli	ITA	Aprilia	119
9	Randy de Puniet	FRA	Aprilia	119
10	Naoki Matsudo	JPN	Yamaha	92

125cc

Pos	Rider	Nat	Machine	Total
1	Arnaud Vincent	FRA	Aprilia	273
2	Manuel Poggiali	RSM	Gilera	254
3	Dani Pedrosa	SPA	Honda	243
4	Lucio Cecchinello	ITA	Aprilia	180
5	Steve Jenkner	GER	Aprilia	168
6	Pablo Nieto	SPA	Aprilia	145
7	Simone Sanna	ITA	Aprilia	106
8	Masao Azuma	JPN	Honda	101
9	Alex de Angelis	RSM	Aprilia	87
10	Gino Borsoi	ITA	Aprilia	82

MOTOGP – THE RULES

The 500cc limit that had been in place since the start of the World Championships in 1949 stayed for two-strokes, but now four-strokes of up to 990cc were permitted. Triples could weigh up to 135kg, four or five cylinders up to 145kg, and if six or more cylinders were desired then the weight limit was 155kg. Oval pistons would attract an extra 10kg in engines with fewer than six cylinders. Two-stroke bikes of two, three and four cylinders had limits of 100, 115 and 130kg, respectively. The bikes also had to be prototypes, a word the FIM had insisted on including in the regulations in order to ensure clear blue water between the new class and the bikes running in the World Superbike Championship.

Fuel-tank capacity was limited to 24 litres and noise output to 130dB – although limit isn't quite the right word since the new bikes were very, very loud. Some riders, notably Rossi, preferred to use silencers. Two-strokes could only make 113dB and could carry 32 litres of fuel. The 25 per cent reduction in fuel use for the new bikes, coupled to massive performance increase, showed why the factories were willing to put development budget into the new class but not into the old 500cc two-strokes.

The move to four-strokes meant electronic fuel injection came to motorcycle racing decades after cars and engineers wrestled with the problems of applying modern digital electronics to two-wheelers. Making power was not a problem; controlling it was. Crude traction control appeared, either using throttle kickers to effectively increase tickover in corners or 'dropping' sparks if rear- and front-wheel speeds differed significantly. Early efforts also centred on coping with engine braking – or back torque. A variety of slipper clutches, some electrically operated, appeared as ways were sought to make 200 plus horsepower usable.

Overnight, the expertise needed to set up carburettors, crucial to any mechanic all through the history of motorcycle racing, became redundant. Making the fuel last was an issue, though, so now the vital men carried a laptop not a box of needles and jets. The most astonishing change was undoubtedly how two-stroke V4s, previously regarded as man-eaters, instantly became obsolete.

BELOW Just how good was the RCV? When Alex Barros got one for the last four races of the year he won two of them. (*Henk Keulemans*)

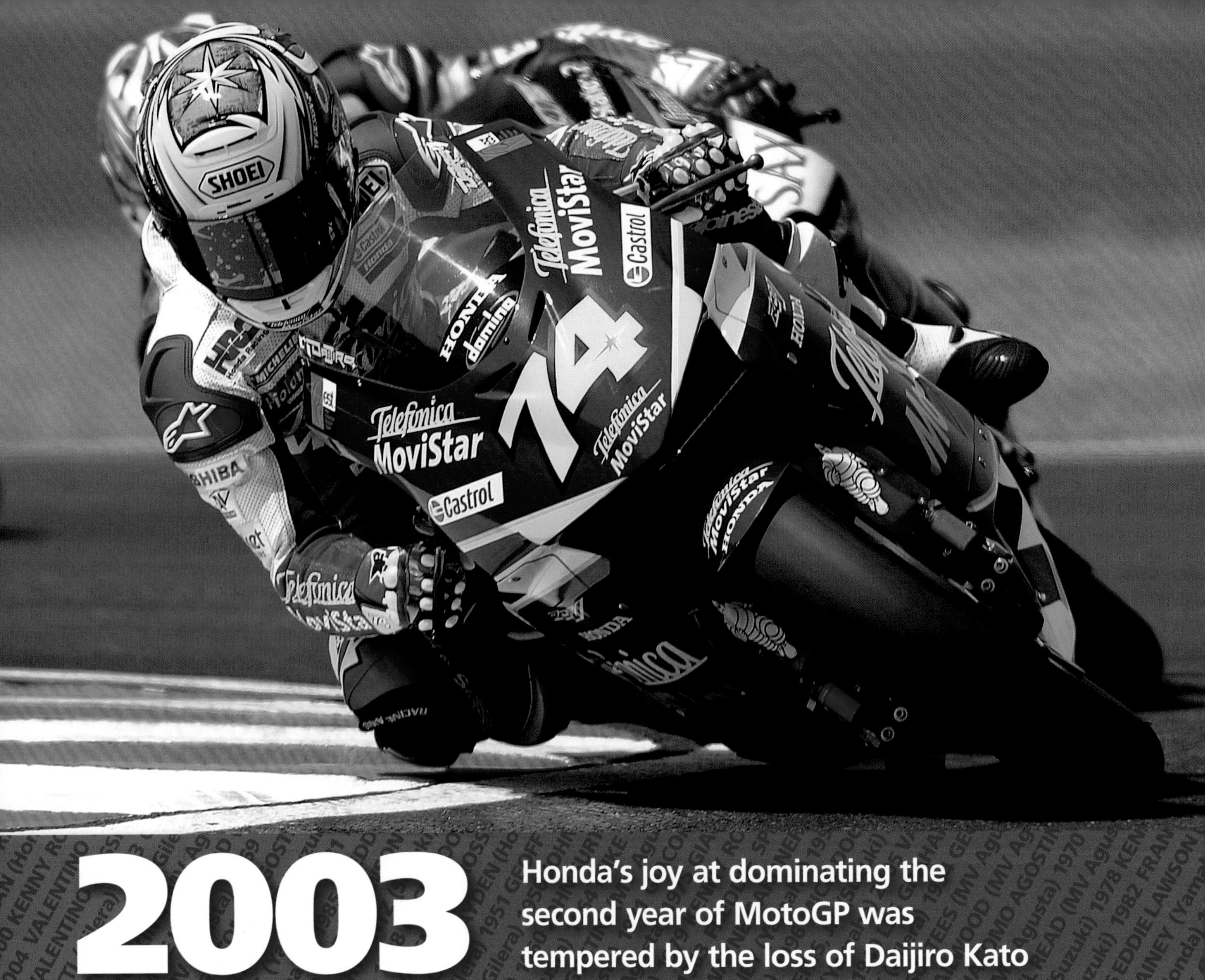

2003

Honda's joy at dominating the second year of MotoGP was tempered by the loss of Daijiro Kato

Ducati and Kawasaki entered MotoGP full time. The Bologna factory recruited Loris Capirossi and teamed him with their Superbike Champion, Troy Bayliss (AUS). Kawasaki picked up Garry McCoy after WCM were unable to guarantee him a ride and teamed him with fellow-Aussie Andrew Pitt, who had ridden the bike as a wild card at the end of the '02 season. Aprilia also upped their game, recruiting double Superbike Champion Colin Edwards (USA) and bringing Noriyuki Haga back to GPs.

At Honda reigning champ Rossi got a new team-mate in Nicky Hayden – the youngest ever AMA champion. Gresini snaffled Sete Gibernau and his sponsor from Suzuki to run alongside Daijiro Kato. Max Biaggi left Yamaha for a Pons Honda, with Tohru Ukawa moving from the factory team to the satellite squad. A seventh RCV was produced for Makoto Tamada who, uniquely among the Honda riders, used Bridgestone tyres. Yamaha retained Carlos Checa and recruited Marco Melandri, Tech 3 kept Olivier Jacque and found a home for Alex Barros while the d'Antin team ran Shinya Nakano.

Having lost both their sponsor and Gibernau, the Suzuki team raced in factory colours, retaining Kenny Roberts Jnr for a fifth season and recruiting American teenager John Hopkins. The WCM team also lost their sponsor, and their Yamahas, so they built their own bikes. As they initially used engine castings from a production bike, they fell foul of the scrutineers and ran their old two-strokes until they could produce their own crankcases, cylinders and heads.

Rossi and Honda were even more dominant than they'd been in the first year of the MotoGP formula, winning nine races, starting from pole nine times and finishing on the rostrum in every race. Valentino set the fastest lap of the race 12 times, with a new lap record each time. Yamaha, their riders hit by early-season injuries, managed only one rostrum all year. The only non-Honda victory came when Loris Capirossi took advantage of a rare Rossi error at Barcelona to give Ducati a victory in only their sixth race in the top class.

ABOVE Daijiro Kato, Honda's great hope for a Japanese champion, who died at Suzuka. (*Henk Keulemans*)

THE 2003 SEASON

MotoGP

JPN/Suzuka

- Japan's champion-in-waiting, Daijiro Kato, suffered fatal injuries after crashing at the end of the third lap
- Loris Capirossi rode the Ducati Desmosedici to a rostrum finish on its competitive debut

SPA/Jerez

- Capirossi gave Ducati their first pole position

FRA/Le Mans

- Sete Gibernau won the MotoGP race, Toni Elias the 250cc and Dani Pedrosa the 125cc, the first time all three of these races had been won by Spanish riders at a GP event
- Team KR debuted their own five-cylinder four-stroke bike in practice but reverted to their two-stroke triple for the race
- First use of the new rain rules: the race was stopped after 15 laps and re-run as a 13-lap dash (so spectators and TV viewers could see the scheduled number of laps)
- Alex Barros, in third, scored Yamaha's only rostrum of the year

ITA/Mugello

- Rossi's victory was the 151st time an Italian had won a premier-class race, making Italy the most successful nation in terms of 500/MotoGP wins, with one more victory than the USA

CAT/Catalunya

- Loris Capirossi took Ducati's first win in the premier class

CZE/Brno

- British rider Chris Burns (WCM) became the last rider to race a two-stroke in the class

RIO/Jacarepagua

- Bridgestone tyres scored their first rostrum thanks to third-placed Makoto Tamada

PAC/Motegi

- American Nicky Hayden was credited with third place but didn't get to stand on the rostrum – original third-placed finisher Tamada was disqualified for an innocuous last-lap move on Gibernau

AUS/Phillip Island

- Rossi received a 10-second penalty for a yellow-flag infringement but still won by 15 seconds (5s on corrected time)
- Rookie of the Year Hayden led a race for the first time and ended up third; this time he did get to stand on the rostrum

VAL/Ricardo Tormo

- Rossi won his last race for Honda sporting a one-off Austin Powers paint scheme designed by the winner of a magazine competition

250cc

JPN/Suzuka

- Ex-125cc World Champion Manuel Poggiali (Aprilia) became the first rider to win on his debut in the 250cc class since Jim Filice took victory in the US GP in 1988

RSA/Welkom

- Chaz Davies (GBR) finished 15th to become the youngest rider to score points in the 250cc class

NED/Assen

- Anthony West's debut GP victory was the first 250cc win for an Australian rider since Gregg Hansford won in Yugoslavia in 1978 riding a Kawasaki

GER/Sachsenring

- A first GP victory for Roberto Rolfo (ITA, Honda), who became the sixth different rider to win in the 250cc class in the first nine races of the year

VAL/Ricardo Tormo

- Poggiali finished third at the final race of the year to clinch the title by six points from Rolfo

125cc

ITA/Mugello

- Casey Stoner (Aprilia) started from pole for the first time in his GP career but failed to finish the race

CAT/Catalunya

- Dani Pedrosa (Honda) gave Spain their 100th GP victory in the 125cc class

GBR/Donington

- Hector Barbera's debut GP win, on an Aprilia, made him the youngest Spanish rider to take a GP victory

POR/Estoril

- Pablo Nieto, son of 13 times World Champion Angel, took his only GP victory

RIO/Jacarepagua

- First GP victory for Jorge Lorenzo (Derbi), the second-youngest rider (after Marco Melandri) to win a GP

MAL/Sepang

- Dani Pedrosa won the race and clinched the world title, becoming the second-youngest World Champion of all time after Loris Capirossi

VAL/Ricardo Tormo

- Casey Stoner won for the first time in his Grand Prix career

DAIJIRO KATO RESULTS AND STATISTICS

- In 2001 Daijiro Kato set the record for highest number of wins in a single season in the 250cc class with 11 victories
- The 322 points Kato scored during the 2001 season was the highest total ever achieved in the 250cc class
- Kato won the 250cc Japanese Grand Prix twice as a wild card before coming to GPs full time

Class	Starts	Wins	Podiums	Poles	Debut	First win
MotoGP	17	0	2	1	JPN/2002	
250cc	36	17	25	10	JPN/1996	JPN/1997
Total	53	17	27	11		

2003 WORLD CHAMPIONSHIP

MotoGP

Pos	Rider	Nat	Machine	JPN	RSA	SPA	FRA	ITA	CAT	NED	GBR	GER	CZE	POR	BRA	PAC	MAL	AUS	VAL	Total
1	Valentino Rossi	ITA	Honda	25	20	25	20	25	20	16	16	20	25	25	25	20	25	25	25	357
2	Sete Gibernau	SPA	Honda	13	25	-	25	9	16	25	20	25	20	13	20	13	20	13	20	277
3	Max Biaggi	ITA	Honda	20	16	20	11	16	2	20	25	-	11	20	13	25	16	-	13	228
4	Loris Capirossi	ITA	Ducati	16	-	-	-	20	25	10	13	13	-	16	10	8	10	20	16	177
5	Nicky Hayden	USA	Honda	9	9	-	4	4	7	5	8	11	10	7	11	16	13	16	-	130
6	Troy Bayliss	AUS	Ducati	11	13	16	-	-	6	7	11	16	16	10	6	-	7	-	9	128
7	Carlos Checa	SPA	Yamaha	6	7	-	-	8	13	13	10	8	13	8	7	-	11	8	11	123
8	Tohru Ukawa	JPN	Honda	-	10	13	9	10	10	4	-	10	8	11	9	9	9	11	-	123
9	Alex Barros	BRA	Yamaha	8	11	11	16	-	8	8	-	-	9	5	4	10	1	-	10	101
10	Shinya Nakano	JPN	Yamaha	7	5	8	2	11	11	3	7	9	2	4	8	7	8	9	-	101
11	Makoto Tamada	JPN	Honda	-	2	10	-	13	9	-	3	3	7	6	16	-	6	6	6	87
12	Olivier Jacque	FRA	Yamaha	1	6	6	13	6	-	11	-	7	5	3	-	3	-	10	-	71
13	Colin Edwards	USA	Aprilia	10	-	2	6	7	-	9	6	2	4	2	3	-	3	-	8	62
14	Noriyuki Haga	JPN	Aprilia	4	-	5	8	-	4	-	9	-	3	1	2	4	4	2	1	47
15	Marco Melandri	ITA	Yamaha	-	-	-	1	5	3	-	-	-	6	9	5	11	5	-	-	45
16	Norick Abe	JPN	Yamaha	5	8	-	5	-	-	-	-	6	-	-	-	-	-	-	7	31
17	John Hopkins	USA	Suzuki	3	3	9	-	-	1	1	5	-	-	-	-	-	-	4	3	29
18	Jeremy McWilliams	GBR	Proton KR	-	-	4	10	-	-	-	-	4	-	-	-	-	-	5	4	27
19	Kenny Roberts	USA	Suzuki	2	1	3	-	-	-	-	-	1	-	-	-	1	2	7	5	22
20	Ryuichi Kiyonari	JPN	Honda	-	-	-	3	3	5	-	2	-	1	-	1	5	-	-	2	22
21	Nobuatsu Aoki	JPN	Proton KR	-	4	7	-	-	-	-	1	5	-	-	-	2	-	-	-	19
22	Garry McCoy	AUS	Kawasaki	-	-	-	7	1	-	-	-	-	-	-	-	-	-	3	-	11
23	Alex Hofmann	GER	Kawasaki	-	-	-	-	2	-	6	-	-	-	-	-	-	-	-	-	8
24	Akira Ryo	JPN	Suzuki	-	-	-	-	-	-	-	-	-	-	-	-	6	-	-	-	6
25	Yukio Kagayama	JPN	Suzuki	-	-	-	-	-	-	-	4	-	-	-	-	-	-	-	-	4
26	Andrew Pitt	AUS	Kawasaki	-	-	1	-	-	-	2	-	-	-	-	-	-	-	1	-	4

Scoring system – 25, 20, 16, 13, 11, 10, 9, 8, 7, 6, 5, 4, 3, 2, 1

250cc

Pos	Rider	Nat	Machine	Total
1	Manuel Poggiali	RSM	Aprilia	249
2	Roberto Rolfo	ITA	Honda	235
3	Toni Elias	SPA	Aprilia	226
4	Randy de Puniet	FRA	Aprilia	208
5	Fonsi Nieto	SPA	Aprilia	194
6	Franco Battaini	ITA	Aprilia	148
7	Anthony West	AUS	Aprilia	145
8	Sebastian Porto	ARG	Honda	127
9	Naoki Matsudo	JPN	Yamaha	119
10	Sylvain Guintoli	FRA	Aprilia	101

125cc

Pos	Rider	Nat	Machine	Total
1	Daniel Pedrosa	SPA	Honda	223
2	Alex de Angelis	RSM	Aprilia	166
3	Hector Barbera	SPA	Aprilia	164
4	Stefano Perugini	ITA	Aprilia	162
5	Andrea Dovizioso	ITA	Honda	157
6	Steve Jenkner	GER	Aprilia	151
7	Pablo Nieto	SPA	Aprilia	148
8	Casey Stoner	AUS	Aprilia	125
9	Lucio Cecchinello	ITA	Aprilia	112
10	Mirko Giansanti	ITA	Aprilia	93

THE DESMOS ARE COMING

Ducati's MotoGP bike, the Desmosedici, bore two of the company's hallmarks: the tubular steel lattice frame and – of course – desmodromic valve operation. Their other characteristic design element – the V-twin motor – was tested but rejected in favour of a V4. The bike was immediately competitive. Loris Capirossi put it on the rostrum in its first race and on the front row in its second. In the third race (SPA/Jerez) Capirossi and team-mate Troy Bayliss were first and second on the grid – the Italian snatching pole by exactly one-hundredth of a second at the very end of qualifying. Three races later, at Catalunya, Capirossi became Ducati's first winner in the top class of racing. He was the first Italian to win on an Italian bike since Agostini won on an MV Agusta at the German GP of 1976. Capirossi finished the season with a tally that included his victory plus five more rostrum finishes. Bayliss scored three rostrums, all third places.

ABOVE Ducati Corse boss Claudio Domenicali and chief engineer Filippo Preziosi. (*Henk Keulemans*)

LEFT Ducati's first winner in the top class of racing – Loris Capirossi at Catalunya. (*Henk Keulemans*)

DUCATI GRAND PRIX HISTORY

- **Alberto Gandossi (ITA) took two wins for Ducati in 1958 on his way to second place in the 125cc World Championship, with one victory going to fellow-countryman Bruno Spaggiari, a rider always closely associated with the Ducati factory. These successes in 1958 placed them second in the manufacturers' championship, just two points behind MV Agusta**

- **The final victory for Ducati in 1959 was at the Ulster GP and was the first Grand Prix win for Mike Hailwood, who was just 19 years old and the youngest ever GP winner at that time. Hailwood was also the rider who had most success with Ducati in the 250 class, with a couple of fourth-place finishes in 1960**

- **Ducati entered a number of machines in the 500cc race at the Italian GP of Nations in both 1971 and 1972. Phil Read was the highest Ducati finisher at Monza in 1971, taking fourth place. Spaggiari scored Ducati's only podium finish in the 500cc class when he finished third at Imola in 1972 behind the MVs of Agostini and Alberto Pagani and just in front of Paul Smart (GBR) on another Ducati. This machine was a V-twin four-stroke with a frame built by British specialist Colin Seeley**

2004

No-one thought it was possible for Valentino Rossi to move from Honda to Yamaha and retain his title; everyone was wrong

Yamaha reduced the number of M1s on the grid from five to four, two for the factory team, two for the Tech 3 satellite team. New signing Valentino Rossi and Carlos Checa rode the works bikes, Marco Melandri moved down from the top team and was joined by Norick Abe, who'd only taken part as a wild-card/replacement rider in five races in 2003. Each Yamaha team ran one of their riders in Gauloises colours and one in Fortuna livery (the brands being owned by the same company).

Honda replaced Rossi with Alex Barros, keeping Nicky Hayden alongside him in the factory Repsol team. The Gresini team retained Sete Gibernau and bought in Colin Edwards from Aprilia to fill the gap left by the death of Daijiro Kato. Honda's second satellite team ran Max Biaggi and Makoto Tamada in Camel colours but on different tyres – Michelin and Bridgestone, respectively.

Suzuki (Kenny Roberts Jnr and John Hopkins) and Ducati (Loris Capirossi and Troy Bayliss) made no alterations to their rider line-ups, but the most significant change to the grid was the arrival of Ducati's first satellite team, entrusted to the care of Luis d'Antin. Ex-World Superbike team-mates Neil Hodgson (GBR) and Ruben Xaus (SPA) were the riders.

Kawasaki had two new riders, gleefully signing Shinya Nakano when Yamaha's cutback made him redundant and pairing him with test rider and impressive 2003 wild-card entrant Alex Hofmann (GER). Aprilia signed Jeremy McWilliams from Team KR and brought in British Superbike Champion Shane Byrne. Team KR kept hold of Nobuatsu Aoki and teamed him with Kurtis Roberts, the team principal's second son. WCM retained Chris Burns and brought in young Italian Michel Fabrizio, who would be lent out to Aprilia and replaced by James Ellison.

Bridgestone now supplied two factory teams – Kawasaki and Suzuki – as well as Tamada's side of the Honda Pons garage. The Japanese factory would get its first MotoGP pole and its first win this season. All the other factory bikes were on Michelins, leaving just WCM and Team KR on Dunlops.

ABOVE The first miracle in a season of miracles, Rossi wins his first race on the M1 in South Africa. (*Henk Keulemans*)

THE 2004 SEASON

MotoGP

RSA/Welkom

- Valentino Rossi took the win, to break the Yamaha factory's longest losing streak, in the process beating Giacomo Agostini's record run of 22 consecutive top-three finishes

SPA/Jerez

- The MSMA announced the first change to MotoGP technical regulations, to come into force for the 2005 season: a two-litre reduction in fuel capacity, from 24 to 22 litres

ITA/Mugello

- Shinya Nakano crashed at over 190mph after his rear Bridgestone tyre delaminated – the fastest crash in GP history – but escaped serious injury
- The race was red-flagged because of rain after 17 laps and, as the rules dictated, then rerun as a six-lap sprint – the shortest GP until 2008, when the 125cc races at both Le Mans and Assen were five-lappers
- This event prompted another review of the rain regulations and led to the 'flag-to-flag' rule being adopted for 2005

CAT/Catalunya

- Marco Melandri finished third, his first rostrum in the top class, then backed it up with another third place next time out at Assen

NED/Assen

- Alex Barros became the first man in Grand Prix history to make 200 starts in the top class

RIO/Jacarepagua

- Kenny Roberts Jnr gave Suzuki their first pole position in the MotoGP class; it was also Bridgestone's first on a four-stroke machine
- Makoto Tamada gave Bridgestone their first win in the top class, ending a run of 92 Michelin victories

GBR/Donington

- Colin Edwards finished second to stand on a MotoGP rostrum for the first time

POR/Estoril

- Team KR tested KTM V4 motors on the Monday after the GP

JPN/Motegi

- Shinya Nakano finished third, his and Kawasaki's first MotoGP rostrum

QAT/Losail

- Ruben Xaus finished third, his and the satellite d'Antin Ducati team's first MotoGP rostrum
- Gibernau and Edwards finished first and second, the first time the Honda Gresini team achieved a one–two

AUS/Phillip Island

- Valentino Rossi took race victory to seal his fourth world title (six in all classes)

250cc

RSA/Welkom

- Dani Pedrosa won on his debut in the 250cc class to become the youngest rider to win a 250cc GP race

CZE/Brno

- Argentine Sebastian Porto's victory was the 100th win for Aprilia in the 250cc class of GP racing

AUS/Phillip Island

- Dani Pedrosa finished fourth to clinch the world title and become the youngest 250cc World Champion
- Pedrosa was the first rider since Carlo Ubbiali in 1960 to win the 125cc and 250cc titles in successive years

VAL/Ricardo Tormo

- Hiroshi Aoyama (Honda) crossed the line in third place but was disqualified because his bike was 0.5kg below the minimum weight

125cc

RSA/Welkom

- First GP victory for Andrea Dovizioso (Honda), the young Italian taking an early lead in the championship that he maintained throughout the season

NED/Assen

- Casey Stoner gave KTM their first pole in Grand Prix racing

GBR/Donington

- Dovizioso's victory at Donington was the 200th win for Italy in the 125cc class

POR/Estoril

- Dovizioso failed to finish the race because of a puncture – the only time all year he was not in the top four

QAT/Losail

- The first occasion since the introduction of timing to an accuracy of one-thousandth of a second when timekeepers were unable to separate the first two riders – Jorge Lorenzo and Dovizioso – across the line. A photo finish gave the win to Lorenzo

MAL/Sepang

- Casey Stoner took the first ever GP victory for the KTM factory
- Andrea Dovizioso finished second to take the world title

YOUNGEST TO WIN A 250cc GRAND PRIX

	Rider	Age	Race
1	Dani Pedrosa	18 years 202 days	RSA/Welkom/2004
2	Alan Carter	18 years 227 days	FRA/Le Mans/1983
3	Jorge Lorenzo	18 years 326 days	SPA/Jerez/2006
4	Marco Melandri	18 years 349 days	GER/Sachsenring/2001
5	Johnny Cecotto	19 years 64 days	FRA/Paul Ricard/1975
6	Valentino Rossi	19 years 131 days	NED/Assen/1998
7	Casey Stoner	19 years 183 days	POR/Estoril/2005
8	Hector Barbera	19 years 193 days	CHN/Shanghai/2006
9	Toni Elias	19 years 194 days	JPN-PAC/Motegi/2002
10	Manuel Poggiali	20 years 51 days	JPN/Suzuka/2003
11	Loris Capirossi	20 years 83 days	NED/Assen/1993

2004 WORLD CHAMPIONSHIP

MotoGP

Pos	Rider	Nat	Machine	RSA	SPA	FRA	ITA	CAT	NED	BRA	GER	GBR	CZE	POR	JPN	QAT	MAL	AUS	VAL	Total
1	Valentino Rossi	ITA	Yamaha	25	13	13	25	25	25	-	13	25	20	25	20	-	25	25	25	304
2	Sete Gibernau	SPA	Honda	16	25	25	20	20	20	-	-	16	25	13	10	25	9	20	13	257
3	Max Biaggi	ITA	Honda	20	20	16	16	8	13	20	25	4	16	-	-	10	20	9	20	217
4	Alex Barros	BRA	Honda	13	16	9	10	-	-	11	20	7	-	16	13	13	16	11	10	165
5	Colin Edwards	USA	Honda	9	9	11	4	11	10	10	11	20	9	7	-	20	5	13	8	157
6	Makoto Tamada	JPN	Honda	8	-	7	-	-	4	25	10	2	13	20	25	6	11	8	11	150
7	Carlos Checa	SPA	Yamaha	6	10	20	-	13	7	6	-	10	10	11	9	-	7	6	2	117
8	Nicky Hayden	USA	Honda	11	11	5	-	-	11	16	16	13	-	-	-	11	13	10	-	117
9	Loris Capirossi	ITA	Ducati	10	4	6	8	6	8	13	-	9	11	9	-	-	10	16	7	117
10	Shinya Nakano	JPN	Kawasaki	4	7	-	-	9	-	7	9	1	4	5	16	-	8	4	9	83
11	Ruben Xaus	SPA	Ducati	-	-	2	11	10	9	4	5	5	-	-	7	16	3	5	-	77
12	Marco Melandri	ITA	Yamaha	5	-	10	7	16	16	3	-	-	7	-	11	-	-	-	-	75
13	Norick Abe	JPN	Yamaha	7	5	-	9	7	5	8	-	-	8	6	-	9	4	-	6	74
14	Troy Bayliss	AUS	Ducati	2	-	8	13	-	-	-	-	11	-	8	-	-	6	7	16	71
15	Alex Hofmann	GER	Kawasaki	-	3	-	2	5	3	5	6	-	3	3	6	7	-	3	5	51
16	John Hopkins	USA	Suzuki	3	1	-	-	-	2	1	7	8	-	10	-	8	-	1	4	45
17	Neil Hodgson	GBR	Ducati	-	-	-	5	4	6	-	3	6	5	-	8	-	-	-	1	38
18	Kenny Roberts	USA	Suzuki	-	8	4	-	-	-	9	8	-	6	2	-	-	-	-	-	37
19	Jeremy McWilliams	GBR	Aprilia	-	-	3	-	-	1	2	4	-	2	4	4	-	1	2	3	26
20	Shane Byrne	GBR	Aprilia	1	-	-	6	3	-	-	2	3	-	-	3	-	-	-	-	18
21	Nobuatsu Aoki	JPN	Proton KR	-	2	-	3	1	-	-	-	-	1	1	2	-	-	-	-	10
22	Michel Fabrizio	ITA	Harris WCM	-	6	-	1	-	-	-	1	-	-	-	-	-	-	-	-	8
23	Yukio Kagayama	JPN	Suzuki	-	-	-	-	-	-	-	-	-	-	-	-	5	2	-	-	7
24	Olivier Jacque	FRA	Moriwaki	-	-	-	-	-	-	-	-	-	-	-	5	-	-	-	-	5
25	James Haydon	GBR	Proton KR	-	-	-	-	-	-	-	-	-	-	-	-	4	-	-	-	4
26	James Ellison	GBR	Harris WCM	-	-	-	-	-	-	-	-	-	-	-	-	3	-	-	-	3
27	Andrew Pitt	AUS	Moriwaki	-	-	-	-	2	-	-	-	-	-	-	-	-	-	-	-	2
28	Youichi Ui	JPN	Harris WCM	-	-	-	-	-	-	-	-	-	-	-	1	-	-	-	-	1
29	Kurtis Roberts	USA	Proton KR	-	-	1	-	-	-	-	-	-	-	-	-	-	-	-	-	1

Scoring system – 25, 20, 16, 13, 11, 10, 9, 8, 7, 6, 5, 4, 3, 2, 1

250cc

Pos	Rider	Nat	Machine	Total
1	Daniel Pedrosa	SPA	Honda	317
2	Sebastian Porto	ARG	Aprilia	256
3	Randy de Puniet	FRA	Aprilia	214
4	Toni Elias	SPA	Honda	199
5	Alex de Angelis	RSM	Aprilia	147
6	Hiroshi Aoyama	JPN	Honda	128
7	Fonsi Nieto	SPA	Aprilia	124
8	Roberto Rolfo	ITA	Honda	116
9	Manuel Poggiali	RSM	Aprilia	95
10	Franco Battaini	ITA	Aprilia	93

125cc

Pos	Rider	Nat	Machine	Total
1	Andrea Dovizioso	ITA	Honda	293
2	Hector Barbera	SPA	Aprilia	202
3	Roberto Locatelli	ITA	Aprilia	192
4	Jorge Lorenzo	SPA	Derbi	179
5	Casey Stoner	AUS	KTM	145
6	Pablo Nieto	SPA	Aprilia	138
7	Alvaro Bautista	SPA	Aprilia	129
8	Steve Jenkner	GER	Aprilia	122
9	Mirko Giansanti	ITA	Aprilia	105
10	Mika Kallio	FIN	Aprilia	86

YAMAHA'S TRIUMVIRATE – ROSSI, BURGESS AND FURUSAWA

It's almost impossible to overstate what bad shape the Yamaha team was in at the end of 2003. The factory was on the longest run in its history without a top-class podium, and they hadn't won a MotoGP race since Max Biaggi's victory in Malaysia towards the end of the 2002 season. (It was also Yamaha's longest ever time without a win across all the GP classes.)

The invaluable contribution of race engineer Jerry Burgess and his mainly Australian pit crew to Valentino Rossi's GP campaign in 2004 cannot be overstated either. Valentino had expended considerable effort in persuading them to move to Yamaha with him, where Burgess's ability to distil complex situations down to the one or two vital factors that he could do something about was second to none. The team gave Rossi a bike that worked in the places where it would enable him to win, while the rider himself could ride around problems on other parts of the track. Yamaha moved Masao Furusawa to head the project: he had already hit on his irregular-firing-order crankshaft design and four-valves per cylinder as the way to go. Rossi concurred the first time he tested the motor. In the tradition of Yamaha's 500c, the M1 was never the fastest bike on track but it worked well everywhere.

Nevertheless, no-one seriously thought Rossi could take the title. In fact, most paddock debate centred on whether he could even win one race in his first season with Yamaha, so by winning the very first race of the year, in South Africa, he effectively removed any lingering doubts about his right to be considered one of the all-time greats. He also made it four crowns in a row, something only Agostini, Hailwood and Doohan had achieved. Geoff Duke, Giacomo Agostini and Eddie Lawson had previously won titles on different makes of bike, but only Lawson achieved that feat in consecutive years. Valentino's win at Welkom also beat Ago's record for consecutive podiums.

Rossi's only serious challenger in both 2003 and '04 was Sete Gibernau, the second most successful rider of the 990cc years with eight wins. When Valentino was relegated to the back of the grid for the Qatar GP because his pit crew illegally cleaned his starting spot, he blamed Gibernau and his crew. Rossi crashed in the race while chasing the Spaniard, but said afterwards that Sete would never win another race … what became known as the 'Curse of Qatar' appeared to work. A week later Rossi won in Malaysia and, on the slow-down lap, he stopped to take a broom from a marshal and proceeded to sweep the track for the benefit of the assembled photographers.

ABOVE Taking the flag at Welkom for that debut win on the Yamaha. (*Henk Keulemans*)

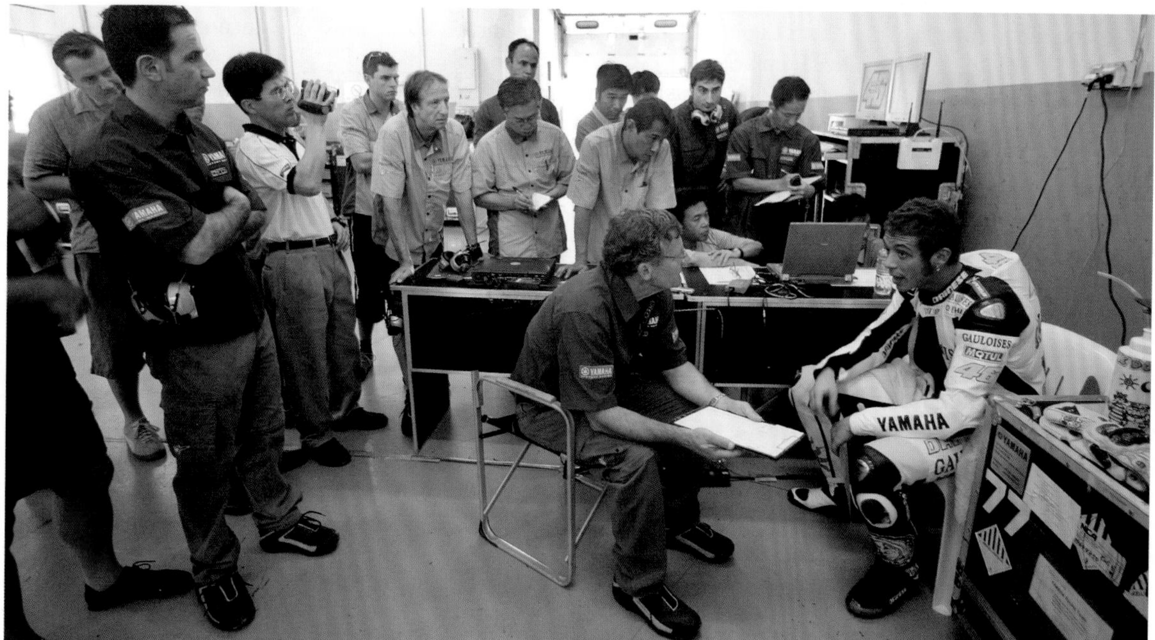

LEFT The first test – you could say Rossi and Burgess have the undivided attention of Yamaha's engineers. (*Henk Keulemans*)

2005

Rossi made it five championships in a row, dominating on the Yamaha as he used to on the Honda

Valentino Rossi got a new Yamaha team-mate in the shape of Colin Edwards, the Texan's third different team in his three years in MotoGP, with both men running in Gauloises colours. Satellite outfit Tech 3 was Fortuna branded and used as a junior team for two promising young Spaniards, rookie Toni Elias and Ruben Xaus.

Repsol Honda brought in Max Biaggi as team-mate to Nicky Hayden while the Gresini team retained Sete Gibernau and signed Marco Melandri, whose relationship with Yamaha had broken down half-way through the previous season. Alex Barros was demoted from the factory team to the satellite Pons outfit and partnered with Troy Bayliss, out of the Ducati family for the first time in his World Championship career. When Bayliss was injured, late in the year, the team used a variety of replacements: Shane Byrne, Tohru Ukawa, Aussie Chris Vermeulen and Ryuichi Kiyonari. A new team, JiR (Japan Italy Racing), was formed to run Makoto Tamada on a seventh Honda with Konica Minolta sponsorship.

Loris Capirossi was retained by Ducati, with Carlos Checa replacing Bayliss, and Roberto Rolfo moving up from 250s to be d'Antin's lone entry on a year-old Ducati. Kawasaki and Suzuki retained their riders: Kenny Roberts Jnr and John Hopkins in blue, Shinya Nakano and Alex Hofmann in green. WCM fielded James Ellison (GBR) and Franco Battaini (ITA). Team KR started the year with KTM engines, but that relationship had soured terminally by the Czech GP. Jeremy McWilliams rode the bike at Brno using the team's own V5, as did Kurtis Roberts at Valencia.

The major surprise of the year was Ducati switching their works team from Michelin to Bridgestone tyres. Clearly this was a gamble, but a clever one. The thinking went something like this: we cannot beat Rossi with the same equipment so we will use something different; that way although we may be at a disadvantage at some tracks there will be others where we have a vital advantage. Kawasaki and Suzuki continued to run Bridgestones, WCM and d'Antin were on Dunlops, and everyone else used Michelins.

ABOVE The pivotal moment of the year came on the last corner of the first race when Rossi barged past Sete Gibernau for the win. (*Henk Keulemans*)

THE **2005** SEASON

MotoGP

SPA/Jerez
- Valentino Rossi won the first race of the season for the fifth successive year, after colliding with Gibernau in the last corner

CHN/Shanghai
- Rossi won the first Grand Prix of China – it was also his first wet-weather win on the Yamaha
- Olivier Jacque replaced the injured Alex Hofmann and gave Kawasaki their best ever MotoGP result – second place

ITA/Mugello
- The MSMA announced that the capacity limit for the MotoGP class would be reduced to 800cc as from 2007 and that – vitally – fuel-tank capacity would be reduced by a litre to 21 litres

NED/Assen
- Valentino Rossi won the final race on the 3.75-mile/6.03-km Assen circuit, becoming the first Yamaha rider to win the Dutch TT twice, and the first to win five MotoGPs races in a row

USA/Laguna Seca
- Grand Prix motorcycle racing returned to the USA for the first time since 1994, and local hero Nicky Hayden won his first GP

GER/Sachsenring
- Rossi won his 50th premier-class race in 90 starts, and equalled Mike Hailwood's 76 victories over all classes

MAL/Sepang
- Loris Capirossi won two races in a row for the first time in the premier class – he was victorious at Motegi the previous week – making it the first back-to-back victories for both Ducati and Bridgestone as well
- Valentino Rossi retained his title with four races still to run

QAT/Losail
- Rossi took his tenth win of the season, a first for a Yamaha rider

TUR/Istanbul Park
- Marco Melandri won the first Turkish GP, his first victory in MotoGP, and backed that up by winning again in Valencia a week later

250cc

POR/Estoril
- Casey Stoner won for the first time in the 250cc class

CHN/Shanghai
- Stoner became the first Australian rider to start from pole in the 250cc class since Gregg Hansford back in 1979

ITA/Mugello
- Jorge Lorenzo became the youngest rider to qualify on pole in the 250cc class

CAT/Catalunya
- The first three riders home – Pedrosa, Stoner and Dovizioso – were all aged under 20 – the first ever all-teenage podium in the 250cc class
- Dani Pedrosa gave Spain its 50th GP win in the 250cc class

QAT/Losail
- Casey Stoner was followed home by Jorge Lorenzo and Andrea Dovizioso – the youngest ever 250cc podium, with an average age of 19 years and 110 days

AUS/Phillip Island
- Dani Pedrosa gave Honda their 600th Grand Prix victory across all classes
- Pedrosa retained his 250cc title after pole-man Stoner crashed out of the lead early in the race

125cc

POR/Estoril
- Mika Kallio became the first Finnish rider to win a 125cc GP

FRA/Le Mans
- Thomas Luthi took his maiden GP victory after qualifying on pole for the first time
- This was the first win in the 125cc class by a Swiss rider since Bruno Kneubuhler at the Swedish GP in 1983

ITA/Mugello
- Gabor Talmacsi's victory was the first ever 125cc GP win by a Hungarian rider, and the first in any class by a rider from Hungary since Janos Drapal won the 350cc race at the Grand Prix of Yugoslavia at Opatija in 1973
- Talmasci was the fifth different rider to win in the first five 125cc races of the year – the first time this had ever occurred

TUR/Istanbul Park
- Mike di Meglio became the youngest French rider to win a Grand Prix

VAL/Ricardo Tormo
- Thomas Luthi finished ninth to take the world title from closest challenger, Mika Kallio, who won the race
- Luthi was the first Swiss rider since Luigi Taveri in 1966 to win the 125cc world title

2005 WORLD CHAMPIONSHIP

MotoGP

Pos	Rider	Nation	Machine	SPA	POR	CHN	FRA	ITA	CAT	NED	USA	GBR	GER	CZE	JPN	MAL	QAT	AUS	TUR	VAL	Total
1	Valentino Rossi	ITA	Yamaha	25	20	25	25	25	25	25	16	25	25	25	-	20	25	25	20	16	367
2	Marco Melandri	ITA	Honda	16	13	16	13	13	16	20	-	-	9	10	-	11	20	13	25	25	220
3	Nicky Hayden	USA	Honda	-	9	7	10	10	11	13	25	-	16	11	9	13	16	20	16	20	206
4	Colin Edwards	USA	Yamaha	7	10	8	16	7	9	16	20	13	8	9	10	6	13	10	9	8	179
5	Max Biaggi	ITA	Honda	9	16	11	11	20	10	10	13	-	13	16	20	10	-	-	4	10	173
6	Loris Capirossi	ITA	Ducati	3	7	4	9	16	4	6	6	10	7	20	25	25	6	-	-	9	157
7	Sete Gibernau	SPA	Honda	20	-	13	20	-	20	11	11	-	20	-	-	-	11	11	13	-	150
8	Alex Barros	BRA	Honda	13	25	5	-	9	13	9	-	16	11	13	-	8	7	-	7	11	147
9	Carlos Checa	SPA	Ducati	6	11	-	-	11	5	7	-	11	-	8	13	16	10	16	11	13	138
10	Shinya Nakano	JPN	Kawasaki	11	8	-	8	6	7	8	7	-	10	4	-	-	9	9	6	5	98
11	Makoto Tamada	JPN	Honda	8	-	-	-	8	-	2	9	9	6	6	16	4	-	8	8	7	91
12	Toni Elias	SPA	Yamaha	4	2	2	7	-	-	-	3	7	4	2	7	5	8	7	10	6	74
13	Kenny Roberts	USA	Suzuki	-	4	-	3	1	1	-	2	20	5	5	8	9	5	-	-	-	63
14	John Hopkins	USA	Suzuki	2	-	9	-	5	-	3	8	5	-	3	11	7	-	6	1	3	63
15	Troy Bayliss	AUS	Honda	10	5	-	6	3	8	5	10	-	-	7	-	-	-	-	-	-	54
16	Ruben Xaus	SPA	Yamaha	-	6	6	4	2	6	4	5	-	3	-	6	1	2	4	2	1	52
17	Olivier Jacque	FRA	Kawasaki	-	-	20	5	-	-	-	-	-	-	-	-	-	-	-	3	-	28
18	Roberto Rolfo	ITA	Ducati	1	3	-	1	-	2	-	-	6	2	-	-	3	4	3	-	-	25
19	Alex Hofmann	GER	Kawasaki	5	-	-	-	4	-	-	4	8	-	1	-	-	-	-	-	2	24
20	Jurgen Goorbergh	NED	Honda	-	-	10	2	-	-	-	-	-	-	-	-	-	-	-	-	-	12
21	Chris Vermeulen	AUS	Honda	-	-	-	-	-	-	-	-	-	-	-	-	-	-	5	5	-	10
22	Franco Battaini	ITA	Blata	-	-	-	-	-	-	-	-	-	1	-	5	-	-	1	-	-	7
23	James Ellison	GBR	Blata	-	1	3	-	-	-	-	-	-	-	-	-	-	1	2	-	-	7
24	Shane Byrne	GBR	Proton/Honda*	-	-	-	-	-	-	-	1	-	-	-	-	2*	3*	-	-	-	6
25	Ryuichi Kiyonari	JPN	Honda	-	-	-	-	-	-	-	-	-	-	-	-	-	-	-	-	4	4
26	David Checa	SPA	Yamaha	-	-	-	-	-	3	1	-	-	-	-	-	-	-	-	-	-	4
27	Tohru Ukawa	JPN	Moriwaki	-	-	1	-	-	-	-	-	-	-	-	-	-	-	-	-	-	1

Scoring system – 25, 20, 16, 13, 11, 10, 9, 8, 7, 6, 5, 4, 3, 2, 1

250cc

Pos	Rider	Nat	Machine	Total
1	Daniel Pedrosa	SPA	Honda	309
2	Casey Stoner	AUS	Aprilia	254
3	Andrea Dovizioso	ITA	Honda	189
4	Hiroshi Aoyama	JPN	Honda	180
5	Jorge Lorenzo	SPA	Honda	167
6	Sebastian Porto	ARG	Aprilia	152
7	Alex de Angelis	RSM	Aprilia	151
8	Randy de Puniet	FRA	Aprilia	138
9	Hector Barbera	SPA	Honda	120
10	Sylvain Guintoli	FRA	Aprilia	84

125cc

Pos	Rider	Nat	Machine	Total
1	Thomas Luthi	SWI	Honda	242
2	Mika Kallio	FIN	KTM	237
3	Gabor Talmacsi	HUN	KTM	198
4	Mattia Pasini	ITA	Aprilia	183
5	Marco Simoncelli	ITA	Aprilia	177
6	Fabrizio Lai	ITA	Honda	141
7	Julian Simon	SPA	KTM	123
8	Tomoyoshi Koyama	JPN	Honda	119
9	Hector Faubel	SPA	Aprilia	113
10	Manuel Poggiali	RSM	Gilera	107

ASSEN

To the sorrow of nearly all the paddock, this was the final season for the classic Assen circuit, the only track to have hosted a Grand Prix for every single year since the World Championships came into being in 1949. In truth the circuit had been gradually modified over the years – the very first Dutch TT was held in 1925 on a 17-mile/27.25-km loop of closed roads – and the wonderful 3.75-mile/6.03-km lap currently in use dated from 1984.

Despite the creeping modifications, the Circuit van Drenthe – to give it its proper name – retained the flavour of a public-roads circuit. No computer would ever have laid out the high-speed snake of tarmac behind the pits – the Veenslang – let alone retained the crown in the road that complicated things so much for riders. Despite having nothing that could honestly be called a straight, Assen remained the fastest track on the calendar. Rossi's lap record from 2004 stood at nearly 113mph/182km/h.

LEFT The classic Assen layout used from 1984 to 2005: the corner at the bottom of the picture is the Duikersloot right-hander that is followed by the ultra-fast run back to the final chicane. (*Henk Keulemans*)

HISTORIC ASSEN

- A total of 238 Grand Prix races for solo motorcycles have been held at the Assen circuit
- Honda have been the most successful manufacturer at Assen, scoring a total of 54 GP victories across all classes, followed by MV Agusta with 36 and Yamaha with 32
- Honda are also the most successful manufacturer in the premier class at Assen with 17 victories, just two more than MV Agusta
- Italy have been the most successful nation at Assen, having scored a total of 70 victories, followed by Great Britain with 43 wins and Spain with 32
- In the premier class Italy have had 18 victories as against Great Britain's total of 16 wins
- A total of 113 riders have scored Grand Prix victories at Assen
- The rider with most GP victories at the circuit was Angel Nieto, with 15 wins in the 125cc and 50cc classes, followed by Giacomo Agostini with 14 wins riding 500 and 350cc machines
- Giacomo Agostini was the most successful rider in the premier class with six victories, followed by Mick Doohan with five, and Mike Hailwood, Geoff Duke, John Surtees and Valentino Rossi all winning four times in the top class
- Both Agostini and Doohan won the Dutch TT five years in a row
- The longest GP ever held at Assen was 1950's 500cc race, run over 18 laps of the then-circuit – a total race distance of 185 miles/297km. It was won by Italian Umberto Masetti riding a Gilera, in a time of 2 hours and 43.2 seconds at an average speed of 92mph/148 km/h
- The youngest rider to win a GP at Assen is Marco Melandri, who was still 15 years old when he took his debut Grand Prix victory in the 125cc race of 1998. The oldest rider ever to win a GP there was Fergus Anderson, who was aged 45 when he won the 350cc race in 1954
- Four Dutch riders have won Grand Prix races at their home circuit: Paul Lodewijkx (50cc, 1968), Wil Hartog (500cc, 1977), Jack Middelburg (500cc, 1980) and Hans Spaan (125cc, 1989)

2006

Nicky Hayden became the only man other than Valentino Rossi to be World Champion under the 990cc formula

Valentino Rossi and Colin Edwards stayed with the factory Yamaha team while the works Honda squad found yet another team-mate for Nicky Hayden. This time, instead of going for experience, double 250 World Champion Dani Pedrosa moved up to the top class, leaving Max Biaggi without a ride. The Ducati factory team went for experience on both sides of the garage, bringing in Sete Gibernau to partner Loris Capirossi. Kawasaki also went for a mix of experience and a young gun up from the 250s, keeping Shinya Nakano and signing Randy de Puniet (FRA). Suzuki retained John Hopkins but brought in their new blood from World Superbike in the shape of 2005 runner-up Chris Vermeulen (AUS).

Gresini, now obviously Honda's senior satellite team, kept Marco Melandri and got Toni Elias (and his sponsor, Fortuna) from Yamaha. Lucio Cecchinello's LCR Honda team moved up from the smaller classes with an RCV for Casey Stoner, while JiR again fielded Makoto Tamada. Honda's most intriguing move was to supply engines to Team KR to wrap their own chassis around, thus coming up with the only truly competitive machine they ever had. Kenny Roberts Jnr rode it.

The d'Antin satellite team had two bikes on the grid, year-old Ducatis for Alex Hofmann and José Luis Cardoso (SPA). Tech 3 Yamaha only got back on the grid with the help of Dunlop and Carlos Checa, who rode for free, alongside James Ellison.

For once, the Rossi/Yamaha/Burgess axis did not come up with an improved motorcycle. Overheating, breakdowns and the first glimmerings of a far-reaching feud with Michelin had an effect. This could have been the year Loris Capirossi added to his 125 and 250cc titles, but a massive crash at the first corner of the Catalan GP ripped the heart out of his season. His form did show, however, that it was now possible to win the title on a tyre other than a Michelin.

In a thrilling end to the season Nicky Hayden overcame all manner of obstacles – developing a new bike on his own, being knocked off by his team-mate – to win the last world title of the 990cc formula.

ABOVE Despite riding a prototype that no other Honda rider used, Nicky Hayden was consistent enough to take the title at the last round. (*Henk Keulemans*)

THE **2006** SEASON

MotoGP

SPA/Jerez
- Loris Capirossi won to lead the MotoGP World Championship for the first time
- Dani Pedrosa finished second and became the first rookie to finish on the rostrum in his first race since Haga and Biaggi (JPN/Suzuka/1998)

QAT/Losail
- Casey Stoner started from pole in only his second MotoGP race

TUR/Istanbul Park
- Nicky Hayden finished third in his 50th MotoGP race and went to the top of the table for the first time
- Stoner's second place made him the youngest Australian to stand on a 500cc/MotoGP podium

CHN/Shanghai
- Dani Pedrosa took his maiden win in only his fourth MotoGP race, becoming the joint second-youngest winner of a premier-class race and the youngest to win in all three classes of GP racing

ITA/Mugello
- Valentino Rossi took his fifth consecutive win at the Tuscan track, becoming the second most successful 500cc/MotoGP racer of all time with 55 wins

CAT/Catalunya
- Kenny Roberts Jnr's third place is the first ever rostrum finish for his father's Team KR

NED/Assen
- Nicky Hayden gave Honda their 200th win in the top class

CZE/Brno
- Loris Capirossi took victory 16 years and 15 days after his first GP win (on a 125 at Donington in 1990) to make his the longest winning career in GP history

AUS/Phillip Island
- Flag-to-flag wet-weather rules were used for the first time, with the whole field changing bikes
- Marco Melandri won, Chris Vermeulen got his first rostrum

POR/Estoril
- Toni Elias won his first MotoGP race by a margin of just 0.002s after qualifying down in 11th place on the grid

VAL/Ricardo Tormo
- Troy Bayliss won, with Capirossi second, to give Ducati their first one–two in MotoGP
- Bayliss was the first (and so far only) replacement or wild-card rider to win a MotoGP race
- Nicky Hayden finished third, becoming the only rider other than Rossi to win the title on a 990

250cc

SPA/Jerez
- Jorge Lorenzo became the third-youngest winner in the 250cc class after Dani Pedrosa and Alan Carter
- This was the first 250cc race with no Yamaha on the grid since the Argentine GP back in 1963

TUR/Istanbul Park
- Hiroshi Aoyama gave KTM their first victory in the 250cc class

CAT/Catalunya
- Sebastian Porto announced his retirement from GP racing after making a record 160 starts in the class

GER/Sachsenring
- Yuki Takahashi gave Honda their 200th win in 250cc GP racing

VAL/Ricardo Tormo
- Jorge Lorenzo clinched the title by finishing in front of his closest challenger, Andrea Dovizioso

125cc

SPA/Jerez
- Alvaro Bautista's first GP victory gave him the championship lead; the Aprilia-mounted Spaniard kept it all year

QAT/Losail
- Bautista's victory ended a record sequence of 56 races in the 125cc class without a rider scoring back-to-back wins, dating back to Arnaud Vincent's results at Donington Park and then the Sachsenring in 2002

TUR/Istanbul Park
- Hector Faubel won for the first time, followed home by Alvaro Bautista and Sergio Gadea – the first all-Spanish podium in the 125cc class

FRA/Le Mans
- Thomas Luthi's victory was the last time a Honda rider won in the 125cc class

CAT/Catalunya
- Pol Espargaro became the youngest rider to score GP points

GER/Sachsenring
- Mattia Pasini (ITA) gave Aprilia their 200th victory in Grand Prix racing

AUS/Phillip Island
- Alvaro Bautista's win clinched his world title with three races remaining

POR/Estoril
- Bautista's victory was his 14th podium finish of the year – a new record for most rostrum finishes in one season in the class

VAL/Ricardo Tormo
- Bautista's fourth-place finish gave him a new record total for the 125cc class of 338 points

LONGEST WINNING CAREERS IN GP RACING

	Rider	First GP win	Last GP win	Length of winning career
1	Loris Capirossi	125cc/GB/1990	MotoGP/JPN/2007	17 years 49 days
2	Angel Nieto	50cc/DDR/1969	80cc/FRA/1985	16 years 8 days
3	Phil Read	350cc/GB/1961	500cc/CZE/1975	14 years 71 days
4	Loris Reggiani	125cc/GB/1980	250cc/CZE/1993	13 years 12 days
5	Valentino Rossi	125cc/CZE/1996	MotoGP/MAL/2008	12 years 62 days

2006 WORLD CHAMPIONSHIP

MotoGP

Pos	Rider	Nation	Motorcycle	SPA	QAT	TUR	CHN	FRA	ITA	CAT	NED	GBR	GER	USA	CZE	MAL	AUS	JPN	POR	VAL	Total
1	Nicky Hayden	USA	Honda	16	20	16	20	11	16	20	25	9	16	25	7	13	11	11	-	16	252
2	Valentino Rossi	ITA	Yamaha	2	25	13	-	-	25	25	8	20	25	-	20	25	16	20	20	3	247
3	Loris Capirossi	ITA	Ducati	25	16	10	8	20	20	-	1	7	11	8	25	20	9	25	4	20	229
4	Marco Melandri	ITA	Honda	11	9	25	9	25	10	-	9	16	20	16	11	7	25	16	8	11	228
5	Dani Pedrosa	SPA	Honda	20	10	2	25	16	13	-	16	25	13	20	16	16	1	9	-	13	215
6	Kenny Roberts	USA	KR211V	8	6	3	3	-	8	16	11	11	-	13	13	9	2	7	16	8	134
7	Colin Edwards	USA	Yamaha	5	7	7	16	10	4	11	3	10	4	7	6	6	-	8	13	7	124
8	Casey Stoner	AUS	Honda	10	11	20	11	13	-	-	13	13	-	-	10	8	10	-	-	-	119
9	Toni Elias	SPA	Honda	13	8	11	5	7	9	-	-	-	5	1	5	-	7	10	25	10	116
10	John Hopkins	USA	Suzuki	7	-	-	13	1	6	13	10	8	6	10	9	10	4	4	10	5	116
11	Chris Vermeulen	AUS	Honda	4	-	9	-	6	2	10	6	-	9	11	4	5	20	5	7	-	98
12	Makoto Tamada	JPN	Honda	6	2	6	10	9	7	9	5	5	-	5	3	2	6	6	11	4	96
13	Sete Gibernau	SPA	Ducati	-	13	5	7	8	11	-	-	-	8	6	-	11	13	13	-	-	95
14	Shinya Nakano	JPN	Kawasaki	9	5	8	6	4	5	-	20	-	10	-	8	-	8	-	-	9	92
15	Carlos Checa	SPA	Yamaha	3	4	1	2	5	1	8	7	6	7	9	1	4	-	2	9	6	75
16	Randy de Puniet	FRA	Kawasaki	-	-	4	4	-	3	-	2	4	-	4	2	3	5	-	6	-	37
17	Alex Hofmann	GER	Ducati	1	1	-	1	3	-	6	4	3	-	2	-	1	3	-	5	-	30
18	James Ellison	GBR	Yamaha	-	3	-	-	2	-	7	-	2	3	3	-	-	-	1	3	2	26
19	Troy Bayliss	AUS	Ducati	-	-	-	-	-	-	-	-	-	-	-	-	-	-	-	-	25	25
20	Jose Luis Cardoso	SPA	Ducati	-	-	-	-	-	-	5	-	1	2	-	-	-	-	-	2	-	10
21	Kousuke Akiyoshi	JPN	Suzuki	-	-	-	-	-	-	-	-	-	-	-	-	-	-	3	-	-	3
22	Garry McCoy	ITA	Ilmor X3	-	-	-	-	-	-	-	-	-	-	-	-	-	-	-	1	1	2

Scoring system – 25, 20, 16, 13, 11, 10, 9, 8, 7, 6, 5, 4, 3, 2, 1

250cc

Pos	Rider	Nat	Machine	Total
1	Jorge Lorenzo	SPA	Aprilia	289
2	Andrea Dovizioso	ITA	Honda	272
3	Alex de Angelis	RSM	Aprilia	228
4	Hiroshi Aoyama	JPN	KTM	193
5	Roberto Locatelli	ITA	Aprilia	191
6	Yuki Takahashi	JPN	Honda	156
7	Hector Barbera	SPA	Aprilia	152
8	Shuhei Aoyama	JPN	Honda	99
9	Sylvain Guintoli	FRA	Aprilia	96
10	Marco Simoncelli	ITA	Gilera	92

125cc

Pos	Rider	Nat	Machine	Total
1	Alvaro Bautista	SPA	Aprilia	338
2	Mike Kallio	FIN	KTM	262
3	Hector Faubel	SPA	Aprilia	197
4	Mattia Pasini	ITA	Aprilia	192
5	Sergio Gadea	SPA	Aprilia	160
6	Lukas Pesek	CZE	Derbi	154
7	Gabor Talmacsi	HUN	Honda	119
8	Thomas Luthi	SWI	Honda	113
9	Julian Simon	SPA	KTM	97
10	Joan Olive	SPA	Aprilia	85

THE 990 YEARS

A surprisingly small number of racers won in the 990cc era (2002–6). Valentino Rossi won on a Honda and a Yamaha, as did Max Biaggi. With hindsight, Biaggi's two wins in the first year of MotoGP look better and better – the Yamaha didn't win again until Rossi got on it – but Max never put a sustained championship challenge together. Biaggi and Rossi were the only men to win on the 990cc M1. However, the Honda RC211V also carried Tohru Ukawa, Alex Barros, Sete Gibernau, Makoto Tamada, Nicky Hayden, Marco Melandri, Dani Pedrosa and Toni Elias to victory. The factory 990cc Ducati Desmosedici was only ridden by four men and two of them won on it – Loris Capirossi and Troy Bayliss – although the Aussie three-times World Superbike Champion won as a replacement rider in the very last race of 2006, not when he was a regular.

That means only a dozen men stood on top of the rostrum in that time, and three of them did so only once, two of them twice, which makes Rossi's tally of 45 wins from the 82 races quite astounding. The next most successful was Sete Gibernau, with eight wins, one of the very few riders to beat Rossi when there were no weather or machinery factors distorting the picture. His 2003 wins in South Africa and Germany were the highlights.

In their five years the 990cc four-strokes obliterated every record set by the old two-strokes. On tracks that remained unaltered and in races unaffected by weather, race times fell by an average of 1m 28s (3.24 per cent) and lap records by 3.4s (3.19 per cent). Qualifying tyres reduced the average pole time by even more: 3.7s. This means a MotoGP machine would on average take 31 laps to gain a full lap on the best 500. The biggest reduction in the record lap time was at Donington Park, (3.9s), the smallest Phillip Island (2.4s), a reflection of the nature of the two tracks. Donington's stop/start final section was tricky for 500s, Phillip Island's sweepers enabled them to maintain corner speed.

All this was done on a third less petrol than the strokers, but the rate of progress is best shown by the fact that in the five years of the 990 era there were only four dry races where the lap record was not broken.

ABOVE The first and last V5 motors. (*Henk Keulemans*)

BELOW HRC lined up every version of the RC211V at Motegi. (*Henk Keulemans*)

2007

The 800cc formula arrived, and Casey Stoner and the Ducati Desmosedici wiped the floor with the Japanese factories

As the regulations underwent the biggest upheaval since the introduction of MotoGP, teams tried to limit the number of variables by retaining both their riders and their brand of tyre. The Honda, Yamaha and Suzuki factory teams did just that, as did Gresini Honda. Hayden, Pedrosa, Rossi, Edwards, Capirossi, Hopkins, Vermeulen, Elias and Melandri all stayed where they had been in 2006. Team KR also kept their rider, Kenny Roberts Jnr, and their link with Honda, but all did not go well and the younger Roberts brother, Kurtis, joined in at Mugello and then saw out the season as the team's lone rider after Junior's retirement.

Ducati had to find a new rider to replace the retired Sete Gibernau and ended up with a man rumoured to be their third choice: Casey Stoner. The Aussie was in turn replaced at LCR Honda by Carlos Checa in what would be the Spanish veteran's last season in MotoGP. Randy de Puniet stayed with the factory Kawasaki team and was, originally, joined by his fellow-countryman Olivier Jacque, lured back to racing from his preferred role as a test rider. OJ didn't last past the Catalan GP, however, a succession of crashes reminding him of why he'd retired the first time round. Anthony West (AUS) eventually replaced him.

The satellite teams, Gresini excepted, shuffled riders. Nakano replaced Tamada at JiR for his first ride on a Honda, while Tamada went to Tech 3 for his first go on a Yamaha. He was joined by top 250 privateer Sylvain Guintoli (FRA). The d'Antin Ducati team kept Alex Hofmann, although his season would be blighted by serious injury, and brought veteran Alex Barros back from World Superbike for a last Grand Prix season. He and the two Gresini men were the only satellite team riders to stand on the rostrum all season.

After their hopeful try-outs in the final two races of 2006 the Ilmor team returned with veterans Jeremy McWilliams and Andrew Pitt as riders. Unhappily, the bike was nowhere near competitive and that, along with the team's failure to raise sponsorship, meant their season lasted just one race.

ABOVE A ski resort in the middle of winter is a strange place to launch a team. (*Henk Keulemans*)

THE 2007 SEASON

MotoGP

QAT/Losail

- Casey Stoner led every lap in his first race on both a Ducati and Bridgestones to win his first MotoGP
- Stoner set a top speed of 201.8mph/324.7km/h, exactly the same as Rossi's mark the previous year on a 990 Yamaha

SPA/Jerez

- Rossi won for the fifth time at Jerez, making him the most successful rider at the track and ending his longest barren spell since his first 500cc victory at Donington Park in 2000

CHN/Shanghai

- John Hopkins finished third, the first time the Suzuki rider was on a GP rostrum

FRA/Le Mans

- Dani Pedrosa became the youngest rider to reach the milestone of 100 Grand Prix starts
- Chris Vermeulen took his, and Suzuki's, first victory in MotoGP and the factory's first since Sete Gibernau's win in Valencia in 2001. It was also Bridgestone's first wet-weather win

ITA/Mugello

- Valentino Rossi's win took him level with Mick Doohan's record of 95 podium finishes in the top class
- It was also Rossi's 27th victory since joining Yamaha in 2004, making him the most successful Yamaha rider in the top class, with one more victory than Eddie Lawson

CAT/Catalunya

- Rossi finished second to Stoner but set a new record for podium finishes in the top class – 96
- For the first time since the Swedish GP in 1972 the first five riders home in a premier-class GP were on bikes from five different manufacturers

NED/Assen

- Rossi's win was Yamaha's 150th in the top class

GER/Sachsenring

- Dani Pedrosa took Honda's first victory of the 800cc formula, but it was the factory's worst start to a season since they re-entered GP racing full time in 1982

USA/Laguna Seca

- Casey Stoner was fastest in every session, led every lap and won by ten seconds
- Chris Vermeulen scored his first dry-weather podium

RSM/Misano

- Stoner took Ducati's first premier-class victory on Italian soil
- Vermeulen and Hopkins finished second and third, Suzuki's first double podium in MotoGP

POR/Estoril

- Rossi took Italy's 200th GP win in the premier class

JPN/Motegi

- Stoner's worst race of the year, but he secured his and Ducati's first title – and Capirossi won on the factory's other bike
- Randy de Puniet's second place was his first podium in the top class and Kawasaki's first under the 800cc formula
- Sylvain Guintoli's fourth place was the best finish by a Dunlop rider in MotoGP

VAL/Ricardo Tormo

- Dani Pedrosa gave Honda their 50th win of the four-stroke MotoGP era

250cc

ITA/Mugello

- Reigning 125cc champion Alvaro Bautista won for the first time in the 250cc class

GER/Sachsenring

- For the first time in the 250cc class KTM riders finished first (Hiroshi Aoyama) and second (Mika Kallio)

RSM/Misano

- Jorge Lorenzo's 16th win in the 250cc class made him the most successful Spanish 250 rider of all time, with one more victory than both Dani Pedrosa and Sito Pons
- Andrea Dovizioso failed to finish after a mechanical problem, ending a run of 31 successive points-scoring rides

JPN/Motegi

- Mika Kallio became the first Finnish rider to win a 250cc GP since Tepi Lansivuori at Imatra in 1973

MAL/Sepang

- Jorge Lorenzo finished third to clinch his second successive 250cc title

125cc

CHN/Shanghai

- Lukas Pesek became the first Czech rider to win a 125cc Grand Prix
- Pesek's victory was the first by a Czech rider in any class of GP racing since Frantisek Stastny won the 1966 500cc race at the Sachsenring, in East Germany

FRA/Le Mans

- Bradley Smith became the first British rider to finish on the podium in the 125cc class since Robin Milton was second at the 1989 Australian GP at Phillip Island

ITA/Mugello

- Just 0.134s covered the first four riders across the line – the closest top-four finish of all time in 125cc GPs

CZE/Brno

- Hector Faubel took the 300th GP victory by Spanish riders

RSM/Misano

- Mattia Pasini's victory was the 100th 125cc win for Aprilia

VAL/Ricardo Tormo

- Gabor Talmacsi finished second behind his closest rival, Hector Faubel, to become the first Hungarian World Champion
- Faubel's victory was the 14th of the year for Aprilia – a new record

YOUNGEST RIDERS TO WIN THE MOTOGP/500CC WORLD CHAMPIONSHIP

	Rider	Age	Year
1	Freddie Spencer	21 years 258 days	1983
2	Casey Stoner	21 years 342 days	2008
3	Mike Hailwood	22 years 160 days	1962
4	John Surtees	22 years 182 days	1956
5	Valentino Rossi	22 years 240 days	2001
6	Gary Hocking	23 years 316 days	1961
7	Giacomo Agostini	24 years 87 days	1966
8	Umberto Masetti	24 years 129 days	1950
9	Nicky Hayden	25 years 91 days	2006
10	Barry Sheene	25 years 318 days	1976

2007 WORLD CHAMPIONSHIP

MotoGP

Pos	Rider	Nation	Machine	QAT	SPA	TUR	CHN	FRA	ITA	CAT	GBR	NED	GER	USA	CZE	RSM	POR	JPN	AUS	MAL	VAL	Total
1	Casey Stoner	AUS	Ducati	25	11	25	25	16	13	25	25	20	11	25	25	25	16	10	25	25	20	367
2	Dani Pedrosa	SPA	Honda	16	20	-	13	13	20	16	8	13	25	11	13	-	20	-	13	16	25	242
3	Valentino Rossi	ITA	Yamaha	20	25	6	20	10	25	20	13	25	-	13	9	-	25	3	16	11	-	241
4	John Hopkins	USA	Suzuki	13	-	10	16	9	11	13	11	11	9	1	20	16	10	6	9	8	16	189
5	Marco Melandri	ITA	Honda	11	8	11	11	20	7	7	6	6	10	16	-	13	11	11	6	20	13	187
6	Chris Vermeulen	AUS	Suzuki	9	7	5	9	25	8	9	16	-	5	20	11	20	3	5	8	9	10	179
7	Loris Capirossi	ITA	Ducati	-	4	16	10	8	9	10	-	-	20	-	10	11	7	25	20	5	11	166
8	Nicky Hayden	USA	Honda	8	9	9	4	-	6	5	-	16	16	-	16	3	13	7	-	7	8	127
9	Colin Edwards	USA	Yamaha	10	16	-	5	4	4	6	20	10	13	5	-	7	6	2	7	6	3	124
10	Alex Barros	BRA	Ducati	7	5	13	2	-	16	8	9	9	-	7	7	-	-	8	11	4	9	115
11	Randy de Puniet	FRA	Kawasaki	-	3	8	8	-	-	11	10	-	-	10	8	-	-	20	10	13	7	108
12	Toni Elias	SPA	Honda	2	13	20	-	-	10	-	4	-	-	-	5	9	8	16	1	10	6	104
13	Alex Hofmann	GER	Ducati	5	-	7	7	11	5	3	7	8	7	-	-	5	-	-	-	-	-	65
14	Carlos Checa	SPA	Honda	-	10	4	6	-	-	-	-	5	2	2	6	10	9	-	5	2	4	65
15	Anthony West	AUS	Kawasaki	-	-	-	-	-	-	-	5	7	8	9	4	8	4	9	4	1	-	59
16	Sylvain Guintoli	FRA	Yamaha	1	1	1	3	6	2	2	-	2	-	3	3	4	2	13	2	-	5	50
17	Shinya Nakano	JPN	Honda	6	6	3	-	-	3	1	2	4	-	4	2	6	5	-	3	-	2	47
18	Makoto Tamada	JPN	Yamaha	-	2	2	-	7	1	4	1	3	3	8	-	2	-	4	-	-	1	38
19	Kurtis Roberts	USA	KR212V	-	-	-	-	-	-	-	3	1	4	-	1	1	-	-	-	-	-	10
21	Michel Fabrizio	ITA	Honda	-	-	-	-	-	-	-	-	-	6	-	-	-	-	-	-	-	-	6
21	Roger Lee Hayden	USA	Kawasaki	-	-	-	-	-	-	-	-	-	-	6	-	-	-	-	-	-	-	6
22	Fonsi Nieto	SPA	Kawasaki	-	-	-	-	5	-	-	-	-	-	-	-	-	-	-	-	-	-	5
23	Olivier Jacque	FRA	Kawasaki	4	-	-	-	-	-	-	-	-	-	-	-	-	-	-	-	-	-	4
24	Kenny Roberts Jr	USA	KR212V	3	-	-	1	-	-	-	-	-	-	-	-	-	-	-	-	-	-	4
25	Nobuatsu Aoki	JPN	Suzuki	-	-	-	-	-	-	-	-	-	-	-	-	-	-	-	-	3	-	3
26	Shinichi Ito	JPN	Ducati	-	-	-	-	-	-	-	-	-	-	-	-	-	-	1	-	-	-	1

Scoring system – 25, 20, 16, 13, 11, 10, 9, 8, 7, 6, 5, 4, 3, 2, 1

250cc

Pos	Rider	Nat	Machine	Total
1	Jorge Lorenzo	SPA	Aprilia	312
2	Andrea Dovizioso	ITA	Honda	260
3	Alex de Angelis	RSM	Aprilia	235
4	Alvaro Bautista	SPA	Aprilia	181
5	Hector Barbera	SPA	Aprilia	177
6	Hiroshi Aoyama	JPN	KTM	160
7	Mika Kallio	FIN	KTM	157
8	Thomas Luthi	SWI	Aprilia	133
9	Julian Simon	SPA	Honda	123
10	Marco Simoncelli	ITA	Gilera	97

125cc

Pos	Rider	Nat	Machine	Total
1	Gabor Talmacsi	HUN	Aprilia	282
2	Hector Faubel	SPA	Aprilia	277
3	Tomoyoshi Koyama	JPN	KTM	193
4	Lukas Pesek	CZE	Derbi	182
5	Mattia Pasini	ITA	Aprilia	174
6	Simone Corsi	ITA	Aprilia	168
7	Sergio Gadea	SPA	Aprilia	160
8	Joan Olive	SPA	Aprilia	131
9	Pol Espargaro	SPA	Aprilia	110
10	Bradley Smith	GBR	Honda	101

Fastest lap times for the new 800s were on average 0.066s slower than for the 990s:
Losail –0.78s; Jerez +0.31s; Istanbul +1.15s; Shanghai +0.54s; Mugello +0.24s; Catalunya +0.2s; Assen +0.33s; Sachsenring –0.27s; Laguna Seca –0.79s; Brno +0.14s; Estoril –0.42s; Phillip Island +0.47s; Sepang –0.02s; Valencia –0.18s

TRIPLE WHAMMY

There were three significant changes in the regulations: first, the reduction in engine capacity from 990 to 800cc; second, the reduction in fuel-tank capacity to 21 litres from 22; and third, MotoGP got its first ever restriction on tyres. Only Honda had a totally new motorcycle, a V4 instead of a V5. All the other factories re-engineered their bikes but stuck to their existing designs.

The first change meant bikes no longer had an excess of power and now relied on high corner speed, much like a pumped-up 250. The fuel restriction had a greater effect than most people predicted, making ignition mapping and engine management the crucial part of race set-up. As for the tyres, riders were now restricted to 31 tyres per weekend, split 14/17 front/rear, to be selected on a Thursday evening and barcoded by the MotoGP scrutineer, Mike Webb. This rule only applied to tyre companies that had won races in the past two years, so the Tech 3 Yamaha riders, the only Dunlop users, had no such restrictions. There was no limit on the number of wet-weather tyres.

This rule obviously favoured the manufacturer that could produce tyres which worked over a broad spectrum of conditions – and that happened to be Bridgestone. The Japanese company had always worked that way, whereas Michelin, thanks to the proximity of their Clermont-Ferrand factory to most European tracks, were known to manufacture new tyres overnight and thus could afford to make their rubber work superbly in a very narrow temperature or humidity range.

One, and only one, combination of rider, tyre and motorcycle got everything right. At the first race of the year Casey Stoner motored past Rossi's Yamaha on the front straight as if the Italian were on a 250; Ducati had got their fuel usage optimised, but only the Aussie could use the peaky motor that was the trade-off for fuel efficiency. His Bridgestone tyres, while not perfect everywhere, did a good job. Rossi and Michelin were falling out with each other, as the shadow of a financial scandal fell across the Italian. Valentino may have had his problems and distractions, but there was no doubt Stoner and Ducati were the perfect combination in 2007.

ABOVE Stoner drove away from the opposition at Qatar like they were standing still. (*Henk Keulemans*)

CASEY STONER RESULTS AND STATISTICS

- **Casey Stoner was the second-youngest rider to win the premier-class title, after 1983 World Champion Freddie Spencer**
- **Stoner won ten races in 2007 – only Giacomo Agostini, Mick Doohan and Valentino Rossi have won more top-class races in a single season**
- **He also became the second-youngest rider to win three consecutive premier-class races – again, only Spencer achieved that at a younger age**
- **Casey was the first rider in the four-stroke MotoGP era to have led every lap for three successive races**
- **Stoner's MotoGP victory in Qatar made him the youngest Australian rider to win in the top class, taking the record from Daryl Beattie, and the first Australian to win in all three current GP classes**
- **His points total for 2007 – 367 – equalled the highest ever single-season total, achieved by Valentino Rossi in 2005**
- **Stoner set a new record in 2007 of 18 points-scoring finishes in a single season**

ABOVE Mr & Mrs Stoner celebrate another win. (*Henk Keulemans*)

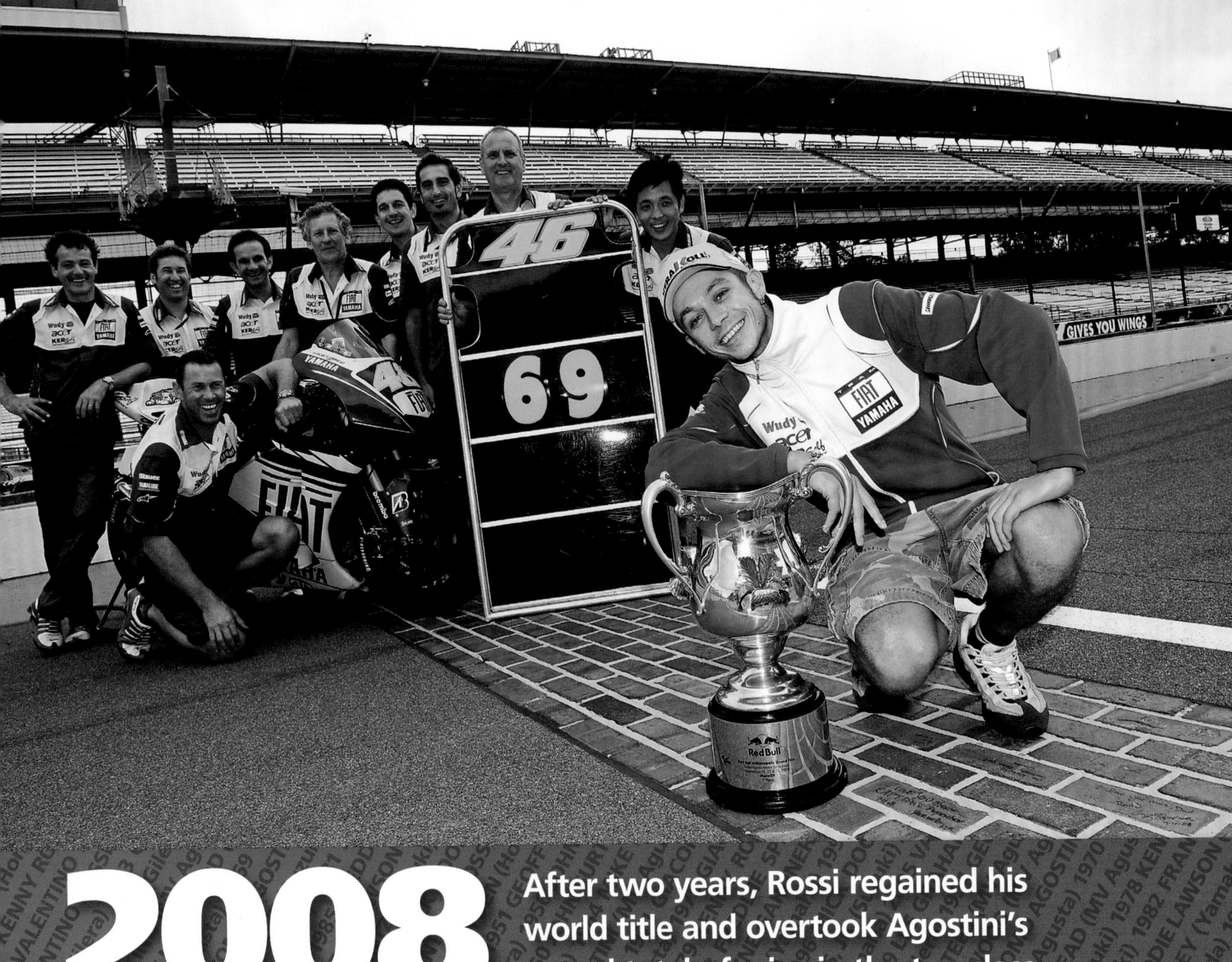

2008

After two years, Rossi regained his world title and overtook Agostini's record total of wins in the top class

World Champion Casey Stoner got a new team-mate at Ducati when team-manager Livio Suppo finally achieved his ambition and signed Marco Melandri. There was a new man at the factory Yamaha team, too, double 250 World Champion Jorge Lorenzo. His arrival meant Colin Edwards moved to Tech 3 to team with another new boy, British double World Superbike Champion James Toseland. Honda stuck with Dani Pedrosa and Nicky Hayden in the factory team, but changed both Gresini riders: Shinya Nakano, whom the factory thought deserved another year, came in alongside another rookie, Alex de Angelis (RSM). JiR formed an alliance with the Scott team to bring another 250 ace to MotoGP, Italian Andrea Dovizioso. Team KR, after a disastrous 2007, could not raise the budget to race in '08.

The big-money signing was John Hopkins's move from Suzuki to Kawasaki; Anthony West, who'd stepped in mid-way through '07, kept his job on the green bike. Hopper's seat at Suzuki was taken by Loris Capirossi, with Chris Vermeulen staying for his third year with the team. Randy de Puniet moved from Kawasaki to the LCR Honda satellite team. Ducati's satellite team started the season under the direction of Spanish founder Luis d'Antin, but when he was levered out after the German GP the Bologna factory started the process of bringing the operation closer to home.

The big subject of the year was tyres. Michelin had a trio of disasters in the middle of the season, and with Rossi having engineered a switch to Bridgestone over winter (for him, not for his team-mate) momentum was building for the move to a single tyre supplier. When, after the San Marino GP, Dani Pedrosa announced that he too (but not his team-mate) would be switching brands with immediate effect the deal was all but done.

Every factory except Honda now used pneumatic valve springs. HRC sent Tadayuki Okada to Mugello to give their system its first outing, and Nicky Hayden finally got to race with them at Assen. Satellite Hondas used conventional engines all season.

ABOVE Rossi and crew celebrate his record-breaking win on the Indianapolis Motor Speedway's line of bricks. (*Henk Keulemans*)

THE 2008 SEASON

MotoGP

QAT/Losail

- Jorge Lorenzo became the first rookie to start from pole in his first premier-class GP since Max Biaggi in 1998
- The average age of the three riders finishing on the podium (Stoner, Lorenzo and Pedrosa) was just 21 years 47 weeks – the youngest ever podium in the premier class

SPA/Jerez

- Dani Pedrosa's win took him to the top of the championship for the first time. It was also the first time he'd been on the rostrum in four consecutive races
- Rossi's second place was his first podium on Bridgestones and his 100th in the premier class
- Lorenzo became the first rider to set poles in his first two rides in the premier class

POR/Estoril

- Lorenzo set his third pole in three races and won, obliterating all previous achievements by a rookie, and in the process becoming the 100th different rider to win a premier-class GP

CHN/Shanghai

- John Hopkins became the youngest rider to make 100 starts in the top class
- Rossi had his first win on Bridgestones, ending his longest streak without a victory – eight months, stretching back to the 2007 Portuguese GP

ITA/Mugello

- Lorenzo became the youngest rider to make his 100th GP start
- Rossi won at Mugello for the seventh time in a row and made it three wins in a row for the first time since 2005

GER/Sachsenring

- Stoner took his third consecutive win from his fourth consecutive pole position – and made this the 100th win for an Australian in the top class
- Valentino Rossi started his 202nd consecutive GP, a new record

RSM/Misano

- Loris Capirossi set a new record for GP appearances – 277. Loris had ridden in an astonishing 37.5 per cent of all GP events
- Toni Elias made it back-to-back rostrums for the first time in his MotoGP career

USA-INY/Indianapolis

- Rossi became the most successful rider in the top class, with 69 wins. This win gave him the full set: wins at every GP track on the calendar
- Ben Spies (USA, Suzuki) was sixth, the best result for a wild-card since Troy Bayliss won at Valencia in 2006

JPN/Motegi

- Rossi won, clinching his eighth career title and his sixth in the top class

AUS/Phillip Island

- All three riders on the podium were either reigning or past MotoGP World Champions, something that had only happened once before in the top class – at the Czech GP in 1990, when Wayne Rainey won the race and in front of previous champions Wayne Gardner and Eddie Lawson

MAL/Sepang

- Rossi won, to stand on a GP rostrum for the 150th time
- Andrea Dovizioso finished third for his first rostrum in MotoGP

250cc

QAT/Losail

- Mattia Pasini (Aprilia) won on his debut ride in the 250cc class

POR/Estoril

- Marco Simoncelli started from pole for the first time since moving up to the 250cc class at the start of 2006 – the first 250cc pole for Gilera
- Following his third-place finish in Portugal, Mika Kallio led the championship for the first time – the first time a KTM rider had topped the table

FRA/Le Mans

- Alex Debon (SPA, Aprilia) took his first victory in his 112th GP start

ITA/Mugello

- Simoncelli won for the first time in the 250cc class and also made it the first win for Gilera in the class

USA-INY/Indianapolis

- The 250cc race was cancelled due to severe weather conditions

JPN/Motegi

- Simoncelli's victory was the 200th consecutive win in the 250cc class for riders using Dunlop tyres

MAL/Sepang

- Marco Simoncelli finished third to clinch his first world title

125cc

QAT/Losail

- Bradley Smith became the first British rider in 35 years to start from pole in a 125cc GP
- On his debut, British teenager Scott Redding became the youngest rider to qualify on the front row for a GP race

FRA/Le Mans

- Mike de Meglio became the first home rider to win in the 125cc class at Le Mans since Guy Bertin in 1979; the win had him leading the World Championship for the first time

ITA/Mugello

- Just 0.036s covered the first three riders across the line – the closest podium of all time in a 125cc GP

GBR/Donington

- Scott Redding became the first British rider to win a 125cc GP since Chas Mortimer at the Spanish GP at Jarama in 1973 – and, at the age of 15 years and 170 days, the youngest GP winner of all time
- The average age of the podium finishers (Redding, di Meglio and Spanish youngster Marc Marquez) was just 17 years 29 days – the youngest ever podium in GP racing

CZE/Brno

- Stefan Bradl took his first victory to become the sixth son of a former GP winner also to win a World Championship race

USA-INY/Indianapolis

- In the first ever GP race to be held at the famous circuit, Nicolas Terol (SPA, Aprilia) took his first victory in a race cut short by rain
- Terol's victory was the 250th win for Aprilia in GP racing

2008 WORLD CHAMPIONSHIP

MotoGP

Pos	Rider	Nation	Machine	QAT	SPA	POR	CHN	FRA	ITA	CAT	GBR	NED	GER	USA	CZE	RSM	INP	JPN	AUS	MAL	VAL	Total
1	Valentino Rossi	ITA	Yamaha	11	20	16	25	25	25	20	20	5	20	25	25	25	25	25	20	25	16	373
2	Casey Stoner	AUS	Ducati	25	5	10	16	-	20	16	25	25	25	20	-	-	13	20	25	10	25	280
3	Dani Pedrosa	SPA	Honda	16	25	20	20	13	16	25	16	20	-	-	1	13	8	16	-	20	20	249
4	Jorge Lorenzo	SPA	Yamaha	20	16	25	13	20	-	-	10	10	-	-	6	20	16	13	13	-	8	190
5	Andrea Dovizioso	ITA	Honda	13	8	-	5	10	8	13	11	11	11	13	7	8	11	7	9	16	13	174
6	Nicky Hayden	USA	Honda	6	13	-	10	8	3	8	9	13	3	11	-	-	20	11	16	13	11	155
7	Colin Edwards	USA	Yamaha	9	-	13	9	16	11	11	13	16	-	2	2	6	1	9	8	8	10	144
8	Chris Vermeulen	AUS	Suzuki	-	6	8	-	11	6	9	8	9	16	16	10	11	7	-	1	7	3	128
9	Shinya Nakano	JPN	Honda	3	7	6	6	6	7	7	7	8	7	6	13	4	-	8	11	11	9	126
10	Loris Capirossi	ITA	Suzuki	8	11	7	7	9	9	-	-	-	9	1	16	9	-	10	6	9	7	118
11	James Toseland	GBR	Yamaha	10	10	9	4	-	10	10	-	7	5	7	3	10	-	5	10	-	5	105
12	Toni Elias	SPA	Ducati	2	1	4	8	5	4	-	5	4	4	9	20	16	4	-	5	1	-	92
13	Sylvain Guintoli	FRA	Ducati	1	-	2	1	3	5	3	3	6	10	4	4	5	9	2	2	3	4	67
14	Alex de Angelis	RSM	Honda	-	2	5	-	4	13	-	1	-	13	3	8	-	6	-	-	2	6	63
15	Randy de Puniet	FRA	Honda	7	-	1	3	7	-	-	4	-	8	10	-	-	3	4	7	6	1	61
16	John Hopkins	USA	Kawasaki	4	9	11	2	-	-	6	-	-	-	-	5	2	2	6	3	5	2	57
17	Marco Melandri	ITA	Ducati	5	4	3	11	1	-	5	-	3	-	-	9	7	-	3	-	-	-	51
18	Anthony West	AUS	Kawasaki	-	3	-	-	2	1	4	6	-	6	-	11	3	5	1	4	4	-	50
19	Ben Spies	USA	Suzuki	-	-	-	-	-	-	-	2	-	-	8	-	-	10	-	-	-	-	20
20	Jamie Hacking	USA	Kawasaki	-	-	-	-	-	-	-	-	-	-	5	-	-	-	-	-	-	-	5
21	Tadayuki Okada	JPN	Honda	-	-	-	-	-	2	-	-	-	-	-	-	-	-	-	-	-	-	2

Scoring system – 25, 20, 16, 13, 11, 10, 9, 8, 7, 6, 5, 4, 3, 2, 1

250cc

Pos	Rider	Nat	Machine	Total
1	Marco Simoncelli	ITA	Gilera	281
2	Alvaro Bautista	SPA	Aprilia	244
3	Mika Kallio	FIN	KTM	196
4	Alex Debon	SPA	Aprilia	176
5	Yuki Takahashi	JPN	Honda	167
6	Hector Barbera	SPA	Aprilia	142
7	Hiroshi Aoyama	JPN	KTM	139
8	Mattia Pasini	ITA	Aprilia	132
9	Roberto Locatelli	ITA	Gilera	110
10	Julian Simon	SPA	KTM	109

125cc

Pos	Rider	Nat	Machine	Total
1	Mike Di Meglio	FRA	Derbi	264
2	Simone Corsi	ITA	Aprilia	225
3	Gabor Talmacsi	HUN	Aprilia	206
4	Stefan Bradl	GER	Aprilia	187
5	Nicolas Terol	SPA	Aprilia	176
6	Bradley Smith	GBR	Aprilia	150
7	Joan Olive	SPA	Derbi	142
8	Sandro Cortese	GER	Aprilia	141
9	Pol Espargaro	SPA	Derbi	124
10	Andrea Iannone	ITA	Aprilia	106

YOUNGEST RIDERS TO WIN A GRAND PRIX (ALL 125CC RACES)

	Rider	Age	Race
1	Scott Redding (GBR)	15 years 170 days	GBR/Donington/2008
2.	Marco Melandri (ITA)	15 years 324 days	NED/Assen/1998
3	Jorge Lorenzo (SPA)	16 years 139 days	RIO/Jacarepagua/2003
4	Ivan Goi (ITA)	16 years 157 days	AUT-A1-Ring/1996
5	Hector Barbera (SPA)	16 years 253 days	GBR/Donington/2003
6	Dani Pedrosa (SPA)	16 years 273 days	NED/Assen/2002
7	Marco Simoncelli (ITA)	17 years 103 days	SPA/Jerez/2004
8	Loris Capirossi (ITA)	17 years 123 days	GBR/Donington/1990
9	Valentino Rossi (ITA)	17 years 184 days	CZE/Brno/1996
10	Mike Di Meglio (FRA)	17 years 279 days	TUR/Istanbul Park/2005

EIGHT AND COUNTING

According to Valentino Rossi this, his eighth world title, was the toughest of the lot. Just how tough can be gauged from the fact that only one other rider, Giacomo Agostini, regained the top-class title after two fallow years. On the way to equalling one of Ago's achievements, Valentino broke another even more significant record. His win at Indianapolis was Rossi's 69th in the top class, a new record. Another of Ago's record totals, 159 podiums in all classes, was in danger as well, because this was Rossi's 147th top-three finish across all classes.

Agostini won 68 500cc GPs from 119 starts, a strike rate of 57.1 per cent, while Valentino's 69 win from 146 starts equates to 47.2 per cent, but do the calculation for rostrum finishes and Vale comes out on top, with 76 versus 74 per cent. However, Rossi himself has said that Agostini's total of 122 wins and 15 world titles are probably out of reach.

The win at Motegi gave Rossi his sixth title in the premier class, one clear of Mick Doohan's total, leaving only Agostini with eight ahead of him. Add in Rossi's 125 and 250 titles to get the total of eight championships and he has only been beaten by Mike Hailwood and Carlo Ubbiali (9 titles apiece), Angel Nieto (13) and, of course, Agostini (15). Rossi's first title came in 1997, and only Angel Nieto's championship career was longer: the Spanish star won the 50cc title in 1969 and his final title was the 125cc crown in 1984.

This was Rossi's first title under the 800cc MotoGP formula, so he became the first man to take the title on four different types of motorcycle, the others being 990cc Yamaha M1, Honda RC211V V5 and the Honda NSR500 two-stroke. The thing that pleased Valentino as much as anything was that this was his 37th win and third title for Yamaha, more than he achieved with any other factory. He is Yamaha's most successful rider of all time (Eddie Lawson won 26 GPs and three titles) and the man himself is more than content that this means he will now be remembered as a Yamaha rider.

LEFT The best crash helmet design ever? Rossi's special self-portrait for the Mugello GP. (*Henk Keulemans*)

LEFT MotoGP under floodlights? Who'd have thought it? (*Henk Keulemans*)

THE WORLD CHAMPIONS

1949		NAT	MOTORCYCLE
500cc	Leslie Graham	GBR	AJS
350cc	Freddie Frith	GBR	Velocette
250cc	Bruno Ruffo	ITA	Moto Guzzi
125cc	Nello Pagani	ITA	Mondial

1950		NAT	MOTORCYCLE
500cc	Umberto Masetti	ITA	Gilera
350cc	Bob Foster	GBR	Velocette
250cc	Dario Ambrosini	ITA	Benelli
125cc	Bruno Ruffo	ITA	Mondial

1951		NAT	MOTORCYCLE
500cc	Geoff Duke	GBR	Norton
350cc	Geoff Duke	GBR	Norton
250cc	Bruno Ruffo	ITA	Moto Guzzi
125cc	Carlo Ubbiali	ITA	Mondial

1952		NAT	MOTORCYCLE
500cc	Umberto Masetti	ITA	Gilera
350cc	Geoff Duke	GBR	Norton
250cc	Enrico Lorenzetti	ITA	Moto Guzzi
125cc	Cecil Sandford	GBR	MV Agusta

1953		NAT	MOTORCYCLE
500cc	Geoff Duke	GBR	Gilera
350cc	Fergus Anderson	GBR	Moto Guzzi
250cc	Werner Haas	GER	NSU
125cc	Werner Haas	GER	NSU

1954		NAT	MOTORCYCLE
500cc	Geoff Duke	GBR	Gilera
350cc	Fergus Anderson	GBR	Moto Guzzi
250cc	Werner Haas	GER	NSU
125cc	Rupert Hollaus	AUT	NSU

1955		NAT	MOTORCYCLE
500cc	Geoff Duke	GBR	Gilera
350cc	Bill Lomas	GBR	Moto Guzzi
250cc	Hermann-Paul Muller	GER	NSU
125cc	Carlo Ubbiali	ITA	MV Agusta

1956		NAT	MOTORCYCLE
500cc	John Surtees	GBR	MV Agusta
350cc	Bill Lomas	GBR	Moto Guzzi
250cc	Carlo Ubbiali	ITA	MV Agusta
125cc	Carlo Ubbiali	ITA	MV Agusta

1957		NAT	MOTORCYCLE
1957			
500cc	Libero Liberati	ITA	Gilera
350cc	Keith Campbell	AUS	Moto Guzzi
250cc	Cecil Sandford	GBR	Mondial
125cc	Tarquinio Provini	ITA	Mondial

1958		NAT	MOTORCYCLE
500cc	John Surtees	GBR	MV Agusta
350cc	John Surtees	GBR	MV Agusta
250cc	Tarquinio Provini	ITA	MV Agusta
125cc	Carlo Ubbiali	ITA	MV Agusta

1959		NAT	MOTORCYCLE
500cc	John Surtees	GBR	MV Agusta
350cc	John Surtees	GBR	MV Agusta
250cc	Carlo Ubbiali	ITA	MV Agusta
125cc	Carlo Ubbiali	ITA	MV Agusta

1960		NAT	MOTORCYCLE
500cc	John Surtees	GBR	MV Agusta
350cc	John Surtees	GBR	MV Agusta
250cc	Carlo Ubbiali	ITA	MV Agusta
125cc	Carlo Ubbiali	ITA	MV Agusta

1961		NAT	MOTORCYCLE
500cc	Gary Hocking	RHO	MV Agusta
350cc	Gary Hocking	RHO	MV Agusta
250cc	Mike Hailwood	GBR	Honda
125cc	Tom Phillis	AUS	Honda

1962		NAT	MOTORCYCLE
500cc	Mike Hailwood	GBR	MV Agusta
350cc	Jim Redman	RHO	Honda
250cc	Jim Redman	RHO	Honda
125cc	Luigi Taveri	SWI	Honda
50cc	Ernst Degner	GER	Suzuki

1963		NAT	MOTORCYCLE
500cc	Mike Hailwood	GBR	MV Agusta
350cc	Jim Redman	RHO	Honda
250cc	Jim Redman	RHO	Honda
125cc	Hugh Anderson	NZE	Suzuki
50cc	Hugh Anderson	NZE	Suzuki

1964		NAT	MOTORCYCLE
500cc	Mike Hailwood	GBR	MV Agusta
350cc	Jim Redman	RHO	Honda
250cc	Phil Read	GBR	Yamaha
125cc	Luigi Taveri	SWI	Honda
50cc	Hugh Anderson	NZE	Suzuki

1965		NAT	MOTORCYCLE
500cc	Mike Hailwood	GBR	MV Agusta
350cc	Jim Redman	RHO	Honda
250cc	Phil Read	GBR	Yamaha
125cc	Hugh Anderson	NZE	Suzuki
50cc	Ralph Bryans	GBR	Honda

1966		NAT	MOTORCYCLE
500cc	Giacomo Agostini	ITA	MV Agusta
350cc	Mike Hailwood	GBR	Honda
250cc	Mike Hailwood	GBR	Honda
125cc	Luigi Taveri	SWI	Honda
50cc	Hans-Georg Anscheidt	GER	Suzuki

1967		NAT	MOTORCYCLE
500cc	Giacomo Agostini	ITA	MV Agusta
350cc	Mike Hailwood	GBR	Honda
250cc	Mike Hailwood	GBR	Honda
125cc	Bill Ivy	GBR	Yamaha
50cc	Hans-Georg Anscheidt	GER	Suzuki

1968		NAT	MOTORCYCLE
500cc	Giacomo Agostini	ITA	MV Agusta
350cc	Giacomo Agostini	ITA	MV Agusta
250cc	Phil Read	GBR	Yamaha
125cc	Phil Read	GBR	Yamaha
50cc	Hans-Georg Anscheidt	GER	Suzuki

1969		NAT	MOTORCYCLE
500cc	Giacomo Agostini	ITA	MV Agusta
350cc	Giacomo Agostini	ITA	MV Agusta
250cc	Kel Carruthers	AUS	Benelli
125cc	Dave Simmonds	GBR	Kawasaki
50cc	Angel Nieto	SPA	Derbi

1970		NAT	MOTORCYCLE
500cc	Giacomo Agostini	ITA	MV Agusta
350cc	Giacomo Agostini	ITA	MV Agusta
250cc	Rod Gould	GBR	Yamaha
125cc	Dieter Braun	GER	Suzuki
50cc	Angel Nieto	SPA	Derbi

1971		NAT	MOTORCYCLE
500cc	Giacomo Agostini	ITA	MV Agusta
350cc	Giacomo Agostini	ITA	MV Agusta
250cc	Phil Read	GBR	Yamaha
125cc	Angel Nieto	SPA	Derbi
50cc	Jan de Vries	NED	Kreidler

1972		NAT	MOTORCYCLE
500cc	Giacomo Agostini	ITA	MV Agusta
350cc	Giacomo Agostini	ITA	MV Agusta
250cc	Jarno Saarinen	FIN	Yamaha
125cc	Angel Nieto	SPA	Derbi
50cc	Angel Nieto	SPA	Derbi

1973		NAT	MOTORCYCLE
500cc	Phil Read	GBR	MV Agusta
350cc	Giacomo Agostini	ITA	MV Agusta
250cc	Dieter Braun	GER	Yamaha
125cc	Kent Andersson	SWE	Yamaha
50cc	Jan de Vries	NED	Kreidler

1974		NAT	MOTORCYCLE
500cc	Phil Read	GBR	MV Agusta
350cc	Giacomo Agostini	ITA	Yamaha
250cc	Walter Villa	ITA	Harley Davidson
125cc	Kent Andersson	SWE	Yamaha
50cc	Henk van Kessel	NED	Kreidler

1975		NAT	MOTORCYCLE
500cc	Giacomo Agostini	ITA	Yamaha
350cc	Johnny Cecotto	VEN	Yamaha
250cc	Walter Villa	ITA	Harley Davidson
125cc	Paolo Pileri	ITA	Morbidelli
50cc	Angel Nieto	SPA	Kreidler

1976		NAT	MOTORCYCLE
500cc	Barry Sheene	GBR	Suzuki
350cc	Walter Villa	ITA	Harley Davidson
250cc	Walter Villa	ITA	Harley Davidson
125cc	Pierpaolo Bianchi	ITA	Morbidelli
50cc	Angel Nieto	SPA	Bultaco

1977		NAT	MOTORCYCLE
500cc	Barry Sheene	GBR	Suzuki
350cc	Takazumi Katayama	JPN	Yamaha
250cc	Mario Lega	ITA	Morbidelli
125cc	Pierpaolo Bianchi	ITA	Morbidelli
50cc	Angel Nieto	SPA	Bultaco

1978		NAT	MOTORCYCLE
500cc	Kenny Roberts	USA	Yamaha
350cc	Kork Ballington	RSA	Kawasaki
250cc	Kork Ballington	RSA	Kawasaki
125cc	Eugenio Lazzarini	ITA	MBA
50cc	Ricardo Tormo	SPA	Bultaco

1979		NAT	MOTORCYCLE
500cc	Kenny Roberts	USA	Yamaha
350cc	Kork Ballington	RSA	Kawasaki
250cc	Kork Ballington	RSA	Kawasaki
125cc	Angel Nieto	SPA	Minarelli
50cc	Eugenio Lazzarini	ITA	Kreidler

1980		NAT	MOTORCYCLE
500cc	Kenny Roberts	USA	Yamaha
350cc	Jon Ekerold	RSA	Yamaha
250cc	Anton Mang	GER	Kawasaki
125cc	Pierpaolo Bianchi	ITA	MBA
50cc	Eugenio Lazzarini	ITA	Kreilder/Iprem

1981		NAT	MOTORCYCLE
500cc	Marco Lucchinelli	ITA	Suzuki
350cc	Anton Mang	GER	Kawasaki
250cc	Anton Mang	GER	Kawasaki
125cc	Angel Nieto	SPA	Minarelli
50cc	Ricardo Tormo	SPA	Bultaco

1982		NAT	MOTORCYCLE
500cc	Franco Uncini	ITA	Suzuki
350cc	Anton Mang	GER	Kawasaki
250cc	Jean-Louis Tournadre	FRA	Yamaha
125cc	Angel Nieto	SPA	Garelli
50cc	Stefan Dorflinger	SWI	Kreidler

1983		NAT	MOTORCYCLE
500cc	Freddie Spencer	USA	Honda
250cc	Carlos Lavado	VEN	Yamaha
125cc	Angel Nieto	SPA	Garelli
50cc	Stefan Dorflinger	SWI	Kreidler

1984		NAT	MOTORCYCLE
500cc	Eddie Lawson	USA	Yamaha
250cc	Christian Sarron	FRA	Yamaha
125cc	Angel Nieto	SPA	Garelli
80cc	Stefan Dorflinger	SWI	Zundapp

1985		NAT	MOTORCYCLE
500cc	Freddie Spencer	USA	Honda
250cc	Freddie Spencer	USA	Honda
125cc	Fausto Gresini	ITA	Garelli
80cc	Stefan Dorflinger	SWI	Krauser

1986		NAT	MOTORCYCLE
500cc	Eddie Lawson	USA	Yamaha
250cc	Carlos Lavado	VEN	Yamaha
125cc	Luca Cadalora	ITA	Garelli
80cc	Jorge Martinez	SPA	Derbi

1987		NAT	MOTORCYCLE
500cc	Wayne Gardner	AUS	Honda
250cc	Anton Mang	GER	Honda
125cc	Fausto Gresini	ITA	Garelli
80cc	Jorge Martinez	SPA	Derbi

1988		NAT	MOTORCYCLE
500cc	Eddie Lawson	USA	Yamaha
250cc	Sito Pons	SPA	Honda
125cc	Jorge Martinez	SPA	Derbi
80cc	Jorge Martinez	SPA	Derbi

1989		NAT	MOTORCYCLE
500cc	Eddie Lawson	USA	Honda
250cc	Sito Pons	SPA	Honda
125cc	Alex Criville	SPA	JJ Cobas
80cc	Manuel Herreros	SPA	Derbi

1990		NAT	MOTORCYCLE
500cc	Wayne Rainey	USA	Yamaha
250cc	John Kocinski	USA	Yamaha
125cc	Loris Capirossi	ITA	Honda

1991		NAT	MOTORCYCLE
500cc	Wayne Rainey	USA	Yamaha
250cc	Luca Cadalora	ITA	Honda
125cc	Loris Capirossi	ITA	Honda

1992		NAT	MOTORCYCLE
500cc	Wayne Rainey	USA	Yamaha
250cc	Luca Cadalora	ITA	Honda
125cc	Alessandro Gramigni	ITA	Aprilia

1993		NAT	MOTORCYCLE
500cc	Kevin Schwantz	USA	Suzuki
250cc	Tetsuya Harada	JPN	Yamaha
125cc	Dirk Raudies	GER	Honda

1994		NAT	MOTORCYCLE
500cc	Mick Doohan	AUS	Honda
250cc	Max Biaggi	ITA	Aprilia
125cc	Kazuto Sakata	JPN	Aprilia

1995		NAT	MOTORCYCLE
500cc	Mick Doohan	AUS	Honda
250cc	Max Biaggi	ITA	Aprilia
125cc	Haruchika Aoki	JPN	Honda

1996		NAT	MOTORCYCLE
500cc	Mick Doohan	AUS	Honda
250cc	Max Biaggi	ITA	Aprilia
125cc	Haruchika Aoki	JPN	Honda

1997		NAT	MOTORCYCLE
500cc	Mick Doohan	AUS	Honda
250cc	Max Biaggi	ITA	Honda
125cc	Valentino Rossi	ITA	Aprilia

1998		NAT	MOTORCYCLE
500cc	Mick Doohan	AUS	Honda
250cc	Loris Capirossi	ITA	Aprilia
125cc	Kazuto Sakata	JPN	Aprilia

1999		NAT	MOTORCYCLE
500cc	Alex Criville	SPA	Honda
250cc	Valentino Rossi	ITA	Aprilia
125cc	Emilio Alzamora	SPA	Honda

2000		NAT	MOTORCYCLE
500cc	Kenny Roberts Jnr	USA	Suzuki
250cc	Olivier Jacque	FRA	Yamaha
125cc	Roberto Locatelli	ITA	Aprilia

2001		NAT	MOTORCYCLE
500cc	Valentino Rossi	ITA	Honda
250cc	Daijiro Kato	JPN	Honda
125cc	Manuel Poggiali	RSM	Gilera

2002		NAT	MOTORCYCLE
MotoGP	Valentino Rossi	ITA	Honda
250cc	Marco Melandri	ITA	Aprilia
125cc	Arnaud Vincent	FRA	Aprilia

2003		NAT	MOTORCYCLE
MotoGP	Valentino Rossi	ITA	Honda
250cc	Manuel Poggiali	RSM	Aprilia
125cc	Dani Pedrosa	SPA	Honda

2004		NAT	MOTORCYCLE
MotoGP	Valentino Rossi	ITA	Yamaha
250cc	Dani Pedrosa	SPA	Honda
125cc	Andrea Dovizioso	ITA	Honda

2005		NAT	MOTORCYCLE
MotoGP	Valentino Rossi	ITA	Yamaha
250cc	Dani Pedrosa	SPA	Honda
125cc	Thomas Luthi	SWI	Honda

2006		NAT	MOTORCYCLE
MotoGP	Nicky Hayden	USA	Honda
250cc	Jorge Lorenzo	SPA	Aprilia
125cc	Alvaro Bautista	SPA	Aprilia

2007		NAT	MOTORCYCLE
MotoGP	Casey Stoner	AUS	Ducati
250cc	Jorge Lorenzo	SPA	Aprilia
125cc	Gabor Talmacsi	HUN	Aprilia

2008		NAT	MOTORCYCLE
MotoGP	Valentino Rossi	ITA	Yamaha
250cc	Marco Simoncelli	ITA	Gilera
125cc	Mike Di Meglio	FRA	Derbi

GRAND PRIX WINNERS

Every rider who has won a Grand Prix from 1949 to 2008, listed in order of number of wins

Full name	NAT	GP wins
Giacomo Agostini	ITA	122
Valentino Rossi	ITA	97
Angel Nieto	SPA	90
Mike Hailwood	GBR	76
Mick Doohan	AUS	54
Phil Read	GBR	52
Jim Redman	RHO	45
Anton Mang	GER	42
Max Biaggi	ITA	42
Carlo Ubbiali	ITA	39
John Surtees	GBR	38
Jorge Martinez	SPA	37
Luca Cadalora	ITA	34
Geoff Duke	GBR	33
Eddie Lawson	USA	31
Kork Ballington	RSA	31
Luigi Taveri	SWI	30
Daniel Pedrosa	SPA	29
Loris Capirossi	ITA	29
Eugenio Lazzarini	ITA	27
Freddie Spencer	USA	27
Pierpaolo Bianchi	ITA	27
Hugh Anderson	NZE	25
Kevin Schwantz	USA	25
Kenny Roberts	USA	24
Walter Villa	ITA	24
Wayne Rainey	USA	24
Barry Sheene	GBR	23
Casey Stoner	AUS	23
Jorge Lorenzo	SPA	22
Marco Melandri	ITA	22
Bill Ivy	GBR	21
Fausto Gresini	ITA	21
Alex Criville	SPA	20
Ralf Waldmann	GER	20
Tarquinio Provini	ITA	20
Carlos Lavado	VEN	19
Gary Hocking	RHO	19
Ricardo Tormo	SPA	19
Kent Andersson	SWE	18
Stefan Dörflinger	SWI	18
Wayne Gardner	AUS	18
Daijiro Kato	JPN	17
Tetsuya Harada	JPN	17
Ernst Degner	DDR	15
Jarno Saarinen	FIN	15
Sito Pons	SPA	15
Alvaro Bautista	SPA	14
Dieter Braun	GER	14
Dirk Raudies	GER	14
Hans-Georg Anscheidt	GER	14
Jan de Vries	NED	14
Johnny Cecotto	VEN	14
John Kocinski	USA	13
Noboru Ueda	JPN	13
Randy Mamola	USA	13
Fergus Anderson	GBR	12
Manuel Poggiali	RSM	12
Mika Kallio	FIN	12
Dave Simmonds	GBR	11
Kazuto Sakata	JPN	11
Takazumi Katayama	JPN	11
Werner Haas	GER	11
Youichi Ui	JPN	11
Toni Elias	SPA	10
Gregg Hansford	AUS	10
Masao Azuma	JPN	10
Ralph Bryans	GBR	10
Rod Gould	GBR	10
Andrea Dovizioso	ITA	9
Bill Lomas	GBR	9
Ezio Gianola	ITA	9
Gabor Talmacsi	HUN	9
Hans Spaan	NED	9
Haruchika Aoki	JPN	9
Mattia Pasini	ITA	9
Roberto Locatelli	ITA	9
Sete Gibernau	SPA	9
Kenny Roberts Jnr	USA	8
Les Graham	GBR	8
Loris Reggiani	ITA	8
Marco Simoncelli	ITA	8
Paolo Pileri	ITA	8
Tepi Lansivuori	FIN	8
Alex Barros	BRA	7
Arnaud Vincent	FRA	7
Chas Mortimer	GBR	7
Christian Sarron	FRA	7
Enrico Lorenzetti	ITA	7
Franco Uncini	ITA	7
Hector Barbera	SPA	7
Hector Faubel	SPA	7
Henk van Kessel	NED	7
Jon Ekerold	RSA	7
Kel Carruthers	AUS	7
Lucio Cecchinello	ITA	7
Olivier Jacque	FRA	7
Reg Armstrong	IRL	7
Sebastian Porto	ARG	7
Aalt Toersen	NED	6
Doriano Romboni	ITA	6
Guy Bertin	FRA	6
Libero Liberati	ITA	6
Manfred Herweh	GER	6
Marco Lucchinelli	ITA	6
Ray Amm	RHO	6
Renzo Pasolini	ITA	6
Shinya Nakano	JPN	6
Tadayuki Okada	JPN	6
Tom Phillis	AUS	6
Tomomi Manako	JPN	6
Umberto Masetti	ITA	6
August Auinger	AUT	5
Bob McIntyre	GBR	5
Bruno Kneubühler	SWI	5
Carlos Cardus	SPA	5
Cecil Sandford	GBR	5
Dario Ambrosini	ITA	5
Fonsi Nieto	SPA	5
Freddie Frith	GBR	5
Garry McCoy	AUS	5
Helmut Bradl	GER	5
Hiroshi Aoyama	JPN	5
Jean-Francois Baldé	FRA	5
John Hartle	GBR	5
Ken Kavanagh	AUS	5
Masaki Tokudome	JPN	5
Mike di Meglio	FRA	5
Peter Öttl	GER	5
Pier-Francesco Chili	ITA	5
Randy de Puniet	FRA	5
Rupert Hollaus	AUT	5
Simone Corsi	ITA	5
Stefano Perugini	ITA	5
Takeshi Tsujimura	JPN	5
Thomas Luthi	SWI	5
Tohru Ukawa	JPN	5
Wil Hartog	NED	5
Barry Smith	AUS	4
Borje Jansson	SWE	4
Bruno Ruffo	ITA	4
Didier de Radigues	BEL	4
Dominique Sarron	FRA	4
Emilio Alzamora	SPA	4
Frantisek Stastny	CZE	4
Gerhard Waibel	GER	4

Gilberto Parlotti	ITA	4
Herbert Rittberger	GER	4
Janos Drapal	HUN	4
John Dodds	AUS	4
Kunimitsu Takahashi	JPN	4
Nello Pagani	ITA	4
Paul Lodewijkx	NED	4
Santiago Herrero	SPA	4
Yoshimi Katayama	JPN	4
Alberto Pagani	ITA	3
Alessandro Gramigni	ITA	3
Alfredo Milani	ITA	3
Bob Foster	GBR	3
Charlie Williams	GBR	3
Daryl Beattie	AUS	3
Emilio Mendogni	ITA	3
Frank Perris	GBR	3
Gianni Leoni	ITA	3
Graziano Rossi	ITA	3
Hideo Kanaya	JPN	3
Jack Findlay	AUS	3
Jacques Cornu	SWI	3
Jean-Philippe Ruggia	FRA	3
Juan Garriga	SPA	3
Julien van Zeebroeck	BEL	3
Keith Campbell	AUS	3
Martin Wimmer	GER	3
Maurice Cann	GBR	3
Michel Rougerie	FRA	3
Mick Grant	GBR	3
Mike Duff	CAN	3
Nicky Hayden	USA	3
Norick Abe	JPN	3
Otello Buscherini	ITA	3
Pat Hennen	USA	3
Patrick Fernandez	FRA	3
Reinhold Roth	GER	3
Roberto Rolfo	ITA	3
Silvio Grassetti	ITA	3
Simone Sanna	ITA	3
Theo Timmer	NED	3
Tommy Robb	GBR	3
Alan Shepherd	GBR	2
Alberto Gandossi	ITA	2
Alex Debon	SPA	2
Angelo Bergamonti	ITA	2
Arthur Wheeler	GBR	2
Bill Doran	GBR	2
Carlos Checa	SPA	2
Cromie McCandless	GBR	2
Dickie Dale	GBR	2
Eric Saul	FRA	2
Gianfranco Bonera	ITA	2
Gianluigi Scalvini	ITA	2
Helmut Kassner	GER	2
Herri Torrontegui	SPA	2
Ivan Palazzese	VEN	2
Jack Middelburg	NED	2
Jan Huberts	NED	2
Lukas Pesek	CZE	2
Makoto Tamada	JPN	2
Manuel Herreros	SPA	2
Maurizio Vitali	ITA	2
Mitsuo Itoh	JPN	2
Pierre Monneret	FRA	2
Salvador Canellas	SPA	2
Sergio Gadea	SPA	2
Stefan Bradl	GER	2
Stuart Graham	GBR	2
Tom Herron	GBR	2
Tommy Wood	GBR	2
Tony Rutter	GBR	2
Virginio Ferrari	ITA	2
Yuki Takahashi	JPN	2
Alan Carter	GBR	1
Alan North	RSA	1
Alberto Puig	SPA	1
Alex de Angelis	RSM	1
Andrea Ballerini	ITA	1
Andrea Iannone	ITA	1
Angelo Copeta	ITA	1
Anthony West	AUS	1
Artie Bell	GBR	1
Benedicto Caldarella	ARG	1
Benjamin Grau	SPA	1
Bert Schneider	AUT	1
Boet van Dulmen	NED	1
Bruno Casanova	ITA	1
Bruno Spaggiari	ITA	1
Cees van Dongen	NED	1
Chris Vermeulen	AUS	1
Dennis Ireland	NZE	1
Derek Minter	GBR	1
Domenico Brigaglia	ITA	1
Duilio Agostini	ITA	1
Edi Stollinger	AUT	1
Edmund Czihak	GER	1
Adu Celso Santos	BRA	1
Fausto Ricci	ITA	1
Fritz Reitmaier	GER	1
Fumio Ito	JPN	1
Gerd Kafka	AUT	1
Gerhard Thurow	GER	1
Ginger Molloy	NZE	1
Giuseppe Colnago	ITA	1
Godfrey Nash	GBR	1
Guido Leoni	ITA	1
Guido Sala	ITA	1
Gyula Marsovszky	SWI	1
Harold Daniell	GBR	1
Hermann-Paul Muller	GER	1
Herve Guilleux	FRA	1
Hiroshi Hasegawa	JPN	1
Horst Fügner	DDR	1
Ian McConnachie	GBR	1
Ingo Emmerich	GER	1
Isao Morishita	JPN	1
Ivan Goi	ITA	1
Jack Ahearn	AUS	1
Jack Brett	GBR	1
Jacques Bolle	FRA	1
Jan Bruins	NED	1
Jean Aureal	FRA	1
Jean-Claude Selini	FRA	1
Jean-Louis Tournadre	FRA	1
Jeremy McWilliams	GBR	1
Jim Filice	USA	1
John Newbold	GBR	1
John Williams	GBR	1
Jorge Kissling	ARG	1
Jos Schurgers	NED	1
Julian Simon	SPA	1
Ken Mudford	NZE	1
Kevin Magee	AUS	1
Kim Newcombe	NZE	1
Leif Gustafsson	SWE	1
Manliff Barrington	IRL	1
Marcellino Lucchi	ITA	1
Mario Lega	ITA	1
Masaru Kobayashi	JPN	1
Michel Frutschi	SWI	1
Nicolas Terol	SPA	1
Nobuatsu Aoki	JPN	1
Olivier Chevallier	FRA	1
Osamu Miyazaki	JPN	1
Pablo Nieto	SPA	1
Paolo Casoli	ITA	1
Pentti Korhonen	FIN	1
Peter Williams	GBR	1
Phil Carpenter	GBR	1
Pierluigi Conforti	ITA	1
Ray McCullough	GBR	1
Regis Laconi	FRA	1
Remo Venturi	ITA	1
Dick Creith	GBR	1
Rod Coleman	NZE	1
Roland Freymond	SWI	1
Romolo Ferri	ITA	1
Rudi Felgenheier	GER	1
Scott Redding	GBR	1
Simon Crafar	NZE	1
Stefan Prein	GER	1
Steve Jenkner	GER	1
Tadahiko Taira	JPN	1
Teisuke Tanaka	JPN	1
Tomoyoshi Koyama	JPN	1
Tony Jefferies	GBR	1
Troy Bayliss	AUS	1
Ulrich Graf	SWI	1
Victor Palomo	SPA	1
Wilco Zeelenberg	NED	1

THE RIDERS

Every racer mentioned in the text in alphabetical order, with the date of their first mention

Norick Abe (JPN) 1994
Duilio Agostini (ITA) 1954
Giacomo Agostini (ITA) 1963
Jack Ahearn (AUS) 1964
Emilio Alzamora (SPA) 1995
Dario Ambrosini (ITA) 1949
Ray Amm (RHO) 1952
Bob Anderson (GBR) 1960
Fergus Anderson (GBR) 1949
Hugh Anderson (NZE) 1962
Kent Andersson (SWE) 1969
Hans-Georg Anscheidt (GER) 1962
Haruchika Aoki (JPN) 1995
Nobuatsu Aoki (JPN) 1993
Takuma Aoki (JPN) 1995
Hiroshi Aoyama (JPN) 2004
Dario Ambrosini (ITA) 1949
Reg Armstrong (IRL) 1949
Hans-Georg Anscheidt (GER) 1962
Arciso Artesiani (ITA) 1950
Karl Auer (AUT) 1976
August Auinger (AUT) 1986
Jean Aureal (FRA) 1969
Masao Azuma (JPN) 1999

Steve Baker (USA) 1977
Jean-Francois Balde (FRA) 1980
Mike Baldwin (USA) 1986
Kork Ballington (RSA) 1976
Carlo Bandirola (ITA) 1949
Hector Barbera (SPA) 2003
Manliff Barrington (IRL) 1949
Alex Barros (BRA) 1990
Franco Battaini (ITA) 2005
Alvaro Bautista (SPA) 2006
Jean-Michel Bayle (FRA) 1996
Troy Bayliss (AUS) 2003
Daryl Beattie (AUS) 1992
Artie Bell (GBR) 1949
Dave Bennett (GBR) 1952
Angelo Bergamonti (ITA) 1968
Silvano Bertarelli (ITA) 1968
Guy Bertin (FRA) 1979
Max Biaggi (ITA) 1992
Pierpaolo Bianchi (ITA) 1976
Rolf Blatter (SWI) 1979
Jacques Bolle (FRA) 1983
Gianfranco Bonera (ITA) 1974
Juan Borja (SPA) 1999
Gino Borsoi (ITA) 1999
Helmut Bradl (GER) 1991
Stefan Bradl (GER) 2008
Dieter Braun (GER) 1970

Walter Brehme (DDR) 1961
Jack Brett (GBR) 1951
Rob Bron (NED) 1971
Bob Brown (AUS) 1957
Norman Brown (GBR) 1983
Ralph Bryans (GBR) 1964
Keith Bryen (AUS) 1957
Chris Burns (GBR) 2003
Jose Busquets (SPA) 1962
Shane Byrne (GBR) 2005

Luca Cadalora (ITA) 1986
Benedicto Caldarella (ARG) 1962
Keith Campbell (AUS) 1957
Salvador Canellas (SPA) 1968
Maurice Cann (GBR) 1950
Loris Capirossi (ITA) 1990
José Luis Cardoso (SPA) 2001
Carlos Cardus (SPA) 1990
Phil Carpenter (GBR) 1974
Kel Carruthers (AUS) 1969
Alan Carter (GBR) 1983
Bruno Casnova (ITA) 1992
Paolo Casoli (ITA) 1987
Corrado Catalano (ITA) 1994
Lucio Cecchinello (ITA) 1998
Johnny Cecotto (VEN) 1975
Adu Celso-Santos (BRA) 1973
Dave Chadwick (GBR) 1958
Doug Chandler (USA) 1991
Carlos Checa (SPA) 1995
Olivier Chevallier (FRA) 1976
Pier-Francesco Chili (ITA) 1986
Giuseppe Colnago (ITA) 1952
Rod Coleman (NZE) 1952
Chris Conn (GBR) 1965
Jacques Cornu (SWI) 1988
Troy Corser (AUS) 1997
Simon Crafar (NZE) 1998
Dick Creith (GBR) 1965
Alex Criville (SPA) 1987
Graeme Crosby (NZE) 1981

Dickie Dale (GBR) 1951
Harold Daniell (GBR) 1949
Chaz Davies (GBR) 2003
David de Gea (SPA) 2000
Randy de Puniet (FRA) 2006
Didier de Radigues (BEL) 1982
Jan de Vries (NED) 1972
Alex Debon (SPA) 2008
Ernst Degner (DDR) 1958
Mike di Meglio (FRA) 2005

John Dodds (AUS) 1970
Mick Doohan (AUS) 1989
Bill Doran (GBR) 1949
Stefan Dorflinger (SWI) 1980
Andrea Dovizioso (ITA) 2004
Ben Drinkwater (GBR) 1949
Janos Drapal (HUN) 1971
Paddy Driver (RSA) 1965
Mike Duff (CAN) 1964
Miguel DuHamel (CAN) 1992
Geoff Duke (GBR) 1950

Colin Edwards (USA) 2003
Jon Ekerold (RSA) 1975
Toni Elias (SPA) 2001
James Ellison (GBR) 2004
Sean Emmett (GBR) 1993
Pol Espargaro (SPA) 2006
Thierry Espie (FRA) 1979

Michel Fabrizio (ITA) 2004
Derek Farrant (GBR) 1954
Hector Faubel (SPA) 2006
Rudi Felgenheier (GER) 1952
Patrick Fernandez (FRA) 1977
Virginio Ferrari (ITA) 1978
Romolo Ferri (ITA) 1956
Jim Filice (USA) 1988
Jack Findlay (AUS) 1968
Carl Fogarty (GBR) 1993
Marc Fontan (FRA) 1982
Bob Foster (GBR) 1950
Ted Frend (GBR) 1949
Freddie Frith (GBR) 1949
Michel Frutschi (SWI) 1982
Horst Fugner (DDR) 1958
Katsuaki Fujiwara (JPN) 1998

Sergio Gadea (SPA) 2006
Alberto Gandossi (ITA) 1958
Bernard Garcia (FRA) 1993
Wayne Gardner (AUS) 1983
Juan Garriga (SPA) 1986
Bo Gehring (USA) 1964
Sante Geminiani (ITA) 1951
Ezio Gianola (ITA) 1987
Sete Gibernau (SPA) 1997
Anthony Gobert (AUS) 1997
Peter Goddard (AUS) 1992
Ivan Goi (ITA) 1996
Rod Gould (GBR) 1968
Ulrich Graf (SWI) 1977
Les Graham (GBR) 1949

Stuart Graham (GBR) 1966
Alessandro Gramigni (ITA) 1991
Mick Grant (GBR) 1975
Ron Grant (USA) 1964
Silvio Grassetti (ITA) 1962
Fausto Gresini (ITA) 1984
Les Griffiths (GBR) 1968
Sylvain Guintoli (FRA) 2007

Werner Haas (GER) 1952
Noriyuki Haga (JPN) 1998
Mike Hailwood (GBR) 1958
Gregg Hansford (AUS) 1978
Tetsuya Harada (JPN) 1993
John Hartle (GBR) 1955
Wil Hartog (NED) 1977
Ron Haslam (GBR) 1983
Nicky Hayden (USA) 2003
John Hempleman (NZE) 1960
Pat Hennen (USA) 1976
Santiago Herrero (SPA) 1969
Manuel Herreros (SPA) 1989
Tom Herron (GBR) 1976
Manfred Herweh (GER) 1983
August Hobl (GER) 1956
Gary Hocking (RHO) 1958
Neil Hodgson (GBR) 2004
Alex Hofmann (GER) 2004
Rupert Hollaus (AUT) 1954
John Hopkins (USA) 2003
Peter Huber (SWI) 1983
Bill Hunt (1959)

Patrick Igoa (FRA) 1988
Dennis Ireland (NZE) 1979
Kenny Irons (GBR) 1987
Fumio Ito (JPN) 1961
Takumi Ito (JPN) 1987
Shinichi Itoh (JPN) 1993
Mitsuo Itoh (JPN) 1963
Bill Ivy (GBR) 1966

Olivier Jacque (FRA) 1996
Borje Jansson (SWE) 1972

Yukio Kagayama (JPN) 1998
Mika Kallio (FIN) 2005
Hideo Kanaya (JPN) 1972
Takazumi Katayama (JPN) 1977
Yoshimi Katayama (JPN) 1965
Daijiro Kato (JPN) 1997
Ken Kavanagh (AUS) 1951
Hiroyuki Kawasaki (JPN) 1981
Jorge Kissling (ARG) 1961
Keiichi Kitagawa (JPN) 1998
Akihiro Kiyohara (JPN) 1977
Ryuichi Kiyonari (JPN) 2005
Bruno Kneubuhler (SWI) 1974
Masaru Kobayashi (JPN) 1987
John Kocinski (USA) 1988
José Kuhn (FRA) 1993

Regis Laconi (FRA) 1998
Tepi Lansivuori (FIN) 1973
Carlos Lavado (VEN) 1979
Eddie Lawson (USA) 1981
Syd Lawton (GBR) 1952
Eddie Laycock (IRL) 1991
Eugenio Lazzarini (ITA) 1978
Mario Lega (ITA) 1977
Gianni Leoni (ITA) 1950
Guido Leoni (ITA) 1951
Christian le Liard (FRA) 1985
Libero Liberati (ITA) 1955
Roberto Locatelli (ITA) 1994
Johnny Lockett (GBR) 1949
Paul Lodewijkx (NED) 1968
Bill Lomas (GBR) 1950
Enrico Lorenzetti (ITA) 1949
Jorge Lorenzo (SPA) 2002
Marcellino Lucchi (ITA) 1998
Marco Lucchinelli (ITA) 1976
Thomas Luthi (SWI) 2005

Rex and Cromie McCandless (GBR) 1951
Ian McConnachie (GBR) 1986
Garry McCoy (AUS) 1995
Rob McElnea (GBR) 1985
Bob McIntyre (GBR) 1954
Ray McCullough (GBR) 1971
Jeremy McWilliams (GBR) 2000
Kevin Magee (AUS) 1987
Niall Mackenzie (GBR) 1986
Randy Mamola (USA) 1979
Tomomi Manako (JPN) 1998
Anton Mang (GER) 1976
Steve Manship (GBR) 1978
Gyula Markovszky (SWI) 1969
Marc Marquez (SPA) 2008
Jorge Martinez 'Aspar' (SPA) 1984
Umberto Masetti (ITA) 1949
Naoki Matsudo (JPN) 1998
Marco Melandri (ITA) 1998
Emilio Mendogni (ITA) 1958
Jack Middelburg (NED) 1980
Alfredo Milani (ITA) 1951
Sammy Miller (IRL) 1957
Derek Minter (GBR) 1959
Osamu Miyazaki (JPN) 2002
Matt Mladin (AUS) 1993
Ginger Molloy (NZE) 1966
Pierre Monneret (FRA) 1954
Isao Morishita (JPN) 1963
Adrien Morillas (FRA) 1991
Chas Mortimer (GBR) 1972
Ken Mudford (NZE) 1953
Hermann-Paul Muller (GER) 1955
Werner Musiol (DDR) 1960

Hideyuki Nakajyo (JPN) 1994
Shinya Nakano (JPN) 1998
Kyoji Nanba (JPN) 1998
Godfrey Nash (GBR) 1969

Billie Nelson (GBR) 1969
John Newbold (GBR) 1976
Kim Newcombe (NZE) 1972
Angel Nieto (SPA) 1964
Fonsi Nieto (SPA) 2002
Pablo Nieto (SPA) 2003

Tadayuki Okada (JPN) 1993
Peter Ottl (GER) 1989

Alberto Pagani (ITA) 1968
Nello Pagani (ITA) 1949
Ivan Palazzese (VEN) 1977
Victor Palomo (SPA) 1974
Gilberto Parlotti (ITA) 1970
Buddy Parriott (USA) 1965
Steve Parrish (GBR) 1977
Renzo Pasolini (ITA) 1968
Mattia Pasini (ITA) 2006
Dani Pedrosa (SPN) 2001
Frank Perris (GBR) 1963
Lukas Pesek (CZE) 2007
Tom Phillis (AUS) 1959
Paolo Pileri (ITA) 1975
Andrew Pitt (AUS) 2003
Katja Poensgen (GER) 2001
Manuel Poggiali (RSM) 2000
Patrick Pons (FRA) 1980
Sito Pons (SPA) 1984
Sebastian Porto (ARG) 2002
Stefan Prein (GER) 1990
Tarquinio Provini (ITA) 1954
Alberto Puig (SPA) 1994

Wayne Rainey (USA) 1984
Dirk Raudies (GER) 1992
Phil Read (GBR) 1961
Scott Redding (GBR) 2008
Jim Redman (RHO) 1961
Loris Reggiani (ITA) 1980
Fritz Reitmaier (GER) 1974
Fausto Ricci (ITA) 1985
Taru Rinne (FIN) 1988
Tommy Robb (GBR) 1962
Kenny Roberts (USA) 1974
Kenny Roberts Jnr (USA) 1996
Kurtis Roberts (USA) 2004
Raymond Roche (FRA) 1984
Roberto Rolfo (ITA) 2003
Doriano Romboni (ITA) 1993
Graziano Rossi (ITA) 1979
Valentino Rossi (ITA) 1996
Reinhold Roth (GER) 1985
Michel Rougerie (FRA) 1975
Bruno Ruffo (ITA) 1949
Jean-Philippe Ruggia (FRA) 1990
Scott Russell (USA) 1995
Akira Ryo (JPN) 2002

Jarno Saarinen (FIN) 1970
Daisaku Sakai (JPN) 2002

BELOW Giacomo Agostini, winner of 122 Grands Prix, with the Senior TT trophy. (*Elwyn Roberts Collection*)

Guido Sala (ITA) 1954
Kazuto Sakata (JPN) 1993
Pierre-Etienne Samin (FRA) 1985
Cecil Sandford (GBR) 1952
Christian Sarron (FRA) 1977
Dominique Sarron (FRA) 1986
Eric Saul (FRA) 1981
Bert Schneider (AUT) 1963
Jos Schurgers (NED) 1973
Kevin Schwantz (USA) 1986
Nikolai Sevostyanov (RUS) 1962
Barry Sheene (GBR) 1970
Alan Shepherd (GBR) 1961
Masahiro Shimizu (JPN) 1988
Bubba Shobert (USA) 1989
Marco Simoncelli (ITA) 2008
Dave Simmonds (GBR) 1967
Barry Smith (AUS) 1968
Bradley Smith (GBR) 2007
Hans Spaan (NED) 1989
Bruno Spaggiari (ITA) 1958
Freddie Spencer (USA) 1980
Frantisek Stastny (CZE) 1960
Hans Stadelmann (SWI) 1977
Casey Stoner (AUS) 2002
John Surtees (GBR) 1955
Giichi Suzuki (JPN) 1959
Junzo Suzuki (JPN) 1959
Beryl Swain (GBR) 1962

Tadahiko Taira (JPN) 1986
Percy Tait (GBR) 1969
Kunimitsu Takahashi (JPN) 1961
Yuki Takahashi (JPN) 2006
Gabor Talmacsi (HUN) 2005
Makoto Tamada (JPN) 2003
Naomi Taniguchi (JPN) 1959
Kenjiro Tanaka (JPN) 1960
Teisuke Tanaka (JPN) 1959
Luigi Taveri (SWI) 1955
Nicolas Terol (SPA) 2008
Aalt Toersen (NED) 1969
Masaki Tokudome (JPN) 1995
Armando Toracca (ITA) 1975
Ricardo Tormo (SPA) 1977
Herri Torrontegui (SPA) 1989
James Toseland (GBR) 2008
Jean-Louis Tournadre (FRA) 1982
Takeshi Tsujimura (JPN) 1994
Keith Turner (NZE) 1971

Carlo Ubbiali (ITA) 1950
Noboru Ueda (JPN) 1991
Youichi Ui (JPN) 2000
Tohru Ukawa (JPN) 1999
Franco Uncini (ITA) 1976

Alessandro Valesi (ITA) 1989
Jurgen van den Goorbergh (NED) 2001
Boet van Dulmen (NED) 1979
Henk van Kessel (NED) 1974

Remo Venturi (ITA) 1959
Chris Vermeulen (AUS) 2005
Francesco Villa (ITA) 1958
Walter Villa (ITA) 1974
Arnaud Vincent (FRA) 1999

Noboyuki Wakai (JPN) 1993
Ralf Waldmann (GER) 1995
Chris Walker (GBR) 2001
Anthony West (AUS) 2003
Jock West (GBR) 1949
Arthur Wheeler (GBR) 1954
Jamie Whitham (GBR) 1999

John Williams (GBR) 1975
Peter Williams (GBR) 1971
Martin Wimmer (GER) 1985
Stan Woods (GBR) 1975

Ruben Xaus (SPA) 2004

Akira Yanagawa (JPN) 2002
Shunji Yatsushiro (JPN) 1986

Wilco Zeelenberg (NED) 1990
Walter Zeller (GER) 1953
Giampiero Zubani (ITA) 1958

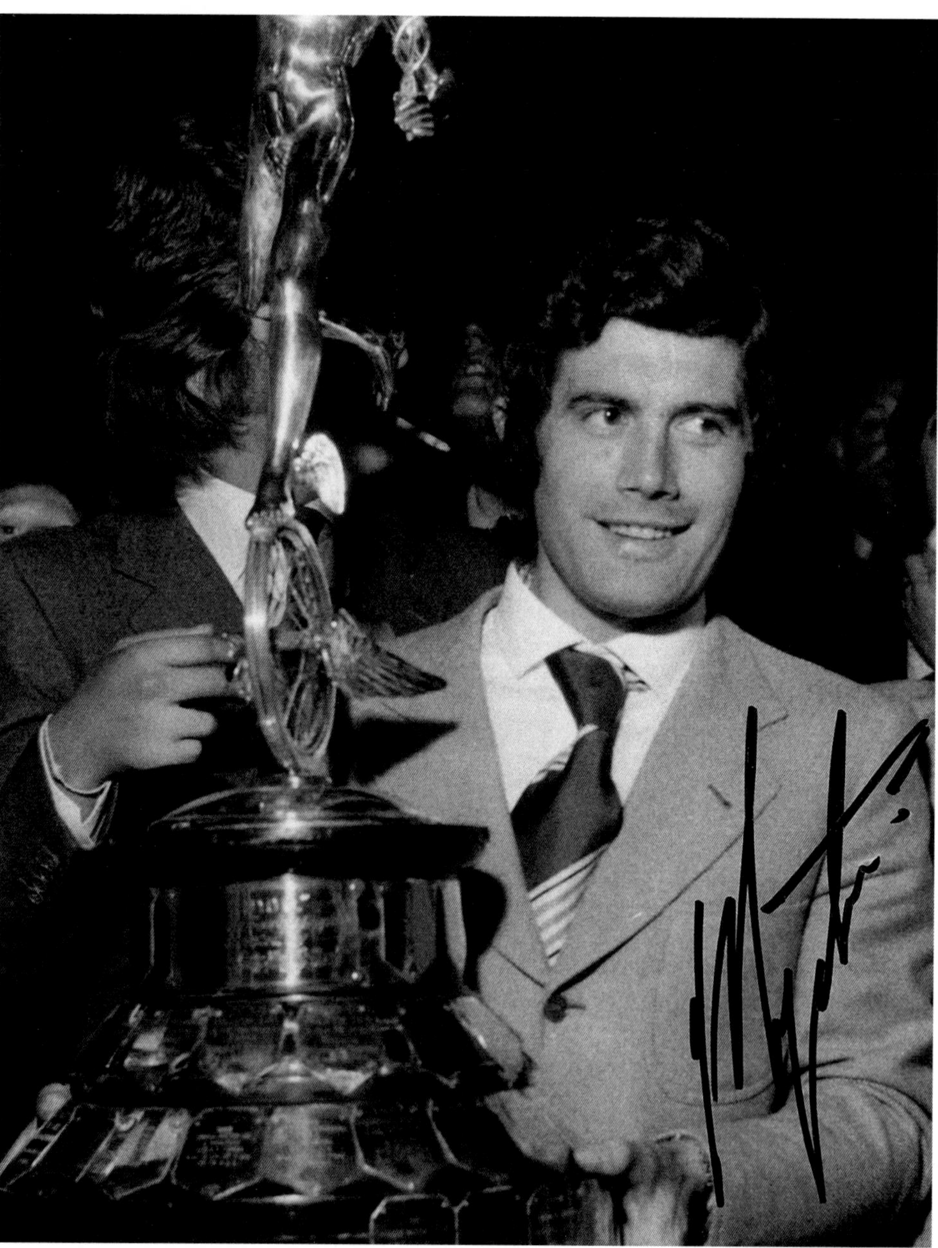